TOEFL® MAP

Reading

New TOEFL® Edition

Advanced

DARAKWON

TOEFL® MAP
New TOEFL Edition
Reading Advanced

Publisher Chung Kyudo
Editor Cho Sangik
Authors Michael A. Putlack, Stephen Poirier, Allen C. Jacobs, Tony Covello
Proofreaders Talib Din, Mark Thorrowgood
Designers Park Narae, Chung Kyuok

First published in April 2023
By Darakwon, Inc.
Darakwon Bldg., 211, Munbal-ro, Paju-si, Gyeonggi-do 10881
Republic of Korea
Tel: 82-2-736-2031 (Ext. 250)
Fax: 82-2-732-2037

ISBN 978-89-277-8034-2 14740
978-89-277-8025-0 14740 (set)

www.darakwon.co.kr

Photo Credits
Shutterstock.com

Components Main Book / Answers, Explanations, and Scripts
8 7 6 5 4 3 2   24 25 26 27 28

Introduction

Studying for the TOEFL® iBT is no easy task and is not one that is to be undertaken lightly. It requires a great deal of effort as well as dedication on the part of the student. It is our hope that by using *TOEFL® Map Reading Advanced* as either a textbook or a study guide, the task of studying for the TOEFL® iBT will become somewhat easier for the student and less of a burden.

Students who wish to excel on the TOEFL® iBT must attain a solid grasp of the four important skills in the English language: reading, listening, speaking, and writing. The Darakwon *TOEFL® Map series* covers all four of these skills in separate books. There are also three different levels in all four topics. This book, *TOEFL® Map Reading Advanced*, covers the reading aspect of the test at the advanced level. Students who want to read passages, learn vocabulary terms, and study topics that appear on the TOEFL® iBT will have their wishes granted by using this book.

TOEFL® Map Reading Advanced has been designed for use both in a classroom setting and as a study guide for individual learners. For this reason, it offers a comprehensive overview of the TOEFL® iBT Reading section. In Part A, the different types of questions that are found on the TOEFL® iBT Reading section are explained, and hints on how to answer these questions properly are also provided. In Part B, learners have the opportunity to build their background knowledge of the topics that appear on the TOEFL® iBT by studying the reading passages of varying lengths that are found in each chapter. Each passage is followed by the types of questions that appear on the TOEFL® iBT, and each chapter also has a section with short passages relevant to the chapter's topic as well as a vocabulary section, which enables learners to test their knowledge of vocabulary that is specific to the particular topic covered in each chapter. Finally, in Part C, students can take several TOEFL® iBT practice tests. These are full-length passages that also have the same numbers and types of questions that appear on actual TOEFL® iBT Reading section passages. Combined, all of these should be able to help learners prepare themselves to take and, more importantly, to excel on the TOEFL® iBT.

TOEFL® Map Reading Advanced has a great amount of information and should prove to be invaluable as a study guide for learners who are preparing for the TOEFL® iBT. However, while this book is comprehensive, it is up to each person to do the actual work. In order for *TOEFL® Map Reading Advanced* to be of any use, the individual learner must dedicate him or herself to studying the information found within its pages. While we have strived to make this book as user friendly and as full of crucial information as possible, ultimately, it is up to each person to make the best of the material in the book. We wish you luck in your study of both English and the TOEFL® iBT, and we hope that you are able to use *TOEFL® Map Reading Advanced* to improve your abilities in both of them.

Michael A. Putlack
Stephen Poirier
Allen C. Jacobs
Tony Covello

TABLE OF CONTENTS

How Is This Book Different?   6

How to Use This Book   7

Part A | Understanding Reading Question Types

Question Type 01   Vocabulary   10

Question Type 02   Reference   12

Question Type 03   Factual Information   14

Question Type 04   Negative Factual Information   17

Question Type 05   Sentence Simplification   19

Question Type 06   Inference   21

Question Type 07   Rhetorical Purpose   23

Question Type 08   Insert Text   25

Question Type 09   Prose Summary   27

Question Type 10   Fill in a Table   30

Practice   33

Part B | Building Background Knowledge of TOEFL Topics

Chapter 01 *History*

Mastering Question Types A1, A2, B1, B2   40

Mastering the Subject A, B, C, D   48

TOEFL Practice Tests A, B   60

Star Performer Subject Topics   68

Star Performer Word Files   70

Vocabulary Review   71

Chapter 02 *The Arts*

Mastering Question Types A1, A2, B1, B2   74

Mastering the Subject A, B, C, D   82

TOEFL Practice Tests A, B   94

Star Performer Subject Topics   102

Star Performer Word Files   104

Vocabulary Review   105

Chapter 03 *Archaeology and Anthropology*

Mastering Question Types A1, A2, B1, B2   108

Mastering the Subject A, B, C, D   116

TOEFL Practice Tests A, B   128

Star Performer Subject Topics   136

Star Performer Word Files 138

Vocabulary Review 139

Chapter 04 *Education, Sociology, and Psychology*

Mastering Question Types A1, A2, B1, B2 142

Mastering the Subject A, B, C, D 150

TOEFL Practice Tests A, B 162

Star Performer Subject Topics 170

Star Performer Word Files 172

Vocabulary Review 173

Chapter 05 *Economics*

Mastering Question Types A1, A2, B1, B2 176

Mastering the Subject A, B, C, D 184

TOEFL Practice Tests A, B 196

Star Performer Subject Topics 204

Star Performer Word Files 206

Vocabulary Review 207

Chapter 06 *Life Sciences*

Mastering Question Types A1, A2, B1, B2 210

Mastering the Subject A, B, C, D 218

TOEFL Practice Tests A, B 230

Star Performer Subject Topics 238

Star Performer Word Files 240

Vocabulary Review 241

Chapter 07 *Physical Sciences*

Mastering Question Types A1, A2, B1, B2 244

Mastering the Subject A, B, C, D 252

TOEFL Practice Tests A, B 264

Star Performer Subject Topics 272

Star Performer Word Files 274

Vocabulary Review 275

Chapter 08 *Environmental Sciences*

Mastering Question Types A1, A2, B1, B2 278

Mastering the Subject A, B, C, D 286

TOEFL Practice Tests A, B 298

Star Performer Subject Topics 306

Star Performer Word Files 308

Vocabulary Review 309

Part C | Experiencing the TOEFL iBT Actual Tests

Actual Test 01 312

Actual Test 02 340

How Is This Book Different?

When searching for the ideal book to use to study for the TOEFL® iBT, it is often difficult to differentiate between the numerous books that are available on a bookstore's shelves. However, *TOEFL® Map Reading Advanced* differs from many other TOEFL® iBT books and study guides in several important ways.

A large number of TOEFL® iBT books arrange the material according to the types of questions that are asked on the test. This often results in learners reading one passage on astronomy, which is then followed by a passage on history, which is then followed by a passage on economics, and so on. Simply put, there is little cohesion except for the questions. However, *TOEFL® Map Reading Advanced* is arranged by subject. There are eight chapters in this book, all of which cover the subjects that appear on the TOEFL® iBT. For instance, there is a chapter on history, there is a chapter on the life sciences, and there is a chapter on the physical sciences, among others. By arranging the chapters according to subjects, learners are able to read passages that are related to one another all throughout each chapter. This enables them to build upon their knowledge as they progress through each chapter. Additionally, since there are many vocabulary terms that are specifically used in certain subjects, learners will be able more easily to recognize these specialized vocabulary terms, understand how they are used in sentences, and, most importantly, retain the knowledge of what these terms mean. Finally, by arranging the chapters according to subjects, learners have the opportunity to cover and become familiar with all of the TOEFL® iBT question types in each chapter rather than just focus on a single type of question.

TOEFL® Map Reading Advanced, unlike many other TOEFL® iBT books and study guides, does not have any translations into foreign languages within its pages. All too often, learners rely on translations of the passages, questions, or difficult vocabulary terms into their native language. They learn to use these translations as a crutch to help them get through the material. However, the actual TOEFL® iBT does not have any translations into foreign languages, so neither does this book. This will better prepare learners to take the actual test in that they must try to learn difficult terms or expressions through context, just as native speakers of English do when they encounter terms or expressions that they fail to understand. Additionally, by not being able to resort to their native language for help through translations of the material, learners will find that their fluency in English will improve more rapidly when they use *TOEFL® Map Reading Advanced*.

Finally, the passages in *TOEFL® Map Reading Advanced* are based on topics that have appeared on the actual TOEFL® iBT in the past. Therefore, by using this book, learners can get the opportunity to see what kinds of topics appear on the TOEFL® iBT. This will enable them to recognize the difficulty level, the style of TOEFL® iBT passages, and the difficulty of the vocabulary that appears on the test. Second, learners will also get the opportunity to enhance their knowledge of topics that have appeared on the TOEFL® iBT before. By knowing more about the topics about which they are reading when they take the actual test, test takers will be sure to improve their TOEFL® iBT scores. Third, learners will also gain knowledge of the specialized vocabulary in particular topics, which will help them more easily to understand passages on the actual test. Finally, many topics appear multiple times on the TOEFL® iBT. Thus, students who study some of these topics will be pleasantly surprised on occasion to find almost the exact same topic when they take the actual TOEFL® iBT, which will no doubt help them improve their test scores.

How to Use
This Book

TOEFL® Map Reading Advanced is designed for use either as a textbook in a classroom in a TOEFL® iBT preparation course or as a study guide for individuals who are studying for the TOEFL® iBT on their own. *TOEFL® Map Reading Advanced* has been divided into three sections: Part A, Part B, and Part C. All three sections offer information that is important to learners preparing for the TOEFL® iBT. Part A is divided into 10 sections, each of which explains one of the question types that appears on the TOEFL® iBT Reading section. Part B is divided into 8 chapters, each of which covers one of the subjects that appears on the TOEFL® iBT. Part C has 2 actual tests consisting of 8 Reading passages and questions that resemble those appearing on the TOEFL® iBT.

Part A Understanding Reading Question Types

This section is designed to acquaint learners with each question type on the TOEFL® iBT Reading section. Therefore, there are 10 sections in this chapter— one for each question type. Each section is divided into 4 parts. The first part offers a short explanation of the question type. The second part shows the ways in which questions of that particular type often appear on the test. The third part provides helpful hints on how to answer these questions correctly. And the fourth part has one or two short passages followed by a question. At the end of Part A, there is a full-length Reading passage with questions from every type that is asked on the Reading section.

Part B Building Background Knowledge of TOEFL Topics

The purpose of this section is to introduce the various subjects that most frequently appear on the TOEFL® iBT. There are 8 chapters in Part B. Each chapter covers one subject and contains 10 Reading passages of various lengths as well as short passages and vocabulary words and exercises. Each chapter is divided into several parts.

Introduction

This is a short description of the subject of the chapter. The purpose of this section is to let learners know what fields of study people focus on in this subject.

Mastering Question Types

This section contains 4 Reading passages that are between 400 and 500 words in length. Following each passage, there are 4 Reading questions. Each question is identified by type. Alongside the questions in the first 2 Reading passages in this section, there are hints on how to answer questions of these types.

Mastering the Subject

This section contains 4 Reading passages that are between 500 and 600 words in length. To the side of each passage are several long notes that provide additional information meant to help learners better understand the passage. Following each passage, there are 5 Reading questions. These questions may be from any of the 10 types of Reading questions. In addition, there is a short summary of the passage after the questions with 4 or 5 blanks for learners to fill in.

TOEFL Practice Tests

This section contains 2 full-length Reading passages. Each passage has 10 Reading questions of any type. The purpose of this section is to acquaint learners with the types of passages and questions they will encounter when they take the TOEFL® iBT.

Star Performer Subject Topics

This section contains 10 short passages that cover topics that have appeared on previous TOEFL® iBT tests. Each passage contains an overview of the information relevant to its topic. There is also a section that includes 10 further topics that have appeared on previous TOEFL® iBT tests. The purpose of this section is to show learners some of the subjects that have appeared on the TOEFL® iBT in the past and that may appear again on the TOEFL® iBT in the future.

Star Performer Word Files

This section contains more than 200 vocabulary words that are related to the subject of each chapter. The words include nouns, verbs, adjectives, and adverbs. The purpose of this section is to teach learners specific words that often appear in passages on certain subjects.

Vocabulary Review

This section contains 20 vocabulary questions. Each question is taken from a passage in the chapter and has a highlighted word for learners to find the meaning of. The purpose of this section is to review the vocabulary words that learners have covered in each chapter.

Part C Experiencing the TOEFL Actual Tests

This section contains 8 full-length TOEFL® iBT Reading section passages and questions. The purpose of this section is to let learners experience actual full-length Reading passages and to see if they can apply the knowledge they have learned in the course of studying *TOEFL® Map Reading Advanced*.

A

Understanding Reading Question Types

Question Type **01** | **Vocabulary**

Vocabulary questions require the test taker to understand specific words or phrases that are used in the passage. These questions ask the test taker to choose another word or phrase that is the most similar in meaning to the highlighted text. The vocabulary words that are highlighted are often important words, so knowing their meanings is often critical for understanding the entire passage. The highlighted words typically have several meanings, so test takers need to be careful to avoid selecting an answer choice simply because it is the word's or phrase's most common meaning.

Vocabulary questions often appear on the test like this:

- The word "X" in the passage is closest in meaning to . . .
- In stating "X", the author means that . . .

Solve Vocabulary questions more easily by doing the following:

○ Remember that many words and phrases in English have multiple meanings. Do not select an answer choice simply because it is a meaning that people most commonly use for that word or phrase.

○ Focus on how the word or phrase is used in the sentence itself.

○ The answer choices can all be substituted into the sentence for the highlighted word. Try inserting every answer choice into the sentence and seeing which one seems to be the most appropriate replacement.

○ Read the other sentences that are near the one that has the highlighted vocabulary word. There are often contextual clues contained in the other sentences in the passage, and they can help you determine the meaning of the word or phrase.

Examples of Vocabulary Questions

Many Egyptian paintings and other works of art were created to decorate tombs. Egyptian paintings have a two-dimensional quality. People and animals were often painted with their heads and faces in profile while their bodies were painted with a frontal view. Furthermore, the figures in the paintings are sized according to their social status; they do not show larger figures in the foreground and smaller ones in the background like some other styles of art do. Although Egyptian paintings seem rather stilted compared to more modern paintings, the Egyptians understood proportion and much about human and animal forms. They simply avoided displaying this knowledge in their artwork.

Q The word "stilted" in the passage is closest in meaning to

- Ⓐ outdated
- Ⓑ unnatural
- Ⓒ minuscule
- Ⓓ simplistic

⊘ Explanation of the above question and answer:

Choice Ⓑ is the one closest in meaning to the highlighted word. Stilted can often mean crude or clumsy. In this case, it means unnatural. Note that the author writes, "Egyptian paintings have a two-dimensional quality," which implies that they do not look natural. Choices Ⓐ, Ⓒ, and Ⓓ are all incorrect.

Attila the Hun's fifth-century invasion of the Roman Empire was for a long time regarded as the epitome of barbarism and cruelty. The Huns first moved from their Eastern European homeland toward Constantinople, where they defeated a Byzantine army, but they were turned away by the city's impregnable defenses. A long march through Gaul resulted in much destruction to the Western Roman Empire. However, Attila was checked and forced to retreat after the Battle of Chalons in 451. He next invaded Italy, but the onset of disease slowed his army. Attila ultimately left Italy and turned again toward Constantinople. Sometime in early 453, he died of either a stab wound or internal hemorrhage, and the Hun threat finally ended.

Q In stating that the Huns were turned away by the city's "impregnable defenses," the author means that the city's defenses

Ⓐ were higher than most others

Ⓑ had few weak points

Ⓒ could not be overcome

Ⓓ were armed with weapons

⊘ Explanation of the above question and answer:

Choice Ⓒ is the one closest in meaning to the highlighted words. Impregnable means that something is unconquerable or cannot be defeated. In the passage, the author notes that the Huns were turned away at Constantinople because of the city's defenses, thereby indicating that they "could not be overcome." Choices Ⓐ, Ⓑ, and Ⓓ are all incorrect.

Reference questions require the test taker to understand the relationships between words and their referents in the passage. These questions most frequently ask the test taker to identify the antecedent of a pronoun. In many cases, the pronouns are words like *he*, *she*, or *they* or *its*, *his*, *hers*, or *theirs*. However, in other cases, relative pronouns like *which* or demonstrative pronouns like *this* or *that* may be asked about instead. Nowadays, these questions seldom appear. Many passages have no Reference questions after them.

Reference questions often appear on the test like this:

- The word "X" in the passage refers to . . .

Solve Reference questions more easily by doing the following:

○ Make sure that the case and number of the pronoun and the antecedent you are looking for are the same. If the pronoun is *this*, eliminate any plural answer choices. Likewise, if the pronoun is *these*, eliminate any singular answer choices.

○ Replace the highlighted words with every answer choice and see which one makes the most sense. This should help you eliminate certain answer choices.

○ The answer choices will appear exactly as they do in the passage. They will also appear in the same order that they do in the passage. Some answer choices may have only one word while others may be phrases.

○ The correct answer usually appears before the highlighted word, but on occasion, it may come after the highlighted word.

Examples of Reference Questions

Natural selection was the basis of Charles Darwin's theory of evolution. He believed that species evolved based on the necessity to change in order to survive and to reproduce. Each successive generation would then have more improved traits that would help its members survive, and these organisms would also evolve as needed lest they perish. Darwin's studies of the differing types of beaks on various species of finches on the Galapagos Islands led him to conclude that the beaks had developed according to the specific types of food they consumed. Darwin theorized that the finches may have all come from one original species. A long time ago though, its members had scattered and developed on separate islands, where the birds then consumed different food sources.

Q The word "they" in the passage refers to
- Ⓐ the differing types of beaks
- Ⓑ various species of finches
- Ⓒ the Galapagos Islands
- Ⓓ the specific types of food

⊘ Explanation of the above question and answer:

> Choice (B) is what the word *they* refers to. Note the word which immediately follows *they*. It is *consumed*. Only a living creature can consume something, so the answer choice must be something alive. The only choice possible is (B). Choices (A), (C), and (D) are incorrect.

Sometimes medical discoveries are of a purely accidental nature. This was the case for Scottish scientist Alexander Fleming, who discovered penicillin in 1928. In his London laboratory, he had left a Petri dish open by mistake, and the resulting bluish mold which had grown in it had isolated a bacteria sample. Although he had discovered a drug that would revolutionize the field of medicine, it took several more years of research to produce penicillin in a medicinal form that could treat infections in patients. The start of World War II gave an impetus to this endeavor. In the United States, processes for increasing the production of medicinal penicillin were swiftly improved, and by the war's end, tens of thousands of lives had been saved by the seemingly miracle cure.

Q The word "it" in the passage refers to

(A) London laboratory

(B) Petri dish

(C) bluish mold

(D) bacteria sample

⊘ Explanation of the above question and answer:

> Choice (B) is what the word *it* refers to. Pay attention to the phrase that the highlighted word is in: "which had grown in it." The key phrase is *grown in*. This eliminates Choice (C) and Choice (D). Choice (A) is incorrect because while the London laboratory was where the penicillin grew, *it* refers to something more specific: the Petri dish. The answer is therefore Choice (B).

Factual Information questions require the test taker to understand and to be able to recognize facts that are mentioned in the passage. These questions may cover any facts or information that is explicitly covered in the passage. These may appear in the form of details, definitions, explanations, or other kinds of data. The facts which the questions ask about are typically found only in one part of the passage—usually in one paragraph but occasionally in two—and do not require a comprehensive understanding of the passage as a whole.

Factual Information questions often appear on the test like this:

- According to the paragraph, which of the following is true of X?
- The author's description of X mentions which of the following?
- According to the paragraph, X occurred because . . .
- According to the paragraph, X did Y because . . .
- According to the paragraph, why did X do Y?
- Select the TWO answer choices from paragraph 1 that identify X. *To receive credit, you must select TWO answers.*

Solve Factual Information questions more easily by doing the following:

- Pay attention to the facts that are mentioned throughout the entire passage.
- Do not be afraid to go back to the passage to check the information that it contains. Do not trust your memory since a passage is likely to have a large number of details.
- Read the answer choices closely. Many answer choices contain factual information from the passage, but one or two words in the answer choice may make it incorrect and therefore wrong.
- Some answer choices have information that may be correct but which is not mentioned in the passage. Make sure that the answer choice you select has information that is found in the passage.

Examples of Factual Information Questions

Included in the defense mechanisms which animals have evolved to protect themselves is camouflage, one of the more effective measures. By using camouflage, animals—both prey and predators—hide themselves somehow so as not to be detected by other creatures. It should be noted though, that predators use camouflage for hunting, not defensive, purposes. Most camouflage techniques can be broken down into two categories: general resemblance and special resemblance. The majority rely upon general resemblance to hide themselves. This frequently comes in the guise of color. Chameleons use color to blend in with their background as do polar bears, grasshoppers, and rabbits, among countless others. The aforementioned animals all utilize one shade to serve as camouflage. Zebras, on the other hand, have stripes, which permit them to blend in with the tall grasses on the African savanna. This is an example of special resemblance. So too is the walking stick, an insect that literally looks like a stick, which allows it to hide in plain sight from predators.

Q According to the passage, which of the following is true of camouflage?

- (A) The animals that use it get caught by predators at a lower rate.
- (B) In some instances, an animal may exactly resemble its surroundings.
- (C) It is much more helpful to prey animals than it is to predators.
- (D) The only camouflage techniques are general and special resemblance.

⊗ Explanation of the above question and answer:

> Choice (B) is the only true statement made about camouflage. The answer may be found in the last sentence in the passage. Because of the walking stick's resemblance to a real stick, it "may exactly resemble its surroundings." The rate at which animals get caught is hinted at but not specifically mentioned in the passage, so Choice (A) is incorrect. The information in Choice (C) is not mentioned at all. Choice (D) is incorrect because the passage mentions that there are other types of camouflage in addition to general and special resemblance.

[3]→ Another result of the Age of Exploration was that the European countries which sent out expeditions frequently wound up with colonies all around the world. Great powers such as Spain, Portugal, England, and France readily established colonies in faraway lands in Africa, Asia, and North and South America. Life for the colonized people was typically harsh, especially when the Spanish, who treated the residents of their colonies like slaves, were their overlords. However, the European colonizers reaped a large number of benefits. Most important of all, they gained access to new supplies of raw materials. These included, but were not limited to, gold, silver, gems, timber, and furs. As these supplies were shipped to Europe, the countries there found their coffers enlarged, and their industries had new supplies of materials from which they could manufacture finished products. Additionally, since many European countries had increasing populations, they could send excess people to their colonies, which helped to alleviate the burdens on their social systems.

Q According to paragraph 3, European countries were eager to establish colonies in other lands because

- Ⓐ they provided places for them to send their rebellious citizens
- Ⓑ they had raw materials which the European countries lacked
- Ⓒ they enslaved the colonies' populations to use as cheap labor
- Ⓓ they became wealthier through exploiting their new lands

✅ Explanation of the above question and answer:

Choice Ⓓ completes the sentence properly. In the passage, the author mentions that gold, silver, and other riches were transported to the colonizing countries. Then the author writes "the countries there found their coffers enlarged." This means they became richer; thus, Choice Ⓓ is correct. Choice Ⓐ is incorrect because European countries sent excess people, not rebellious citizens, to their colonies. For Choice Ⓑ, while colonies provided raw materials, the passage does not mention whether or not the European countries lacked them. And Choice Ⓒ is only partially correct because although the Spanish treated the people living in their colonies like slaves, nothing is mentioned about how the other European countries behaved toward them.

Negative Factual Information questions require the test taker to understand and to be able to recognize facts that are mentioned in the passage. These questions may be about any facts or information that is explicitly covered in the passage. However, these questions ask the test taker to identify the incorrect information in the answer choices. Three of the four answer choices will therefore have correct information that can be found in the passage. The answer the test taker must choose will either have incorrect information or information that is not found in the passage.

Negative Factual Information questions often appear on the test like this:

- According to the passage, which of the following is NOT true of X?
- The author's description of X mentions all of the following EXCEPT:
- In paragraph 2, all of the following questions are answered EXCEPT:

Solve Negative Factual Information questions more easily by doing the following:

○ Pay attention to the facts that are mentioned throughout the entire passage.

○ Do not be afraid to go back to the passage to check the information that it contains. Do not trust your memory since a passage is likely to have a large number of details.

○ The information in the answer choices is often found in a single paragraph or occasionally in two paragraphs. The question will identify the paragraph or paragraphs the information is in, so focus only on the identified section to find the answer.

○ The correct answer is often the exact opposite of some of the information that appears in the passages. In other cases, the correct answer may contain information that is not even mentioned in the passage.

Examples of Negative Factual Information Questions

One of the most notable aspects of Frank Lloyd Wright's work was his association with two areas of architecture that somewhat overlapped. He was a proponent of organic architecture as well as a leading figure in the Prairie School of architecture. Organic architecture focused on the notion that homes and other buildings should be in harmony with nature and should therefore integrate certain aspects of nature in their design. This included using natural materials such as wood and rock to construct buildings. Meanwhile, the Prairie School of architecture developed out of a desire to make homes and buildings that were appropriate for their natural surroundings. Even today, prairie homes can be found in various states in the Midwest. They are typically one-story, wide, and spacious since they were built to fit in with the flat vastness of the prairies in the United States. The Prairie School was also uniquely American, and it arose not only out of a love of nature but also as a way to construct homes and buildings without being influenced by European styles.

Q According to the passage, which of the following is NOT true of the Prairie School of architecture?

(A) It was created to avoid using European architectural methods.

(B) The founder of the movement was Frank Lloyd Wright.

(C) One of its goals was to make buildings blend in with nature.

(D) Homes influenced by this style often lacked a second floor.

⊘ Explanation of the above question and answer:

Choice (B) is the only one of the statements in the passage which is NOT true. According to the passage, Frank Lloyd Wright was "a leading figure in the Prairie School of architecture," but the passage does not mention whether he was the founder or not. Choice (A) is a correct statement. It is noted in the last sentence of the paragraph. The importance of being in harmony with nature is also noted, so Choice (C) is a true statement. And the passage states that Prairie School homes are "typically one-story," so Choice (D) is also a correct statement.

³➡ Many of the indigenous people living in the world's rainforests have long known how to cure various ailments by using plants. Pharmaceutical companies from around the world have also been aware of this, but nowadays there is a greater urgency to find natural remedies. First, there is competition. Countless groups of experts are rushing to rainforests, particularly those found in South America, in the hope of discovering various exotic plants in order to determine their medicinal value. The companies are hoping to find cures for cancer or other deadly diseases. The second reason for their haste is the ongoing rapid deforestation of the rainforests in many countries. Independent farmers and farming companies are both clearing land for agriculture, but, in the process, they are possibly destroying plants that could someday be utilized as medicinal cures. As the world's rainforests shrink, the pharmaceutical companies are increasing the rapidity with which they explore the forests' interiors looking for cures from Mother Nature herself.

Q In paragraph 3, all of the following questions are answered EXCEPT:

(A) How long does it take to create medicines from plants in rainforests?

(B) How are some rainforests being caused to become smaller?

(C) Why are people interested in discovering plants in rainforest?

(D) Why are pharmaceutical companies in a hurry to explore rainforests?

⊘ Explanation of the above question and answer:

Choice (A) is the only one of the questions in the paragraph that is NOT answered. There is nothing in the passage about how long it takes to create medicines from plants in rainforests. The paragraph explains why some rainforests are getting smaller, so the question in Choice (B) is answered. The question in Choice (C) is also answered because people want to discover plants in rainforests to make medicines with them. And the question in Choice (D) is answered because the paragraph explains why pharmaceutical companies are in a hurry to explore rainforests.

Sentence Simplification questions require the test taker to select a sentence that best restates one that has been highlighted in the passage. These questions ask the test taker to note the main points in the sentence and to make sure that they are mentioned in the rewritten sentence. These sentences use words, phrases, and grammar that are different from the highlighted sentence. They also sometimes do not appear in a passage. When they are asked, there is only one Sentence Simplification question per passage.

Sentence Simplification questions often appear on the test like this:

- Which of the sentences below best expresses the essential information in the highlighted sentence in the passage? *Incorrect* answer choices change the meaning in important ways or leave out essential information.

Solve Sentence Simplification questions more easily by doing the following:

○ The highlighted sentences can often be broken down into separate clauses. Determine what the main point of each clause is.

○ Make sure that the answer choice you select covers all of the essential information in the highlighted sentence.

○ Make sure that the answer choice you select does not have any information that disagrees with or is in opposition to the main sentence.

○ Avoid selecting answer choices that omit essential information. Sometimes an answer choice may accurately restate a part of the sentence yet leave out an important point. This makes it an incorrect answer.

Example of Sentence Simplification Questions

The positive effects of dams have been well chronicled, yet for whatever reason, their negative effects are often ignored. Dams actually have many disadvantages, primarily in the manner in which they affect their local area. For one, dams interrupt the natural cycle of the environment for both plants and animals. The construction of most dams results in the formation of a large lake. This means that land that was once above water is now submerged. In many cases, both people and animals are obligated to depart from areas where they had once lived. The forming of a lake can also result in the disappearing of animals' breeding or feeding grounds, and it can also kill many plants that once lived in the now water-covered area. In addition, dams remove sediment, which had once flowed freely, from the river. While this frequently results in water that is crystal clear in most places downriver from the dam, the absence of silt removes invaluable nutrients from the water. This can have a dramatic effect on the fish and the plants living in the river's waters. As their habitat is destroyed, the fish either die out or flee to other areas while the plants merely die. Additionally, many animals use water muddied by silt to hide from predators. Once the silt is removed because of the dam, these animals become easy targets and are often quickly devoured.

Q Which of the sentences below best expresses the essential information in the highlighted sentence in the passage? *Incorrect* answer choices change the meaning in important ways or leave out essential information.

(A) The crystal-clear water downriver from the dam lacks silt, which means that it has more nutrients in it.

(B) Without nutrients in the water, the water will turn a different color so that it is very easy to see through.

(C) Dams are meant to remove silt and nutrients from the water, and this is what makes some rivers so clear.

(D) The water flowing in places downstream from the dam is clear, but it lacks the nutrients that silt provides.

✅ Explanation of the above question and answer:

Choice (D) best restates the important information from the highlighted sentence. The highlighted sentence can be broken down into two parts: 1) The water downriver from the dam is crystal clear, and 2) the lack of silt means the water is missing nutrients. Choice (D) includes both of those essential pieces of information. Choice (A) is incorrect because it states that the water has more nutrients, not fewer nutrients. Choice (B) is incorrect because it fails to mention silt, which is important to both parts of the sentence. Choice (C) is incorrect because it adds information about the purpose of dams. This is information that did not appear in the highlighted sentence.

Question Type 06 | Inference

Inference questions require the test taker to understand the argument that the passage is attempting to make. These questions ask the test taker to consider the information that is presented and then to come to a logical conclusion about it. The answers to these questions are never explicitly stated in the passage. Instead, the test taker is asked to infer what the author means. These questions often deal with cause and effect or comparisons between two different things, ideas, events, or people.

Inference questions often appear on the test like this:

- Which of the following can be inferred about X?
- The author of the passage implies that X . . .
- Which of the following can be inferred from paragraph 1 about X?

Solve Inference questions more easily by doing the following:

○ Learn to read between the lines. Understand that the words written by the author often have a second meaning. However, this meaning is not stated; it is only hinted at.

○ Think about cause-effect relationships in the passage. The author may describe an event, idea, or phenomenon in the passage. Consider what some possible effects of these may be.

○ Remember that the correct answer will never contradict the main point of the passage. Do not choose an answer that does not agree with the central idea of the passage.

○ Do not simply choose an answer because it contains words that appear in the passage. These are often intentionally misleading.

Examples of Inference Questions

² → Italian teacher Maria Montessori developed the method of education that has been named for her in Rome at the beginning of the twentieth century. The premise behind the Montessori Method of education centers on the concept that children are different from adults in the ways they think, learn, and develop. For the most part, the Montessori Method is used with preschool and elementary school children, not with older children. At a Montessori-directed school, the teachers act as observers, not lecturers. They provide direction to the students and initiate projects and study sessions, but the students are essentially on their own since the teachers merely observe them in silence. The children are not given a set of problems to solve, nor do the teachers provide them with the correct answer if they cannot discover it. Instead, in Montessori classrooms, children are allowed to find the answers to their questions and to discover why they are the answers all by themselves.

Q In paragraph 2, the author implies that the Montessori Method
- Ⓐ is the primary education method used by the Italians
- Ⓑ encourages the students to communicate with their teacher
- Ⓒ rewards students who work well with others in their class
- Ⓓ is seldom used to teach students who are in high school

⊘ Explanation of the above question and answer:

Choice Ⓓ is implied about the Montessori Method in the passage. The author writes, "For the most part, the Montessori Method is used with preschool and elementary school children, not with older children." This implies that high school students are only seldom taught with this method. Italy is only mentioned because it is Montessori's home country, so Choice Ⓐ is incorrect. The students at Montessori-directed schools are not encouraged to speak with their teacher, so Choice Ⓑ is incorrect. There is nothing hinted as to whether or not students should work together with their classmates, so Choice Ⓒ is also incorrect.

³➙ When a volcano erupts, a pyroclastic flow is one possible result. This is a massive cloud of hot gases, rocks, and ash which emerges from the volcano, flows with rapid speed down its slopes, and utterly destroys anything in its path. Volcanologists have clocked pyroclastic flows at more than 400 miles per hour and at temperatures that nearly reached 2,000 degrees Fahrenheit. If a pyroclastic flow has more gas and ash than it does rock, it can flow swiftly over geographical features such as ridges, and it can even travel across open water. In the few instances where human settlements were in the path of a pyroclastic flow, the devastation was complete. When Mount Pelee on the French island of Martinique erupted in 1902, the resulting pyroclastic flow struck the town of Saint Pierre and killed more than 30,000 people—most of them in a very short time—from heat, fires, and poisonous gases.

Q In paragraph 3, which of the following can be inferred about pyroclastic flows?
- Ⓐ The presence of a river might not be enough to stop them.
- Ⓑ They are comprised of equal amounts of gas, rock, and ash.
- Ⓒ They can move at high rates of speed for several hours.
- Ⓓ It is possible for people to survive close encounters with them.

⊘ Explanation of the above question and answer:

Choice Ⓐ can be inferred about pyroclastic flows by reading the passage. The author notes that pyroclastic flows "can even travel across open water." Thus, it can be inferred that they may be able to cross a river and that the presence of water will not prevent them from crossing. The passage notes that pyroclastic flows can have unequal amounts of gas, rock, and ash, so Choice Ⓑ is incorrect. While pyroclastic flows can move very fast, nothing is hinted as to how long they can move that quickly, so Choice Ⓒ is incorrect. And the author notes that they "utterly" destroy everything in their way, so it is doubtful that people can survive encounters with them.

Rhetorical Purpose questions require the test taker to understand why the author mentions or writes about something in the passage. These questions ask the test taker to consider the reasoning behind the information that is being presented in the passage. For these questions, the function—not the meaning—of the material is the most important aspect to be aware of. The questions often focus on the relationship between the information mentioned or covered either in paragraphs or individual sentences in the passage and the purpose or intention of the information that is given.

Rhetorical Purpose questions often appear on the test like this:

- The author discusses "**X**" in paragraph 2 in order to . . .
- Why does the author mention "**X**"?
- The author uses "**X**" as an example of . . .

Solve Rhetorical Purpose questions more easily by doing the following:

○ Identify the part of the passage to which the question refers. Then, try to understand how the topic mentioned in the question relates to the passage as a whole.

○ Look for clues in the passage that will help identify the author's purpose. These clues often appear in the language itself when the author uses words such as *definition, example, illustrate, explain, contrast, compare, refute, note, criticize,* or *function.*

○ To answer these questions, there is no need to consider the passage as a whole. Instead, merely focus on the section which mentions the topic of the question.

Examples of Rhetorical Purpose Questions

While Greenland today is primarily an inhospitable land known mostly for its extensive glaciers, it did not always have the same harsh weather conditions. In fact, Greenland received its name during a time of warming in the Middle Ages, when, to offshore observers, it appeared to be a land of green grass and forests. The years from around 800 to 1300 were a period of high temperatures all around the world. This made the Atlantic Ocean more ice-free and allowed the Vikings, some of whom were led by Leif Ericson, to sail to various islands in the Atlantic Ocean. Iceland, Greenland, and even the more distant Newfoundland in North America were all settled. Unlike today, during this warm period, the settlers on Greenland could actually cultivate parts of the land. Some academics have speculated that Ericson, who named Greenland, gave the island its name in order to attract more people to his settlement. There may be some truth to this theory, but at the time, he was hardly exaggerating; Greenland really was a fertile place.

Q Why does the author mention "Leif Ericson"?

- (A) To give the name of the person who discovered Greenland
- (B) To mention him as one of the Vikings who sailed to Greenland
- (C) To discuss the reason why he gave Greenland its name
- (D) To claim that the name he gave Greenland was misleading

⊘ Explanation of the above question and answer:

Choice (C) best explains why the author mentioned Leif Ericson. The paragraph notes that vegetation once grew on Greenland, and it also mentions that Leif Ericson named the island. The end of the paragraph explains why Greenland got its name, which makes Choice (C) the correct answer. Choice (A) is incorrect. The person who discovered Greenland is not mentioned. While the passage mentions that Leif Ericson sailed to Greenland, it is a minor point, so Choice (B) is incorrect. Choice (D) is incorrect because the author mentions that the name Greenland was not misleading since it really had vegetation on it.

3→ Through countless generations, animals have evolved to protect themselves from cold temperatures, especially in extreme climates. These changes include having fur and feathers and also using blubber. Mammals such as the polar bear have fur, which can protect them from the cold. Birds, on the other hand, have feathers, which can grow to be very thick and thus can provide comfort when the cold of winter arrives. Fortunately for these animals, they have also developed ways to keep themselves from overheating when warmer weather arrives. Mammals can shed fur, which enables them to have less dense coats, while birds molt. This is a process that causes them to lose many of their feathers. Other animals, however, rely upon blubber, which is a thick layer of fat, to insulate themselves from the cold. These animals—which include seals and walruses—overeat, and this causes them to develop a large amount of blubber. They can then utilize their blubber to keep warm as well as to provide them with nourishment when food is in short supply.

Q The author discusses "blubber" in paragraph 3 in order to

- (A) compare its effects with fur and feathers
- (B) explain how animals develop and use it
- (C) name some animals that rely upon it
- (D) prove that it protects animals from the cold

⊘ Explanation of the above question and answer:

Choice (B) best describes why the professor discusses blubber. Both the passage and the answer choice contain the word "develop," and the passage has "utilize" while the answer choice has "use." The similarities in word choice help indicate the correct answer. Choice (A) is incorrect because while fur and feathers are mentioned, they are not compared with blubber. Choice (C) is incorrect. The author names two animals that rely on blubber, but that is a minor point. Choice (D) is incorrect because the author does not try to prove anything about the effectiveness of blubber.

Insert Text questions require the test taker to determine where in the passage another sentence should be placed. These questions ask the test taker to consider various aspects, including grammar, logic, connecting words, and flow, when deciding where the new sentence best belongs. This question always appears just before the last question. Nowadays, there is almost always one Insert Text question for every passage.

Insert Text questions often appear on the test like this:

- Look at the four squares [■] that indicate where the following sentence could be added to the passage.

  [**You will see a sentence in bold.**]

  Where would the sentence best fit?

  Click on a square [■] to add the sentence to the passage.

Solve Insert Text questions more easily by doing the following:

○ Insert the sentence in all four places where squares appear and then read the resulting passage. This will help you determine where the sentence best goes.

○ Pay attention to connecting words that can help maintain the flow of the passage. Words or phrases such as *therefore, similarly, in contrast, for example, for instance, finally, meanwhile, on the other hand,* and *as a result* are often used as connecting words. Note how they fit in with the other sentences in the passage.

○ Make sure that the place for the new sentence which you select fits logically with the other sentences in the passage.

Example of an Insert Text Question

No society exists in a vacuum; therefore, ideas, inventions, and social practices often move from one culture to another. This is what is known as cultural diffusion. It happens when people from various societies observe something in another place, and they subsequently introduce it to their own culture, thereby altering it. These changes can occur for a number of different reasons. Defeated people may have changes forced upon them by their conquerors. Merchants traveling to faraway lands may bring new ideas, or even religions and philosophies, back home with them when they return from their trips. **1** And immigrants may bring with them ideas, languages, or even inventions from their homelands. **2** Whatever the case may be, cultural diffusion has had a tremendous effect on many societies. **3** One of the most prominent—and repeating—examples of cultural diffusion happens to be the introduction of religions to various places. **4** For instance, Christianity was once a minor cult in the Roman Empire. However, it was introduced to the many cultures living in the Roman Empire and was accepted by so many that it ultimately managed to become the sanctioned religion of an empire that covered much of Europe and parts of Asia and Africa. Buddhism also spread through cultural diffusion. While Buddhism's origins lie in India, it spread throughout Asia, eventually reaching China, Korea, and Japan, where it went on greatly to affect and influence the cultures in those three areas.

Q Look at the four squares [■] that indicate where the following sentence could be added to the passage.

Finally, people may actively attempt to spread ideas through methods such as those that missionaries utilize.

Where would the sentence best fit?

Click on a square [■] to add the sentence to the passage.

⊘ Explanation of the above question and answer:

After the second square is where the sentence best fits. Notice the presence of the word *finally*. The three sentences prior to the second square all mention different reasons why culture diffusion occurred. The new sentence also discusses cultural diffusion. Since it begins with *Finally*, it should be the last sentence in the series. The first square is incorrect because putting the sentence there would mean that the series would not flow logically. The third square is incorrect since the two sentences are about different topics. The fourth square seems as if it could potentially be the correct answer because the sentence in the passage mentions religion while the new sentence mentions missionaries. Thus, they appear to have a connection. However, they are actually discussing different topics, so the fourth square is incorrect as well.

Prose Summary questions require the test taker to understand the main point of the passage and then to select sentences which emphasize the main point. These questions present a sentence which is essentially a thesis statement for the entire passage. The sentence synthesizes the main points of the passage. The test taker must then choose three out of six sentences which most closely describe points mentioned in the introductory sentence. This means that three of the choices are minor points, have incorrect information, or do not appear in the passage, so they are all therefore incorrect. These are always the last question asked about a Reading passage, but they do not always appear. Instead, a Fill in a Table question may appear in its place. However, nowadays, Prose Summary questions are much more common than Fill in a Table questions.

Prose Summary questions often appear on the test like this:

- *Directions:* An introductory sentence for a brief summary of the passage is provided below. Complete the summary by selecting the THREE answer choices that express the most important ideas of the passage. Some sentences do not belong because they express ideas that are not presented in the passage or are minor ideas in the passage. *This question is worth 2 points.*

Solve Prose Summary questions more easily by doing the following:

○ Recognize that the statement sums up the main themes or ideas of the passage.

○ Focus on selecting answer choices that refer to these main themes or ideas.

○ Ignore answer choices that refer to minor themes in the passage.

○ Some answer choices may have correct information, but this information is not mentioned in the passage. Ignore these answer choices as they are incorrect.

Example of a Prose Summary Question

Print and Online Newspapers

Technology can have a tremendous effect on certain industries. Sometimes the changes can come swiftly, such as when the automobile replaced the horse and buggy virtually overnight. In other situations, the transformation can be more drawn out. One such instance of technology having a slower effect on a particular industry is currently happening with the modern news media. Because of the Internet, traditional print media is undergoing various radical changes.

For years, many people woke up, retrieved their morning paper from the front porch, and read it over breakfast. Others waited to read the evening edition of the local newspaper until they returned home from work. Whatever the case may have been, for millions, reading the daily newspaper was their primary source of local, domestic, and international news. However, when the World Wide Web began gaining popularity in the 1990s, newspapers almost immediately began publishing online editions. These electronic versions typically had the same articles that were published in the print version. But there were two major differences: Online stories could be updated or revised almost instantly, and people no longer had to wait until the next day to read the news. Since breaking news updates could be posted as soon as noteworthy events happened, people started to make the switch from printed to online news.

Unfortunately for newspapers, few of them actually charge their readers to peruse their content. Most simply make it available for free. While newspapers sell online ads, they cost much less than ads sold in printed versions. Additionally, as the number of subscribers to printed newspapers began decreasing and as advertisers started making the transition to the Internet, newspapers saw the amount of money they could charge for ads decrease as well. Once highly profitable, in recent years, newspapers have watched their revenues and profits plummet, and some major American newspapers have even been forced to declare bankruptcy.

These changes brought about by the Internet are forcing newspapers to engage in a certain amount of introspection. Clearly, the traditional model of the newspaper—one which employed large numbers of reporters, editors, copywriters, and other employees—is no longer valid. Newspapers must find a way to make themselves profitable once again. This will surely involve using the Internet in some manner. It is up to them, however, to determine the method they will use. Only then will they be able to prevent modern technology from making them the twenty-first century equivalent of the horse and buggy: something today only seen in museums.

Q **Directions:** An introductory sentence for a brief summary of the passage is provided below. Complete the summary by selecting the THREE answer choices that express the most important ideas of the passage. Some sentences do not belong because they express ideas that are not presented in the passage or are minor ideas in the passage. *This question is worth 2 points.*

Drag your answer choices to the spaces where they belong.
To remove an answer choice, click on it. To review the passage, click on **View Text**.

The rise of the Internet and online versions of newspapers has created problems for the modern newspaper industry.

-
-
-

Answer Choices

① Some newspapers in the United States are completely out of money.

② Technological changes have caused many industries to go out of business.

③ In the 1990s, online papers gained popularity while printed versions lost popularity.

④ Newspapers get paid less for online advertisements, so their ad revenue is going down.

⑤ Newspapers must come up with a new paradigm to make themselves competitive.

⑥ Newspapers typically hire a large number of people to do specialized jobs.

⊘ Explanation of the above question and answer:

Choices ③, ④, and ⑤ are all correct. Choice ③ refers to a problem in the modern newspaper industry—how their printed versions are losing popularity—and notes the effect of the Internet on them. Choice ④ shows how the Internet has negatively affected newspapers. And Choice ⑤ mentions that newspapers need a new method—a new paradigm—that will let them become competitive with online businesses. Choices ①, ②, and ⑥ are all incorrect. Choice ① notes how some newspapers are out of money, which is true, but is a minor point. Choice ② is true but is a minor point in the passage. Choice ⑥ is also true, but it is a minor point as well.

Fill in a Table questions require the test taker to have a comprehensive understanding of the entire passage. These questions typically break the passage down into two—or sometimes three—main points or themes. The test taker must then read a number of sentences or phrases and determine which of the points or themes the sentences or phrases refer to. These questions often ask the test taker to consider cause and effect, to compare and contrast, or to understand various theories or ideas covered. These are always the last question asked about a Reading passage, but they do not always appear. Instead, a prose summary question may appear in its place. Nowadays, Fill in a Table questions are much lesson common than Prose Summary questions.

Fill in a Table questions often appear on the test like this:

- *Directions:* Select the appropriate sentences [phrases] from the answer choices and match them to the type of X to which they relate. TWO of the answer choices will NOT be used. ***This question is worth 3 [4] points.***

Solve Fill in a Table questions more easily by doing the following:

○ Recognize the major ideas or themes that are covered in the passage. Note any significant differences between them.

○ Pay attention if you are reading a cause-effect passage, a compare-contrast passage, or a problem-solution passage. These passages frequently have Fill in a Table questions.

○ Take notes on the main ideas or themes. Focus primarily on the major points rather than the minor ones. Fill in a Table questions usually have statements about the main points but ignore the minor ones.

○ Ignore answer choices that are not connected to either of the two or three categories. There will always be two answer choices that are incorrect and should not be selected.

Example of a Fill in a Table Question

Egyptian and Sumerian Civilizations

The first successful human attempts at developing civilization occurred in the area of the Middle East known as the Fertile Crescent. Two distinct societies—Egyptian and Sumerian—developed, and both lasted for thousands of years. They shared some resemblances regarding their geographic locale, dependence on irrigated agriculture, religious practices, use of writing, and architecture. Yet upon closer observation, many of these similarities were merely superficial in nature and only somewhat comparable.

Both civilizations arose near river systems. The Egyptians lived along the Nile River, and the Sumerians settled around the Tigris and Euphrates rivers in Mesopotamia, which is located in modern-day southern Iraq. Agriculture based on irrigated land served as the basis for their food supply. The Egyptians' irrigation methods depended not so much on their skills but on the annual flooding of the Nile, which brought nutrient-rich waters to their farms. In contrast, the Sumerians established an extensive irrigation system that drew water from the two great rivers and brought it to farmlands. So enormous was this undertaking that some scholars believe the rise of the Sumerian bureaucracy was a direct result of the necessity of harnessing the manpower and resources to construct this system.

Each civilization had a hierarchical governing structure, with the godlike pharaohs dominating in Egypt and a priest class ruling in Sumerian culture. Additionally, both cultures erected massive structures, but in design and purpose, they had some differences. The pharaohs built the pyramids to serve as their tombs while the Sumerians constructed ziggurats to worship and honor their gods. The Egyptian pyramids had an almost uniform progression of stones from bottom to top, giving them a smooth appearance from a distance. But the ziggurats were steplike structures.

Significantly, both cultures developed systems of writing, a true indicator of a highly developed culture. Initially, both the Sumerians and the Egyptians used pictures to represent words and to express ideas. The Egyptians continued using their hieroglyphics for thousands of years. However, the Sumerians managed to change their picture writing into what scholars today call cuneiform. It consisted of wedge-like marks made on wet clay, which were then dried. While based on pictures, cuneiform can arguably be considered the world's first distinct writing system.

In the end, the Egyptians outlasted the Sumerians. Sheltered in the Nile valley and surrounded by deserts, the Egyptians were afforded protection by their geographical location. Thus, they remained long after the Sumerians had declined and been assimilated into other cultures in the Mesopotamian area. While ancient Egyptian monuments still stand for all to see, virtually nothing of early Sumerian civilization now exists.

Q **Directions:** Select the appropriate sentences from the answer choices and match them to the type of civilization to which they relate. TWO of the answer choices will NOT be used. **This question is worth 3 points.**

Drag your answer choices to the spaces where they belong.
To remove an answer choice, click on it. To review the passage, click on **View Text**.

Answer Choices	TYPE OF CIVILIZATION
1 It was founded along the banks of two separate rivers.	**Egyptian**
	•
2 It failed to develop a writing system more advanced than pictures.	•
	•
3 It survived into the present day in southern Iraq.	**Sumerian**
4 Its people worshipped gods in ziggurats they constructed.	•
	•
5 Its rulers were considered to be similar to divine beings.	
6 Its farmers relied upon water from a flooding river.	
7 It constructed pyramids that had steplike structures.	

✅ Explanation of the above question and answer:

The second, fifth, and sixth choices refer to Egyptian civilization. The second choice describes hieroglyphics—a form of picture writing—which was the most advanced form of writing for the Egyptians. The fifth choice refers to the phrase "godlike pharaohs" that appears in the passage. And the sixth choice refers to the fact that Egyptian farmers relied upon the annual flooding of the Nile River to irrigate the land. The first and fourth choices refer to Sumerian civilization. The first choice refers to the Tigris and Euphrates rivers, upon which Sumerian civilization was founded. The fourth choice mentions ziggurats, which was where the Sumerians worshipped. The third and seventh choices refer to neither civilization.

The Creation of the Solar System

¹➜ Earth is part of a larger celestial group called the solar system, which consists of the sun, eight planets, several dwarf planets, including Pluto, comets, asteroids, meteoroids, and the numerous moons orbiting planets. How the solar system was formed is a matter of speculation for astronomers. There are three main theories that describe its creation. They are the core accretion theory, the tidal theory, and the exploding supernova theory. All three agree the sun was formed first; however, they disagree about how the planets and everything else were created. Although each one has its supporters and detractors, the core accretion theory is widely considered the most plausible explanation as to how the planets came into existence.

²➜ Supporters of the core accretion theory generally agree that in the beginning, the universe consisted primarily of dark matter, helium, and hydrogen. Gradually, these gathered together to form galaxies, and then within these galaxies, stars, solar systems, and all of their internal components were formed. Some stars were short lived and exploded, thereby becoming supernovas. A spinning disk comprised of around 98% helium and hydrogen formed from the remnants of one of these supernovas, and it gradually produced a gravitational attraction that pulled other elements from space together to form the sun. As these elements collided, they created heat and eventually formed the fusion process through which the sun generates its own heat and energy. At this point, the sun had become a star.

³➜ After the creation of the sun, the planets were formed. It is at this point, however, that astronomers cannot agree on what happened. Nevertheless, the core accretion theory is the most probable explanation of the process by which Earth, the other planets, and everything else came into being. According to some astronomers, as the center of the spinning disk became the sun, the remaining elements in that cloud of dust and gas collided, and through accretion, they began forming larger masses, which created their own fields of gravity and therefore attracted more and more matter. At this point, the solar system had a flattened appearance and was something which astronomers call a protoplanetary disk. Its shape was the result of the forces of gravity, rotation, and magnetism working together. The remaining gases in the spinning disk became the gas planets—or Jovians—Jupiter, Saturn, Uranus, and Neptune. Meanwhile, the dust and the heavier elements coalesced to become the terrestrial planets—Mercury, Venus, Earth, and Mars—as well as the dwarf planets and asteroids. The main reason why rocky planets developed close to the sun while gaseous planets formed farther away is that the sun's heat was too great for the molecules that comprise gaseous planets to condense. Only elements with high melting points, such as iron, could form planets so close to the sun's heat.

The core accretion theory is rejected by some scientists, however, who favor either the tidal theory or the exploding supernova theory. According to both theories, by the time the sun had formed, there were neither planets nor a spinning disk of matter that would become the planets. The tidal theory proposes that the strong gravitational pull of a passing star ripped away parts of the sun. These pieces of matter were then dropped like breadcrumbs marking a trail as the itinerant star moved away from the sun. Eventually, these chunks became the planets. Finally, scientists who believe in the exploding supernova theory postulate that the sun had a nearby twin that exploded and left behind the material which became the planets. It is similar to the core accretion theory except it claims the material which created the planets and everything else came from a star other than the sun.

As of today, it is impossible to know which theory, if any, is correct, but the core accretion theory seems the most plausible since astronomers have observed protoplanetary disks, which appear to be the beginnings of new solar systems, near other stars. **1** Because of the limits of scientific knowledge, many questions about the formation of the solar system remain. **2** Astronomers hope, however, that by examining the planets and solar systems of other stars, they will be able to learn more about Earth's solar system. **3** Perhaps then the mystery of its creation will be solved. **4**

📚 *Glossary*

detractor: an opponent
remnant: something that is left over

---

1 In paragraph 1, why does the author mention "Pluto"?

   Ⓐ To compare it with the other planets in the solar system

   Ⓑ To provide an example of one of the first planets to be formed

   Ⓒ To argue that it should be considered a part of the solar system

   Ⓓ To identify it as one of the solar system's dwarf planets

Rhetorical Purpose Question (0-2 questions per passage)

Ⓓ | Pluto is mentioned in the phrase "including Pluto," which shows that the author is identifying it as a dwarf planet.

2 According to paragraph 1, which of the following is NOT true of the creation of the solar system?

   Ⓐ One theory concerning its creation has more adherents than the others do.

   Ⓑ The exploding supernova theory is opposed by the greatest number of people.

   Ⓒ The manner in which it came into being is still unknown to experts.

   Ⓓ The main theories on its creation have some aspects they share in common.

Negative Factual Question (0-2 questions per passage)

Ⓑ | There is nothing mentioned about how many people oppose the exploding supernova theory.

3 The word "it" in the passage refers to

   Ⓐ a spinning disk

   Ⓑ hydrogen

   Ⓒ a gravitational attraction

   Ⓓ space

Reference Question (0-1 questions per passage)

Ⓐ | The second half of the sentence is also about the spinning disk, so that is the correct answer.

4 According to paragraph 2, which of the following is true of supernovas?

   Ⓐ They are what remain of a star after it explodes.

   Ⓑ The majority of their composition is dark matter.

   Ⓒ They were stars prior to becoming supernovas.

   Ⓓ They emit a tremendous amount of energy.

Factual Question (1-3 questions per passage)

Ⓒ | The passage reads, "Some stars were short lived and exploded, thereby becoming supernovas," which shows that supernovas were once stars.

5 According to paragraph 2, the sun managed to transform into a star because

- (A) it became self-sustaining since it created its own energy
- (B) it gathered together all of the elements scattered by the supernova
- (C) it is comprised almost entirely of hydrogen and helium
- (D) it emitted light throughout the solar system for a sustained period of time

Factual Question
(1-3 questions per passage)

(A) | The passage states that the sun generates its own heat and energy, which is what makes it a star.

6 Which of the sentences below best expresses the essential information in the highlighted sentence in the passage? *Incorrect* answer choices change the meaning in important ways or leave out essential information.

- (A) The high temperatures caused by the sun made rocky planets, which formed close to it, practically devoid of any gaseous elements.
- (B) The terrestrial planets were created close to the sun while the Jovian planets wound up being created at distances far from it.
- (C) The gaseous planets were created far away from the sun, so its heat could not affect their gas molecules, but this was not true for the rocky planets.
- (D) The terrestrial and Jovian planets formed in different parts of the solar system on account of the intense heat emitted by the sun.

Sentence Simplification Question
(0-1 question per passage)

(D) | The highlighted sentence notes that the sun's heat made the terrestrial and Jovian planets form in different parts of the solar system.

7 In paragraph 3, the author implies that the protoplanetary disk

- (A) was much wider in the areas where the Jovian planets are now located
- (B) was responsible for the creation of comets, asteroids, and meteors
- (C) dissipated into nothingness once the planets were completely formed
- (D) was a unique phenomenon that is unlikely to form in other star systems

Inference Question
(0-2 questions per passage)

(B) | The passage mentions that because of the disk, the planets and "everything else came into being," which implies that the disk created the comets, asteroids, and meteors.

8 The word "itinerant" in the passage is closest in meaning to

- (A) wandering
- (B) hermetic
- (C) invading
- (D) encroaching

Vocabulary Question
(1-3 questions per passage)

(A) | In the sentence with "itinerant," it is noted that the sun is moving, which indicates that it is wandering through outer space.

9 Look at the four squares [■] that indicate where the following sentence could be added to the passage.

This has been made possible thanks to their having access to more advanced equipment, such as the Hubble Space Telescope, which currently orbits Earth.

Where would the sentence best fit?

Click on a square [■] to add the sentence to the passage.

10 *Directions:* Select the appropriate statements from the answer choices and match them to the theory on the creation of the solar system to which they relate. TWO of the answer choices will NOT be used. *This question is worth 3 points.*

Drag your answer choices to the spaces where they belong.
To remove an answer choice, click on it.
To review the passage, click on **View Text**.

Answer Choices

1. Is the least believed of the three main creation theories
2. Was caused by the appearance of another star near the solar system
3. Accounts for the placement of the planets in the solar system
4. Has the greatest number of believers in the astronomy community
5. Came about through the disappearance of the sun's twin
6. Made planets because of a star's gravitational effects
7. Explains where the leftover elements in the solar system have gone

THE CREATION OF THE SOLAR SYSTEM

Core Accretion Theory

-
-

Tidal Theory

-
-

Exploding Supernova Theory

-

Insert Text Question
(0-1 question per passage)

*Always appears just in front of the last Reading to Learn question

■ | The phrase "since astronomers have observed protoplanetary disks" is crucial because it indicates that they are able to look at objects far away; the sentence to be inserted includes what astronomers used to observe these disks.

Fill in a Table Question

*Partial-Credit Item

5 key items
3 correct answers: 1 point
4 correct answers: 2 points
5 correct answers: 3 points

7 key items
4 correct answers: 1 point
5 correct answers: 2 points
6 correct answers: 3 points
7 correct answers: 4 points

Core Accretion Theory: ③, ④

Tidal Theory: ②, ⑥

Exploding Supernova Theory: ⑤

According to the passage, the core accretion theory tells why the Jovian and terrestrial planets are in their locations and is also supported by the most astronomers. The tidal theory states that another star helped create the solar system and also mentions that the gravity of a star affected the solar system's creation. The exploding supernova theory claims that another star near the sun exploded and became a supernova, which thereby helped create the solar system.

11 *Directions:* An introductory sentence for a brief summary of the passage is provided below. Complete the summary by selecting the THREE answer choices that express the most important ideas of the passage. Some sentences do not belong because they express ideas that are not presented in the passage or are minor ideas in the passage. ***This question is worth 2 points.***

> Drag your answer choices to the spaces where they belong.
> To remove an answer choice, click on it.
> To review the passage, click on **View Text**.

Despite the fact that they generally agree upon how the universe was formed, astronomers are in disagreement about the manner in which Earth's solar system was created.

-
-
-

Answer Choices

1. Until astronomers obtain more information about the solar system, they will be unable to state with any certainty how it came in to being.

2. There are three main theories, one of which is the core accretion theory, that explain how the solar system formed.

3. There are a huge number of objects in the solar system, and they include planets, dwarf planets, asteroids, and comets.

4. Scientists have observed the creation of solar systems around other stars, which is teaching them about Earth's solar system.

5. Most astronomers believe that the sun was created in the aftermath of the explosion of a supernova.

6. The tidal theory and the exploding supernova theory are the two least likely explanations for the formation of the solar system.

☑ 2, 5, 6

According to the passage, there are three main theories on the formation of the solar system. The core accretion theory, which is the most believed, is also based on the explosion of a supernova. Since the core accretion theory is the most believed, the other two theories receive less support from astronomers.

B

Building Background Knowledge of TOEFL Topics

Chapter 01   History

History is the study of the past. Historians typically concern themselves with important names, dates, places, and events, but history is not simply about memorizing facts. On the contrary, historians attempt to interpret various events that happened in the past. In other words, not only do they study what happened, but they also try to explain why specific events happened. For this reason, many historians often disagree with one another about various interpretations of historical events. While it is difficult to dispute facts, it is simple to argue about why something happened and what its effects were. For this reason, history is full of different theories which seek to explain various past events. In fact, historians take many different approaches to their field. This is known as historiography. Some historians closely examine political events. Others study military, economic, or diplomatic history. Nowadays, social history, women's history, and cultural history are popular fields of study.

The Change from English to American

When the American Revolution started in 1775, around two and a half million people lived in the thirteen colonies. The vast majority had emigrated from England or were descendants of English settlers. Most called themselves English and still felt a strong bond with the customs and traditions of their faraway homeland. When war erupted, this connection was put to the test. Many saw the colonists' reasoning behind their revolt but could not bring themselves to lift a hand against mother England; therefore, they tried to remain neutral. Others were so fiercely devoted to England that they instead formed loyalist groups that aided the English military forces.

2→ Before the revolution, there was one major difference between an Englishman in England and one in America. Men with property in England had the right to vote for representatives in **Parliament**. Their grievances were heard, and they had the power to effect changes. This was not so in America as the American colonies lacked representatives in Parliament. The colonists had their own legislatures as well as some measure of autonomy, but even this power was subject both to British law and the rule of a local British governor. Thus, men who considered themselves Englishmen in America were treated as American colonists by their counterparts in England.

3→ Many American colonists were of the opinion that they possessed rights beyond what their supposed rulers in England were willing to grant them. The king of England, while subject to restrictions by Parliament, was still invested with the power to govern the British Empire. In essence, England was an **aristocracy** that ruled millions of people from afar and had little concern for what they desired. The majority of American colonists wanted to rid themselves of English rule and to form a republic to rule themselves. Calls for revolution started because of these aspirations. The actual break between the two groups came as a result of the heavy debt England incurred following the Seven Years' War. Since the war had been fought primarily to protect the American colonies from the French, the English thought the colonies should pay the debt. The series of taxes subsequently levied on the colonists so angered them that they revolted—by waging war. In the end, the Americans won, driving the English back to England and most Loyalists to Canada. After the war, any ties the colonists had previously with England were severed. From then on, those who had fought against England became Americans.

≋ *Glossary*

Parliament: the legislature in Great Britain
aristocracy: a monarchy

1 Which of the sentences below best expresses the essential information in the highlighted sentence in the passage? *Incorrect* answer choices change the meaning in important ways or leave out essential information.

   (A) While they disagreed with the colonists' motivations, they still remained neutral in the fight against the English.

   (B) The revolt forced people to choose sides, so those who wanted to rebel against England tried to remain neutral yet could not do so.

   (C) Despite understanding the colonists' feelings, many people avoided choosing sides since they did not want to fight England.

   (D) Wishing to stay neutral, many people refused to choose sides or to examine the logic behind the colonists' actions.

2 The word "grievances" in the passage is closest in meaning to

   (A) complaints

   (B) decisions

   (C) institutions

   (D) elections

3 According to paragraph 2, which of the following is true of the American colonists?

   (A) They were respected as Englishmen by people living in Britain.

   (B) They were given the right to rule themselves to some extent.

   (C) They were allowed to vote for representatives in Parliament.

   (D) They were actively involved in the British government.

4 In paragraph 3, why does the author mention "the Seven Years' War"?

   (A) To point out when the American Revolution actually started

   (B) To sympathize with the British position on taxing the American colonists

   (C) To explain how England went bankrupt during the eighteenth century

   (D) To note what caused the Americans to rebel against the English

[Sentence Simplification Question]

Break down the sentence into its individual clauses to make sure that you understand all of its parts.

[Vocabulary Question]

Make sure you understand the context in which the word is used.

[Factual Question]

Read the entire paragraph to learn which answer is accurate and which ones are not.

[Rhetorical Purpose Question]

Look for key expressions such as "as a result of," which can often give hints as to why an event is mentioned.

The Punic Wars and Their Aftermath

1➡ Prior to 264 B.C., Rome had not yet expanded so was not a powerful force in the Mediterranean region but merely controlled the majority of the Italian peninsula. The Mediterranean's most powerful city was located across the sea on land occupied by modern-day Tunisia. The city was Carthage, which possessed immense wealth, a powerful navy, and a strong **mercenary** army, thereby allowing it to trade throughout the entire Mediterranean as the undisputed regional power. Then, from 264 to 146 B.C., Rome and Carthage engaged in three wars, collectively called the Punic Wars, which altered the balance of power there forever.

Before the First Punic War began in 264 B.C., Rome and Carthage had signed a **treaty** banning Rome from trading anywhere in the western Mediterranean. At that time, Rome lacked a navy, so when Carthaginian ships caught Roman ones breaking the treaty, they seized the ships and drowned the sailors without fear of retribution. This, in combination with a desire to control Sicily, caused war to break out between Carthage and Rome. Despite having no navy, the Romans swiftly built hundreds of ships and mastered the art of shipboard fighting. The war lasted for more than two decades, but Rome ultimately won several battles, thereby resulting in Carthage suing for peace to conclude hostilities in 241 B.C.

The Second Punic War started in 218 B.C. when Hannibal Barca, the leader of the Carthaginian forces and the son of Hamilcar Barca, who had led Carthage during the first war, attacked a Roman ally. The Romans took offense and initiated direct hostilities against Carthage. **1** Hannibal, a brilliant leader, invaded the Italian homeland and won several victories, frequently thanks to innovative tactics which included using elephants. **2** At the Battle of Cannae, his forces annihilated a Roman army, killing 44,000 Romans while losing approximately 6,000 soldiers. **3** Nevertheless, the Romans invaded North Africa, forcing Hannibal to leave Italy, and managed to defeat Carthage at the Battle of Zama, whereupon the city surrendered. **4**

Carthage paid reparations to Rome for five decades, but when the payment was complete, it once again became bellicose. The Romans concluded that Carthage would never cease hostilities, so they determined to destroy the city. Romans such as Cato the Elder, who ended every speech by exclaiming, "Carthage must be destroyed," heartily supported the war effort. The war lasted from 149 to 146 B.C. and was essentially the siege of Carthage. When the city walls fell, the Romans sacked Carthage, burned it to the ground, and permitted nothing to be built there for a century. With Carthage destroyed, the entire Mediterranean was open to the Romans. They had gained invaluable experience in warfighting and shipbuilding and would proceed to dominate much of the Western world for the next few centuries.

≋ *Glossary*

mercenary: being hired to serve as a soldier in a foreign army

treaty: a signed agreement between two or more states that concerns war, commerce, or international relations

1 In paragraph 1, the author's description of Carthage mentions all of the following EXCEPT:

Ⓐ The place in the Mediterranean where it could be found

Ⓑ The time period when it was stronger than Rome was

Ⓒ The type of government that ruled over it

Ⓓ Some of the reasons that it was such a powerful city

[Negative Factual Question]

The correct answer may often be something that is not even hinted at or implied in the passage.

2 The word "it" in the passage refers to

Ⓐ Carthage

Ⓑ Rome

Ⓒ the payment

Ⓓ every speech

[Reference Question]

Substitute each answer choice into the sentence where the pronoun is in order easily to find the correct answer.

3 Look at the four squares [■] that indicate where the following sentence could be added to the passage.

Along with the Battle of the Teutoburg Forest, it ranked among the worst defeats Rome ever suffered during its entire history.

Where would the sentence best fit?

[Insert Text Question]

Determine the subject of the sentence to be inserted and then use that knowledge to match it with the correct sentence in the passage.

4 *Directions:* Select the appropriate statements from the answer choices and match them to the Punic War to which they relate. TWO of the answer choices will NOT be used. *This question is worth 4 points.*

[Fill in a Table Question]

Be careful of the two answer choices that are not used. They typically contain information that is mentioned in the passage, but that information is either incorrect or refers to something else.

Answer Choices	Punic War
① Resulted in the destruction of the Carthaginian navy	**First Punic War** • •
② Involved the father of Hannibal Barca	
③ Started when Carthage attacked a Roman ally	**Second Punic War** • • •
④ Involved the complete destruction of Carthage	
⑤ Included a great defeat of Roman forces	
⑥ Saw Roman forces led by Cato the Elder	**Third Punic War** • •
⑦ Took place because of incidents happening at sea	
⑧ Happened after reparations to Rome ceased	
⑨ Involved some warfare using elephants	

Roman Citizenship

1➜ In ancient Rome, not everyone was a Roman citizen. Only a select few possessed that honor along with the power and privileges that went with it. As first the republic, and later the empire, expanded, the right to citizenship also expanded. Rome's leaders often used the promise of citizenship to attract allies to their side. Ultimately, on the empire's frontier, the Romans frequently assimilated **barbarians** by a Romanization process which made them citizens of the empire that had conquered their people.

Only males could have Roman citizenship as all women were placed first under the rule of their fathers and then their husbands. The state automatically conferred citizenship to all males born to citizens. Slaves became partial citizens upon being emancipated by their masters, but the state granted a freed slave's sons full citizenship. During Rome's early years, those in the Latin provinces in the Italian mainland were first partial citizens and later became full citizens. This practice spread as Rome's holdings did, and, eventually, virtually all free males in the empire possessed some form of partial or full citizenship.

3➜ Along with citizenship came several rights and obligations. Roman citizens could vote and hold political office. Only citizens could own property and make business contracts. Furthermore, they had the right to sue someone, and only they could be sued. Citizens had the right to a fair trial and the right to appeal a court's verdict. The state did not enforce corporal punishment on citizens, who could only be sentenced to death for **treason** against the state. For these rights, citizens had to offer themselves as soldiers in the Roman army for a period of time. During times of emergency, the state offered citizenship to freemen willing to join the army.

On the empire's frontiers were many barbarian tribes that often threatened war. Rome's leaders decided to absorb them into the empire by offering their leaders Roman citizenship, and at times, every male in certain tribes was granted citizenship. Some historians believe this practice eventually weakened the empire while others claim it strengthened Rome and delayed its collapse by several centuries. As Roman citizens, these former barbarians and their descendants fought as Romans, not as allies with no stake in the empire's fate. In the end though, the granting of citizenship was not enough when unassimilated barbarians overran and conquered Rome itself in the late fifth century.

📚 *Glossary*

barbarian: a person from an uncivilized land; a person who behaves in an uncivilized manner
treason: betrayal; treachery, typically against a government

1 According to paragraph 1, Rome often gave citizenship to people because

[Factual Question]

- (A) these new citizens were attempting to avoid barbarian tribes
- (B) Rome wanted to make friends out of its enemies
- (C) this action enabled the empire to conquer other people
- (D) a population with many citizens strengthened the empire

2 The word "conferred" in the passage is closest in meaning to

[Vocabulary Question]

- (A) required
- (B) requested
- (C) bestowed
- (D) decreed

3 The author discusses suing people in paragraph 3 in order to

[Rhetorical Purpose Question]

- (A) show how citizens' rights were different from noncitizens'
- (B) explain the fairly complicated Roman legal system
- (C) contrast that with a citizen's inability to be sentenced to death
- (D) explain one of the rights granted during times of emergency

4 *Directions:* An introductory sentence for a brief summary of the passage is provided below. Complete the summary by selecting the THREE answer choices that express the most important ideas of the passage. Some sentences do not belong because they express ideas that are not presented in the passage or are minor ideas in the passage. ***This question is worth 2 points.***

[Prose Summary Question]

Roman citizenship was often used to grant certain rights to people in the empire and even succeeded in turning Rome's enemies into its allies.

Answer Choices

- ① Sometimes the males in an entire tribe were made citizens in order to secure their allegiance to Rome.

- ② Neither women nor slaves were permitted to become citizens of Rome at any time during its history.

- ③ Under the policy of Romanization, barbarians were assimilated into Roman culture in part by being granted citizenship.

- ④ Rome was finally conquered by unassimilated barbarians from Germanic tribes that invaded in the fourth century.

- ⑤ Corporal punishment was often enforced in Rome, and there was capital punishment for people who committed treason.

- ⑥ Roman citizens were able to do many things, such as own property and sue others, which noncitizens could not do.

Railroads and the Local Economy

1➡ Throughout history, the ease of transportation has been crucial to the placement and growth of population centers. It is no accident that most ancient cities were beside or near major waterways since water transportation was the fastest and best way to travel. Many years later, the Romans built extensive networks of roads throughout Europe, and major settlements grew up alongside them. And although the exploration of North America from the sixteenth to eighteenth centuries followed its rivers and lakes, the vast majority of the continent never truly opened to human habitation until the nineteenth century advent of railroads.

2➡ Railroads are an **offshoot** of the steam engines and rail systems which transported coal from mines in England. Later converted to carry people, the first passenger railroad in the United States began operating in 1830. As America grew, so did railroads. A town in the path of railroad construction was fortunate indeed. Railroads brought immigrants to towns, delivered west products from the great eastern cities, and transported east food produced on western farms. Railroad companies were numerous, and they competed for ideal places to lay new tracks and for fees from carrying freight and passengers.

Chicago is a perfect example of how railroads profoundly influenced cities' growth. Ideally situated at the southern end of Lake Michigan, Chicago serves as a gateway between the east and west as well as the northern states of Wisconsin and Minnesota. The first railway opened there in 1838 and helped transform Chicago into a major urban and manufacturing center. The invention of the refrigerated railroad car turned it into a meatpacking hub, and its Union Stock Yards was the world's busiest meatpacking center for decades. Animals came in by rail from the north and west. Then, they were slaughtered and processed, and the meat was transported on refrigerated cars to American markets everywhere.

The dream of many American railroad companies was to build a **transcontinental** railroad. **1** This desire was realized in 1869 when the final spike that connected two railroads was driven into a track in Utah. **2** From that time, Americans could travel from coast to coast in a few days and could avoid the rough overland trip by covered wagon or the long ocean journey. **3** Ultimately, virtually all corners of the country were connected by railroads. **4** Even today, railroads are vital to freight transportation despite having been largely replaced by cars and airplanes as passenger carriers in the twentieth century.

⯈ *Glossary*
offshoot: a branch; a result
transcontinental: spanning an entire continent

1   In paragraph 1, the author implies that

- Ⓐ much of North America was unsettled in the eighteenth century
- Ⓑ some Roman roads are still being used in Europe today
- Ⓒ cities not on waterways in ancient times were typically small
- Ⓓ the first settlers in North America arrived in the sixteenth century

2   According to paragraph 2, which of the following is NOT true of railroads?

- Ⓐ They were vital to moving people and products in America.
- Ⓑ They were invented in the United States around 1830.
- Ⓒ The first ones were used to transport materials.
- Ⓓ They were operated by many companies.

3   The word "it" in the passage refers to

- Ⓐ railway
- Ⓑ Chicago
- Ⓒ urban and manufacturing center
- Ⓓ refrigerated railroad car

4   Look at the four squares [■] that indicate where the following sentence could be added to the passage.

Despite the speed of the journey, it was not without its own difficulties as Native Americans frequently attacked trains on their way across the western United States.

Where would the sentence best fit?

American Western Migration

Note

Between the 1830s and 1870s, the population of the United States west of the Mississippi River increased dramatically. There were several reasons for this, the foremost being the availability of cheap farmland. Additionally, gold was discovered in California, cheaper and faster means of transportation west were established, and there was a burgeoning immigrant population seeking its place in America. However, the new denizens did not always have an easy time as they faced hostile Native Americans and unscrupulous businessmen, and the land itself was often harsh. But they persisted, so the western lands were filled with people, and the United States was transformed.

2→ In 1803 and 1804, when Lewis and Clark made their famous expedition to the west coast, the land was empty except for the natives and a few white hunters and trappers. Initially, the number of people moving west was just a trickle. The journey was long and difficult; there were no railways, and the sailing time to California in the days before the Panama Canal opened was measured in months. Then, in 1848, everything changed. Men discovered gold near San Francisco, so people began **flocking** there. The California Gold Rush resulted in the first large increase in the western population. Many people found gold, yet most did not; but they stayed, established businesses or farmed, and raised their families.

3→ The land between California and the Mississippi did not see great migration until after the Civil War, when the transcontinental railroad was completed and cheap, fertile land became available for farming. Some people who moved west came from the east and south to seek better, more fertile farmland. Others were immigrants, coming from Italy, Germany, Poland, and **Scandinavia**. Promises of wide-open rich land drew tens of thousands of people who moved to the great, open plains to begin new lives. Armed clashes with natives did not deter them, nor did problems between farmers who wanted to fence in their lands and ranchers who wanted open plains. They lived rough and tumble lives. Towns were built and died, lawlessness was common, and many only had their faith in religion along with the fact that they had nowhere else to go to sustain them.

As steamboat and rail transportation reduced the costs of shipping from west to east, more land was broken, and great fields of wheat and corn began covering the prairies. The expectation of profits from farming drew greater numbers of migrants, including freed slaves from the south, businessmen seeking a share of the new wealth, and discharged war veterans looking for a fresh start. As the population increased, the lands were eventually incorporated first as territories and then as American states.

Native Americans were once commonly called Indians, yet this name is seldom used today and is considered an offensive term by many.

In 1803, President Thomas Jefferson made the Louisiana Purchase from France. This greatly increased the size of the U.S. He immediately sent the Lewis and Clark expedition to explore and to survey the new land. From 1803 to 1806, Lewis and Clark and their men crossed the entire continent, reached the Pacific Ocean, and then went back east. Their trip helped open the American west to further exploration and settlements.

The American Civil War lasted from 1861 to 1865. It started when eleven southern states tried to secede from the Union. One of the main issues of the war between the North and South was that of slavery. Eventually, President Abraham Lincoln freed all Southern slaves with the Emancipation Proclamation in 1862. After the war ended, the Thirteenth Amendment to the Constitution, which abolished slavery, was ratified in 1865.

By 1870, one third of America's population lived in the west whereas only one twelfth of the population had done so in 1830. The country's population had tripled between 1830 and 1870, going from twelve million to more than thirty-eight million. Additionally, western migration continued long after the westward rush for gold and land. Today, California is America's most populous state, with around forty million people, almost equivalent to the entire country's numbers in 1870.

≋ Glossary

flock: to move quickly; to gather quickly

Scandinavia: the countries Norway, Sweden, and Denmark and sometimes Finland

---

1 The word "denizens" in the passage is closest in meaning to

- (A) emigrants
- (B) residents
- (C) citizens
- (D) pioneers

2 In paragraph 2, the author implies that Lewis and Clark

- (A) traveled by rail for part of their journey to the west
- (B) found employment in the west working as hunters
- (C) were some of the first settlers to live in the American west
- (D) met few people during their journey from east to west

3 According to paragraph 3, which of the following is true of people who migrated to the west?

- (A) They came mostly from various European counties.
- (B) Large numbers of them died in fights with natives and each other.
- (C) Many of them were seeking land on which they could raise crops.
- (D) They moved west because they had fought for the losing side in the Civil War.

4 Which of the sentences below best expresses the essential information in the highlighted sentence in the passage? *Incorrect* answer choices change the meaning in important ways or leave out essential information.

- (A) People wanting to start their lives over, such as former slaves, businessmen, and soldiers, looked for business opportunities from migrants.
- (B) Expecting to make a lot of money, many people, excepting freed slaves, businessmen, and veterans, became farmers out west.
- (C) A variety of people, including freed slaves, businessmen, and soldiers, were attracted to farming by the possibility of making money.
- (D) Because so many people were making money from farming, this led to difficulties for former slaves, businessmen, and soldiers.

5 *Directions:* Select the appropriate sentences from the answer choices and match them to the American west before and after the Civil War. TWO of the answer choices will NOT be used. ***This question is worth 3 points.***

Answer Choices

① The price of land there was extremely high.

② European immigrants went there to settle the land.

③ Less than ten percent of the population lived in the west.

④ It often took months to get from east to west.

⑤ There were no Native Americans living there.

⑥ The transcontinental railroad connecting the country was completed.

⑦ About thirty-three percent of the American population lived in the west.

THE AMERICAN WEST

Before the Civil War
-
-

After the Civil War
-
-
-

Summarizing ▶ Complete the summary by filling in the blanks.

The American population in the western part of the country increased between 1830 and 1870. In the early 1800s, the land was mostly empty of settlers. However, several events happened to change this. In 1848, gold was discovered in _____ , so many people moved there. Additionally, after _____ , a transcontinental railroad connecting east and west was finished. This opened _____ to people. Both Americans and immigrants moved west to farm and to start new lives. In addition, as _____ improved, it became easier to make money, so even more people moved west to take up farming.

Agricultural Methods in Medieval Europe

Note

1 → The years after the fifth-century fall of the Roman Empire were dark times in Europe as the few people scratched out a meager existence from the land, often barely growing enough food to survive. This changed sometime in the tenth and eleventh centuries. The medieval European population slowly but steadily rose, and innovative farming methods helped yield greater amounts of food. However, whether the increase in food caused the growth in population or the growth in population allowed more food to be cultivated is unclear. Whatever the case, the two went hand in hand and enabled Europe to begin a revival that has never really stopped.

The Roman Empire fell in 476 although the Byzantine Empire in Eastern Europe lasted until 1453. In Western Europe, the Dark Ages began in the fifth century and lasted for a few hundred years. Little of note occurred during this period.

2 → Several factors were involved in increasing agricultural production. First, animal husbandry produced higher-quality stocks of oxen and horses, which peasant farmers then utilized to till the land. Animal power from oxen and horses meant that the thick, heavy, moisture-laden soil in the northern lands could be **plowed** and planted. Draft animals could pull heavy wooden and iron plows, some of which had wheels, thereby allowing for the easier breaking of the fertile ground. New crops, like oats, with higher energy returns for the amount of labor invested, were planted, so both peasants and animals enjoyed better diets. Finally, crop rotation systems were implemented, ensuring that the soil was not depleted of nutrients and enabling long-term farming in one area. These factors led to more stable lifestyles, the growth of urban centers, and a return to more civilized lives.

Draft animals include horses, oxen, donkeys, and mules. Known as beasts of burden, they are used because of their physical strength. Farmers may have them drag plows to till their fields, or they may be tied to carts and wagons and used to transport goods from one place to another.

3 → All of these things did not happen overnight though, and historians still argue over the **chronological** course of events and which ones had the greatest impact. The main debate centers on whether having more food permitted a higher population or if the higher population forced peasants to find ways to grow more food. The latter seems more logical, and studies of modern subsistence farming societies in Asia and Africa suggest it is correct. With more mouths to feed, farmers are forced to find ways to produce more food. They either increase their own labor or become more willing to try unproven ideas to produce more food. As a population increases, having more people means more labor is available to work the land, build irrigation systems, raise animals, and do other tasks associated with agriculture.

Europe's population did not always increase after the eleventh century. At times, it decreased dramatically. One such instance happened because of the Black Death. From 1347 to 1352, this disease, thought to be the bubonic plague, spread through Europe and killed somewhere around fifty percent of the entire population of the continent.

4 → The exact population of Europe in the tenth century is unknown, but most estimates put it at around forty million people, the vast majority being peasants who farmed. Signs of rising populations there do not appear until the eleventh-century revival of towns and trade. Yet the population did not steadily and continuously increase until modern times, for war, disease, and famine all took their toll. Famine, in particular, was a constant threat since increasing numbers meant that whatever food farmers grew had to sustain more people. In times of poor harvests, the larger population was a burden, not a benefit, and many died. Despite these occasional setbacks, the revolution in agriculture was the first step to putting Europe on the path that eventually led it to dominate the world.

≋ *Glossary*
plow: to till the soil, typically for farming
chronological: relating to time

1   Which of the following can be inferred from paragraph 1 about Europe's population?
  Ⓐ In the tenth century, it had the same population as Rome once did.
  Ⓑ It directly resulted in better agricultural methods being used worldwide.
  Ⓒ Its increased number of people has enabled it to prosper for centuries.
  Ⓓ It was at its lowest point in history during the fourth century.

2   In paragraph 2, why does the author mention "oats"?
  Ⓐ To note a part of many Europeans' improved daily diets
  Ⓑ To compare their nutritional value with other foods Europeans ate
  Ⓒ To mention one of the crops planted in the crop rotation system
  Ⓓ To explain why Europeans' horses and cattle were so much healthier

3   According to paragraph 3, why did farmers try unproven methods to raise their crops?
  Ⓐ They wanted to improve the irrigation systems on their farms.
  Ⓑ They were forced to employ more people to work in their fields.
  Ⓒ They were imitating methods once used in both Africa and Asia.
  Ⓓ They were responsible for feeding a larger number of people.

4   In paragraph 4, all of the following questions are answered EXCEPT:
  Ⓐ What happened to people in Europe in years when harvests were not good?
  Ⓑ Why did the European population not always increase up until modern times?
  Ⓒ How did the Europeans manage to dominate the world after medieval times?
  Ⓓ What do some people believe that the European population was in the tenth century?

5   ***Directions:*** An introductory sentence for a brief summary of the passage is provided below. Complete the summary by selecting the THREE answer choices that express the most important ideas of the passage. Some sentences do not belong because they express ideas that are not presented in the passage or are minor ideas in the passage. ***This question is worth 2 points.***

While European agriculture struggled after the fall of Rome, agricultural production eventually improved due to new farming methods that revitalized Europe.

-
-
-

Answer Choices

1. No one is exactly sure how many people lived in Europe during the medieval period, but it is estimated at around forty million.

2. Farmers were eventually able to produce more food in Europe due to factors such as improved crops, better domestic animals, and a new crop rotation system.

3. European wars, such as the Hundred Years' War, led to declining European populations, and outbreaks of diseases and poor crop yields led to famines.

4. European plows were made of iron and wood, and they had wheels, which made them easier for animals to pull through the earth.

5. Researchers still debate whether larger populations enabled greater food production; however, it seems likely that this is the case.

6. While Europe encountered some obstacles to increasing its population, the revolution in agriculture was the first step to it attaining a preeminent global position.

Summarizing ▷ Complete the summary by filling in the blanks.

From the fifth to tenth centuries, the European population was rather small. However, in the tenth and eleventh centuries, it began _____. Historians note that the Europeans began producing more agricultural products, which let them live healthier lives. One reason the farmers became more successful was that they made good use of animals to _____. They also grew better and more nutritious crops like oats and used _____ to avoid wearing out the soil. As the population began growing, _____, and people engaged in trade. Ultimately, Europe's greater population helped it become a world power.

Note

James Watt and the Industrial Revolution

The modern world would not be the same without James Watt's improvements to the steam engine. There had been steam engines before James Watt's time, but none achieved the efficiency and practicality of Watt's improved design. His engine wound up transforming the world and was crucial to the Industrial Revolution. Thanks to Watt, steam pushed and pulled the pistons and drove the wheels that turned the world from an agrarian society into the modern technologically driven one that exists today.

²➜ Watt trained as an instrument maker and worked at the University of Glasgow during the mid-eighteenth century. While there, he became interested in the use of steam as a source of power. He subsequently built some steam engine models which barely worked, and he also worked on the Newcomen steam engine, a type that had its own problems. Watt studied his creations until he discovered why they had failed to produce much energy. The result was that he invented a key device crucial to a practical steam engine: a condenser that cooled the steam even while the cylinder was hot. This enabled his steam engine to be four times more efficient than those currently in use.

Coal miners during Watt's time used early steam engines to pump water out of deep mines. The engines used low-pressure steam and operated on a vacuum **principle** to move a piston back and forth. Watt, however, was interested in developing steam engines for use in factories. He installed the first practical factory steam engine in 1776 and changed the way the world worked. Factory steam engines allowed more work to be accomplished in less time. In addition, they were not dependent on falling water as a power source, so factories could be built anywhere. Finally, steam engine-powered factories needed workers, and the mass movement of people from the English countryside to expanding urban centers was the result. Within fifty years, steam power had transformed England from a countryside cottage industry and **agrarian** society to a factory-based urban-dwelling industrial powerhouse.

The world soon transformed as well with Watt's steam engines and their improved descendants spreading abroad. The mass industrialization of Western Europe and the United States quickly followed, and it eventually occurred in Eastern Europe, parts of the British Empire, and Japan. By the end of the twentieth century, industrialization was the norm. With it, though, came various issues, including crowded cities and the numerous problems, such as crime and pollution, which occur in them. In addition, the exploitation of workers by factory owners ultimately led to the rise of communism and socialism as well as the advent of labor unions, all of which greatly affected society.

The Industrial Revolution began in the eighteenth century and continued throughout the nineteenth century. Thanks to improvements in machines, there were vast changes in the textile and manufacturing industries, transportation, mining, and agriculture. While it began in Britain, the Industrial Revolution soon spread to North America, Europe, and the rest of the world.

Thomas Newcomen invented the Newcomen steam engine in 1712. While a simple machine that was eventually improved upon, it was the first device that used steam to do mechanical work.

Urbanization was one direct result of the Industrial Revolution. Before it occurred, the vast majority of people made their living from farming and also lived in rural areas. After the Industrial Revolution started, people abandoned farms and moved to the cities. This caused cities greatly to increase in size. Soon, cities with populations of 100,000 or more people were not unusual, and some cities even had populations of 1,000,000 or more people.

James Watt continued improving his steam engines, eventually retiring in 1800 and passing on his business to his son and others. He was still tinkering around in his private workshop until his death in 1819. Today, he is hailed as the inventor of the steam engine. While not literally true, it was Watt's improvement of others' creations that was the key to initiating the Industrial Revolution and shaping the modern world.

≋ Glossary
principle: a method; a theory
agrarian: related to farming

1 Which of the sentences below best expresses the essential information in the highlighted sentence in the passage? *Incorrect* answer choices change the meaning in important ways or leave out essential information.

- (A) Pistons and wheels were not the only things that worked on steam, yet they were able to transform the world into a more modern one.
- (B) The technology needed to change the world from being agrarian-based to more modern was found in the piston, which Watt invented.
- (C) Because of Watt, steam engines became much more prevalent, both in agricultural as well as modern-day technological settings.
- (D) Watt's work with steam helped make the world much more advanced and based on technology than it had previously been.

2 According to paragraph 2, which of the following is true of the steam engine?

- (A) It was the result of a joint project between Watt and Newcomen.
- (B) It was created after the condenser as a way of cooling it off.
- (C) It was first invented by researchers at the University of Glasgow.
- (D) Its original design was greatly improved upon by Watt.

3 The word "them" in the passage refers to

- (A) various issues
- (B) crowded cities
- (C) numerous problems
- (D) crime and pollution

4 The word "tinkering" in the passage is closest in meaning to

- (A) fiddling
- (B) designing
- (C) inventing
- (D) discussing

5 ***Directions:*** An introductory sentence for a brief summary of the passage is provided below. Complete the summary by selecting the THREE answer choices that express the most important ideas of the passage. Some sentences do not belong because they express ideas that are not presented in the passage or are minor ideas in the passage. ***This question is worth 2 points.***

Because of James Watt's improvements on the steam engine, the Industrial Revolution got underway, and parts of the world began the process of industrialization.

-
-
-

Answer Choices

1. Some people still claim that the Industrial Revolution is continuing to this very day.

2. The U.S. and much of Western Europe started developing industry soon after Britain did.

3. England transformed from being an agrarian society to one that was filled with factories.

4. The steam engine that Watts designed was much more efficient than Newcomen's was.

5. Big urban centers often have to deal with issues like crime and overpopulation.

6. The first steam engines were used by miners to help them get water out of mineshafts.

Summarizing ▶ Complete the summary by filling in the blanks.

While James Watt did not invent _____, he improved it greatly. This helped spark the Industrial Revolution and change the world into _____. Watt was fascinated by using steam as power, so he worked with Newcomen's engine to make a much more efficient one. He then _____ in factories, thereby increasing their productivity. As a result, factories sprang up everywhere as England became _____. Other places, such as the U.S. and Western Europe, also became more industrialized during this period.

Athens and Sparta

Athens and Sparta were the greatest city-states in ancient Greece. Occasionally allies yet frequently enemies, their rivalry shaped much of classical Greek history. In modern history books, Sparta's reputation is that of a ruthless, slave-owning military state while Athens is praised for being a shining example of early democracy and meritocracy. While both points have merit, neither is exactly true as each city could, at times, resemble the reputation that was traditionally **accorded** to the other.

2➜ Sparta was the preeminent land power in Greece in the fifth century B.C., which was when the Spartan-Athenian rivalry was at its peak. Spartan men were trained in the use of combat arms since childhood, and the Greeks considered the Spartan army the most formidable in the land. **1** Sparta was also unique in that it had a standing army which was ready to go to war instantly. **2** Athens, like most Greek city-states, depended on its mass of landowning men who wielded political power and thus owed military service to the state when called upon. **3** Additionally, Athens was more accomplished in naval warfare, and it was at sea that the Athenians were usually the masters of the Spartans. **4**

Sparta was able to maintain a professional standing army thanks to the unusual nature of its economic organization. Spartans did not engage in agriculture but instead depended on a vast horde of peasant slaves, called helots, to farm the land and provide them with food. The Spartans kept the more numerous helots in abject servitude; naturally, the helots were constantly eager to rebel—another reason why Sparta maintained a standing army. Athens had its own share of lower classes, mostly poor farmers, craftsmen, and laborers, but they were primarily free men. Contrary to popular belief, Athenians practiced slavery—as did most ancient societies—but nowhere near the degree the Spartans did.

4➜ Despite treating their slaves so harshly, the Spartans were **enlightened** in at least one way: Spartan women were considered equals with men, and they took part in politics and even had some military training. The logic behind this was that women were needed to help raise strong warriors from childhood. Indeed, Spartan women were no wilting flowers when it came to feats of arms. On the other hand, in Athens, the so-called birthplace of democracy, women had no voice in politics, and Athenian men expected their women to maintain the home and to do nothing else. Even when men without property were later given rights in Athenian politics, women still remained excluded from participation in the political arena.

Note

A city-state is an independent city and the territory in its immediate area. It is typically a self-ruling place. In ancient Greece, city-states like Athens, Sparta, Thebes, and Corinth were the dominant forms of government. Throughout history, other city-states have existed. Most famous and powerful among them were the Italian city-states of Venice and Florence.

While Athens and Sparta were often allied against common enemies such as the Persians, they also went to war with each other. The Peloponnesian War, which lasted from 431 to 404 B.C., was one example of this. The war, which affected almost all of Greece, as well as other areas, eventually ended with Athens losing to Sparta.

Artistically, the Athenians were far more accomplished than the Spartans. Craftsmen constructed the great Athenian buildings that remain standing today. In literature, philosophy, science, and history, no Spartan ever compared to the Athenians. While Athens earned its reputation in numerous fields, Sparta's rests solely on its military triumphs. Yet even the Spartans could be defeated as the Thebans, led by Epaminondas, crushed them in the early fourth century B.C., leading to the long decline of Spartan society. Today, Athens is the capital of Greece while Sparta is but a part of its history.

There are countless famous Athenians in history. Socrates, Plato, and Aristotle are known for their contributions to philosophy. Alcibiades and Pericles are known for their military leadership. And Demosthenes is known for his statesmanship.

📚 **Glossary**

accord: to give; to grant; to bestow
enlightened: advanced; progressive

---

1   In paragraph 2, the author implies that

Ⓐ   the Athenians often defeated the Spartans on land

Ⓑ   some other Greek city-states had standing armies

Ⓒ   the Spartan navy was not as good at fighting as its army was

Ⓓ   the way the Athenians ran their army was atypical of Greek city-states

2   The word "abject" in the passage is closest in meaning to

Ⓐ   long-term

Ⓑ   violent

Ⓒ   continual

Ⓓ   wretched

3   According to paragraph 4, which of the following is NOT true of Spartan women?

Ⓐ   They had more rights than did Athenian women.

Ⓑ   They were thought to be on the same level as slaves.

Ⓒ   They were allowed to engage in political matters.

Ⓓ   They helped raise their boys to become warriors.

4   Look at the four squares [■] that indicate where the following sentence could be added to the passage.

One need only consider some of Athens's overwhelming victories against the Persians, like at Salamis, to be reminded that no other Greek city-state had such a potent naval force.

Where would the sentence best fit?

5   ***Directions:*** Select the appropriate statements from the answer choices and match them to the Greek city-state to which they relate. TWO of the answer choices will NOT be used. ***This question is worth 3 points.***

Answer Choices	**GREEK CITY-STATE**

Answer Choices

① It avoided having a full-time army.

② It was led at one time by the general Epaminondas.

③ It was defeated by the Persians in a naval battle.

④ Its army was considered the greatest in all Greece.

⑤ Its people used slaves to cultivate their crops for them.

⑥ Its women were excluded from participation in politics.

⑦ Its primary accomplishments were related to the military.

GREEK CITY-STATE

Athens
 •
 •

Sparta
 •
 •
 •

Summarizing ▶ Complete the summary by filling in the blanks.

Athens and Sparta were ancient Greece's _____. However, they were quite different from one another. The Spartans had a very militaristic society. They kept a standing army and even used their women to help _____. The Spartans also enslaved large numbers of helots and forced them to raise their crops. Athens, meanwhile, was the birthplace of _____. Ironically, though, Athenian women were less free than Spartan women. While its navy was strong, Athens is known more for _____ in fields like architecture, literature, philosophy, science, and history.

The Legacy of Jamestown

¹➡ Jamestown was the first successful British colony in the New World, but its early years were disastrous. However, its transition from a failing, disease-ridden economic venture into a full-fledged profitable colony had a resounding and lasting impact on the New World and the indigenous American people and their environment. Conceived as a business enterprise financed by English merchants in search of gold, silver, and other riches, Jamestown was founded in 1607 on the shores of the James River near Chesapeake Bay. Over the next twenty years, the colony came perilously close to being destroyed by disease, starvation, and gross incompetence. Only when the colonists turned away from their desire for quick wealth and began building a farming community based on the English model did the colony begin to thrive. The cash crop tobacco became the gold they had been searching for. Yet, unwittingly, the colonists would wreak havoc on the native population and their land.

²➡ Prior to the arrival of the colonists, the natives in the Chesapeake region were flourishing. Around 15,000 natives—the majority belonging to the Powhatan tribe—lived in the immediate area. The site chosen by the English colonists was empty, though, and for good reason: The James River lacked sufficient flow during hot summers to prevent saltwater from Chesapeake Bay from entering as far inland as the new settlement. Since the colonists were inept at handling their human waste and dead, the waters near Jamestown became a salty, disease-ridden cesspool. ❶ Colonists often succumbed to dysentery and other water-borne illnesses during Jamestown's first few years. ❷ Of the approximately 6,000 people who came to Jamestown between 1607 and 1624, almost seventy-five percent died. ❸ The local native leaders could have easily wiped them out at any time yet failed to press their advantage, believing the colonists would soon abandon their efforts. ❹

³➡ The natives lived off the land, managing their crops and fishing and hunting grounds, so the land and the sea provided them a renewable bounty. Corn, squash, and beans were cultivated together, and the nitrogen-replenishing beans kept the soil fertile and moist. When crop yields became low, the natives abandoned their fields and cleared trees for new plots. They erected no fences to denote land ownership, nor did they have any large domestic animals other than dogs. In contrast, the colonists, when they began farming, followed the English practices of fencing and land ownership. For them, open land was free for animal grazing, and the cows, pigs, goats, and sheep they brought frequently destroyed native crops. Soon, the countryside was filled with fenced lands, keeping the natives from their traditional plots and hunting grounds and causing great tension between both sides.

⁴➡ When the colonists arrived, they brought other instruments of change, many of which negatively altered the land. Chief among these were worms, which were uncommon in the Americas before the arrival of the Europeans. Worms destroyed the dead leaves and other vegetation on the forest floors, which had previously replenished the soil. However, other insects they introduced provided some benefits. These included bees, which spread pollen and let new plants grow far and wide. Still, the natives did not regard the bees as a boon but as a sign that colonists were not far behind.

⁵➡ The English decision to start systematically planting and selling tobacco caused the major change in the fortunes of the colony and America itself. Virginia tobacco, as it was soon called, was sweet and smooth and became a hit in Europe. The colonists—at least those who survived—had found their fortune

after all. Land was quickly cleared, and great fields of tobacco were planted. Unfortunately, tobacco sucks the life out of the soil in just a few years, so new lands were constantly being sought and forests cut down. Simultaneously, the natives were often too weak from Old World diseases such as smallpox and malaria, so they could offer only a token defense of their lands. Then, in 1619, the first African slaves arrived in Jamestown to work the tobacco fields, thus beginning another long, sad chapter in American history. The legacy of Jamestown is not only as the first English colony but also as the harbinger of change—both good and bad—for the natives and the continent itself.

≋ **Glossary**
bounty: a reward; a prize
boon: a benefit; an advantage

---

1   The word "indigenous" in the passage is closest in meaning to
   - (A) independent
   - (B) native
   - (C) unique
   - (D) apparent

2   Which of the following can be inferred from paragraph 1 about the Jamestown colonists?
   - (A) They did not intentionally set out to harm the Native Americans.
   - (B) After several years of searching, they managed to find gold and silver.
   - (C) The colonists never managed to overcome the diseases that afflicted them.
   - (D) They abandoned their hopes for the colony after two decades.

3   According to paragraph 2, what was the importance of Jamestown's geographical location?
   - (A) It was located right beside Chesapeake Bay.
   - (B) Crops did not grow well because of the hot summers there.
   - (C) The water in its river was sometimes rather salty.
   - (D) It was situated on land that thousands of tribes called home.

4   Which of the sentences below best expresses the essential information in the highlighted sentence in the passage? *Incorrect* answer choices change the meaning in important ways or leave out essential information.
   - (A) The natives built fences around their farms and hunting grounds in an effort to reduce the tension between the colonists and themselves.
   - (B) With the land full of fences, the natives increased tension between the colonists and themselves since they had no access to the land.
   - (C) Without land to farm or hunt on, the colonists had to fence in the land, which increased the tension with the natives.
   - (D) The natives could neither hunt nor farm because of the fenced-in lands, which was an issue between the colonists and them.

5   According to paragraph 3, which of the following is true of the natives' farming practices?

    Ⓐ They used irrigation techniques to water the land.

    Ⓑ They cleared new fields for farming every year.

    Ⓒ They raised crops that helped improve the soil.

    Ⓓ They always got the highest possible yields from their crops.

6   The author discusses "worms" in paragraph 4 in order to

    Ⓐ show an indirect way in which the Europeans harmed the natives

    Ⓑ explain why the amount of forest vegetation began to decrease

    Ⓒ note that the soil in the forests began to be replenished

    Ⓓ compare their positive effects on the environment with those of bees

7   The word "harbinger" in the passage is closest in meaning to

    Ⓐ description

    Ⓑ image

    Ⓒ portent

    Ⓓ oracle

8   According to paragraph 5, the colonists regularly cleared new land for farming because

    Ⓐ they were attempting to drive the natives away from the land

    Ⓑ the tobacco they planted quickly exhausted the soil's nutrients

    Ⓒ more and more immigrants were coming to the colonies from Europe

    Ⓓ they wanted to deforest the land to make it safer to work on

9   Look at the four squares [■] that indicate where the following sentence could be added to the passage.

Despite this appalling rate, there was still a steady supply of people in England willing to sail across the Atlantic to become American colonists.

Where would the sentence best fit?

Click on a square [■] to add the sentence to the passage.

10 **_Directions:_** Select the appropriate statements from the answer choices and match them to the people to which they relate. TWO of the answer choices will NOT be used. **_This question is worth 3 points._**

> Drag your answer choices to the spaces where they belong.
> To remove an answer choice, click on it. To review the passage, click on **View Text.**

Answer Choices	**PEOPLE**

Answer Choices

1. They avoided using fences to mark their territory.

2. They suffered greatly from imported diseases.

3. They found gold and silver in large amounts.

4. They raised a number of domesticated animals.

5. They failed to attack their opponents when they had the opportunity.

6. Their objective was to make money off of the land.

7. Their people were governed by competent leaders.

PEOPLE

Native Americans
-
-
-

Jamestown Colonists
-
-

Roman Britain

1→ For almost 400 years, Britain belonged to the Roman Empire. This profoundly changed the island, and the legacy of the Roman period is evident even today. Many of Britain's motorways run along old Roman roads, and virtually every major urban center is located where a Roman town once existed. Although most of the historical record is lost, the Romans left behind a treasure **trove** of archaeological evidence, including buildings, roads, coins, and weapons, and a multitude of other relics at various sites. Through an examination of these places and artifacts, researchers have produced a fairly accurate picture of Roman life in Britain.

2→ Julius Caesar actually invaded Britain twice—in 55 and 54 B.C. as an offshoot of his campaign to subdue Gaul—nevertheless, his forces failed to conquer it. However, his efforts produced alliances with individual British Celtic tribal leaders, resulting in ties with Rome being established. A full-scale Roman invasion occurred in 43 A.D., but it took several decades to defeat the numerous tribes. In fact, the Romans never succeeded in maintaining complete control over the entire island. Rebellions constantly flared up, especially in the north. Since territory in practically constant rebellion required a large military presence, several legions plus allied barbarian troops were stationed in Britain during the Roman period.

3→ As the Roman military moved throughout Britain, it constructed roads and established camps. Some became permanent settlements that included a Roman fortress as a center of defense. Among the more famous settlements were the beginnings of modern-day London, Canterbury, York, and Manchester. The road system was vital for ensuring the speedy transportation of troops and supplies across the island. This infrastructure typically allowed the Romans to move quickly to a rebelling region with enough forces to quell the uprising. The primary exception was in the north: The fierce Pict warriors, living in the region of modern-day Scotland, refused to ally themselves with Rome, and the Romans, despite multiple invasions and attempts at occupation, failed to conquer them. As a result, during Emperor Hadrian's time, the Romans built the famous wall named after him as a bulwark against the northern tribes.

Britain is far from Rome, so most Roman legionnaires posted there became permanent settlers. They intermarried with the local population, started farms, and stayed after retirement from the military. The locals became used to the Romans, their laws and customs were adopted, and they even granted the honor of citizenship to some of the so-called barbarians. To encourage trade in Britain and to maintain its standing army, the Romans transported much coinage, which was used to pay soldiers and to purchase commodities, to the island. The coins remained in circulation and contributed to the region's economic prosperity. Britain became one of Rome's major sources of mineral deposits and for some time supplied it with much tin as well as gold, iron, lead, silver, and marble. Animal skins, furs, timber, and wool were also prized products from Britain paid for with Roman funds.

5→ The end of Roman rule in Britain was slow in coming. Some historians blame economic decline and a decrease in the amount of circulating **funds**. Others place the blame on increasing barbarian attacks and the Roman administration's inability to deal with them. ■1 The Roman army in Britain itself underwent a series of rebellions, and by 410 A.D., Rome had had enough and decided to part ways with the region by refusing to send any more troops or assistance there. ■2 At some point, the new leaders in Britain invited the Saxons from the Germanic lowlands on the European continent to assist them in maintaining order. **3** The Saxons, however, chose to conquer the island instead. **4**

⁶→ After their formal withdrawal, the Romans continued to influence Britain, but their power rapidly declined. Roman buildings, aqueducts, and other structures were torn down for material to build castles. Roads fell into disrepair, currency disappeared, and trade returned to a primitive barter system. Even the Latin language failed to survive. All that remained from 400 years of Roman civilization were the names of the towns, pathways of roads with but a few stones remaining, some artifacts buried in the ground, and structures such as Hadrian's Wall, which remains to this day.

Glossary
trove: a collection
fund: money; currency

---

1 According to paragraph 1, which of the following is true of Britain during the Roman Period?

Ⓐ There is little written evidence of the events that happened during it.

Ⓑ The period of Roman rule in Britain began around the year 400 A.D.

Ⓒ It was a time when most of Britain's population centers contracted.

Ⓓ The Romans found an enormous amount of treasure while they were there.

2 In paragraph 2, why does the author mention "Julius Caesar"?

Ⓐ To note who the person that ultimately conquered Britain was

Ⓑ To compare his campaign there with his other one in Gaul

Ⓒ To explain why his tactics for invading Rome were unsuccessful

Ⓓ To state he was responsible for the first Roman invasion of Britain

3 The phrase "flared up" in the passage is closest in meaning to

Ⓐ exploded

Ⓑ started

Ⓒ extinguished

Ⓓ threatened

4 In paragraph 2, the author implies that Rome

Ⓐ preferred to negotiate with the Picts than to fight them

Ⓑ felt that conquering Britain was more crucial than defeating Gaul

Ⓒ failed to experience a continual state of peace in Britain

Ⓓ recruited a number of British soldiers to staff its legions

5   According to paragraph 3, the Romans built such good roads in Britain because

   Ⓐ they were hoping to encourage the expansion of trade

   Ⓑ they felt it assisted in civilizing the people living alongside the roads

   Ⓒ they needed to move soldiers rapidly from place to place

   Ⓓ the roads permitted the Romans to communicate easily with the Picts

6   Which of the sentences below best expresses the essential information in the highlighted sentence in the passage? *Incorrect* answer choices change the meaning in important ways or leave out essential information.

   Ⓐ The Romans needed a large amount of money in order to pay their soldiers and to purchase necessary items from the British.

   Ⓑ The Romans brought lots of money to Britain to pay wages, to purchase items, and to promote commerce there.

   Ⓒ There had been no previous trading in Britain, so the Romans brought money with them to encourage it to occur.

   Ⓓ Without trade, the Romans would never have had sufficient funds to pay soldiers' wages and to purchase equipment.

7   According to paragraph 5, which of the following is true of the end of Roman rule in Britain?

   Ⓐ Historians are unable to agree on what its exact causes were.

   Ⓑ It ultimately ended because the Roman army itself revolted.

   Ⓒ The Saxons were responsible for driving the last Romans out.

   Ⓓ The final Romans to leave retreated to the Germanic lowlands.

8   Which of the following can be inferred from paragraph 6 about life in Britain after the Romans left?

   Ⓐ The British continued to follow Roman architectural styles.

   Ⓑ More wars were started as Britain moved toward a state of anarchy.

   Ⓒ The people continued to remember Roman influences such as the Latin language.

   Ⓓ It became much less civilized than it had previously been.

9   Look at the four squares [■] that indicate where the following sentence could be added to the passage.

   Its leaders decided it was necessary that Roman troops be closer to the capital, which itself would fall to barbarian attacks slightly more than half a century later.

   Where would the sentence best fit?

   Click on a square [■] to add the sentence to the passage.

10 ***Directions:*** An introductory sentence for a brief summary of the passage is provided below. Complete the summary by selecting the THREE answer choices that express the most important ideas of the passage. Some sentences do not belong because they express ideas that are not presented in the passage or are minor ideas in the passage. ***This question is worth 2 points.***

> Drag your answer choices to the spaces where they belong.
> To remove an answer choice, click on it. To review the passage, click on **View Text.**

Roman rule in Britain led to the establishing of invaluable infrastructure, and the Romans themselves had a great effect on the people there.

-
-
-

Answer Choices

1. The British wound up forgetting the Latin language after the Romans left.

2. Many modern-day British cities are located on sites that once held Roman towns.

3. The Romans built roads in order to travel quickly to various parts of the country.

4. Julius Caesar ordered two invasions of Rome, both of which were unsuccessful.

5. The British took some Roman laws and customs and made them their own.

6. Trade in Britain decreased once the Romans imported large amounts of currency there.

❶ The Renaissance

After the fifth-century fall of the Roman Empire, Europe endured several centuries of stagnation now called the Dark Ages. There were few advances in science and the arts, and little was done to promote human knowledge. However, in the thirteenth century, Europe began changing. This happened first in Italy, where there was a rebirth—a renaissance—of knowledge and learning. Indeed, this time would become known as the Renaissance. Scientists began making discoveries and exploring the natural world. Ancient Greek and Roman knowledge once believed lost was found, translated, and commented and improved upon. Artists experimented with new styles and forms. Ultimately, the Renaissance led directly to the Age of Reason and the Industrial Revolution, both of which are still influencing the world today.

❷ The California Gold Rush

In the late 1840s, the large majority of the American population lived along the East Coast. But a mass exodus west began in 1849. The reason was that, in 1848, gold was found near John Sutter's mill in the American River in California. Once news of the discovery spread, thousands of people made their way west. In approximately three years' time, the nonnative American population in California increased from slightly over 10,000 to a quarter of a million people. Many prospectors found gold, got rich, and left. Others found nothing. Yet many stayed and made new lives in California. This prompted more people to settle in the west and eventually resulted in the populating of the country from the Atlantic to the Pacific oceans.

❸ The Influence of the Roman Empire

The Roman Empire, which lasted from around 27 B.C. until 476 A.D.—and which had been a republic for 500 years prior—was one of history's most influential empires. While Rome did not avoid making war to defeat its enemies, it often subsequently brought civilization to its defeated foes. Enemies were usually not oppressed but were converted into Roman citizens. Additionally,

Rome's cultural influence was enormous. Its art and architecture spread widely, and some Roman roads are still traveled today. Even Rome's language—Latin—remains used, both in its original form as well as in its direct descendants: the Italian, Spanish, and French languages.

❹ Life in the American South after the Civil War

The Civil War ended in 1865 with the defeat of the South. The North then faced the issue of how to reintegrate the South into the country. Three major issues were dealt with during Reconstruction, which lasted from 1865 to 1877. They were how to rebuild the South, what to do with the emancipated slaves, and how to punish leading Southerners such as Jefferson Davis and Robert E. Lee. Ultimately, the South was rebuilt, yet many Southerners were taken advantage of and mistreated. Freed slaves were given land, yet racism persisted against them for decades. And there were no treason trials against leading Southerners. Reconstruction left mostly bitter memories for those involved.

❺ Hellenism

By the time Alexander the Great died in 323 B.C., he had conquered a huge swath of land in Europe, Asia, and Africa. Immediately after his death, the period of Hellenism reigned in these lands. Hellenism arose from the Greek influence on these places. City-states, such as Alexandria and Seleucia, were founded in conquered areas and based on Greek models. Trade flourished in many places, and there were advances in science, art, philosophy, and architecture. However, Hellenism was short-lived, lasting only about 200 years. Alexander's empire quickly fractured, and wars between rival factions and outside states led to Hellenism's eventual downfall.

❻ The Brazilian Independence Movement

The nineteenth century—and the late eighteenth century as well—was a time of revolution not only in Europe but also in other areas. Brazil was once such place. From 1821 to 1825, the Brazilian independence movement occurred. Unlike most other revolutions, though, it was fought with a minimum of bloodshed. The Brazilians, led by Dom Pedro, wanted their freedom from Portugal, their colonial master. Through a series of maneuvers, set battles were avoided, and, after four years, Portugal recognized Brazilian independence. Thanks to British intervention, the newly freed state was assured that Portugal would not try to regain its lost colony.

❼ The Role of Geography in the Development of Cities

Geography has long played a crucial role in where cities are founded and in their growth and influence. But cities can use their geographical location to gain power in different ways. London, England, sits along the banks of the River Thames. While it does not adjoin the North Sea, seafaring ships can still sail up the river to London. Given England's tradition as a naval power, this enabled London to become exceedingly important. Paris, France, meanwhile, has never wielded naval power but has been a land power instead. Located at a crossroads for routes north, south, and east, Paris used its geographical setting to make it powerful on land over the years.

❽ Northern and Southern Europe in the Middle Ages

The eleventh and twelfth centuries in Europe are commonly called the High Middle Ages. In both Northern and Southern Europe, populations increased, urbanization took place, and the quality of life in general improved. However, each region's method of governance differed. In Northern Europe, particularly England and France, feudalism dominated. A king ruled the land, and under him were various nobles—dukes, earls, and barons—who themselves ruled the peasants that lived on and worked the land. Southern Europe, like in Italy, eschewed kings and instead centralized power in various cities. Venice and Florence became two powerful city-states during this period.

❾ The Effects of Movable Type

In 1352, Johannes Gutenberg, a German, developed a form of movable type enabling the invention of the printing press. Its initial effects were to lower the prices of books and to increase dramatically the number of books. Gutenberg's invention quickly spread, thereby enabling other places to benefit from movable type. First, the literacy rate in Europe increased. Books were no longer sole possessions of the wealthy or the Catholic Church; now, common people were learning to read. This would directly lead to the sixteenth-century Reformation, as people began reading the Bible for themselves and, more importantly, started interpreting it in ways other than those approved by the Church.

❿ The Development of the Telegraph

The inventing of the telegraph in the mid-nineteenth century tremendously affected the communications of the day. Previously, letters or messages took days, weeks, or even months to be delivered. However, the telegraph permitted communications to proceed at a much faster rate. The first public telegram was sent in 1844. After that, telegraph lines were rapidly set up, first in the eastern United States and Great Britain. By the 1850s, people were laying telegraph wires all over the world. In 1865, a transatlantic cable was successfully set up. Essentially, the telegraph enabled people to share news and to transmit messages much quicker than before, serving to bring people worldwide closer together.

Star Performer Topic Files | **History**

- The development of moveable type in Europe and China
- Italy during the Middle Ages
- The history of various Iranian tribes
- The effects of the telegraph on the United States and Europe
- The events leading up to the Industrial Revolution in Great Britain
- The development of China in the twentieth century
- The industrialization of the United States in the nineteenth century
- The status of women in colonial America
- International exchanges between Japan and China
- The roles of the state and federal governments in the early United States

abolish	declare	immigrant	province
absolutism	defend	immigrate	radical
adapt	defense	imperial	railway
admiral	defy	import	rebel
age	delegate	incite	rebellion
agrarian	democracy	independence	reform
agriculture	democratic	industrialization	refugee
alliance	descendant	infrastructure	regime
ally	destructive	inhabitant	reign
amendment	develop	institution	renaissance
ancient	development	integrate	reparation
antiquity	dictator	invade	repeal
apprentice	diplomacy	isolate	representative
aristocracy	diplomat	isolationism	republic
armada	dissident	knight	resist
artisan	dissolve	legacy	resolution
assault	doctrine	legalize	revolt
authoritarian	dominate	liberal	revolution
autonomous	dynasty	liberate	riot
barbarian	election	lord	ritual
battle	embargo	loyalist	route
belligerent	emigrant	mandate	royalist
betray	emigrate	manipulate	rural
bloc	enemy	market	sail
blockade	enact	medieval	sect
boycott	era	merchant	siege
brink	erupt	military	slavery
canal	ethnic	mob	socialism
capitalism	exile	moderate	sovereignty
captive	expand	modernize	steamboat
captivity	expansion	monarchy	succession
castle	explore	nationalism	suffrage
centralize	export	naval	tariff
chivalry	factory	navy	taxation
class	famine	neutral	terrorize
classical	feudalism	noble	testify
clash	figurehead	palace	trade
colonize	fleet	parliament	traitor
colony	flourish	partisan	transcontinental
commerce	found	patrician	treason
communism	general	patriot	treaty
congress	globalization	patron	tribal
conquest	growth	persecute	tribute
conscription	guardian	pioneer	turmoil
conservative	guerrilla	piracy	unify
consolidate	heir	pirate	unrest
corruption	heresy	plague	urban
coup	heritage	plebian	vassal
crisis	hierarchy	plot	violence
crusade	historian	population	warfare
declaration	humanism	propaganda	waterway

Vocabulary *Review*

✎ Choose the words closest in meaning to the highlighted parts of the sentences.

1 In 1803 and 1804, when Lewis and Clark made their famous expedition to the west coast, the land was empty except for the natives and a few white hunters and trappers.

Ⓐ course
Ⓑ journey
Ⓒ mission
Ⓓ travel

2 Rome's leaders often used the promise of citizenship to attract allies to their side.

Ⓐ competitors
Ⓑ mercenaries
Ⓒ armies
Ⓓ partners

3 The colonists had their own legislatures as well as some measure of autonomy, but even this power was subject both to British law and the rule of a local British governor.

Ⓐ support
Ⓑ strength
Ⓒ independence
Ⓓ commercialism

4 There had been steam engines before James Watt's time, but none achieved the efficiency and practicality of Watt's improved design.

Ⓐ power
Ⓑ affordability
Ⓒ potential
Ⓓ effectiveness

5 Even when men without property were later given rights in Athenian politics, women still remained excluded from participation in the political arena.

Ⓐ land
Ⓑ possessions
Ⓒ money
Ⓓ freedom

6 The city was Carthage, which possessed immense wealth, a powerful navy, and a strong mercenary army, thereby allowing it to trade throughout the entire Mediterranean as the undisputed regional power.

Ⓐ potential
Ⓑ competing
Ⓒ acknowledged
Ⓓ hopeful

7 Prior to the arrival of the Jamestown colonists, the natives in the Chesapeake region were flourishing.

Ⓐ thriving
Ⓑ hunting
Ⓒ wandering
Ⓓ establishing

8 When the colonists arrived, they brought other instruments of change, many of which negatively altered the land.

Ⓐ imperiled
Ⓑ enhanced
Ⓒ poisoned
Ⓓ transformed

9 Armed clashes with natives did not deter them, nor did the problems between farmers who wanted to fence in their lands and ranchers who wanted open plains.

Ⓐ threats
Ⓑ events
Ⓒ fights
Ⓓ wars

10 Watt, however, was interested in developing steam engines for use in factories.

Ⓐ creating
Ⓑ utilizing
Ⓒ procuring
Ⓓ selling

11 Although most of the historical record is lost, the Romans left behind a treasure trove of archaeological evidence, including buildings, roads, coins, and weapons, and a multitude of other relics at various sites.

Ⓐ possessions
Ⓑ institutions
Ⓒ sites
Ⓓ artifacts

12 However, its transition from a failing, disease-ridden economic venture into a full-fledged profitable colony had a resounding and lasting impact on both the New World and the indigenous American people and their environment.

Ⓐ alternate
Ⓑ attempt
Ⓒ prohibition
Ⓓ evolution

13 Others were so fiercely devoted to England that they instead formed loyalist groups that aided the English military forces.

Ⓐ recruited
Ⓑ supported
Ⓒ battled
Ⓓ located

14 Later converted to carry people, the first passenger railroad in the United States began operating in 1830.

Ⓐ expanding
Ⓑ running
Ⓒ charging
Ⓓ using

15 Finally, steam engine-powered factories needed workers, and the mass movement of people from the English countryside to expanding urban centers was the result.

Ⓐ residential
Ⓑ manufacturing
Ⓒ municipal
Ⓓ commercial

16 However, whether the increase in food caused the growth in population or the growth in population allowed more food to be cultivated is unclear.

Ⓐ planned
Ⓑ produced
Ⓒ picked
Ⓓ planted

17 By the end of the twentieth century, industrialization was the norm.

Ⓐ transportation
Ⓑ globalization
Ⓒ automation
Ⓓ mechanization

18 The Romans concluded that Carthage would never cease hostilities, so they determined to destroy the city.

Ⓐ fighting
Ⓑ anger
Ⓒ negotiations
Ⓓ planning

19 The local native leaders could have easily wiped them out at any time yet failed to press their advantage, believing that the colonists would soon give up and abandon their efforts.

Ⓐ warriors
Ⓑ travelers
Ⓒ settlers
Ⓓ seafarers

20 The locals became used to the Romans, their laws and customs were adopted, and they even granted the honor of citizenship to some of the so-called barbarians.

Ⓐ practices
Ⓑ regulations
Ⓒ language
Ⓓ requirements

B

Chapter 02   The Arts

The arts encompass a number of fields, but they are all concerned with the creation of works that are pleasing to the eye and ear. Among the most prominent fields are art, music, literature, and architecture. There are many types of art; among them are painting, drawing, etching, sculpting, and photography. Likewise, music has many genres, and there are also a large number of periods of music which have been crucial to its development over the years. Literature too takes many forms and may include poetry, novels, and dramatic productions such as plays. Architecture can be a form of art in that one of the primary concerns of architects is the aesthetic quality of their designs. Most artists are creative individuals, yet they also are influenced by the people and works in their fields from previous times. This makes it imperative to understand the history of each field and to understand how the different ages, movements, and eras are all related to one another.

Elizabethan Acting Troupes

The Greeks and the Romans wrote both dramas and comedies and then performed them on the stage. While they had theaters in which actors could stage their performances, times changed after both the Greek and Roman empires vanished. By the time of the Middle Ages, wandering <u>minstrels</u> traveled from town to town to give dramatic performances, which were most often passion plays related to the Bible. Nevertheless, by the sixteenth century, plays were making a comeback of sorts in Britain, and there were several changes in the acting culture.

2➡ In sixteenth-century Britain, actors—who were always men—were considered among the lowest members of society. They were frequently called "rogues" or "scoundrels" by the populace, and they performed under constant threat of punishment by the law. Actors were even forced to get permits that indicated their profession and which gave them permission to travel throughout the country. However, in 1559, an acting troupe called Leicester's Men was founded. They were given that moniker since they were sponsored by the Earl of Leicester. Soon afterward, more groups—which came to be called Elizabethan acting troupes after Queen Elizabeth, who was the reigning monarch at that time—were formed. Among them were Lord Strange's Men, Admiral's Men, King's Men, and Chamberlain's Men. Chamberlain's Men would eventually become the most important troupe of the period.

These groups were backed by various nobles, which gave them slightly more rights. Even so, they were still regulated by officials and could be censored at times. The reason for this suppression was primarily that many actors felt at liberty to give their thoughts on religious or political issues of the day while in the middle of a performance. When actors got carried away and then improvised by expressing unpopular opinions—or at least ones that the crown disagreed with—officials would fine or imprison them as punishment.

At first, the troupes had to tour the British countryside to stage performances. They typically acted in the courtyards of inns. However, in 1576, James Burbage, who was a leading figure in the British theatrical world, opened the first theater in England, called, appropriately enough, The Theatre. This gave his group a permanent home. Not much later, other theaters were built, and more and more <u>thespians</u> could abandon their itinerant lifestyles. Fortunately, before these troupes entirely stopped traveling, several of them visited the town of Stratford, where a young William Shakespeare was inspired enough by them that he followed one group back to London to begin his career as a playwright.

📚 *Glossary*

minstrel: a medieval performer who could often play musical instruments, sing, and act
thespian: an actor

1 The word "comeback" in the passage is closest in meaning to

- (A) reappearance
- (B) resource
- (C) revision
- (D) recital

2 According to paragraph 2, which of the following is true of actors in Britain in the sixteenth-century?

- (A) They were not allowed to perform unless they belonged to an acting troupe.
- (B) Thanks to the Earl of Leicester, people came to respect the work they did.
- (C) They were obligated to wander the country on their own until the mid-1500s.
- (D) They were treated with disdain by a large portion of British society.

3 Which of the sentences below best expresses the essential information in the highlighted sentence in the passage? *Incorrect* answer choices change the meaning in important ways or leave out essential information.

- (A) The British monarchy often stopped plays before they could become too unpopular.
- (B) If actors said anything controversial while on stage, they were likely to be punished.
- (C) Officials frequently punished actors when they gave poor performances for the audience.
- (D) Part of the appeal of plays was waiting to see how the actors would express themselves.

4 ***Directions:*** An introductory sentence for a brief summary of the passage is provided below. Complete the summary by selecting the THREE answer choices that express the most important ideas of the passage. Some sentences do not belong because they express ideas that are not presented in the passage or are minor ideas in the passage. ***This question is worth 2 points.***

In the sixteenth century, actors began to band together in troupes sponsored by nobles, and they toured the countryside to perform until the first theaters were founded.

Answer Choices

1. The first Elizabethan acting troupe, which was called Leicester's Men, was created.

2. When actors went to other towns to act, they typically staged their performances in the yards of inns.

3. Williams Shakespeare saw an acting troupe, which caused him to begin his life as a playwright.

4. Some actors improvised while on stage and made political statements that the monarchy disagreed with.

5. Because noblemen supported the groups of actors, they were given a few more rights than normal.

6. Theater underwent many changes from the times of the Greeks and Romans to the Middle Ages.

Traditional Chinese Paintings

Over countless centuries, Chinese traditional paintings have managed to maintain many of the same characteristics and consequently have changed little in style and subject matter. In fact, artists often choose to **duplicate** the paintings of the great masters of Chinese art, and they are highly praised when their works come close to resembling the originals. It is therefore unsurprising that many of the elements that influence the painters themselves have remained unchanged as time has passed. Among them are calligraphy, Zen Buddhism, and the manner in which objects in the paintings are depicted.

2→ Calligraphy is the art of penmanship in which letters are written in a stylistic manner. The Chinese use calligraphy to express beauty in the letters themselves as they are drawn by an artist. Most Chinese paintings are created by using the same style that **calligraphists** use. First, the artist uses a brush to apply ink either on paper or silk. While the ink can be black or colored, the majority of artists paint in monochrome, and most opt for black ink. Additionally, like calligraphists, the artists paint their pictures in a formal and meticulous manner while ascribing great importance to every brushstroke, no matter how small it may be.

Buddhism—especially Zen Buddhism—has long been influential in Chinese traditional painting. Thus, an artist focuses on the painting and visualizes how it will appear when complete before a single drop of ink touches the paper. Unlike many Western artists, who draw pictures on canvas and then paint over them, this is never done in Chinese traditional painting. Instead, the painter, in a Zen-like trance requiring a great deal of concentration, keeps the image to be painted in mind while making every brushstroke. Fortunately for the artists, Chinese painting is so formalized that there are specific brushstrokes that are used to create certain features. For instance, one type of brushstroke is used for mountains, another is used for trees, and yet another is used for water or any other feature which commonly appears in the paintings.

4→ Finally, when one observes a Chinese traditional painting, the objects do not appear completely as they do in reality. However, they are not abstract images, for it is clear what the artist had intended to paint. Instead of being entirely realistic, the essences of the people, the animals, and the landscapes are painted by the artist. This look—neither realistic nor abstract—gives Chinese traditional paintings a distinctive appearance that is unmatched by any other style of painting.

≋ *Glossary*
duplicate: to imitate; to replicate
calligraphist: a person who does calligraphy

1 They word "they" in the passage refers to

(A) artists   (B) the paintings

(C) the great masters   (D) their works

[Reference Question]

The correct answer choice is often not adjacent to the pronoun. It is frequently far away from it instead.

2 According to paragraph 2, which of the following is NOT true of calligraphy?

(A) It requires the use of a brush to apply ink to some kind of surface.

(B) All of the brushstrokes that a calligraphist makes are of tremendous importance.

(C) The people who excel at it are those who make Chinese traditional paintings.

(D) There is a proper way for the people who do calligraphy to draw the characters.

[Negative Factual Question]

By finding all of the answer choices that have information which appears in the passage, use the process of elimination to find the correct answer.

3 In paragraph 4, the author implies that Chinese traditional painting

(A) has a dissimilar look to the abstract art created by Western artists

(B) is gaining popularity due to the unique look that its artists create

(C) focuses primarily on scenes that take place somewhere outside

(D) can be imitated by others if they have the requisite artistic skills

[Inference Question]

Incorrect answers often have information that may be true but which was not hinted at in the passage. Be sure to avoid those answer choices.

4 *Directions:* Select the appropriate sentences from the answer choices and match them to the influence on Chinese traditional painting to which they relate. TWO of the answer choices will NOT be used. ***This question is worth 3 points.***

[Fill in a Table Question]

Review the information in the passage on each of the main topics. Then, look for key words in the answer choices that match with those that appear in the passage itself. This should make finding the correct answers somewhat easier.

Answer Choices

1 The artists strive to capture the essence of the subjects they are depicting.

2 The artists painstakingly apply each stroke of the brush to the paper or silk.

3 The artists typically create works depicting people, animals, or landscapes.

4 The artists use a stylistic way of painting that they have been taught to do.

5 The artists are obliged to maintain strict focus on what they are painting.

6 The artists expect their brushstrokes to be works of art themselves.

7 The artists consider the work they will create prior to starting painting.

INFLUENCE ON CHINESE TRADITIONAL PAINTING

Calligraphy

•

•

•

Zen Buddhism

•

•

Roman Sculpture

The Romans created countless impressive sculptures, many of which have survived until today. Roman sculpture is noted for its seriousness of tone. There are many depictions of battles won done in **bas-reliefs** on walls and columns as well as statues of emperors done as **busts**, shown in serious full-scale portrait sculptures, and sometimes riding on horseback in full military regalia. Publicly displayed sculptures in Rome itself and later throughout the empire were intended to impress people with Rome's power and majesty.

2➜ Roman sculptures were influenced by their Etruscan neighbors in the early years of Rome. Many Etruscan artists were trained in Greek methods of sculpture art, and eventually, by the third century B.C., the Romans began inviting Greek artists to Rome to create artwork. In fact, most sculptures in Rome from that time on were designed and created by Greek artists. It must be noted that Greeks in Rome commonly imitated or even outright copied sculptures from their homeland; however, the Romans also demanded that Greek artists create sculptures in line with their own tastes of seriousness and power. It is these types of sculptures that modern art historians categorize as Roman sculpture art.

Most early Roman sculptures were done in stone, but later sculptors employed marble, bronze, and even ivory for smaller objects. Some of the most impressive Roman sculptures depict emperors. One is the statue of Emperor Augustus, which is named *Augustus of Prima Porta* because it was discovered in the mid-nineteenth century in the Prima Porta section of Rome at a villa owned by Livia, Augustus's third wife. The statue stands more than two meters high and shows the emperor clad in armor and a cloak with his right arm stretched out as if commanding troops in battle. The sculpture features incredible detail and was painted at one time, but the colors have long since faded, a problem common to many Greek and Roman sculptures.

4➜ Another common form of Roman sculpture was bas-reliefs created on walls and columns that frequently depicted historical events, particularly military victories. Bas-reliefs had an advantage over portrait statues and busts in that they could portray a wide variety of subjects in great detail. Of particular note are the ones on Trajan's Column, a thirty-five-meter-high column of marble built from 106 to 113 A.D. to celebrate and record the military victories of Emperor Trajan. The bas-reliefs wind around the column's exterior in a continuous band over a meter high and about 190 meters long. It is considered one of the greatest examples of Roman sculpture art ever created.

🕮 *Glossary*
bas-relief: a sculpture in which the figures project from the background
bust: a work of art showing the upper body, particularly the head and shoulders, of a person

1 The author discusses "Greek artists" in paragraph 2 in order to

    (A) contrast the works that they created with those of Etruscan artists

    (B) argue that they were the real creators of Roman sculpture art

    (C) describe their influence on the development of Roman sculpture art

    (D) claim the Etruscans first invited them to come to Rome to work

2 Which of the sentences below best expresses the essential information in the highlighted sentence in the passage? *Incorrect* answer choices change the meaning in important ways or leave out essential information.

    (A) The sculpture is very detailed, and the colors that it was painted in have not even faded over time.

    (B) The colors of the highly detailed sculpture have faded, something that happened to many Greek and Roman statues.

    (C) This statue was different from other Greek and Roman sculptures in that it was once painted, but the colors have disappeared.

    (D) Many Greek and Roman sculptures were painted in the past, but the colors frequently vanished during the passage of time.

3 According to paragraph 4, the Romans created many bas-reliefs because

    (A) they were easy to create thanks to the types of stones the Romans made sculptures with

    (B) they were frequently ordered to be created by Roman emperors such as Trajan

    (C) they depicted historical events and could be sculpted with relative speed

    (D) they enabled their creators to depict many subjects with a large amount of detail

4 ***Directions:*** An introductory sentence for a brief summary of the passage is provided below. Complete the summary by selecting the THREE answer choices that express the most important ideas of the passage. Some sentences do not belong because they express ideas that are not presented in the passage or are minor ideas in the passage. ***This question is worth 2 points.***

Roman sculpture art became well developed over time and often depicted emperors or historical events.

Answer Choices

    [1] The Romans often created bas-reliefs, letting them portray various events in great detail.

    [2] Many Roman sculptures, including *Augustus at Prima Porta* and Trajan's Column, were impressive works.

    [3] The Romans made statues not only to display in their capital city but also to erect in places throughout the empire.

    [4] Many creators of Roman sculptures came from Greece, but they created art in the style that the Romans preferred.

    [5] Some Roman sculptors used ivory, especially when making fairly small statues.

    [6] Modern-day art historians consider Roman sculpture to be the equal of anything that the Greeks ever created.

Gothic and Renaissance Architecture

1➡ The Gothic Age of art and architecture began during the High Middle Ages and lasted for several centuries, but it came to an end when the Renaissance, which had its own unique style, started. While the Renaissance followed the Gothic Age <u>chronologically</u>, both periods produced architecture that was dramatically different. It was almost as if the ordered Renaissance were a response to the irregularity that was common during Gothic times. A look at the differing styles of these two ages bears witness to this supposition.

First and foremost, the style of the buildings themselves was diametrically opposite during these two periods. Gothic architecture was the culmination of the medieval style. Many of the buildings in this age, particularly the cathedrals, were enormous structures that both figuratively and literally seemed to be stretching toward the heavens. Thanks to new methods in architecture, buildings could be constructed much higher than ever before. Indeed, it was during this period that the Great Pyramid of Giza was surpassed as the highest manmade structure in the world and replaced at the top of the list by Lincoln Cathedral in England. Meanwhile, Renaissance architecture did not continue the trend of focusing on the height of the buildings constructed during the period. In fact, no building constructed during the Renaissance exceeded the heights of Europe's tallest cathedrals.

On the other hand, unlike Gothic buildings, Renaissance architecture was concerned with symmetry. Just as the Renaissance was a period which saw a rebirth of learning in the arts and sciences, the field of architecture witnessed a renewal in ancient styles as well. Greek and Roman architecture became the ideal for Renaissance architects. The buildings were square and were designed to be symmetrical. There was a certain preciseness that the great buildings of this period were constructed with. **1** Among the prototypical buildings of this time were St. Peter's Basilica in the Vatican, San Giorgio Maggiore in Venice, and the Louvre in Paris. **2** The orderliness of Renaissance buildings stands in stark contrast to those of the Gothic Age, where asymmetry reigned supreme. **3** While beautiful, the arches, spires, and statues in Gothic architecture seemed to have been arranged with no specific plan in mind. **4**

While buildings from both ages are exceptional in terms of their architecture, it is virtually impossible to confuse a Gothic cathedral with a Renaissance building. Even the building materials were different, so much so that Gothic cathedrals today appear dark and <u>foreboding</u> while Renaissance buildings look bright and appealing. That difference, as well as their height and style, serves to highlight their dissimilarity.

📚 *Glossary*
chronologically: related to time
foreboding: ominous

1 The word "it" in the passage refers to

    Ⓐ the Gothic Age of art and architecture

    Ⓑ the High Middle Ages

    Ⓒ the Renaissance

    Ⓓ its own unique style

2 Which of the following can be inferred from paragraph 1 about Renaissance architecture?

    Ⓐ Its architects intentionally made it as opposite to Gothic architecture as possible.

    Ⓑ The architects at that time had access to improved engineering and building methods.

    Ⓒ It lasted for a considerably longer time than the Gothic Age managed to.

    Ⓓ People in contemporary times consider it to be superior to Gothic architecture.

3 Look at the four squares [■] that indicate where the following sentence could be added to the passage.

There were, of course, a large number of other buildings, many of which have survived into modern times.

Where would the sentence best fit?

4 ***Directions:*** Select the appropriate statements from the answer choices and match them to the architectural style to which they relate. TWO of the answer choices will NOT be used. ***This question is worth 3 points.***

Answer Choices	**ARCHITECTURAL STYLE**
① Was inspired by studying styles from the past	**Gothic**
② Had buildings with a somewhat shadowy style	• •
③ Employed the same concepts used to make the Pyramid of Giza	**Renaissance**
④ Used a certain level of preciseness to construct buildings	• • •
⑤ Relied upon construction materials that were unavailable in the past	
⑥ Had architects concerned with making buildings as high as possible	
⑦ Was less focused on the sizes of the buildings than their appearances	

Realism

Realism was an artistic movement centered in France in the mid- to late-nineteenth century. It sought to recreate realistic settings by using everyday scenes and common people as subjects for the canvas. Realism came about as a reaction to the Romanticism of the late eighteenth and early nineteenth centuries. Romanticism sought to inject emotion and lofty notions of humanity into the art, literature, and music of its day while Realism attempted to show the bare realities of human existence. There were strong public reactions to Realism; some intensely disliked having common people and scenes be called "art" while others embraced it as a social leveler during a time of great social disparity.

The development of photography in France in the mid-nineteenth century was, surprisingly enough, the **catalyst** for Realism. Photographs—images that were frozen in time forever—captured the truth of both people and the world. The growing popularity of photography led artists to begin to paint in a similar style as they tried to imitate the commonness of life. Previously, during the Romantic Period and earlier, artists sought to bring to the canvas idealized images of people and scenarios. Their subjects were typically heroic figures, political or religious leaders, and symbolic characters and scenes from mythology and literature. Realism, on the other hand, portrayed everyday people doing ordinary things such as working in the fields, meeting people on the road, and sitting with their families. It had a far wider appeal to the general public, who could see the truth of the subject as well as the artist's sincerity.

3➡ The center of the French Realism movement was Gustave Courbet. He is often credited with **coining** the term "Realism" for his own work. Courbet wanted to portray the customs, ideas, and settings of his time as he saw them. He claimed to be independent of any artistic movement, yet in doing so, he created his own. In actuality, Courbet and his followers were influenced by the school of landscape artists that used the countryside near Paris as their subject and also by a trend toward using more rural settings in works of art. Courbet's large canvas, *A Burial at Ornans*, provoked strong criticism. It depicted the funeral of his uncle and showed rows of mourners at the graveside. It had no religious significance and no grand moral theme of life and death. It was just a simple painting of a man's funeral that showed some common people laying to rest one of their own.

Realism also saw its practitioners become involved in the politics of the day. Courbet and other artists in the Realist school were often accused of being socialists because of their depictions of common people and their struggles. Ultimately, the influence of Realism spread to other countries and other fields

Note

Realism was greatly affected by the ongoing technological advances in the nineteenth century. The world was becoming increasingly more based on technology at that time. The telegraph and the telephone made communications easier. Railroads made travel faster. Even electric lights were contributing to the development of society.

Many people were working on cameras in the nineteenth century. Louis Daguerre, a Frenchman, was one of them. He invented the daguerreotype, an early camera, in 1839. It required about twenty-five minutes of exposure to produce a permanent image.

Gustave Courbet lived from 1819 to 1877. His paintings often had a political element in them since he believed in democracy and was a fierce critic of Emperor Napoleon III, who ruled France in the mid-nineteenth century. However, in the later years of his life, his work lost its democratic element, and he began painting landscapes and portraits instead.

of work, including theater, sculpture, and even literature. Furthermore, Realism is considered to be the forerunner of the artistic schools of Naturalism and Impressionism. Its legacy is that it gave artists the freedom to paint as they wished without having to follow a particular school, thus enabling them to paint their personal visions.

≋ **Glossary**

catalyst: something which causes change

coin: to create; to come up with

1   The word "embraced" in the passage is closest in meaning to

   Ⓐ hugged

   Ⓑ regarded

   Ⓒ accepted

   Ⓓ portrayed

2   Which of the sentences below best expresses the essential information in the highlighted sentence in the passage? *Incorrect* answer choices change the meaning in important ways or leave out essential information.

   Ⓐ By showing people doing things they sometimes did, they created the Realist school.

   Ⓑ There was nothing ordinary about Realism despite its subject matter.

   Ⓒ The art of showing regular people doing typical activities was called Realism.

   Ⓓ Everyday activities were captured on the canvas by some of these painters.

3   According to paragraph 3, which of the following is true of Gustave Courbet?

   Ⓐ He set out to establish a movement of art unique from the others which existed.

   Ⓑ He instructed his followers in how to create art with a more realistic look to it.

   Ⓒ His work *A Burial at Ornans* received widespread acclaim by contemporary art critics.

   Ⓓ Although he strived to be independent, his work was affected by the paintings of others.

4   The word "them" in the passage refers to

   Ⓐ theater, sculpture, and even literature

   Ⓑ the artistic schools of Naturalism and Impressionism

   Ⓒ artists

   Ⓓ their personal visions

5 **Directions:** An introductory sentence for a brief summary of the passage is provided below. Complete the summary by selecting the THREE answer choices that express the most important ideas of the passage. Some sentences do not belong because they express ideas that are not presented in the passage or are minor ideas in the passage. ***This question is worth 2 points.***

In the second half of the nineteenth century, the Realist school sought to create art which portrayed people, places, and objects as they appeared in real life.

-
-
-

Answer Choices

1. Many art experts found fault with Gustave Courbet and complained about his works, particularly *A Burial at Ornans.*

2. Gustave Courbet, an important Realist painter, tried to depict the subjects of his paintings as he saw them.

3. Romanticism and Realism both took place in the nineteenth century, yet their adherents created different-looking works.

4. The lives of regular people were often topics that Realist artists sought to reproduce on canvas.

5. The Realist school helped influence other art movements that took place later in the twentieth century.

6. The advent of photography and the type of images it produced had a profound effect on certain painters.

Summarizing ▷ Complete the summary by filling in the blanks.

In the mid-nineteenth century, _____ began. It was a reaction against Romanticism in that it tried to represent _____ and people as they actually were. One reason Realism developed was that _____ showed people exactly as they appeared. So the artists sought to imitate the pictures. _____ was the man who came up with the term "Realism." He and his followers created the art movement after being influenced by certain landscape artists. Realism did not just affect the world of art; its followers became involved in _____ and also influenced other art movements such as Naturalism and Impressionism.

African Masks

Note

¹→ In sub-Saharan Africa, which is the part of the continent south of the Sahara Desert, African tribes used masks as a part of their ceremonial rituals long before European explorers ever reached the continent's shores. These masks were made of leather, wood, cloth, and even metal. Some fit over a person's entire head while others were simply worn on the face or on the top of the head. During a ceremony, a dancer wore a mask and performed a frenzied dance ritual. A translator often accompanied the dancer in order to interpret the dancer's guttural utterances, which were in no recognizable language. After falling into disuse during the colonial era, many of these traditions from past centuries are making a comeback, and the masks themselves are highly prized by collectors worldwide.

The shapes, the sizes, and the materials used in African masks were heavily influenced by the tribe they represented and the purpose of the mask itself. Wood was a favorite material since African mask carvers believed that spirits resided in trees, which meant that the wood in a mask was a natural place for a new spirit to enter during a ceremonial dance. In addition, trees were—and still are today—plentiful in Africa, so wood was not nearly as expensive as other materials such as metal were.

There are four basic types of African masks: the headdress, the facemask, the horizontal plank mask, and the helmet mask. Even today, the facemask is the most common, and as its name suggests, it covers the face and is fastened either to the head or to a costume. The headdress mask sits on top of the head, is very high, may be stiff or flexible, and may have feathers or dried grasses in a **plume** at the top. **1** Horizontal plank masks also sit on top of the head and have extensions like wings sticking out from the main piece. **2** They are designed to represent a bird in flight. **3** Finally, helmet masks encase the entire head and are usually made of a piece of wood carved from a solid tree trunk. **4**

⁴→ Today, African tribes use the masks and the costumes in religious and social ceremonies. Typical events include manhood initiations, ceremonies asking the gods for a good harvest, preparations for war, ceremonies asking for peace, and events begging the gods for relief from troubles like famines and epidemics. The mask used in a particular ceremony represents a spirit the tribe wishes to appease. It may be a deity, an animal spirit, or even a family member. Many families have masks that resemble their ancestors, and they frequently appeal to spirits for guidance. During a ceremony, the dancer becomes possessed by a spirit, which then gives guidance to the tribe or family through the dancer's utterances.

One reason for the wide variety of masks used was the large number of tribes in Africa. Most of these tribes had their own language, culture, and traditions, and this led them to create masks out of materials and in styles that were the most suitable to them.

Masks were also made of materials such as ivory, which came from elephant tusks, and copper, which could be mined. Some tribes created brass or bronze masks if they had the technology to make those alloys. Some even made masks out of various ceramic materials.

Dances in modern-day Africa may or may not make use of masks. As more Africans look to the past in an attempt to recover old traditions, mask dances are beginning to gain in importance.

The colonization of Africa by the Europeans did not begin until the nineteenth century, which was when explorations on the inner part of the continent began. Before then, Africa was known as the "Dark Continent" because so little was known about it. Great Britain, France, and Belgium were the countries that possessed the largest number of colonies in Africa.

⁵➡ With the arrival of white settlers and the European colonial masters, the importance of African masks began to **wane**. Many tribes were uprooted as large numbers of their members were sent to the New World to become slaves and lost their traditional homes. This loss of contact with their traditional roots and the forced education of Africans in colonial languages and schooling caused a decline in those interested in African masks and traditional ceremonies. With the independence they gained in the late twentieth century, however, many Africans sought out their roots, so mask ceremonies, while still not common, are making a comeback.

📚 *Glossary*

plume: a feather or group of feathers that is attached to the top of something
wane: to decrease

1 Which of the following can be inferred from paragraph 1 about African mask dances?

Ⓐ Most people were unable to understand the dancer's words during the ritual.

Ⓑ The dancers who wore the masks were also the ones who made them.

Ⓒ The European colonists forbade Africans from using masks during their dances.

Ⓓ Today, the masks are expensive and difficult to find by people who want to buy them.

2 According to paragraph 4, which of the following is NOT true of ceremonies in which masks are used?

Ⓐ People may hold them to plead for relief from natural disasters.

Ⓑ The masks used in these ceremonies may represent divine figures.

Ⓒ Just one dancer may wear a mask during an entire ceremony.

Ⓓ The ceremonies are always of a religious nature.

3 The author discusses "the European colonial masters" in paragraph 5 in order to

Ⓐ mention the first time that white settlers reached the shores of Africa

Ⓑ explain why the popularity of mask dances has returned to Africa

Ⓒ state the time when masks began to lose their prominence in Africa

Ⓓ describe how many Africans were forced to move to the Americas

4 Look at the four squares [■] that indicate where the following sentence could be added to the passage.

These often come from whichever birds are native to the area where the masks are made.

Where would the sentence best fit?

5   *Directions:* Select the appropriate sentences from the answer choices and match them to the cause and effect of the mask dance in Africa to which they relate. TWO of the answer choices will NOT be used.
This question is worth 3 points.

Answer Choices

1. The masks have become collectors' items and are valued by many.

2. A war between two opposing tribes had already come to an end.

3. The people were making preparations to gather the year's crops.

4. The people in the tribe were given advice as to how they should act.

5. An interpreter was necessary to explain the ramblings of the dancer.

6. A young boy was nearly ready to become a man in the eyes of the tribe.

7. It was thought that some kind of spirit took hold of the dancer.

MASK DANCE

Cause
-
-

Effect
-
-
-

Summarizing ▶ Complete the summary by filling in the blanks.

In parts of Africa south of _____ , tribes used to wear masks when they held various _____ , but the practice ended when the colonialism period began. The shapes, the sizes, and the _____ of the masks depended upon the tribes that made them, so they all looked different. But there were four basic types of masks: the headdress, the facemask, the _____ , and the helmet mask. Each was different from the others. Mask dances are _____ in Africa these days and are used in ceremonies held for various reasons.

The Greek and Roman Influence on Renaissance Art

The Renaissance was a period of profound intellectual change in Europe that took place from the fourteenth to the seventeenth century. It was initially centered in Italy but soon spread throughout most of Western Europe. Renaissance means "rebirth," and in a way, the literature, art, and architecture of the period constituted a rebirth of classical Greek and Roman styles. Following the fall of the Roman Empire in the fifth century, for years, the dominant influence on Western European life was Christianity, and all artistic endeavors were heavily affected by it. Then, starting in the late fourteenth century, lost writings of ancient Greek scholars came to light primarily due to the actions of academics centered in Constantinople in the Byzantine Empire. At the same time, many writings of Roman scholars were rediscovered in monasteries in Italy. As this knowledge was assimilated, a revival of interest in classical Greece and Rome began, and the roots of the Renaissance took hold.

Prior to the Renaissance, medieval painters and sculptors were considered skilled craftsmen who performed jobs like carpenters and **masons** did. Paintings were done when they were commissioned by rich patrons, and the subjects were often portraits or religious-themed paintings of Biblical events. These works were very two dimensional and flat and had a dearth of emotion while the lack of the proper use of lighting or shading gave them no depth or perspective. In addition, little thought was given to using the correct human **anatomical** form or geometric shapes. However, when the ideas of Greek and Roman artists, mathematicians, and scientists began spreading, an entirely new form of art developed.

The Greeks and Romans used the human form in much of their artwork. This greatly influenced the Italian Renaissance masters. The human form was revered as God's symbol of perfection, so nude humans became a constant theme in Renaissance art both in paintings and sculptures. The linear perspective of Greek and Roman art, which allowed for depth in an otherwise flat surface, also heavily influenced Renaissance art and architecture. Architects sought to recreate the style of classical Greek and Roman architecture while artists attempted to create perfect replicas of buildings and natural backgrounds to create a heightened sense of realism in their work. Foreshortening, the use of shorter lines, gave depth to paintings, allowing a painting to seem like a window looking at a scene from life.

⁴➡ The peak of Italian Renaissance art was the period known as the High Renaissance, which took place in the late fifteenth and early sixteenth centuries. Masters such as Michelangelo, Leonardo da Vinci, and Raphael employed

---

Note

It is generally agreed that the Renaissance began in Florence, Italy, around 1350. As many scholars began fleeing the Byzantine Empire, which was being threatened by the Ottoman Turks, they often found their way to Italy. There, they took on students, who were introduced to the Greek language and ancient Greek knowledge for the first time. The works of Greek philosophers, scientists, architects, historians, and others had a profound effect on Western Europeans.

It was the huge influence of the Church in the Middle Ages that caused most art made in this period to be of a religious nature.

The Renaissance introduced the notion of humanism to society. This ideal sought to promote the interests and desires of humans and also resulted in the lessening of the influence of religion on people's lives.

The High Renaissance lasted from around the 1490s to the 1520s and

notions of human perfection to their work but added a new element—human emotion—to make them superior to their Greek and Roman forbearers. Leonardo's paintings *The Last Supper* and the *Mona Lisa* are remarkable for the expressions on the faces of the figures he painted. Michelangelo's sculpture *David* is often said to have been influenced by a Greek statue known as *The Spear Bearer*, yet David's face has more expression in it. Raphael's painting of the Virgin Mary and baby Jesus is also renowned for the depth of human emotion shown. Thanks to the new skills that they learned from the past, these Renaissance artists were without peer and have rarely been matched since.

was most prominent in Florence and Rome. Its painters were extremely technically competent, and they typically painted heroic scenes from mythology, the Bible, or other stories. During this time, Pope Julius II was the patron of many artists, which helped Rome become a base for artists during this period of the Renaissance.

≋ Glossary

mason: a person who builds with stones or bricks

anatomical: pertaining to the structure of an organism, often a human one

---

1 The word "it" in the passage refers to

(A) the Roman Empire

(B) the fifth century

(C) Western European life

(D) Christianity

2 Which of the sentences below best expresses the essential information in the highlighted sentence in the passage? *Incorrect* answer choices change the meaning in important ways or leave out essential information.

(A) Some Renaissance artists were able to create nude paintings and sculptures that showed the body perfectly.

(B) Nude artwork was valued in the Renaissance since God was said to have made the human body perfect.

(C) God made the human body perfect, so Renaissance artists made their artwork as close to flawless as possible.

(D) In the Renaissance, the artists learned the proper way to make nude artwork since it was revered so much then.

3 In paragraph 4, the author uses "*David*" as an example of

(A) a Renaissance statue that was essentially a copy of an ancient Greek work

(B) the first time that a Renaissance sculptor successfully depicted human emotions

(C) the kind of work that the creator of *The Spear Bearer* was trying to do during his time

(D) a statue that was based on a past work but which made improvements in the style

4 According to paragraph 4, which of the following is true of the High Renaissance?

(A) It was a period of innovation in art that improved upon the works of ancient masters.

(B) Michelangelo worked on *The Spear Bearer* to make it an even better piece of art.

(C) Leonardo da Vinci was acclaimed to be the one of the greatest artists of that time.

(D) Human emotions were added to artwork for the first time since ancient Greece.

5 *Directions:* Select the appropriate sentences from the answer choices and match them to the period of art to which they relate. TWO of the answer choices will NOT be used. *This question is worth 3 points.*

Answer Choices	PERIOD OF ART
① Artists learned the proper way to use the method called foreshortening.	**Medieval Art** • •
② The artists were unable to add the dimension of depth to their works.	
③ The sculptures were very realistic but lacked the element of human emotion.	**Renaissance Art** • • •
④ There was an attempt to look back at the past and to imitate art from other periods.	
⑤ The way that humans really looked was not essential to the painting.	
⑥ Expressions were added to the work that made them appear more human.	
⑦ Artists painted for themselves and therefore determined their own subject matter.	

Summarizing ▷ Complete the summary by filling in the blanks.

Life in Europe during _____ changed in many ways. It even affected the type of art that was created. Before the Renaissance, medieval artists painted in _____, did not use light well, and did not depict anatomically correct humans. But thanks to the influence of _____, Renaissance artists painted in a new style. They used depth in their paintings and also accurately depicted the human body. The greatest art was created during _____. Masters such as Michelangelo, Leonardo da Vinci, and Raphael incorporated human emotions into their works to make them masterpieces. This was true of both the paintings and the sculptures that they made.

Commedia dell'arte

Note

In Italy in the fourteenth century, a new form of stage presentation called commedia dell'arte emerged. As the name suggests, it was comedy, but it was improvised. It had no set dialog, yet it included common situations for structure and a **troupe** of stock characters that appeared in most productions. This form of stage production lasted for about 400 years until the eighteenth century and was extremely popular in the middle period of its timeframe. It also enjoyed a revival in France during the middle of the nineteenth century and has even influenced some modern entertainment.

2→ A commedia dell'arte production employed some common themes, including love intrigues, jealousy, and efforts to obtain money or to outwit someone. The details could include two family members in love with the same person, a hero mistaken for a villain, and devious servants involved in various schemes. The actors would prepare for the performance by establishing the basic scenario, determining the course of the performance and how the play would end, and deciding the role each character would play as well as their relationships with the other characters. Then, the actors would take to the stage and play off of one another while entertaining the audience. Because of its impromptu manner, commedia dell'arte is often considered one of the most difficult types of performances, and actors who excelled at it were highly praised.

3→ The stock characters in a commedia dell'arte performance included, but were not limited to, the following: Harlequin, an acrobatic figure who is a servant and loves Columbina, who is also a servant, but who rejects Harlequin's advances; a Captain who is either a hero or a **buffoonish** coward: a doctor who serves as a source of wisdom; a rich man, usually called Pantalone, who is greedy and without feeling; the Innamorati, two young lovers who must overcome some obstacles—usually their parents' objections—to be together; and Punch, a physically deformed person—often a hunchback—whose character is foolish or, at times, clever.

There were some stock gestures, phrases, and situations that a commedia dell'arte audience expected during each performance. **1** Comic relief in a tragic situation was one such scene. **2** Something funny often occurred right when someone received bad news. **3** In addition to these situations, most of the characters wore elaborate costumes and masks. **4** Harlequin's costume, a suit with a colorful diamond pattern, is perhaps the best-known one outside of Italy and theater circles. The doctor and Pantalone wore old-man masks to show their age and wisdom while the Captain wore the mask of a younger man. The only ones who did not wear masks were the two young lovers.

Theatrical productions began centuries before commedia dell'arte emerged. The ancient Greeks performed plays—both dramas and comedies—and they produced three of the world's most famous and influential playwrights: Sophocles, Aeschylus, and Euripides.

A typical commedia dell'arte production required only six to twelve actors. These performances were often much more popular than the more literary productions that were put on at courts.

Despite the limited number of characters, the actors were able to come up with hundreds of different plots in the course of their performances.

Women actually performed the roles of the female characters. This was unusual for the time since in many other places, such as England, women were not permitted to perform on the stage.

Despite its revival in the nineteenth century, the classic form of commedia dell'arte has perhaps been lost forever. Its influence, however, is still felt. William Shakespeare's play *Twelfth Night*, with its comedy of errors and mistaken identities, is an example, yet there are also modern versions of the same story. Harlequin is perhaps the most famous contribution of the commedia dell'arte form to modern entertainment as his costume and acrobatic skills have been imitated numerous times by characters similarly named in literature, comics, and cinema.

Some of the works of Moliere also show how much he was influenced by commedia dell'arte.

📚 **Glossary**

troupe: a group of actors or other performers
buffoonish: foolish; silly

1 The word "impromptu" in the passage is closest in meaning to

   Ⓐ unrehearsed

   Ⓑ ribald

   Ⓒ complicated

   Ⓓ thematic

2 Which of the following can be inferred from paragraph 2 about commedia dell'arte?

   Ⓐ The actors needed little time in order to prepare for their roles.

   Ⓑ Good actors became wealthy because they were in high demand.

   Ⓒ The performances given were all closely related to one another.

   Ⓓ Most of the plays centered on someone's need for more money.

3 According to paragraph 3, which of the following is NOT true of the stock characters in commedia dell'arte?

   Ⓐ The handicapped individual would sometimes play the fool.

   Ⓑ One of the characters has his affections for another spurned.

   Ⓒ One of the people in the play had money yet lacked emotions.

   Ⓓ All of the characters' personalities could change from play to play.

4 Look at the four squares [■] that indicate where the following sentence could be added to the passage.

Yet the people watching always looked forward to seeing how the actors would portray these various scenes.

Where would the sentence best fit?

5 **_Directions:_** An introductory sentence for a brief summary of the passage is provided below. Complete the summary by selecting the THREE answer choices that express the most important ideas of the passage. Some sentences do not belong because they express ideas that are not presented in the passage or are minor ideas in the passage. **_This question is worth 2 points._**

Commedia dell'arte performances all shared the same characters and basic themes, yet the plays still became popular in Europe for some time.

-
-
-

Answer Choices

1. The person who played the hunchback had to pretend to be deformed in some way.

2. The actors had no set lines but merely gave spontaneous performances.

3. Many playwrights, like Shakespeare, wrote works that were in this genre.

4. It was in Italy during the fourteenth century that commedia dell'arte was born.

5. Harlequin's love for Columbina was unrequited in all of the performances.

6. Some of the plays focused on feelings of jealousy between the characters.

Summarizing ▷ Complete the summary by filling in the blanks.

In fourteenth-century Italy, commedia dell'arte was created as a new form of _____ . It remained popular for 400 years but is no longer practiced today. It had common themes like love, jealousy, and mistaken identities, but it had no set dialog. The actors would discuss roughly how the play would go and would then give _____ . There were a number of _____ in the form, and they always had certain features which defined them. There were also certain gestures, _____ , and situations that always occurred in each performance. Writers such as Shakespeare created works in this genre, and characters like _____ are still imitated in literary forms today.

The Dada Movement

¹→ Dada was a twentieth-century intellectual and artistic movement that started in Switzerland. It was mainly a reaction to the carnage of World War I and was characterized by irrationalism, **anarchy**, cynicism, and a disregard for social conformity. It began in Zurich, Switzerland, in 1916 and faded away by the mid-1920s. Its ephemeral lifespan corresponded with the war and its aftermath. Most professing to belong to Dada drifted away to other movements, and a majority turned to Surrealism. The legacy of the Dada movement is that it marked the beginning point in the twentieth century for social protests expressed through artistic displays. This legacy can be witnessed in such diverse realms as performance art and punk rock music.

²→ The beginning of the Dada movement is disputed, but the generally accepted history is that sometime in 1916, a group of intellectuals at the Cabaret Voltaire in Zurich, Switzerland, founded the movement. These artists and performers had mostly come from nations like France, Germany, and Romania, which were involved in the war. They escaped to neutral Switzerland to protest their countries' involvement in something they did not support. They frequently gathered at the Cabaret Voltaire to protest the war and to discuss their feelings about it through various performances they put on. All of them had lost faith in their cultures and in the ideas of nationalism and colonialism, which had helped drag many countries into the war, and they decided they needed to shock the establishment to make it see its own idiocy. Regarding the origin of the word "Dada," one story claims it was picked at random from a French dictionary and referred to a child's toy hobbyhorse. Another legend is that the Zurich group chose it as a word that made the least amount of sense, which is exactly what they were striving for.

³→ The Dada movement used various methods to shock the establishment and to spread the movement. The publication of a **manifesto** that described Dada in a rambling, nonsensical stream of consciousness was one such step. Other methods were public displays of art or performances. In one famous example, a moustache was drawn on a copy of the *Mona Lisa*, and an obscenity was written next to her mouth as if she were actually speaking the words. Another piece, supposedly a sculpture, was actually a urinal turned upside down. The title given to this piece was *Fountain*, and it evoked harsh criticism and outrage. Artistically, the Dadaists, as they were called, proclaimed Dada art was not art but was anti-art instead. **1** Their paintings had no purpose or theme but were to be interpreted by individuals in whichever way they wanted to. **2** Using chaotic images, misplaced perspectives, and seemingly random and unconnected themes, Dada art offended the sensibilities of most that saw it, so it is no surprise that it is the root of Surrealism. **3** Ironically, by trying not to be art, Dada became a recognized form of art. **4**

⁴→ To spread the word about Dada, the group published a literary-art journal, yet they printed few issues. The founders used Zurich as a base to spread the word abroad by appealing to artists and writers in other nations. After the war ended, the movement attracted veterans who had a wealth of experience in the chaos of war. The Zurich enclave broke up after the war, and most members returned to their home countries to start Dada movements. Some groups, such as the one in Berlin, became political and got involved in various movements while using art as a form of political protest.

⁵→ The Dada movement died out because those who had founded it realized it was actually becoming

an established form of art, something its founders were adamantly against. The movement also had no center; there was no dominant city or country after the breakup of the Zurich group. The brief revival in Paris in the 1920s seems to belie this, but the move toward Surrealism had already begun and was, in fact, accelerated by disagreements between members in the Paris Dada movement. Despite its brief life and its founders' desires not to be anything, Dada did become something, and its legacy is found in the artists' protests of the established order, something that remains commonplace today.

≋ *Glossary*
anarchy: chaos; lawlessness
manifesto: a public declaration of one's intentions or policies

---

1   The word "ephemeral" in the passage is closest in meaning to
   Ⓐ influential
   Ⓑ effective
   Ⓒ brief
   Ⓓ systematic

2   In paragraph 1, why does the author mention "Surrealism"?
   Ⓐ To name one art movement that Dada had an influence upon
   Ⓑ To explain the reason why Dada did not remain important for long
   Ⓒ To compare its effects on the twentieth century with those of Dada's
   Ⓓ To note what happened to Dada's followers after the movement died

3   Which of the sentences below best expresses the essential information in the highlighted sentence in the passage? *Incorrect* answer choices change the meaning in important ways or leave out essential information.
   Ⓐ Because so many countries were involved in the war, it was clear that something had to be done to stun people.
   Ⓑ Nationalism and colonialism were complete failures, so the Dadaists tried to convince people to bring the war to an end.
   Ⓒ They acted in a flamboyant manner because they were reacting to the horrors of the war, which was caused by their cultures.
   Ⓓ They became disillusioned with modern life and the war, so they determined to show people the error of their ways.

4   In paragraph 2, the author implies that Switzerland
   Ⓐ was known as a breeding ground for discontented artists
   Ⓑ had programs in place to help support struggling artists
   Ⓒ encouraged people to live there rather than to fight in the war
   Ⓓ had no battles fought on its territory during World War I

5 According to paragraph 3, which of the following is NOT true of Dada?

  (A) While the art appeared chaotic, there was actually a method the artists followed.

  (B) The subject matter chosen by some artists caused others to become upset.

  (C) Some artists took established works of art and adapted them in various manners.

  (D) Despite not wanting their works to be considered art, that was the end result.

6 According to paragraph 4, the Dada movement produced a literary-art journal because

  (A) it was a way for some of the artists to be compensated for their work

  (B) the artists were stuck in Switzerland and had no other way to display their work

  (C) the Dadaists considered it necessary to publicize what they were doing

  (D) the movement needed some way to record its works for posterity

7 The word "belie" in the passage is closest in meaning to

  (A) emphasize

  (B) contradict

  (C) approve of

  (D) consider

8 Which of the following can be inferred from paragraph 5 about Surrealism?

  (A) It was not as outrageous as Dada, nor did it seek to offend people.

  (B) It took the ideas of Dada and brought them to an entirely new level.

  (C) It had a short lifespan yet managed to last longer than Dada did.

  (D) Many of its founding members had once been in the Dada movement.

9 Look at the four squares [■] that indicate where the following sentence could be added to the passage.

This was yet another movement which produced work that was radically different than what most people were used to seeing.

Where would the sentence best fit?

Click on a square [■] to add the sentence to the passage.

10 ***Directions:*** Select the appropriate sentences from the answer choices and match them to the cause and effect of the Dada movement to which they relate. TWO of the answer choices will NOT be used. ***This question is worth 3 points.***

> Drag your answer choices to the spaces where they belong.
> To remove an answer choice, click on it. To review the passage, click on **View Text.**

Answer Choices

1. There is some disagreement as to how the name "Dada" came to be used.

2. The settlement that ended World War I was unsatisfactory to many artists.

3. More artists in the twentieth century began to protest various issues.

4. Artists wanted to show people how absurd the world they were living in was.

5. Certain individuals were protesting the current events that were taking place.

6. The Surrealism movement was founded by a number of former Dadaists.

7. People often felt that the works the Dadaists produced were not art at all.

THE DADA MOVEMENT

Cause

-
-

Effect

-
-
-

Music and Instruments in the Classical Era

1➜ The Classical Era of music comprises the second half of the eighteenth century and most of the nineteenth. During this period, most musical instruments used in orchestras were developed into their present-day forms. In addition, the great composers of the period—Ludwig van Beethoven, Wolfgang Amadeus Mozart, and Frederic Chopin, to name but three—created the musical styles known today as classical music. This did not occur in a **vacuum** though, and the creation of musical instruments and music alike was influenced by what came before them. Prior to the Renaissance, which occurred in the fifteenth and sixteenth centuries, most music was composed for the church, and the organ was the main instrument. During the Renaissance and the Baroque Period following it, the main instruments of the modern orchestra, with the exception of the piano, were developed. During the Classical Era, instrument makers and composers refined them and, relying upon past influences, created the classical music people today love.

2➜ By the eighteenth century, the basic orchestra consisted of woodwind, brass, percussion, and stringed instruments. The woodwind family included the flute, the oboe, the clarinet, and the bassoon while the trumpet, the trombone, and other horns were in the brass family. Numerous percussion instruments were made, and violins, violas, and cellos were the most popular members of the string family. Finally, there was the piano, which is classified as either a stringed or percussion instrument. It was a descendant of the harpsichord, yet there were distinct differences between the two in form and sound. The piano's creation is credited to Bartolomeo Cristofori of Italy. The exact date of his first piano is unknown, but three of Cristofori's pianos from the 1720s have survived, making them the world's oldest pianos. An article dated to 1711 extolling the virtues of a Cristofori piano implies that the invention came much earlier. Cristofori's great discovery was a way to allow a hammer to strike a string and then to return to its original position so that it did not press on the string and dampen its sound. In addition, the hammer did not bounce and could be struck again immediately. This gave the piano a richer, deeper, and more sustained sound than the harpsichord.

3➜ Classical Era music was based on the sonata, which was composed of four movements, or sections. The first was the sonata-allegro and had three main themes: the exposition, the development, and the restatement. **1** The exposition was the main theme, the development was an expansion of the theme, and the restatement was a return to the main theme. **2** There were many variations on the form, all of which depended on the composer. **3** The sonata was used in three different instrumental arrangements: symphonies, concertos, and chamber music. **4** In addition, many sonatas were composed solely for the piano. The piano therefore began to stand out as a singular instrument upon which an entire complex piece of music could be played by one individual. Many great composers of the era, like Mozart and Beethoven, composed sonatas solely for the piano.

4➜ A symphony consisted of the main instruments grouped together. There were usually eight woodwinds, consisting of pairs of flutes, oboes, bassoons, and clarinets. The brass instruments were also in pairs, but their numbers varied widely. Stringed instruments were dominant in classical music, and the violin was the prime instrument in symphonies. They were divided into first and second violins; first violins played the overall theme while second violins played the harmonies. The concerto differed from the symphony in that one instrument—often the piano, violin, or cello—performed the main piece while the orchestra accompanied it. Chamber music was written for smaller groups of musicians—usually strings and woodwinds—while brass and percussion instruments were infrequent in it. The most common format was the stringed quartet, which had two violins, a viola, and a cello.

The **legacy** of the musical instruments developed in the eighteenth century and the forms of music composed in the Classical Era have had a profound influence on the history of music. The music of the era is still played in the same form and style. The great composers of the Classical Period have stood the test of time and are revered as masters of the art. Their music, which has lasted for more than two hundred years, is sure to continue into the distant future.

≋ *Glossary*
vacuum: a void space; a state or condition of isolation
legacy: a heritage

---

1   The author discusses "the Renaissance" in paragraph 1 in order to
　　Ⓐ state that there were new musical instruments made in that period
　　Ⓑ name the period of music that came immediately before the Classical Era
　　Ⓒ imply that the kind of music played was the same as in previous eras
　　Ⓓ compare its effect on musical genres with that of the Classical Era

2   In paragraph 1, which of the following can be inferred about the Baroque Period?
　　Ⓐ It lacked influential composers such as Mozart and Beethoven.
　　Ⓑ It was slightly less influential than the Renaissance was.
　　Ⓒ Orchestral music began to be played for the first time during it.
　　Ⓓ It happened sometime after the sixteenth century had begun.

3   In paragraph 2, why does the author mention "the harpsichord"?
　　Ⓐ To name the instrument from which the piano evolved
　　Ⓑ To compare the music that it made with that of the piano
　　Ⓒ To describe the deepness and the tone of music that it created
　　Ⓓ To give the name of the person who first created it

4   Which of the sentences below best expresses the essential information in the highlighted sentence in the passage? *Incorrect* answer choices change the meaning in important ways or leave out essential information.

    Ⓐ Cristofori invented a hammer and put it in the piano so that it could play the strings as the musician pressed the keys.

    Ⓑ What Cristofori managed to do was to improve the way that the hammer moved in the piano.

    Ⓒ The hammer installed by Cristofori did not cause there to be any loss of sound when the piano was played.

    Ⓓ Cristofori replaced the hammer with something that would improve the quality of the piano's sound.

5   In paragraph 2, the author's description of the basic orchestra mentions all of the following EXCEPT:

    Ⓐ The names of various percussion instruments in it

    Ⓑ The most common string instruments played in it

    Ⓒ The reason woodwinds were more common than strings in it

    Ⓓ The number of families of instruments appearing in it

6   According to paragraph 3, which of the following is true of the sonata?

    Ⓐ It aided many of the improvements made to the piano during the Classical Era.

    Ⓑ There were three main themes covered in its first movement.

    Ⓒ It could be played by many instruments but sounded best on the piano.

    Ⓓ It was the predominant form of music during the Classical Era.

7   In paragraph 4, the author's description of the symphony mentions which of the following?

    Ⓐ The number of singers featured in it

    Ⓑ The major instrument played in it

    Ⓒ The types of brass instruments appearing in it

    Ⓓ The length that one typically lasted

8   The word "profound" in the passage is closest in meaning to

    Ⓐ diametrical

    Ⓑ exhaustive

    Ⓒ positive

    Ⓓ considerable

9   Look at the four squares [■] that indicate where the following sentence could be added to the passage.

This, in part, is what has made the Classical Era such a rich source of all kinds of musical sounds.

Where would the sentence best fit?

Click on a square [■] to add the sentence to the passage.

10 ***Directions:*** An introductory sentence for a brief summary of the passage is provided below. Complete the summary by selecting the THREE answer choices that express the most important ideas of the passage. Some sentences do not belong because they express ideas that are not presented in the passage or are minor ideas in the passage. ***This question is worth 2 points.***

> Drag your answer choices to the spaces where they belong.
> To remove an answer choice, click on it. To review the passage, click on **View Text.**

During the Classical Era, not only were musical instruments developed and new ones invented, but new styles of music were also created.

-
-
-

Answer Choices

1. Much of the music that was written in earlier ages was of a religious nature and was meant to be played in church.

2. Composers often wrote sonatas, which were flexible enough to be used in three different kinds of arrangements.

3. Symphonies and concertos were common during this time, but music written for smaller groups of musicians, called quartets, also gained popularity.

4. The creating of new instruments, including drums and the piano, greatly influenced the type of music played during this era.

5. Bartolomeo Cristofori invented the piano in the early 1700s by basing it on the harpsichord.

6. Mozart, Beethoven, and Chopin were three of the major composers who lived during the Classical Era.

1 Quilts

Quilts are a type of bedding that originated in Asia yet became highly developed in the United States. In fact, quilt making—at events called quilting bees—was once a popular pastime for many American women. There were three main types of quilts: pieced quilts, applique quilts, and crazy quilts. Pieced quilts used many types of cloth and were simply pieced together by individuals, like those at quilting bees, making them all unique in appearance. Applique quilts were often composed of expensive materials like silk and were frequently made by professionals. Finally, crazy quilts were developed during Victorian times. They were creative designs often assembled in a seemingly random order.

2 Murals

Artists have many mediums upon which they create their works. The most common way is to paint on canvas, but some artists prefer instead to work on walls. These works of art, which are often of great size, are called murals. The Romans occasionally painted them, but murals did not become very popular until the Renaissance. Italian painters such as Michelangelo and Leonardo da Vinci both were muralists. Thanks mostly to the size of murals, they can show much more and be more detailed than normal paintings. However, it is a type of art that is neglected more than many others.

3 Pottery in Ancient Greece

An enormous amount of pottery from ancient Greece has survived until modern times, which has enabled scholars to study it extensively. They have been able to divide the pottery created into five separate periods, the last two of which are the Black Figure Period and the Red Figure Period. As there were numerous city-states in Greece, they all developed their own individual styles and standards. Many Greek ceramics were painted in a highly decorative style, with figures from mythology frequently being depicted on them. However, not all Greek pottery was of high quality. It was often mass-produced, and much of it—even to the Greeks—was considered worthless.

4 Musical Instruments in the 1800s

The 1800s was a century in which there were several innovations in the world of music. This is particularly true of musical instruments as many were either created during this time or adapted in some way. For instance, the saxophone was invented in the mid-1800s by Adolphe Sax. He created several variations of it over a period of years. Likewise, the clarinet, while made earlier, had its keying system changed to the one that is used today. The piano, meanwhile, drastically changed in the 1800s. It was given a wider range, and felt hammers, which are still used today, were added to it as well.

5 The Camera Obscura

Nowadays, cameras are ubiquitous, appearing even on cell phones. But camera technology has only been around for a relatively short time. Prior to the invention of photographic cameras in the 1800s, people sometimes used the camera obscura instead. However, it was unable to reproduce pictures on film like cameras do. If one is in a dark room while a small hole emits light into the room, then an inverted picture of the outside will appear on the opposite surface. This is the premise by which the camera obscura works. Some artists actually traced around the images to make their paintings more realistic. The camera obscura enjoyed popularity in the 1800s until cameras made it obsolete.

6 Stage Blocking

In any staged performance, several actors and actresses are often on stage at the same time. Therefore, their movements, and even the places where they stand, must be precisely choreographed; otherwise, the performers run into each other or make movements that appear unnatural or incompatible with the particular scene. So directors engage in something called stage blocking. When they do this, they carefully determine exactly where the performers will stand and move during their time on stage. By precisely establishing where the actors will be, the directors can avoid clutter and also give the actors space to improvise without affecting any others who happen to be on stage at the same time.

7 Roman Masks

Dramatic productions during both the Roman Republic and the Roman Empire required the actors to wear masks. These enabled the audience more easily to determine what kind of character was being played by a particular actor. Over the centuries, the masks underwent many changes in styles. However, they all tended to have exaggerated expressions. For instance, for comedies or characters with comedic roles, masks usually had enormous smiles and wide eyes, thereby making the characters look funnier. For dramas, masks possessed more serious expressions that were suitable for serious roles.

8 French Academic Salons

Starting in the Renaissance, a number of art academies began in France, most notably in Paris. They were established mostly to preserve and to instruct people on the various arts. They continued for hundreds of years and achieved some measure of prominence in the nineteenth century. In fact, during this time, many French artists were formally trained at these salons. The salons became incredibly influential as they held exhibitions to promote the works of their members. While its members clearly benefitted, those who were not in salons were excluded from the events, thus causing their works to be ignored while other more connected artists were supported.

9 J. M. W. Turner

Prior to the nineteenth century, most paintings were either portraits or depicted historical or Biblical events. J.M.W. Turner, however, focused on creating landscapes instead. Turner often painted the Thames River as well as other landscapes throughout Britain. He was especially noted for the way he incorporated light into his paintings, and this fact has caused some to believe he had a great deal of influence on the Impressionist Movement, which was founded after he died. Turner lived during the Industrial Revolution, so he also made paintings that showed the contrast between the traditional and the modern. For instance, the groundbreaking work *Rain, Steam, and Speed* shows a train barreling through the natural landscape.

10 William Wordsworth

Among the many Romantic poets of the 1800s, William Wordsworth was among the greatest. His poems were typically concerned with nature. Among his most famous works are *Lines Composed a Few Miles above Tintern Abbey* and *Daffodils*, both of which focus on nature and the beauty of the land Wordsworth was observing. Wordsworth was unique for his period in that he believed poetry should be for everyone. So he eschewed language that was too confusing or highbrow and instead wrote in the language that ordinary people used. This has helped him maintain his popularity in the decades since his death.

Star Performer Topic Files | **The Arts**

- The evolution of ancient Greek drama
- The development of the American film industry
- The different styles of photographs taken of people
- The process involved in making a film
- The connection between photography and painting
- American colonial gardens
- The use of makeup in the theater
- The development and spread of comedy throughout Europe
- The changing focus of Chinese art
- Various genres of movies

abstract
abstraction
academy
accent
act
ad lib
alto
applaud
applause
application
apply
architect
architecture
aria
arrange
arrangement
artistic
arts
artwork
art deco
audience
avant-garde
bass
beat
bedding
blanket
blur
blurry
bronze
brush
brushstroke
calligraphy
camera obscura
canvas
carve
ceramics
ceremonial
ceremony
charcoal
choreography
classical
collage
comedy
compose
composer
composition
concert
concerto
conduct
conductor
contemporary
cosmetics

cover
crafts
Cubism
decorate
decoration
depict
depiction
design
detach
dialogue
display
dissolve
dissonance
drama
dramatic
dramatization
dramatize
duet
dynamics
easel
element
etch
exhibit
exhibition
express
expression
facial
fake
film
filmmaking
form
function
fresco
garden
genre
gild
harmonize
harmony
hue
idealization
idealize
illustrate
illustration
Impressionism
Impressionist
influence
influential
instrument
interpret
interpretation
juxtapose
juxtaposition

keyboard
landscape
lens
lyrics
makeup
mask
mask dance
master
masterpiece
material
medium
melody
modernize
montage
mosaic
movement
mural
oil paint
opera
operetta
orchestra
organ
pedal
percussion
perform
performance
perspective
pigment
poetic
photograph
photography
pictorial
pitch
plant
play
playwright
porcelain
portable
portrait
portraiture
pose
pottery
print
realism
realistic
reed
refrain
rehearsal
rehearse
reproduce
reproduction
resolution

rhythm
rite
ritual
ritualistic
scale
scenario
sculpt
sculpture
sequence
serious
sew
shadow
shoot
sketch
silk
silkworm
snapshot
solo
soprano
spontaneous
stage
statue
still life
storytelling
string
style
stylistic
Surrealism
symmetrical
symmetry
technique
theater
theatrical
tradition
traditional
quilt
quilting bee
tempo
tenor
tone
troupe
tune
valuable
value
vase
verse
vocalize
vocals
watercolor
weave
weld
woodwind

✍ Choose the words closest in meaning to the highlighted parts of the sentences.

1 Finally, helmet masks encase the entire head and are usually made of a piece of wood carved from a solid tree trunk.

- Ⓐ restrict
- Ⓑ involve
- Ⓒ cover
- Ⓓ disguise

2 Another piece, supposedly a sculpture, was actually a urinal turned upside down.

- Ⓐ purportedly
- Ⓑ theoretically
- Ⓒ definitely
- Ⓓ systematically

3 Additionally, like calligraphists, the artists paint their pictures in a formal and meticulous manner while ascribing great importance to every brushstroke, no matter how small it may be.

- Ⓐ painstaking
- Ⓑ unobstructed
- Ⓒ transparent
- Ⓓ abstract

4 The Zurich enclave broke up after the war, and most members returned to their home countries to start Dada movements.

- Ⓐ foundation
- Ⓑ commune
- Ⓒ brigade
- Ⓓ charity

5 There were strong public reactions to Realism; some intensely disliked having common people and scenes be called "art" while others embraced it as a social leveler during a time of great social disparity.

- Ⓐ upheaval
- Ⓑ misfortune
- Ⓒ reorganization
- Ⓓ inequality

6 First and foremost, the style of the buildings themselves was diametrically opposite during these two periods.

- Ⓐ traditionally
- Ⓑ uniquely
- Ⓒ entirely
- Ⓓ fortunately

7 The publication of a manifesto that described Dada in a rambling, nonsensical stream of consciousness was one such step.

- Ⓐ tedious
- Ⓑ whimsical
- Ⓒ coherent
- Ⓓ broad

8 The orderliness of Renaissance buildings stands in stark contrast to those of the Gothic Age, where asymmetry reigned supreme.

- Ⓐ modest
- Ⓑ general
- Ⓒ austere
- Ⓓ extreme

9 Architects sought to recreate the style of classical Greek and Roman architecture while artists attempted to create perfect replicas of buildings and natural backgrounds to create a heightened sense of realism in their work.

- Ⓐ duplicates
- Ⓑ images
- Ⓒ renovations
- Ⓓ reflections

10 While they had theaters in which actors could stage their performances, times changed after both the Greek and Roman empires vanished.

- Ⓐ coalesced
- Ⓑ disappeared
- Ⓒ reunited
- Ⓓ endured

11 Paintings were done when they were commissioned by rich patrons, and the subjects were often portraits or religious-themed paintings of Biblical events.

(A) sponsors
(B) artisans
(C) bureaucrats
(D) nobles

12 This look—neither realistic nor abstract—gives Chinese traditional paintings a distinctive appearance that is unmatched by any other style of painting

(A) unexpressed
(B) unrewarded
(C) unsurpassed
(D) undermined

13 During the Classical Era, instrument makers and composers refined them and, relying upon past influences, created the classical music people today love.

(A) created
(B) perfected
(C) polished
(D) tuned

14 They were given that moniker since they were sponsored by the Earl of Leicester.

(A) privilege
(B) name
(C) advantage
(D) lesson

15 A commedia dell'arte production employed some common themes, including love intrigues, jealousy, and efforts to obtain money or to outwit someone.

(A) outsmart
(B) outgo
(C) outreach
(D) outsource

16 During a ceremony, a dancer wore a mask and performed a frenzied dance ritual.

(A) passionless
(B) stylized
(C) customary
(D) frantic

17 The details could include two family members in love with the same person, a hero mistaken for a villain, and devious servants involved in various schemes.

(A) irritable
(B) amusing
(C) lovable
(D) wily

18 Thus, an artist focuses on the painting and visualizes how it will appear when complete before a single drop of ink touches the paper.

(A) considers
(B) imagines
(C) proposes
(D) sketches

19 There were some stock gestures, phrases, and situations that a commedia dell'arte audience expected during each performance.

(A) rare
(B) humorous
(C) typical
(D) ad-libbed

20 The statue stands more than two meters high and shows the emperor clad in armor and a cloak with his right arm stretched out as if commanding troops in battle.

(A) dressed
(B) portrayed
(C) discussed
(D) visualized

Chapter 03   Archaeology and Anthropology

Archaeology and anthropology are both concerned with the study of prehistoric and ancient humans. Archaeologists primarily focus on ancient cultures and civilizations by studying the remnants of their cultures. This can come in the form of ruins, artifacts, and sometimes written texts. Anthropologists focus more on how humans developed over time. This can include conducting research on humans' beliefs, cultures, and social and physical development. Both of these areas require their practitioners to engage in fieldwork at various sites in order to do hands-on work to learn about the past. Unfortunately, due to the lack of written records, both fields involve a certain amount of guesswork, which means that these scholars can rarely be certain about the results of their research. Still, they continue to try to explain the mysteries of the past to give people a better look at how men used to live thousands of years ago.

Prehistoric Musical Instruments

The origins of music date back to the beginning of mankind. Perhaps the first sounds that can be called music emerged from human mouths through the acts of singing, humming, and whistling. Archaeologists theorize that music may have developed around the same time as early humans surely used stones to shape tools by beating them in a rhythmic manner, thereby creating the first percussion sounds. From these humble beginnings, humans took the next step of creating purpose-built musical instruments.

The first prehistoric musical instruments made for the **sake** of creating music were wind and percussion instruments. All over the world, archaeologists have discovered wind instruments made from animal bones at sites where early humans lived. Typically, the bones were hollowed out and then had a series of holes drilled into them with stone tools, giving them the appearance of a modern-day recorder. The **femur** was a particular favorite for creating wind instruments, possibly due to its size since it would not crack during the process of hollowing it out and drilling holes in it. Other favorite raw materials for making wind instruments were large horns of animals and large shells, such as conches, from the ocean. A rarer material used for ancient wind instruments was ivory from mammoth tusks. Despite producing higher-quality instruments, ivory was rarely used because it was difficult to drill holes in it with only stone tools.

3➡ Percussion instruments were possibly the first type of musical instruments as they can be essentially anything that is beaten or beaten together and therefore require little work to produce. Early humans may have discovered the joyous sound of clapping their hands together and, coupled with the noise of beating stones to make tools, they were inspired to become more creative. Wooden sticks beaten together or against hollowed-out tree trunks perhaps served as the earliest percussion instruments, but evidence is lacking since wood does not survive as well as bone and stone. Eventually, humans learned to stretch animal skins over wooden frames to produce the first drums, but there is no evidence for this dating back further than around 5500 B.C. in Egypt, Mesopotamia, and China.

4➡ Even with modern dating methods, it is not easy to determine the precise dates of origin for these instruments. In southern Germany, archaeologists found several pieces of bone flute made from **vulture** bones in Hohle Fels Cave which have been dated between 35,000 and 42,000 years ago. Even older, a bone flute made from a bear femur was found in a cave in Slovenia and has been dated to around 43,000 years ago. In yet another cave in Germany, a bone flute and an ivory flute were found and are also believed to have been created 43,000 years ago. Assuming these dates are accurate, these flutes are the oldest known musical instruments.

≋ *Glossary*
femur: the thighbone; the bone going from the knee to the pelvis
vulture: a large bird of prey that primarily feeds on carrion

1 The word "sake" in the passage is closest in meaning to

   Ⓐ appearance

   Ⓑ purpose

   Ⓒ idea

   Ⓓ possibility

Question Type

[Vocabulary Question]

Pay attention if a preposition follows the highlighted word. The correct answer must also be able to be used with that preposition.

2 According to paragraph 3, people probably made percussion instruments first because

   Ⓐ they liked the sounds that they made

   Ⓑ they were not difficult for early humans to create

   Ⓒ they enjoyed beating sticks together to make sounds

   Ⓓ they could use wood, bones, or stones to make them with

[Factual Question]

Avoid choosing answer choices simply because they have some information that is mentioned in the paragraph.

3 In paragraph 4, why does the author mention "Hohle Fels Cave"?

   Ⓐ To claim that the people who lived there in prehistoric times invented music

   Ⓑ To argue that the ivory flute found in it is more than 35,000 years old

   Ⓒ To point out that it is the only cave where intact musical instruments have been unearthed

   Ⓓ To name a place where one of the oldest known musical instruments was found

[Rhetorical Purpose Question]

Focus on the verbs that are used at the beginning of each answer choice. They can help you find the correct answer and eliminate incorrect ones.

4 ***Directions:*** An introductory sentence for a brief summary of the passage is provided below. Complete the summary by selecting the THREE answer choices that express the most important ideas of the passage. Some sentences do not belong because they express ideas that are not presented in the passage or are minor ideas in the passage. ***This question is worth 2 points.***

During prehistoric times, the first musical instruments that people made were wind and percussion instruments.

[Prose Summary Question]

Think about the main idea of each paragraph and then look for answer choices that describe those main ideas.

Answer Choices

⓵ Humans learned how to stretch skin over wooden frames to make drums around 5500 B.C.

⓶ Hohle Fels Cave is the site of an excavation where an old flute made from a bird's bone was found.

⓷ Many wind instruments were made from bones, horns, or shells and had holes drilled in them.

⓸ The oldest known prehistoric instruments are flutes made of bone and ivory that are around 43,000 years old.

⓹ The earliest humans probably created percussion instruments from various things, such as stones, that they beat together.

⓺ Prehistoric people most likely discovered music by accident by doing actions such as whistling and humming.

The Development of Early Writing Systems

Today, people take writing systems and the ability to write for granted, but for most of human history, the vast majority of cultures lacked writing systems, and in those few with them, only small numbers of people could read and write. Over time, however, humans developed writing independently in four separate areas: Mesopotamia, Egypt, China, and Mesoamerica. In addition, the people of the ancient Indus valley civilization located in modern-day Pakistan may have developed writing, yet there is some dispute as to the nature of the symbols found in ruins there. Furthermore, there is evidence that the Egyptian hieroglyphic writing system is an offshoot of one of the Mesopotamian systems, which means there may be only three distinct, unique writing systems in the world. Since the Mayans of Mesoamerica never spread their writing to other cultures and their system has largely disappeared, most of the world's writing systems can trace their roots back to Mesopotamia or China.

One of the questions archaeologists strive to answer is why and how writing systems developed. The simplest answer is that they developed out of necessity. The most commonly accepted theory is that, as people began living in farming societies and, later, in more complex civilizations, bureaucracies expanded to organize and regulate people's affairs. **1** They desired to keep accurate counts of certain things, so as a result, various systems of counting and noting what was being calculated were developed. **2** From this, scholars have <u>surmised</u> that the Sumerian writing system called cuneiform developed in Mesopotamia. **3** Interestingly, most of the extant clay tablets with cuneiform on them deal with bureaucratic matters such as the amount of grain produced somewhere. **4**

³→ Cuneiform did not just suddenly emerge from the minds of Mesopotamian bureaucrats though. Prior to its formation, there was something which scholars call proto-writing. These are symbols or sets of symbols that represented certain objects or ideas. Scholars believe it developed between the eighth and sixth millennium B.C. How and when proto-writing became cuneiform is unknown, but around the fourth millennium B.C., an early form of it was in use in Mesopotamia. Scholars have found proto-writing in many societies around the world, but only the few cultures already mentioned advanced from proto-writing to <u>full-fledged</u> writing systems.

Many early writing systems used pictures or symbols, like the marks on clay tablets in cuneiform, Egyptian hieroglyphics, or Chinese logograms. Alphabets, using what are now called letters, first appeared in ancient Egypt and were later adopted by many other cultures, including the Phoenicians, the Greeks, and the Romans. Through a long and meandering process, the modern alphabet most Western languages employ emerged from these early beginnings.

📚 *Glossary*
surmise: to conclude; to determine
full-fledged: mature; complete

1   The word "They" in the passage refers to

    Ⓐ Farming societies

    Ⓑ Complex civilizations

    Ⓒ Bureaucracies

    Ⓓ People's affairs

Question Type

[Reference Question]

Pronouns may sometimes refer to multiple words in a sentence—in this case, "people" is a possible answer. However, it is not an answer choice, so look for another word that also refers to the pronoun.

2   According to paragraph 3, which of the following is NOT true of proto-writing?

    Ⓐ Proof of its existence has been found in many places on the Earth.

    Ⓑ It was developed prior to the creation of cuneiform.

    Ⓒ Many cultures never developed it into an actual writing system.

    Ⓓ It was first developed during the fourth millennium B.C.

[Negative Factual Question]

Read the entire paragraph carefully. This will keep you from being fooled by answer choices that use words from the paragraph but in an incorrect manner.

3   Look at the four squares [■] that indicate where the following sentence could be added to the passage.

In other instances, however, literature, such as the *Epic of Gilgamesh*, was recorded in cuneiform.

Where would the sentence best fit?

[Insert Text Question]

The connecting words that start the sentences to be inserted often give valuable hints as to where they should be inserted in the text.

4   ***Directions:*** Select the appropriate statements from the answer choices and match them to the type of writing system to which they relate. TWO of the answer choices will NOT be used. ***This question is worth 3 points.***

[Fill in a Table Question]

The answer choices do not always appear as complete sentences. Instead, they may appear as phrases. When this happens, the categories into which you are placing the answer choices can serve as the subjects of the sentences.

Answer Choices

1. Was first developed between the eighth and sixth millennium B.C.

2. Was a collection of symbols which represented various ideas

3. Was used by the Egyptians when they developed hieroglyphics

4. Is thought to have been created in Mesopotamia

5. Has several modern-day alphabets worldwide based on it

6. Has been found in various forms in many primitive cultures

7. Was used by bureaucrats to keep track of certain items

TYPE OF WRITING SYSTEM

Cuneiform

•

•

Proto-Writing

•

•

•

The Domestication of the Dog

1➡ Since ancient times, animals have served humans as sources of food, means of transportation, beasts of burden, protectors, and companions. Out of the millions of animal species living on the planet, however, humans have domesticated a **miniscule** number. Domesticated animals are tame and do not lash out and attack humans or flee in their presence. Most farm animals are domesticated; so are common pets such as dogs and cats. Yet the great majority of the world's animals are wild, and despite repeated attempts by humans to domesticate many species, unlike humans' success with the dog, they have ended in failure.

Domesticating animals requires a special kind of conditioning. First, the animals must be made to abide interaction with humans so that their basic instincts do not **incite** them to attack people or to run away, both of which are common urges even among animals which have been domesticated. Domesticated animals were once wild, so some may still have feral tendencies. Most horses, for example, need to be "broken" before they will permit a person to ride them. Likewise, dogs are the descendants of wolves that were domesticated by humans centuries ago, so even today some may require a certain amount of training before they are comfortable being around people.

The relationship between humans and dogs is so close that it suggests there is a powerful attraction which draws them together. Anthropologists speculate that the origins of the human-wolf relationship are important in understanding human-dog relationships. After the last ice age, many large animals roamed the Northern Hemisphere. Humans and wolves frequently combined forces to hunt these beasts. For humans, wolves added the advantages of speed and the power of their claws and teeth as additional weapons. For wolves, when humans killed animals, they could share the meat from the kill. Out of this mutual need, perhaps a growing companionship developed.

4➡ Wolves and humans also share certain characteristics. Both tend to form tightknit family groups, to mate for life, and to take care of abandoned young. Indeed, history is replete with stories of wolves suckling abandoned human infants. The most famous is probably the story of the wolf which raised Romulus and Remus, the legendary founders of Rome. Perhaps many thousands of years ago, a human found an abandoned wolf cub and raised it. This wolf felt no danger and had no fear of humans; thus, its instinct to avoid humans, which remains in modern-day wolves, was overcome by the companionship it felt with them. This wolf then found a mate and raised cubs, or perhaps the cubs were also raised alongside humans. Many generations later, dogs emerged as a new, domesticated animal species.

≋ *Glossary*
miniscule: extremely small
incite: to stimulate; to cause to happen

1 In paragraph 1, the author's description of domesticated animals mentions which of the following?

  Ⓐ The manner in which they usually behave around humans

  Ⓑ The number of them that have been tamed by humans

  Ⓒ The amount of time it takes to tame most of them

  Ⓓ The names of the animals which are the easiest to tame

[Factual Question]

2 In paragraph 4, the author uses "Romulus and Remus" as an example of

  Ⓐ two people who were the founders of an ancient civilization

  Ⓑ babies who were reared after being found by a wild animal

  Ⓒ children who grew up with wolves and assumed some of their traits

  Ⓓ two people who were responsible for helping to tame wolves

[Rhetorical Purpose Question]

3 Which of the sentences below best expresses the essential information in the highlighted sentence in the passage? *Incorrect* answer choices change the meaning in important ways or leave out essential information.

  Ⓐ Modern-day wolves, unlike wolves in the past, have a sense of companionship with many humans.

  Ⓑ Wolves both in the past and today sometimes do not follow their instincts to flee when around humans.

  Ⓒ Some wolves make good companions for humans, so they prefer to live with them and not to avoid them.

  Ⓓ Unthreatened by humans, the wolf felt a connection to them and overcame its instinct to live apart from them.

[Sentence Simplification Question]

4 ***Directions:*** An introductory sentence for a brief summary of the passage is provided below. Complete the summary by selecting the THREE answer choices that express the most important ideas of the passage. Some sentences do not belong because they express ideas that are not presented in the passage or are minor ideas in the passage. ***This question is worth 2 points.***

[Prose Summary Question]

For a wild animal to be domesticated, its instinct to flee in the presence of humans must be overcome, something which dogs have managed to do.

Answer Choices

1 All modern dogs are descendants of wolves, which were once tamed by humans but are no longer domesticated.

2 Horses retain some of their wildness so that they must always be broken in order to let someone ride them.

3 People today mostly use animals as sources of companionship and to transport them to various places.

4 Dogs and humans have a connection with one another that anthropologists attempt to understand.

5 Wolves, the ancestors of dogs, were likely tamed when abandoned wolves conquered their fear of humans.

6 Despite attempting to domesticate many animals, humans have often failed because the animals remained afraid of them.

The Tribes of the Central Asian Steppes

The steppes of Central Asia have been the homelands of tribes that have significantly influenced humanity. These tribes have been called by various names throughout history: Huns, Turks, and Mongols are just a few of the many tribes that have come from the steppes. In particular, these tribes are responsible for the domestication of the horse, which helped them make the mass migrations that brought them to Europe and the Middle East and eventually led to the overthrow of civilizations such as Rome and Byzantium. The reasons for migrating varied, but some of them were population pressures, quests for food and fodder, and in the case of the Mongols, the desire for conquest.

2→ None of this would have been possible without horses. Without them, the movement of the steppe people would have been severely limited and their prowess in battle also **curtailed**. How and when the horse was first domesticated is a matter of speculation, but archaeological evidence recently unearthed suggests the Botai, a group of people that lived in what is Kazakhstan today, were the earliest culture to domesticate the horse. They did this sometime around 3500 B.C. Wild horses lived in this region for thousands of years and were often hunted for food. Archaeologists speculate that at some point, the Botai managed to tame, bridle, and ride them. In addition, they selectively bred their horses to be larger and stronger. From these beginnings, methods for domesticating horses spread far and wide.

Migrations of people take place for various reasons. In some cases, like those of nomads, they are a way of life. The tribes of the central Asian steppes were more akin to modern **pastoral** nomads. They raised large herds of livestock which they moved through certain regions to graze. They typically followed a routine pattern—often associated with the seasons—over these grazing grounds. However, they were sometimes forced to make major movements, which led to mass migrations.

4→ Most of these migrations were based on necessity since population pressure at one end of the steppes could prompt tribes to move further west in search of food. Tribes battled one another for resources, and they sometimes experienced such pressure that their leaders decided to move to new lands, thereby causing a domino effect across the steppes. Tribes frequently moved west; for example, the Turks went into Anatolia and parts of the Middle East, the Huns and other tribes migrated to Europe, and much later, the Mongols assaulted both regions. In essence, conquest, search for new grazing lands, and pressure from other tribes all contributed to these mass migrations.

≋*Glossary*
curtail: to limit; to restrain
pastoral: rustic; relating to rural areas

1 The word "them" in the passage refers to

- (A) civilizations
- (B) Rome and Byzantium
- (C) the reasons for migrating
- (D) population pressures

2 According to paragraph 2, which of the following is NOT true of the domestication of the horse?

- (A) It is thought to have been done first by the Kazakhstani people.
- (B) It enabled the people of the steppes to be more mobile.
- (C) It is believed that it first happened more than 5,000 years ago.
- (D) It was quickly followed by the breeding of horses for various purposes.

3 Which of the following can be inferred from paragraph 4 about mass migrations from the Central Asian steppes?

- (A) They led to the importing of new cultural ideas.
- (B) They resulted in the migrating tribes choosing one king to rule them.
- (C) They happened in the past on a fairly regular basis.
- (D) They often involved a certain amount of bloodshed.

4 *Directions:* Select the appropriate sentences from the answer choices and match them to the cause and effect of mass migration from the Central Asian steppes to which they relate. TWO of the answer choices will NOT be used. *This question is worth 3 points.*

Answer Choices

MASS MIGRATION

1. The domestication of the horse happened sometime around 3500 B.C.

Cause
-
-
-

2. The tribes battled people in lands as far away as Europe.

3. There was not enough food in the steppes to support the local populations.

Effect
-
-

4. Various civilizations, such as that in Rome, suffered defeat.

5. Tribes on the steppes began fighting each other for resources.

6. Some tribes were interested in defeating people in other places.

7. The tribes on the Central Asian steppes have been given various names over time.

Problems in Archaeology

¹➡ Archaeology is the study of human cultures through the examination of artifacts like tools and weapons that have been left behind, the ruins of buildings, and human remains. Archaeologists hope to understand how humans lived together and how they developed historically. Yet it is not an exact science, and there are several problems related to archaeological studies. The most significant has always been the lack of written records to give clues as to what actually happened in the past. In addition, at times, several different groups of people may have occupied the same site, thereby making it difficult to determine which relics belonged to which culture. Finally, archaeologists must deal with modern-day governments and their frequent desire to prohibit the removal of artifacts and to shape history or to leave its interpreting as they wish it to be.

For much of history, there were no written records, and even when they do exist, determining the truth can be troublesome. Archaeologists must employ a wide variety of methods to overcome this daunting obstacle. Three steps are frequently taken when ancient ruins or a place with artifacts is discovered. First, a careful survey of the area is taken to determine the size of the site and to plan the next steps. Second, the site is excavated. This requires careful digging in order to preserve the site as well as possible. Third is the process of analysis. All the information is gathered and examined in detail. Experts use carbon dating and other methods to determine how old the objects are. **1** Archaeologists peruse garbage pits to find out what kinds of food the people ate. **2** Others examine tree rings to determine rainfall patterns. **3** These and a wide variety of other methods help archaeologists discover the history of an ancient people in the absence of written documentation. **4**

³➡ At times, however, even these actions are insufficient. Some sites have been occupied continuously for thousands of years. Modern buildings sometimes even lie on top of ancient ruins, so there are fewer traces of the ancient cultures remaining. Determining who did what and when now becomes more difficult. This is a common problem that archaeologists face when examining ruins from the Roman Empire and ancient Middle Eastern societies. While high-tech equipment such as ground **sonar** can find ruins and artifacts under buildings, permission to excavate must still be sought and then granted. On occasion, though, when construction projects inadvertently uncover ruins, archaeologists may be given a limited amount of time to conduct surveys of the newly unearthed sites.

One of the greatest obstacles archaeologists face today is obtaining permission from governments to examine and excavate a site. Many

Note

Archaeology does not merely focus on finding ruins or relics and then analyzing them. Much of archaeology is conducted in libraries as archaeologists seek to learn as much about their topic prior to excavating a site.

Most archaeological digs are conducted very slowly. Archaeologists avoid using shovels or any kind of digging tools that could cause accidental damage to their site. Instead, using trowels or even small instruments like toothbrushes, they slowly brush away dirt and catalog everything that they find. While time consuming, this meticulous behavior enables them better to preserve various sites.

Athens, Rome, Istanbul, and Jerusalem are just a few of the cities where people live alongside and above ancient sites. It is quite common for construction projects in these cities—and others—to be halted by the discovery of a long-forgotten ancient site.

Grave robbers have looted countless sites of

governments fear that pseudo-archaeologists and <u>looters</u> will use the cover of an archaeological expedition to rob the sites and to steal ancient treasures from their land. In addition, many cultures have a vested interest in maintaining the mythological stories of their people's history, but archaeological discoveries might poke holes in the image they have of themselves. In some cases, this leads to the authorities restricting access to various excavation sites.

archaeological value over the course of time. Ancient Egyptian sites in particular have been robbed of their relics and treasures.

📚 *Glossary*

sonar: a method for detecting objects by using echolocation

looter: a person who steals from an unattended place

---

1   According to paragraph 1, which of the following is NOT true of problems related to archaeology?

   (A) Many artifacts are removed from sites by governments.

   (B) Governments are reluctant to assist some archaeologists.

   (C) Not enough records exist for the time periods in question.

   (D) The dig sites may have evidence from multiple settlements.

2   The word "daunting" in the passage is closest in meaning to

   (A) frightening

   (B) impenetrable

   (C) discouraging

   (D) reluctant

3   Which of the following can be inferred from paragraph 3 about the Roman Empire?

   (A) The artifacts from it that have been found by archaeologists are not helpful.

   (B) The land it once controlled has been continuously occupied since its downfall.

   (C) The ruins from that period can often be found by using sonar.

   (D) Many of its ruins are still standing and are open to the public to observe.

4   Look at the four squares [■] that indicate where the following sentence could be added to the passage.

This has enabled archaeologists not only to determine ancient people's diets but also to learn what plants and animals were native to specific regions.

Where would the sentence best fit?

5 ***Directions:*** An introductory sentence for a brief summary of the passage is provided below. Complete the summary by selecting the THREE answer choices that express the most important ideas of the passage. Some sentences do not belong because they express ideas that are not presented in the passage or are minor ideas in the passage. ***This question is worth 2 points.***

Despite their use of modern methods, there are still many problems that archaeologists encounter as they attempt to learn about the past.

-
-
-

Answer Choices

1. Many archaeologists explore ruins of the Roman Empire and Middle Eastern cultures.

2. Pseudo-archaeologists often loot invaluable cultural treasures from some countries.

3. Governments may interfere with archaeologists when they conduct digs.

4. Most archaeologists first research the sites that they intend to excavate.

5. The lack of written records often makes researching the past difficult.

6. Traces of past civilizations can be erased because people live in the same places.

Summarizing ▶ Complete the summary by filling in the blanks.

For many reasons, archaeology is not an exact science, so its practitioners often have problems conducting it. There were no _____ in the past, so archaeologists cannot rely on them for their research. Instead, they must carefully inspect ancient sites as they excavate them and unearth _____ to analyze. In addition, many modern-day cultures have built on ancient sites, so remains from the past are hard to get at or have even been destroyed. Finally, _____ are reluctant to let some people dig in places. They are concerned about looting and that their carefully crafted _____ may be disproven.

Early Food Preservation

Note

Most modern homes have refrigerators; however, for much of human history, preserving food was a tremendous problem since with few exceptions, food spoils after some time. The spoilage rates depend on the food, temperature, and whether or not it has been preserved with salt or something else. All food contains microorganisms or can get ones like bacteria from the environment. These microbes eventually reproduce and are the main reason that food spoils. Preventing food from spoiling has been an objective of humans since practically the beginning of history.

One of the earliest known methods of food preservation involved utilizing burial pits. People frequently placed their food underground, where a combination of factors enabled it to remain fresh for a longer period of time than when it was above the ground. There are several theories concerning when and why people first started doing this. No one is certain, but using burial pits to preserve food likely began shortly after man started practicing agriculture, which happened soon after the last ice age ended around ten to twelve thousand years ago. During that time, humans depended mostly on hunting to obtain their food supplies. As the ice and glaciers began to **retreat**, wild grains started growing in the warmer southern climates. Humans discovered they were edible and soon developed ways to plant, maintain, and harvest them. This was the beginning of agriculture. Research suggests that agriculture started in the area of the Middle East known as the Fertile Crescent, which is where modern-day Iraq and Syria are located.

Sometimes, the farmers had bumper crops, and more food was grown than could be readily consumed in a short period of time. Of course, the opposite sometimes occurred when a harvest failed and food supplies **dwindled**. What was therefore needed was a method to preserve food during good harvests in order to tide the people over during the inevitable lean years. Additionally, farmers needed to preserve grain for use in planting the next year's crops. Underground burial pits accordingly became the first method of food storage. Burial pits are dark, cool places and thus enabled food to keep from spoiling quickly because of the absence of oxygen and heat, which cause microorganisms on food to grow faster.

⁴➡ Caves may also have been among the first places humans used to store food. Excavations of many ancient sites around the world have proven that caves were steadily used as storage sites for thousands of years. In areas without caves, which are often quite cool themselves, humans learned to bury grain seeds underground through the process of trial and error. The more widespread development of pottery can perhaps be attributed to the use of

As soon as living matter dies, it begins to decompose. This is true of both animals and vegetation. However, they all decompose at separate rates. Various factors, such as heat in particular, can accelerate the rate at which something decomposes.

In some societies, dehydration, or drying, was also used as a food preservation method. Essentially, the food was left in the sun, which removed the water from it and enabled it to be preserved for a long period of time. In places where salt was in abundance, it was used to preserve food. Fish was one food frequently preserved with salt.

Seed grain was and is essential to all farmers. Without it, they would not be able to plant their next year's crop. Even during times of famine, most farmers have been hesitant to eat their seed grain since it would guarantee that they would have no food to eat the next year.

The temperatures in many caves, particularly those located deep underground, are usually much lower than the temperatures outside of the caves. This enabled people in many

burial pits and caves as places of food storage since people needed containers to place their grain in and to keep animals and insects from consuming it.
In the modern age, the use of burying food underground is still practiced. In places with cold climates, even meat can be placed underground, and cold temperatures will act like a natural refrigerator.

places to preserve their food with a minimum of effort.

📚 *Glossary*

retreat: to recede

dwindle: to disappear; to become smaller and smaller

1   Which of the sentences below best expresses the essential information in the highlighted sentence in the passage? *Incorrect* answer choices change the meaning in important ways or leave out essential information.

     Ⓐ   Because they were able to farm the land after the ice age ended around ten thousand years ago, people felt the need to use burial pits for their food.

     Ⓑ   At the end of the last ice age over ten thousand years ago, people probably began burying food underground to preserve it once they started farming the land.

     Ⓒ   It is well known that burial pits and agriculture developed at virtually the same time, which was right at the end of the world's last ice age.

     Ⓓ   Archaeologists speculate that the need for food burial pits is what prompted people to discover agriculture sometime between ten and twelve thousand years ago.

2   The word "lean" in the passage is closest in meaning to

     Ⓐ   slim

     Ⓑ   frigid

     Ⓒ   unproductive

     Ⓓ   famished

3   The word "it" in the passage refers to

     Ⓐ   pottery

     Ⓑ   food storage

     Ⓒ   grain

     Ⓓ   the modern age

4   According to paragraph 4, people preserved food in caves because

     Ⓐ   they were unable to dig burial pits to put their supplies in

     Ⓑ   they were easier to protect from other humans or animals

     Ⓒ   they had the same effect on their food as burial pits did

     Ⓓ   they lacked enough pottery to preserve their food in

5 ***Directions:*** Select the appropriate sentences from the answer choices and match them to the cause and effect of using food burial pits to which they relate. TWO of the answer choices will NOT be used. ***This question is worth 3 points.***

Answer Choices

[1] It took longer for microorganisms to reproduce and to spoil the food.

[2] People used caves because they worked better than burial pits did.

[3] Modern refrigerators were developed and now appear in most homes.

[4] Farmers began growing more food than could be eaten in a short time.

[5] People needed to keep grain so that they could plant it the next year.

[6] Pottery was developed so that people could put their food in it.

[7] People were able to eat enough in years when harvests were insufficient.

FOOD BURIAL PITS

Cause
-
-

Effect
-
-
-

Summarizing ▶ Complete the summary by filling in the blanks.

Humans have always been concerned about preserving their food, so they have sought ways to keep _____ from spoiling it. Mostly, they used burial pits to do this. They kept their food underground since the cooler temperatures there help food remain edible longer. Once _____, having burial pits became imperative since people could keep their surplus food and _____ for planting in them. Other cultures used caves to keep their food in since they were cool. This also led to the invention of _____ because people needed containers to keep their food in before burying them.

Populating the Americas

¹➡ When the Europeans first arrived in the Americas, they discovered an entire landmass already populated by millions of people. One question they asked themselves was where these people initially came from. This has been something people have pondered for centuries. The most widely accepted theory concerning the origins of humans considers Africa to be the cradle of humanity. From there, people later spread to Asia and Europe. While this migration took ages to accomplish, there were no real obstacles since all three continents are interconnected. However, how humans reached the Americas, which are unconnected to other landmasses, is a matter of conjecture. There are two main theories which account for this movement. The first states that humans walked across a **land bridge** that connected northern Siberia and modern-day Alaska. The second claims that humans arrived in the Americas by boat.

The land bridge theory is the more logical of the two and has a plethora of evidence to defend it. First, there is ample evidence that during the end of the last ice age—about ten to twelve thousand years ago or perhaps even earlier— global sea levels were lower, thereby causing the revealing of a land bridge between Asia and North America. Humans likely followed herds of animals across the bridge and eventually migrated south into North and South America. Supporting evidence for this is the large number of stone spear points carbon dated to the same time period—but not before it—which have been found throughout North America. There are also numerous fossilized animal bones in various places which show evidence of having been gnawed upon by human teeth. These bones have additionally been dated to the same time period as the spear points.

³➡ The theory that humans first came to the Americas by ship is partially based on the superior **navigational** skills of the Pacific Polynesian islanders. The Polynesians moved east from New Guinea and the Solomon Islands and spread across the Pacific, eventually reaching as far east as Easter Island near Chile, as far north as the Hawaiian Islands, and as far south as New Zealand. Some people believe they could have made it as far east as North or South America. While that possibility exists, the evidence is scanty. First of all, most of the Pacific islands were only reached during the last two or three thousand years whereas there is evidence of humans in the Americas going back at least ten thousand years. In addition, no evidence, such as similar pottery, spear points, or anything else, links the Americas with Polynesia.

One more promising theory is that people sailed to the Americas by following the northern Siberian coastline, passing the Aleutian Islands off Alaska, and then

The earliest form of what could arguably be considered "human" is a hominid that lived approximately three million years ago. It is called Australopithecus. It is often considered one of the missing links between humans and apes. In 1974, about forty percent of the skeleton of one, since called Lucy, was unearthed in Ethiopia.

The Bering Land Bridge is what once connected Asia and North America to one another. Today, parts of it lie about fifty meters beneath the surface of the Bering Sea. It is believed that migrating humans in Asia passed over it until it finally submerged around 10,000 to 11,000 years ago.

The languages of the people in Oceania, that is, islands in the Pacific that include New Zealand, Hawaii, Fiji, Tonga, Samoa, and Easter Island, all belong to the same family. The genetic evidence shows that the natives of these islands share common ancestors, which proves that early Polynesians succeeded at sailing extremely long distances to settle these islands.

heading down the coast of British Columbia. This theory is being investigated by some archaeologists. But there is one major obstacle. Sea levels are higher today than they were in the past, meaning that many potential coastal settlement sites are now underwater, which therefore makes excavations extremely difficult. Nevertheless, there is mounting evidence that people somehow managed to travel southward along the coast. Whether they first came across a land bridge or sailed the ocean waters is unknown. For the time being, the land bridge theory remains the strongest explanation of how people began populating the Americas.

≋ *Glossary*

land bridge: a strip of land connecting other landmasses and that may be underwater at times

navigational: relating to the act of guiding a ship, plane, or other form of transportation

1   According to paragraph 1, which of the following is true of early human migration?
   Ⓐ Early humans migrated first to the continent of Africa.
   Ⓑ Migrating to some continents was easier than to others.
   Ⓒ All the continents are interconnected, so migrating was relatively simple.
   Ⓓ The last place to which early humans migrated was Europe.

2   The word "it" in the passage refers to
   Ⓐ the land bridge theory
   Ⓑ a plethora of evidence
   Ⓒ ample evidence
   Ⓓ the last ice age

3   In paragraph 3, why does the author mention "Easter Island"?
   Ⓐ To stress its nearness to Chile, showing how impressive the Polynesian sailors were
   Ⓑ To give the name of one of the most famous islands discovered by the Polynesians
   Ⓒ To note the easternmost extent of the migration by Pacific Polynesian islanders
   Ⓓ To compare its location in the Pacific with that of New Zealand and Chile

4   Which of the sentences below best expresses the essential information in the highlighted sentence in the passage? *Incorrect* answer choices change the meaning in important ways or leave out essential information.

(A)   The sites that were located along the water have been revealed due to the current state of sea levels.

(B)   It is hard to discover the many sites that once were established along the coast because they are currently underwater.

(C)   Due to rising water levels, any sites formerly located alongside the water are now under it, so they are difficult to investigate.

(D)   The changing temperature caused sea levels to rise, so it is harder to find and to excavate any coastal sites.

5   *Directions:* Select the appropriate statements from the answer choices and match them to the theory on human migration to the Americas to which they relate. TWO of the answer choices will NOT be used. *This question is worth 3 points.*

<table>
<tr><td align="center">**Answer Choices**</td><td align="center">**THEORY ON HUMAN MIGRATION
TO THE AMERICAS**</td></tr>
<tr><td>

1   Supposes that the Polynesians were the first to visit the Americas

2   Can no longer be duplicated by people wishing to get to the Americas

3   Involves the seeking of the bones of animals as well as ancient spear tips

4   Is the more likely explanation for how the Americas became peopled

5   Has scanty archaeological evidence because of higher ocean levels

6   Involved people migrating while pursuing various game animals

7   Saw Polynesian islanders sail to many islands in the South Pacific Ocean

</td><td>

The Land Bridge Theory
-
-
-

The Sailing Theory
-
-

</td></tr>
</table>

Summarizing ▶ Complete the summary by filling in the blanks.

The Americas were _____ that humans settled. There are two competing theories on how this happened. The first is that lower sea levels exposed _____ between modern-day Siberia and Alaska. People from Asia followed herds of animals across the bridge and migrated to the two continents. Some archaeological evidence supports this theory. The other theory is that people _____ to the Americas. Some claim _____ sailed to the Americas. Others say that sailors went up the coast of Asia, past the Aleutian Islands, and down into the Americas. Finding _____ has been hard because any possible sites are beneath the ocean now.

Stonehenge

1→ Stonehenge is one of the world's most recognizable ancient sites. This circular group of large stones is found in southwest England and has been a source of mystery since before written records existed. The main questions surrounding it involve who built it and how it was constructed. Even more curious is what purpose it served. While Stonehenge today is a major tourist attraction, at some point in the past, experts speculate that it was a place of worship, an astronomical observatory, or a **sacred** burial ground. Despite decades of research on the site, archaeologists remain no closer to answering these questions than they were in the past.

2→ Stonehenge consists of dozens of stones set upright in a circular fashion. Some top stones connect to the upright stones, and they all lie within a raised circular earthen **embankment**. Archaeologists believe that ancient Britons constructed the site at various times between 3100 and 1900 B.C. At first, Stonehenge may have been used as a burial ground since excavations there have revealed the remains of numerous bodies. Originally, the circular monument was built of wood, but it was later replaced with stones. Over forty different types of stones may be found there, and careful studies have shown that some come from as far as 200 kilometers from the Stonehenge site.

How these stones were moved and how they were shaped and erected by people without modern equipment have long baffled experts. **1** Some have suggested that supernatural forces were involved, but that notion is widely disregarded. **2** Humans have constructed much larger monuments—the pyramids of Egypt, the Mayan temples, and the Great Wall of China—with nothing but muscle and animal power. **3** While there is no evidence explaining which methods they used, the ancient Britons obviously managed to move, shape, and erect the stones in some fashion. **4**

4→ The site's function is a question that has gripped many people's imaginations. Unfortunately, early studies of Stonehenge in the seventeenth century clouded the judgment of later researchers. Those initial examiners suggested it was a place of worship by ancient Druids, who may or may not have even been involved in its construction. Others believed the Romans or Saxons built Stonehenge, but it was not until the late nineteenth century that experts realized it was much older—at least 5,000 years old—than those two civilizations. In fact, the ancient site showed enough signs of wear and tear that, in the mid-twentieth century, the British government restored Stonehenge to what was believed to be its ancient form.

The other main theory concerning Stonehenge's function is that it was an

---

Note

There is little about Stonehenge that is known with any certainty. Many archaeologists believe that the construction of the monument that stands there today took place in three distinct stages occurring over a period of several centuries.

There are some experts who believe that there was some type of construction on Stonehenge around 6,000 to 7,000 years ago. Evidence in the neighboring area shows signs of construction dating back at least 8,000 years in the past.

Some of the stones used at Stonehenge weigh up to fifty tons. Many of them are known to have come from quarries tens of kilometers away. This only increases the mystery of how they were transported there.

The stories and the folklore about Stonehenge go back centuries. Geoffrey of Monmouth, an Arthurian chronicler, believed that they were connected with Merlin the magician, who was a legendary member of King Arthur's court. The Druids were said to be connected to Stonehenge since the Celts, to whom they belonged, were known to have predated the Romans in Britain. This possible link to the Druids has made Stonehenge ancient astronomical research site. The alignment of the stones corresponds with the rising and setting of the sun and moon at various times of the year. Another possibility is that Stonehenge was used to worship the sun and moon, which were extremely important for many ancient customs. None of these theories can be proven with any amount of certainty. No matter who built it or why, Stonehenge will remain a curiosity for a long time to come.

a popular site with many practitioners of new age religions.

📚 *Glossary*
sacred: holy
embankment: a mount, typically made of earth; a mound

---

1 In paragraph 1, all of the following questions are answered EXCEPT:

Ⓐ What are some of the mysteries that exist around Stonehenge?

Ⓑ What do people believe that Stonehenge was used for in the past?

Ⓒ What kinds of excavations have archaeologists done at Stonehenge?

Ⓓ In which part of England is Stonehenge located?

2 According to paragraph 2, which of the following is true of Stonehenge?

Ⓐ It took more than one thousand years for the entire site to be constructed.

Ⓑ There were at least two hundred giant stones used to build Stonehenge.

Ⓒ The stones that exist there today were not a part of the original construction.

Ⓓ Stonehenge was used as a cemetery by cultures throughout the centuries.

3 In paragraph 4, the author implies that the Druids

Ⓐ are known to have constructed other monuments in England

Ⓑ existed in England prior to both the Romans and the Saxons

Ⓒ are said by some to have possessed supernatural powers

Ⓓ were interested in using Stonehenge as an observatory

4 Look at the four squares [■] that indicate where the following sentence could be added to the passage.

Others have even gone so far as to suggest that extraterrestrials were responsible for erecting many of the more massive blocks of stone.

Where would the sentence best fit?

5 **Directions:** An introductory sentence for a brief summary of the passage is provided below. Complete the summary by selecting the THREE answer choices that express the most important ideas of the passage. Some sentences do not belong because they express ideas that are not presented in the passage or are minor ideas in the passage. ***This question is worth 2 points.***

> **Stonehenge is an ancient monument erected thousands of years ago, yet no one knows exactly when, how, or why it was actually constructed.**

-
-
-

Answer Choices

1 Stonehenge was originally a monument made of wood, which was later replaced by the stones that are there today.

2 Some people have written books claiming that Stonehenge is a site of magic and that aliens inspired humans to construct it.

3 Stonehenge may have been used to look at the stars, or it may have been sacred to the people who made it.

4 The stones used in its construction came from many places, leaving people to wonder how they were moved there.

5 Once thought to have been a Saxon construction, Stonehenge is believed to be around 5,000 years old.

6 Stonehenge is a popular tourist site in England and thus attracts large numbers of visitors annually.

Summarizing ▸ Complete the summary by filling in the blanks.

One of the oldest and most mysterious ancient sites is Stonehenge in southwest England. Very little is known about it. It is a monument made of _____ sitting upright in a circle. No one knows how the stones got there or who erected them. Some think supernatural forces were responsible, but this is highly unlikely. People have proposed that the ancient _____, Romans, and Saxons were all responsible, but no one is certain. Nevertheless, it appears to be at least _____. Some believe Stonehenge was _____, and others claim it was a sacred spot for worshippers.

The Rise of Mayan Civilization

¹➜ In 1839 in the jungles of the Yucatan Peninsula of Mexico and in nearby Belize and Guatemala, explorers rediscovered the lost Mayan civilization. More than forty cities were found in one of the most fascinating archaeological discoveries of modern times. The Mayans once numbered in the millions, but by 1839, they had all but disappeared, in the process becoming one of the great mysteries of history. The archaeologists learned that Mayan life had centered on agriculture with a mass of peasant farmers supporting kings, priests, **bureaucrats**, and soldiers in the cities. The relationship between these farmers and the upper elements of Mayan society was fundamental both to the rise and eventual collapse of Mayan civilization.

²➜ Thanks to careful archaeological excavations, it is clear that the Mayans began as farmers in small villages, where they cultivated crops like beans, corn, and squash. They later gradually began to form more sophisticated societies. Strong leaders emerged and started attracting followers, and by 250 A.D., the first evidence of kings and dynasties appeared. Massive building programs were initiated, and huge temples and palaces, many of which have survived to this day, were constructed. Unlike most ancient civilizations, the Mayans never united under one king. Instead, more than forty small kingdoms arose, and the virtually constant warfare between them was a bane to Mayan unity. No king could grow strong enough to overcome the others, mainly because of the nature of the land, the farming conditions, and the Mayans' lack of mobility.

³➜ The lands the Mayans lived on were not very suitable for farming, so the peasants grew little surplus food. There was barely enough for themselves and a few others. The peasants toiled on the land while the kings, who also often acted as high priests, promised them rain to grow their crops. Like people in most ancient cultures, the Mayans were highly superstitious and believed the annual rainfall was a divine gift. During bountiful years, all was well; the kings' and priests' prayers brought rain, the peasants planted and harvested crops, and there was enough food to support the growing population. Indeed, archaeologists estimate that anywhere from two to ten million people lived in the area at the height of Mayan civilization.

Mayan cities consisted of the temples, palaces, and homes of the elites. The peasants lived on the land, and most only ventured into the cities during ceremonies to pray for rain or for other religious events. These took place a few times a year, for Mayan society was quite immobile, having no beasts of burden, wheeled vehicles, or boats with sails. All movement, building projects, farming, and transportation in it were achieved with human muscle power. Kings could never unite the entire Mayan civilization because the inefficient farmers could not grow enough food to supply large armies in the field and the armies were never fast and mobile enough to subdue the numerous neighboring kingdoms.

1 Soon, thanks to the growing population, suitable farmland grew scarce, and perhaps civil warfare among the peasantry broke out. **2** Swaths of jungle were cut down to make more farmland, but this, in turn, caused soil erosion and the loss of valuable nutrients. **3** Then, there came a long period of reduced rainfall and some years of drought starting in the eighth century. **4** Crop yields decreased, the population became too large to be fed, starvation and famine reared their ugly heads, and the peasants became desperate. The kings and the elites, their promises of rain broken, soon lost any mystical hold they had over the masses.

6➡ By the ninth century, Mayan civilization had begun to collapse. Kings' achievements are no longer recorded after this time either on palace and temple **inscriptions** or in other Mayan writings. It can be surmised that they died alongside their people. Archaeologists estimate that approximately 90% of the Mayan population disappeared over the next few centuries. Mayan civilization thus did not end with one catastrophe; it was a long, gradual collapse. Indeed, the Mayans were still numerous when the Spanish arrived in the early sixteenth century. However, disease and the Spaniards' ruthlessness rapidly decimated the remaining population. The cities grew silent, the jungle reclaimed the land, and the Mayans disappeared, their cities not to be rediscovered for almost 300 years.

≋ Glossary
bureaucrat: an official who works for a government
inscription: something written or painted on stone, brick, or some other hard surface

---

1   Which of the following can be inferred from paragraph 1 about the Mayans?
    Ⓐ They were the largest group of people in the Mexican area.
    Ⓑ Some of them were still alive during the nineteenth century.
    Ⓒ The peasant farmers were more important than the kings were.
    Ⓓ Much of their culture remains unknown to modern archaeologists.

2   According to paragraph 2, there was never a unified Mayan kingdom because
    Ⓐ the Mayans were more concerned with construction projects than warfare
    Ⓑ several factors combined to keep one kingdom from becoming all powerful
    Ⓒ all forty of the kingdoms could never agree to unite under one leader
    Ⓓ most armies lacked the weaponry needed to conquer their opponents

3   According to paragraph 2, which of the following is NOT true of Mayan society?
    Ⓐ It began to emerge around the year 250 A.D.
    Ⓑ There were wars going on almost all of the time.
    Ⓒ Its people started as farmers and then became more developed.
    Ⓓ It constructed religious buildings for its people.

4   The word "them" in the passage refers to
    Ⓐ peasants
    Ⓑ kings
    Ⓒ high priests
    Ⓓ the Mayans

5 The author discusses "rainfall" in paragraph 3 in order to

Ⓐ prove that Mayan society collapsed from a lack of rain

Ⓑ explain why the kings were also the priests

Ⓒ demonstrate why the Mayan population increased

Ⓓ show the importance of religion to the Mayans

6 Which of the sentences below best expresses the essential information in the highlighted sentence in the passage? *Incorrect* answer choices change the meaning in important ways or leave out essential information.

Ⓐ Inefficient farmers were the reason why kings could not unite the Mayans since they refused to grow enough food for the kings' armies, which were neither fast nor mobile.

Ⓑ Various kings' armies would move slowly into other kingdoms, so they were unable to conquer enough land, and they were not well fed since the farmers were too inefficient.

Ⓒ The inability of farmers to supply armies with food as well as the relative slowness and immobility of the armies prevented anyone from uniting the Mayans under one ruler.

Ⓓ The lack of a united Mayan civilization was a result of farming practices that could not provide enough food and questionable military leadership on the part of the kings.

7 The word "yields" in the passage is closest in meaning to

Ⓐ profits

Ⓑ harvests

Ⓒ advancements

Ⓓ revenues

8 According to paragraph 6, which of the following is true of the Spanish?

Ⓐ The Mayans would have survived had they not appeared.

Ⓑ They helped the Mayans to overcome certain diseases.

Ⓒ They contributed to the disappearance of Mayan civilization.

Ⓓ They first visited Mayan culture when it was at its peak.

9 Look at the four squares [■] that indicate where the following sentence could be added to the passage.

There is evidence in the historical records that farmers engaged in rebellions in various provinces.

Where would the sentence best fit?

Click on a square [■] to add the sentence to the passage.

10   ***Directions:*** An introductory sentence for a brief summary of the passage is provided below. Complete the summary by selecting the THREE answer choices that express the most important ideas of the passage. Some sentences do not belong because they express ideas that are not presented in the passage or are minor ideas in the passage. ***This question is worth 2 points.***

> Drag your answer choices to the spaces where they belong.
> To remove an answer choice, click on it. To review the passage, click on **View Text.**

Mayan civilization had its roots in agriculture yet slowly became a series of independent kingdoms; however, due to inefficient farming practices and natural disasters, the Mayans slowly disappeared as a viable civilization.

-
-
-

Answer Choices

1. Many of the construction projects finished by the Mayans have managed to survive even up to the present day.

2. It took several hundred years for the Mayans to disappear since no singular event was responsible for their downfall.

3. The Spaniards appeared in the sixteenth century, but the Spaniards only dealt with the Mayans when they were extremely weak.

4. The Mayans were forced to cut down much of the jungle to use as farmland when their crops began to fail.

5. The Mayans were constantly at war with one another, but no one army was able to defeat all of the others.

6. The early Mayans farmed the land and only later began to construct cities with palaces and temples.

Nomadic Life

¹➡ Early humans were nomads by necessity, not by choice. The first humans to walk the Earth were constantly moving in search of food. With the advent of agriculture approximately eight to ten thousand years ago, the movement of humans became less frequent, but it never really ended. There are still approximately thirty million people on the planet that can be called nomadic. Most modern nomads are pastoral nomads. They maintain herds of animals and travel with these animals to their regular feeding grounds. Nomads throughout history have had distinctive ways of life common to most **itinerant** groups, including their relations with civilized people, methods of travel, possessions, social structure, and the reasons why they move about so frequently.

²➡ In the beginning, humans were hunter-gatherers who gained sustenance from the berries and fruits of plants they gathered and the animals they hunted. Occasionally, these early people found a large area with edible plant life and abundant game, so they stopped there for a time, but in no way were permanent settlements developed. ❶ However, as agriculture began and spread, more people settled down; they built towns and then cities, and eventually civilizations appeared. ❷ Yet there were always those outside of civilized life—nomads—wandering about, refusing to take part in agriculture, and occasionally coming into conflict with settled people. ❸ One constant theme throughout human history is the clash of nomads with more civilized people. ❹

³➡ Nomadic life was based on family and tribal organizations. An occasional strong leader, such as Attila the Hun or Genghis Khan, could unite many tribes for a common purpose such as military conquest. The domestication of the horse, the ox, and the camel made movement much easier. As nomads became more sophisticated, they raised their own herds of livestock and became less dependent on hunting and gathering. Others, like the North American Indians, followed herds of wild animals such as the buffalo. These herds, whether wild or somewhat domesticated, needed plant matter to eat, and the nomads followed them as they moved around. The necessity of moving constantly meant that nomads carried few possessions. These usually amounted to their food, clothing, weapons, shelters, and some trinkets. An armed party on the warpath traveled even lighter, for the nomadic way of war was to strike fast and damage the enemy but to flee if necessary. When an entire nation of nomads moved, as did the Germanic tribes when invading the Roman Empire in the late fifth century or the Mongols when moving across Central Asia in the thirteenth century, they frequently used ox-drawn wagons to carry their women, children, and possessions.

⁴➡ Generally speaking, within nomadic tribes, there was a strong sense of equality. Nomad leaders typically equally shared any **plunder** they acquired. Of course, this practice varied from tribe to tribe, but observations of modern nomads and evidence from the past indicate this was quite common. Gender roles usually involved men being dominant, but with some people, such as the Mongols, women were expected to learn to ride a horse and to fight if necessary. Fathers raised their sons to be warriors and to use spears, swords, and bows and arrows to hunt animals and to kill men from horseback. Customs regarding marriage varied, but one constant theme was that nomads used marriage to establish alliances with other families and tribes. Many of these customs survive today among remaining nomads.

⁵➡ For most nomads, the notion of living in towns or cities was distasteful. They enjoyed wide-open

spaces, fresh air, and constantly moving from place to place. In modern times, Mongols speak of the romantic vistas of the Asian plains, and Bedouins feel they are one with the desert. The nomadic Mongols of Genghis Khan's time looked at the southern Chinese cities and their teeming hordes as disease-ridden places to be avoided at all costs. Nomads sometimes conquered cities, but most did not stay long. On some occasions, such as during the Germanic conquests of Rome, nomads adopted agricultural methods and assimilated into civilized lands; however, this was not common. In modern times, nomads' territories are shrinking as civilization encroaches, so perhaps one day even these few civilization-resisting nomads will become part of the urban masses.

≋ *Glossary*
itinerant: wandering; nomadic
plunder: treasure, which has usually been stolen or taken in battle

---

1   According to paragraph 1, which of the following is true of nomads?

Ⓐ There were once more than thirty million of them on the planet.

Ⓑ In the past, they had to lead their type of life in order to survive.

Ⓒ They avoided traveling in large groups and were more independent.

Ⓓ In general, they got along fairly well with people who lived in cities.

2   The word "sustenance" in the passage is closest in meaning to

Ⓐ vitamins

Ⓑ replenishment

Ⓒ abundance

Ⓓ nourishment

3   Which of the following can be inferred from paragraph 2 about nomads?

Ⓐ They often made war against people living in settled areas.

Ⓑ They frequently raided farming villages to steal their crops.

Ⓒ They were sometimes more developed than people living in cities.

Ⓓ They were eager to abandon their hunter-gatherer ways.

4   Why does the author mention "Attila the Hun" in paragraph 3?

Ⓐ To compare his conquests with those of Genghis Khan

Ⓑ To cite him as an example of a leader who united several tribes

Ⓒ To describe his conquests as a military leader of the nomads

Ⓓ To mention his place in the organization of his tribe of Huns

5 In paragraph 3, the author implies that nomads

    (A) were capable of crossing entire empires in short periods of time

    (B) were interested in accumulating large numbers of possessions

    (C) encouraged their families to go to war with them

    (D) did not have a policy of fighting to the death in battle

6 According to paragraph 4, which of the following is true of nomads' domestic lives?

    (A) The men and women were treated as equal members of the tribe.

    (B) They preferred to get married to other members of their own tribe.

    (C) It was expected that everyone, not just the men, would fight in wars.

    (D) The role of procuring food was often left to the women and children.

7 The word "teeming" in the passage is closest in meaning to

    (A) looming

    (B) packed

    (C) ominous

    (D) sweltering

8 According to paragraph 5, which of the following is NOT true of nomads' attitudes toward settlements?

    (A) They considered most of them to be unsanitary places.

    (B) They occasionally felt it was fine to move to them and to live in them.

    (C) The vast majority of them were very much against living in them.

    (D) They thought that too many cities were being established in their lands.

9 Look at the four squares [■] that indicate where the following sentence could be added to the passage.

No matter in which era that happened, much blood was shed on both sides when unfortunate events like this occurred.

Where would the sentence best fit?

Click on a square [■] to add the sentence to the passage.

10 ***Directions:*** An introductory sentence for a brief summary of the passage is provided below. Complete the summary by selecting the THREE answer choices that express the most important ideas of the passage. Some sentences do not belong because they express ideas that are not presented in the passage or are minor ideas in the passage. ***This question is worth 2 points.***

> Drag your answer choices to the spaces where they belong.
> To remove an answer choice, click on it. To review the passage, click on **View Text.**

For centuries, nomads have lived their lives by wandering through certain areas since the majority of them have disliked the idea of residing in urban areas.

-
-
-

Answer Choices

1. Many nomads believe cities to be places filled with numerous diseases so are not interested in visiting them.

2. Attila the Hun, along with Genghis Khan, was one of the greatest conquerors to come from a nomadic culture.

3. Some people believe that living a life in the desert or all alone away from others has a tinge of romance to it.

4. Thanks to the fact that they learned to domesticate certain animals, the migrations of nomads were made easier.

5. The North American Indians used to follow herds of buffaloes all across the great plains of the continent.

6. Even after people learned the secrets of farming, most nomads refused to abandon their wandering ways.

1 The First City

For thousands of years, humans were nomadic hunter-gatherers. They typically followed herds of animals—their food sources—as the animals migrated from place to place. But people slowly began settling in certain areas. While evidence exists that actual cultures began arising about 5,000 years ago, there were small cities even before that. Many archaeologists believe that Catalhoyuk, located in modern-day Turkey, was the world's first city. According to them, a few thousand people may have lived there around 9,000 years ago. To date, Catalhoyuk is the largest city discovered from the Neolithic Period. However, archaeologists have found other settlements almost as old in areas throughout the Middle East.

2 Mayan Urban and Rural Dwellers

The ancient Mayan Empire was centered in the area around modern-day Guatemala and Honduras in Central America. It had cities as well as many smaller settlements that were located outside of the cities. However, the Mayans had a very segregated culture. Their cities were meant almost exclusively for the religious class in their society. Mostly priests and their servants lived in these cities, which had numerous buildings. Meanwhile, members of the lower classes, such as farmers, were forced to live outside the cities and to raise crops and animals to provide for the priestly class.

3 The First People in Oceania

The South Pacific Ocean has numerous islands, including Polynesia, Micronesia, and the Hawaiian Islands. For most of human history, they were unpopulated. However, humans eventually made their way by sailing to many of them. While each island culture has its own myths about how the islands came to be settled, anthropologists have their own theories as well. Some have claimed that ancient Egyptians were the first to sail to them. However, a more widely accepted theory is that people from South Asia made their way to the islands, slowly hopping from one island to another over centuries until the majority of them came to be populated.

4 Native American Tribes in the Southeast

Typically, Native American tribes in the west, like the Sioux, the Hopi, and the Apache, receive more attention from scholars. However, there were numerous tribes in the Southeast part of North America that left their own mark on the continent. Among them were the Cherokees, the Chickasaws, the Choctaws, the Creeks, and the Seminoles. When the first Europeans came, some engaged in warfare against them. The Seminoles, for instance, fought hard against them and later against the Americans, too. Others, such as the Cherokees and the Creeks, actually fought with the Americans against the British in the Revolutionary War. As for cultural achievements, the Cherokee named Sequoyah developed a writing system for his tribe to record their language.

5 Egyptian Civilization

Egypt, centered on the Nile River Valley, was one of the first human civilizations. Around 6,000 B.C., people began establishing something resembling a civilization there. Still, it took a few more millennia, until around 3100 B.C., before the pharaohs—Egyptian kings—appeared in Egypt. The pharaohs, who ruled as god-kings, dominated Egyptian life and culture. The people were essentially slaves and were forced to do their bidding. There were several dynasties over the next few thousand years, and it was during this time that Egyptian civilization reached the peak of its glory. Today, the pyramids and Sphinx are the most famous structures left from early Egyptian times.

6 The Role of Water in Mayan Civilization

The land occupied by the Mayan Empire was varied in its topography. While much of the land was covered with rainforests, other parts were forested in spite of getting little rainfall, and still other regions were covered in volcanic mountains. Essentially, the southern part of Mayan territory received abundant amounts of rainfall while the northern region did not. This made much of the empire dependent on one area for most of its food supplies. Around 900 A.D., the empire suddenly collapsed. Some have speculated that an extended drought in the south subsequently caused an extensive famine, which, in turn, led to widespread starvation and the end of the Mayan Empire.

7 The Importance of Maize in Aztec Culture

The Aztec Empire occupied parts of Central America, especially much of the area of modern-day Mexico. Although the Aztecs grew many crops, the primary one was maize. Maize is a variety of corn sometimes referred to as "Indian corn." The Aztecs grew maize in abundance; thus, it became a staple for them like rice was to Asian cultures and wheat was to European cultures. Its extreme importance has been determined by researchers in other ways though. The Aztecs had numerous words to describe maize, and they even wrote poems and hymns in honor of it, proving how vital it was to their existence.

8 The Pueblo Indians

In the Southwest United States in Arizona and New Mexico, the Anasazi Indians once lived on the land. They dominated it for hundreds of years, but around 1100, they quickly and quietly disappeared. However, their descendants lived on in the guise of the Pueblo Indians. The Pueblo Indians were actually divided into several different tribes, including the Hopi, the Zuni, and the Laguna. Mostly farmers, they used irrigation methods to water their fields in the parched land of the Southwest. They also became skilled basket weavers, creating works that were desired by other tribes in the area.

9 Human Migrations out of Africa

It is widely accepted that humans originated in Africa. From there, they migrated to the other continents. Over time, there were countless migrations out of Africa. The first occurred almost two million years ago. However, the earliest migrants were not *Homo sapiens*, modern man. Instead, they were *Homo ergaster* and *Homo erectus*, two early species of man. The first instance of *Homo sapiens* migrating from Africa happened about 70,000 years

ago. All these species likely migrated for food. They were either following wandering herds of animals, or their numbers in Africa were too big for them to support. Hence, they left for other areas and ended up populating the planet.

10 Theories on Populating Islands

There are competing theories about how islands, particularly those in the South Pacific Ocean, were populated. Many anthropologists theorize that the people who ended up living on islands did so accidentally. Their boats simply drifted wherever the current took them. Upon landing on an island, they settled it and started their own civilization there. Others, however, believe that people intentionally moved there. For various reasons—war, famine, or overpopulation—people sailed on boats for new lands to inhabit. When they arrived at a suitable island, they stopped and settled it. These competing theories remain a point of contention among anthropologists today.

Star Performer Topic Files **Archaeology and Anthropology**

- The development of Sumerian culture
- The development of Egyptian culture
- The nomadic tribes of Iran
- Trade in Mayan culture
- The lives that the Sumerian people lived
- The effects of drought on Mayan culture
- The development of civilization in Mexico
- The ways that civilizations develop over time
- Cultural exchanges between the Mayans and other cultures
- Native American culture in the Southwest United States

abandon
acculturation
adapt
adaptation
agricultural
agriculture
amulet
analysis
analyze
ancient
animism
antique
apocryphal
aqueduct
armor
arrowhead
artifact
artistic
artwork
assault
assimilate
assimilation
battle
battlefield
biblical
breed
bronze
burial
bury
buried
carbon dating
caste
castle
cave art
ceramics
characteristic
chief
civilization
civilize
clan
clash
clay
class
coastal
conquer
construct
construction
cranium
Cro-Magnon
cross-cultural
cult
cultural

culture
cuneiform
cultivate
cultivation
data
decipher
develop
development
diffusion
dig
discover
discovery
domesticate
domestication
dowry
drift
drought
erect
erosion
ethnic
ethnicity
excavate
excavation
excursion
evolution
evolve
factual
famine
farmland
fieldwork
folklore
folktale
footprint
forage
forager
fortification
glyph
grain
grave
graze
growth
harvest
hidden
hierarchy
hieroglyph
hieroglyphics
hoard
Homo erectus
Homo sapiens
hunter-gatherer
ice age
indigenous

inscribe
inscription
instinct
instinctual
interpret
interpretation
iron
irrigate
irrigation
kiln
kin
kinship
land bridge
language
legend
legendary
linguistics
logogram
loot
looter
lore
migrate
migration
missing link
mound
mummy
mummified
myth
mythological
mythology
Neanderthal
Neolithic
nomad
nomadic
observatory
overpopulate
palace
Paleolithic
pastoral
pharaoh
populate
population
potlatch
pottery
prehistoric
preservation
preserve
priest
primeval
primitive
proto-writing
pyramid

race
raid
relic
religious
remains
research
rite
ritual
rural
sacrifice
sacrificial
settle
settlement
shaman
shard
site
slash and burn
spear
spear tip
structure
superstition
superstitious
sustenance
survey
sword
symbol
symbolism
tablet
tame
technique
temple
tomb
totem
tracks
transformation
transformative
translate
translation
treasure
tribal
tribe
unification
unify
urban
urbanization
wander
warfare
wheel
wild
worship
writing system
ziggurat

Vocabulary Review

📝 Choose the words closest in meaning to the highlighted parts of the sentences.

1 Through a long and meandering process, the modern alphabet most Western languages employ emerged from these early beginnings.

   Ⓐ regard
   Ⓑ hire
   Ⓒ utilize
   Ⓓ interpret

2 Nevertheless, there is mounting evidence that people somehow managed to travel southward along the coast.

   Ⓐ convincing
   Ⓑ rising
   Ⓒ trivial
   Ⓓ potential

3 Early humans may have discovered the joyous sound of clapping their hands together and, coupled with the noise of beating stones to make tools, they were inspired to become more creative.

   Ⓐ combined
   Ⓑ doubled
   Ⓒ heard
   Ⓓ played

4 Most modern homes have refrigerators; however, for much of human history, preserving food was a tremendous problem since, with few exceptions, food spoils after some time.

   Ⓐ desiccates
   Ⓑ rots
   Ⓒ shrinks
   Ⓓ stinks

5 For most nomads, the notion of living in towns or cities was distasteful.

   Ⓐ avoidable
   Ⓑ unimaginable
   Ⓒ possible
   Ⓓ repulsive

6 Archaeologists peruse garbage pits to find out what kinds of food the people ate.

   Ⓐ overlook
   Ⓑ excavate
   Ⓒ collect
   Ⓓ scrutinize

7 Stonehenge consists of dozens of stones set upright in a circular fashion.

   Ⓐ erect
   Ⓑ adjacent
   Ⓒ apace
   Ⓓ exposed

8 Sometimes the farmers had bumper crops, and more food was grown than could be readily consumed in a short period of time.

   Ⓐ malnourished
   Ⓑ surplus
   Ⓒ nutritious
   Ⓓ enormous

9 Like people in most ancient cultures, the Mayans were highly superstitious and believed the annual rainfall was a divine gift.

   Ⓐ fortunate
   Ⓑ considerate
   Ⓒ heavenly
   Ⓓ well-timed

10 From these humble beginnings, humans took the next step of creating purpose-built musical instruments.

   Ⓐ creative
   Ⓑ unique
   Ⓒ modest
   Ⓓ obvious

11. While this migration took ages to accomplish, there were no real obstacles since all three continents are interconnected.

   (A) opponents
   (B) barriers
   (C) recriminations
   (D) detours

12. However, disease and the Spaniards' ruthlessness rapidly decimated the remaining population.

   (A) primitiveness
   (B) effectiveness
   (C) insensitivity
   (D) brutality

13. Out of this mutual need, perhaps a growing companionship developed.

   (A) joint
   (B) basic
   (C) ephemeral
   (D) considerable

14. Finally, archaeologists must deal with modern-day governments and their frequent desire to prohibit the removal of artifacts and to shape history or to leave its interpreting as they wish it to be.

   (A) restrict
   (B) forbid
   (C) postpone
   (D) cancel

15. One of the questions archaeologists strive to answer is why and how writing systems developed.

   (A) endeavor
   (B) rush
   (C) fail
   (D) struggle

16. The relationship between these farmers and the upper elements of Mayan society was fundamental both to the rise and eventual collapse of Mayan civilization.

   (A) partial
   (B) subordinate
   (C) essential
   (D) connected

17. Without them, the movement of the steppe people would have been severely limited and their prowess in battle also curtailed.

   (A) expertise
   (B) desire
   (C) method
   (D) opposition

18. Some have suggested that supernatural forces were involved, but that notion is widely disregarded.

   (A) mocked
   (B) imitated
   (C) considered
   (D) ignored

19. The land bridge theory is the more logical of the two and has a plethora of evidence to defend it.

   (A) pattern
   (B) surfeit
   (C) dearth
   (D) smattering

20. Domesticated animals were once wild, so some may still have feral tendencies

   (A) cruel
   (B) cautious
   (C) untamed
   (D) rabid

Part
B

Chapter 04 Education, Sociology, and Psychology

Education, sociology, and psychology are three of the most prominent of the social sciences. The field of education is concerned both with how people learn and how they are taught. For this reason, teaching and learning methods are examined, and studies into the past to explore previous learning methods are done as well. Sociology is the study of every aspect of human society. This encompasses an enormous period of time, for while many sociologists focus on contemporary society, there are others who look back to past societies to conduct their research on. Essentially, sociologists examine how societies develop, organize, progress, and function. Psychology is the study of the mind and how it works. Psychologists try to determine how people think and why they think the way they do. Some of them also examine the mental health issues which some people are afflicted by. Altogether, all three disciplines are concerned with the thought processes of humans and the results that these thought processes create.

Family Roles in Colonial America

Life in colonial America centered on the family unit from its earliest days until far past the time the colonies became independent from Britain. Colonial America was primarily a rural society with the vast majority of people dwelling on family farms. Frequently, multiple generations of the same family lived beneath the same roof. Within the family structure, each individual had certain daily tasks and duties they were responsible for.

Life in colonial times was harsh, so the primary requirement for each family to survive was to find a sufficient food supply for their daily needs. Accordingly, farming was a key activity for colonial families. Food was also obtained by hunting and fishing, especially in coastal regions such as New England. Most farms had cows for milk and chickens for eggs as well. While fathers and older sons typically did heavy **manual labor**, women, young children, and even grandparents shared in the daily work, which usually lasted from sunrise to sunset. Everyone took part in planting and harvesting while also hewing wood from nearby forests for building and for heating homes. Successful farmers who had surpluses traded with residents of nearby towns to obtain clothing, coffee, tea, tools, and other necessary supplies.

³➡ The father was almost universally the master of the home, being the person who made every decision while serving as the religious leader by taking charge of prayers with the family. He also assumed responsibility for disciplining the children. The mother ran the household, handling the cooking and the cleaning as well as any servants employed there. She also educated the children, especially in areas lacking schools. Mothers taught their daughters to sew, to cook, and to run a household while fathers taught their sons about farming, hunting, fishing, and conducting business. **Inheritance** passed through the male line in most cases, so sons normally waited until their father passed away to obtain land. Sometimes the eldest son would marry and obtain the farm before his father died if he lived until a very old age. Daughters were expected to marry young and to leave to start their own families. Fathers also had the right to decide whom their daughters would marry.

⁴➡ Many colonial families had multiple children, who, when old enough, were expected to assist in the family's quest for survival. Additionally, having many children was necessary because colonial life was harsh, so many children failed to survive infancy. As more children were born, older daughters were expected to help their mother care for newborn infants. Most children did not receive much of an education beyond learning reading, writing, and arithmetic; however, children in prosperous families might have private tutors or attend college, something beyond the reach of most colonial children.

≋ *Glossary*
manual labor: work people do by hand
inheritance: the act of receiving money, land, or personal items from a family member upon that person's death

1 The word "surpluses" in the passage is closest in meaning to

   (A) crops

   (B) seeds

   (C) excesses

   (D) supplies

[Vocabulary Question]

Think of the common synonyms for the highlighted word. If one of these is not an answer choice, think of similar words to the synonyms you have thought of.

2 In paragraph 3, the author uses "farming, hunting, fishing, and conducting business" as examples of

   (A) some of the skills that people considered very important in the past

   (B) skills that most men in colonial times did not need to be taught by anyone

   (C) skills that sons in colonial families were taught to do by their fathers

   (D) a few of the skills sons and daughters were expected to learn in colonial times

[Rhetorical Purpose Question]

Focus on the sentence that the highlighted section of the question appears in. The answer can often be found in that sentence or in the ones directly before or after it.

3 In paragraph 4, the author's description of colonial families which of the following?

   (A) The type of learning most colonial children received

   (B) The percentage of children who died in infancy

   (C) The locations of colleges some children might attend

   (D) The number of children that the average family had

[Factual Question]

When the question asks about a specific paragraph, focus exclusively on that paragraph for the information you need in order to find the correct answer.

4 ***Directions:*** An introductory sentence for a brief summary of the passage is provided below. Complete the summary by selecting the THREE answer choices that express the most important ideas of the passage. Some sentences do not belong because they express ideas that are not presented in the passage or are minor ideas in the passage. ***This question is worth 2 points.***

Each person in an American family during colonial times had various duties and responsibilities that had to be carried out.

[Prose Summary Question]

Think about the main idea or ideas of the passage. The answer choices will always have information which relates to them.

Answer Choices

   ☐1 Some people who ran successful farms were able to sell some of their produce to people who lived in towns.

   ☐4 People in the southern colonies relied more upon farming than those who lived in the New England colonies did.

   ☐2 Fathers and sons usually handled the work outside while mothers and daughters took care of domestic chores.

   ☐5 Sons and daughters were taught different skills by their parents to help them master a variety of abilities.

   ☐3 Very few people in colonial times could afford to attend college or pay for private tutors in their homes.

   ☐6 Families had many children because they were needed to work on the farms and so many died during infancy.

Preschool Education

In North America, most children start school at the age of five and continue for thirteen years until they graduate from high school when they are seventeen or eighteen. Some children, however, start preschool at an earlier age, sometimes as early as three or four. The advantages and disadvantages of sending children to preschool depend on the points of view of both the parents and children.

From many parents' points of view, preschool is wonderful. As any parent can attest, raising children is a time-consuming task because they need constant attention to keep them both safe and entertained. So even if children attend preschool for only a few hours each day, this gives parents time to run **errands**, to take care of household chores, and simply to take a break from watching over them. In cases where preschool lasts for most of the day, both parents can have jobs, thereby increasing the family's income.

3➡ Meanwhile, from the children's point of view, preschool is also advantageous. They get to meet other children and to enjoy themselves. Children begin to develop their social skills by interacting with others, and they also learn the basics of sharing and playing nicely. They get a head start on their basic education, including learning how to read, write, and count. In some cases, they also play games, engage in artistic endeavors, and even learn to play musical instruments. Many doctors also concur that exposing children to other children at young ages and allowing them to build up their immunities to common childhood diseases will make them stronger in the future.

1 Some people, on the other hand, disagree with the concept of preschool and believe that parents should spend as much time as possible with their children so as to form a special child-parent bond. **2** They argue that once children get older, the majority of their time will be in school, so there is no need to rush them out of the house at an early age. **3** Still, even children attending preschool spend a considerable part of every day at home with their parents and other family members. **4**

Finally, some supporters of preschool argue that it helps children more easily to overcome separation **anxiety**. Preschoolers benefit from having been in a school setting prior to attending elementary school. Thus, when their first day of elementary school arrives, those children who attended preschool already know what to expect, which gives them a leg up on those who merely stayed home.

📚 *Glossary*

errand: a quick trip to do something specific, such as buying groceries
anxiety: a feeling of nervousness or apprehension

1 The word "them" in the passage refers to

(A) children

(B) parents

(C) errands

(D) household chores

[Reference Question]

By substituting all of the answer choices for the highlighted word, obviously incorrect choices can easily be eliminated. This will reduce the number of possible correct answers.

2 According to paragraph 3, which of the following is NOT true of preschool?

(A) The children there can learn how to behave around others their age.

(B) The students become weak after being exposed to diseases there.

(C) Some students have the opportunity to learn special skills there.

(D) The children who go there get to have fun with the other students.

[Negative Factual Question]

Many times, the correct answer choice contains words from the passage; however, they are phrased differently than they were written in the passage.

3 Which of the following can be inferred from paragraph 3 about preschools?

(A) Music is not a part of the standard curriculum at the majority of them

(B) The children who attend them need fewer vaccinations than other children.

(C) Children become good at socializing there so seldom argue with one another.

(D) The schools teach their students to read at an elementary school level.

[Inference Question]

Look for key expressions like "in many cases." These will often provide hints as to what the author is implying.

4 Look at the four squares [■] that indicate where the following sentence could be added to the passage.

Instead, they encourage parents to keep their children at home for as long as possible.

Where would the sentence best fit?

[Insert Text Question]

Pay attention to words such as "instead." The presence of this word indicates that the sentence to be included contains a contrary argument or action to the sentence in the passage that it should be placed after.

Schooling and Education

While it is frequently believed that the terms schooling and education are synonymous, this is far from the truth. In reality, while there is some overlap between the two, schooling is a limiting term while education is a more **all-encompassing** expression as there are several ways in which the two differ from one another.

2→ To begin with, schooling is merely instruction or training that a person receives at school. This may refer to any kind of school, be it kindergarten, elementary, middle, or high school, or college or graduate work. For individuals who graduate from high school, schooling takes up at least twelve years of their lives, and should they attend college, they receive even more schooling. Nevertheless, despite the amount of time they invest, their schooling covers a limited number of topics. In many American public schools, students are required to take math, English, history, and science. They may take other classes— economics, foreign languages, and home economics, for example—but these are typically electives and may not even be offered at some schools. Essentially, schooling is limited in two ways: It covers only academic topics and is restricted in scope. Additionally, it is usually formalized in that, at most schools, students are taught in a specific manner: The teachers lecture, assign homework, and give tests while the students listen, take notes, complete their assignments, and take tests.

Meanwhile, education, which is the act of learning general knowledge and skills, is not so restrictive. However, it must be noted that while all schooling is considered education, not all education is considered schooling. Schooling is merely a small aspect of education which, as its name implies, takes place only at school. But education can occur in a wide variety of environments, including the workplace, home, outdoors, and school. This makes education unlimited in scope as it literally covers everything a person learns.

Education is, as a general rule, not learned as formally or as rigidly as the way students are taught in school. For instance, in workplaces, people may be educated by serving as an apprentice, or veteran employees may be assigned to mentor new trainees in how to carry out their duties. Children may be educated in life by their parents, siblings, or other relatives as they are taught how to socialize, how to behave around others, how to take care of themselves, and other skills. Finally, some people are **autodidactic** and have taught themselves all kinds of skills, from cooking to languages to rocket science.

📚 *Glossary*
all-encompassing: inclusive
autodidactic: self-taught

1 Which of the sentences below best expresses the essential information in the highlighted sentence in the passage? *Incorrect* answer choices change the meaning in important ways or leave out essential information.

Ⓐ High school graduates study for at least a dozen years while college students attend school for even longer.

Ⓑ It takes the average person twelve years to finish high school and another four if that person goes to college.

Ⓒ By the time a person graduates from college, that individual will have attended school for well over a dozen years.

Ⓓ Twelve years in high school enables one to graduate and then to be able to go to college for a few more years.

2 In paragraph 2, the author uses "home economics" as an example of

Ⓐ a class that students do not have to take

Ⓑ a subject that is taught at most schools

Ⓒ a class which is required for students

Ⓓ a subject of less value than foreign languages

3 The word "mentor" in the passage is closest in meaning to

Ⓐ regale

Ⓑ instruct

Ⓒ order

Ⓓ demonstrate to

4 ***Directions:*** An introductory sentence for a brief summary of the passage is provided below. Complete the summary by selecting the THREE answer choices that express the most important ideas of the passage. Some sentences do not belong because they express ideas that are not presented in the passage or are minor ideas in the passage. ***This question is worth 2 points.***

Schooling is learning that takes place in a formal academic environment while education can assume a number of different forms.

Answer Choices

1 It is possible to improve one's knowledge base at home or at the office.

2 People may instruct their relatives on how they should behave and live their lives.

3 There is a limit to how much a person can learn when he or she is at school.

4 Most people need someone to advise them when they are learning a new job.

5 A large number of subjects may be unavailable for students to take at some schools.

6 Students tend to take tests and to do assignments for their teachers in their classes.

The Family and the Industrial Revolution

1➜ Prior to the advent of the Industrial Revolution at the end of the eighteenth century, most European families lived together in rural <u>agrarian</u> settings. People typically farmed, with all family members taking part. Sons learned how to work the land while daughters prepared for married life by learning housekeeping and how to care for children by helping raise their younger siblings. The majority of children were educated at home by their parents while public schooling beyond the elementary level was for the rich and privileged. Families lived together, and most individuals never ventured more than a few miles from where they were born. With the coming of the Industrial Revolution, everything changed.

Britain was the first nation to **industrialize** on a massive scale. It managed this first by undergoing an agricultural revolution during the eighteenth century. Changes in the use of the land as well as farming methods produced more food with fewer people working the land. This created a population surplus and also caused many people to be unemployed. Many sons had no hope of inheriting land from their fathers, so in one of the first changes to the family unit, large numbers of them went off to seek their fortunes in the growing urban centers.

Soon, many fathers joined their sons; whole families were often uprooted from rural areas as they moved to cities in Britain and in other nations when industrialization spread. **1** In an era with few labor laws, young children frequently found themselves involved in the struggle to make money and to make ends meet. **2** Factory work was done in shifts, and children sometimes worked as many as twelve or fourteen hours a day in this early, unregulated period of industrialization. **3** Family members barely saw one another as they shuffled back and forth between their homes and factories, and often the only day entire families spent time with each other and rested was Sunday. **4**

The plight of children working in factories and the poor conditions of factory work brought about changes to labor conditions. The age limit when children were allowed to work was raised in many lands, and governments mandated universal education for all children up to a certain age. Children still did not spend all of their time with their families, but they were at least being educated. In addition, shift hours decreased until eight hours a day became the norm in most places. While families now had more time together, industrialization had forever changed the lifestyles of millions of people in Europe and around the world.

🕮 *Glossary*
agrarian: relating to farming
industrialize: to introduce manufacturing

1 Which of the following can be inferred from paragraph 1 about European families at the end of the eighteenth century?

  (A) All classes of them sent their children to public schools for higher learning.

  (B) A minority of them could be found living and working in cities.

  (C) They had mostly small families since raising children was difficult.

  (D) Both sons and daughters contributed by helping raise crops and animals.

2 The word "them" in the passage refers to

  (A) people

  (B) sons

  (C) fathers

  (D) large numbers

3 Look at the four squares [■] that indicate where the following sentence could be added to the passage.

The works of the writer Charles Dickens vividly depict this and some of the other hardships which minors endured during this period.

Where would the sentence best fit?

4 *Directions:* Select the appropriate sentences from the answer choices and match them to the lifestyles of people in the time period to which they relate. TWO of the answer choices will NOT be used. *This question is worth 3 points.*

Answer Choices

1. The populations of many countries became greater than before.

2. Individual family members spent a smaller amount of time together.

3. People primarily remained in the areas where they had been born.

4. Children were required to attend school for a specific number of years.

5. Countries around the world began to develop and become more industrialized.

6. The men and boys in a family were responsible for running the farm.

7. Workers were often spending more than half of the day doing their jobs.

PEOPLE'S LIFESTYLES

Before the Industrial Revolution
-
-

During the Industrial Revolution
-
-
-

Misconceptions

Note

¹➡ Misconceptions are false ideas people can have about virtually anything. Most are related to the everyday interactions people have with others and are influenced by both internal and external factors. The internal factors can include people's self-image as based on their experience, their level of confidence, and their perceptions of how others judge them. Some external factors that can cause misconceptions are how other people react to an individual and how people respond in certain situations. There is often a lack of information that causes the misconception. For the most part, misconceptions have no consequences except perhaps that they may lead to small misunderstandings. In some cases, however, misconceptions can have dire consequences.

Most people have an internal self-image which is built on their experiences, their confidence, and how they perceive that others view them. Each individual's belief in him or herself is based on so many factors that simply cannot be known to others; therefore, others may not understand why a person behaves in a certain way. This is the most common cause of misconceptions. For instance, a man who seems relatively confident in most situations may lack confidence when it comes to speaking to women. **1** A woman who is attracted to him may assume the man does not like her since he does not speak with her and does not ask her out no matter how often she hints that she would like to date him. **2** The man simply has no confidence and fears that the woman does not like him and will reject him. **3** The woman, unfortunately, lacks this information and thus makes a misconception which may prevent the two of them from ever getting together. **4**

³➡ Other misconceptions may result from how people react to an individual. A professor giving a lecture may believe some of his students are yawning because they are bored and his lecture is **uninspired**. But in actuality, they may have been up late studying for exams or writing papers. He lacks enough information to make a correct assessment of the situation; thus, he may react negatively to those students who are yawning. This, in turn, will cause the same students to develop negative feelings toward their professor since he has no sympathy for their current situation, which was caused by them working hard.

Some misconceptions can be long lasting and will not change until a person comes forward with new information that can change the misconception. Others are based on people's experiences related to external events. If a metropolitan area has many homeless drunks, for instance, then seeing a shabbily dressed man passed out on a street corner will **elicit** no reaction from the hundreds of people walking by. In fact, he may be deathly ill and require medical attention.

Propaganda is one kind of misconception that is often utilized by governments. Propaganda is the deliberate spreading of information with the desire to influence people. While it is not necessarily false information, it often results in misconceptions and can therefore conceal the truth.

People's beliefs are the main cause of their self-image. When told that their beliefs are wrong, this can have a tremendous negative effect on people's self-images.

Some people have no desire to get rid of their misconceptions. The reason is that what they believe is a strong part of who they are. Thus, upon finding out that what they believe is actually wrong, they are unwilling to give up their misconceptions since it would require them to change some or all of their beliefs. This is a common feature in politics. When confronted with evidence that is contrary to their political beliefs, many people will reject the evidence and continue to believe in their misconceptions.

However, if that same man were clean shaven and wearing a business suit, some people may believe he has suffered a heart attack and will attempt to assist him when, in fact, he may simply be inebriated. In instances like these, it takes a great deal of effort to alter how one perceives various situations.

≋ *Glossary*
uninspired: dull
elicit: to evoke

---

1   According to paragraph 1, which of the following is NOT true of misconceptions?

Ⓐ Their cause is most often a person's lack of information.

Ⓑ They may result in either minor or major problems.

Ⓒ They may be caused by a number of different factors.

Ⓓ They cause people to make accurate judgments of things.

2   Which of the following can be inferred from paragraph 3 about the professor mentioned in the example?

Ⓐ It is not unusual for him to make misconceptions about his students.

Ⓑ He dislikes what he perceives as disrespect on the part of his students.

Ⓒ His lectures are so boring that the students have trouble paying attention to them.

Ⓓ He teaches a class with a relatively small number of students in it.

3   The word "shabbily" in the passage is closest in meaning to

Ⓐ hurriedly

Ⓑ smartly

Ⓒ vulgarly

Ⓓ poorly

4   Look at the four squares [■] that indicate where the following sentence could be added to the passage.

Essentially, the only way they will ever end up dating is through the actions of a third party.

Where would the sentence best fit?

5 **Directions:** An introductory sentence for a brief summary of the passage is provided below. Complete the summary by selecting the THREE answer choices that express the most important ideas of the passage. Some sentences do not belong because they express ideas that are not presented in the passage or are minor ideas in the passage. ***This question is worth 2 points.***

People can have misconceptions about others for a wide variety of reasons.

-
-
-

Answer Choices

1. Misconceptions frequently happen between teachers and students in classrooms.

2. What commonly occurs with misunderstandings is that little or no harm is done.

3. How people feel about themselves can cause misunderstandings to occur.

4. An experience a person has can cause that individual to form a misconception.

5. When people lack information, they are prone to misunderstanding a situation.

6. It is very difficult for people to change the misconceptions they have of others.

Summarizing ▶ Complete the summary by filling in the blanks.

When people have _____ about others, they are said to have misconceptions. While they are typically not harmful, misconceptions can arise because of a variety of _____ factors. People's self-image—how they look at themselves—is one factor that often creates misconceptions. This happens because others cannot know exactly what another person is _____ . Likewise, some misconceptions can result from how people _____ another individual. And some misconceptions may last _____ and may be difficult for a person to change without the presence of new information that could possibly change a person's opinion about a preconceived notion.

Children and Parental Dependence

Attachment to their parents is something most children eventually get over despite being utterly dependent on parental care during their early years. At first, babies do not recognize their parents and will react with equal friendliness to their parents, other family members, or anyone else. As their cognitive abilities develop, they learn to recognize their parents and understand who they are, and they also realize that other people are strangers and are not their parents. At some point, babies develop what is called separation anxiety. This is the fear of being removed from the presence of one or both of their parents. Simultaneously, many of them develop a fear of strangers. Both fears eventually diminish, and as they age, children come to be no longer totally dependent on their parents.

2➡ It is believed that children form an attachment to a parent—or even to a nonparental primary caregiver such as a grandparent or an adoptive parent—on an **instinctual** level. This attachment is related to their need to be taken care of and to feel secure. From around the age of six months to two years, children form a bond with their caregivers. It is often stronger with one caregiver—typically the mother—than the other. This is logical since, in many societies, mothers are the primary caregivers whereas fathers tend to have less interaction with their children. Yet in their early months, children have no attachments to anyone and will attempt to attract the attention of anyone they see no matter who it is. Later, as children develop a growing attachment to one or more people, they will seek out these individuals and will be dissatisfied when they are not available. This displeasure is often expressed through crying and the throwing of **temper tantrums**.

3➡ Crying and tantrums are familiar behavior to most parents. Oftentimes, children become so attached that their parents find it hard to leave them alone with anyone else. In many cases, especially when both parents work and the mother returns to her job soon after giving birth, children will become accustomed to having other people like grandparents and babysitters around. This helps lessen the attachment bond and makes separation from parents more tolerable. On the other hand, children who spend all of their time with one primary caregiver will display strong emotions when that caregiver departs. They will scream, cry, refuse to be held by other people, and cling to the person they feel most attached to. When that person returns, children will rush to meet that person and to reassert the bond.

Perhaps the biggest change in early childhood occurs when children start attending school. Many children, and even caregivers, feel acute distress on the first day of school. On this day, children are thrust into a classroom full of

Note

When human babies are born, they are utterly helpless and would quickly die if they were left alone. In fact, for the first several years of humans' lives, they are dependent upon others in order to live.

The bond between a mother and her child is crucial to the psychological well-being of the child. Studies show that children who have strong bonds with their mothers grow up to become self-reliant individuals and also have high self-esteem. Those who fail to bond with their mothers frequently develop various psychological issues, including low self-confidence and a sense of insecurity.

Divorce can have a negative effect on young children, particularly if the child does not live with the parent with whom he or she is most closely bonded. The resulting separation may cause the child to develop several types of problems. Among them are anger issues, a loss of self-confidence, withdrawal, and sadness.

new people with a strange—to them at least—person in charge of everything. Hopefully, the children have already met their teacher and have some friends in their class, which will lessen the stress they feel. After some time, the children's dependence on parental attachment diminishes as they form new bonds with their peers at school.

≋ **Glossary**

instinctual: related to one's instincts

temper tantrum: an outburst, often by a child and which features screaming and crying

1. Which of the sentences below best expresses the essential information in the highlighted sentence in the passage? *Incorrect* answer choices change the meaning in important ways or leave out essential information.

    Ⓐ They begin to understand that the majority of people they see are not their parents.

    Ⓑ They start learning to tell the difference between their parents and other people.

    Ⓒ They become better able to distinguish their parents and other family members.

    Ⓓ They understand their parents much better than they do strangers and other people.

2. The word "them" in the passage refers to

    Ⓐ babies

    Ⓑ parents

    Ⓒ strangers

    Ⓓ fears

3. The author discusses children forming bonds in paragraph 2 in order to

    Ⓐ explain why children may get so attached to their caregivers

    Ⓑ contrast this with children's attitudes toward complete strangers

    Ⓒ excuse their behavior when they begin to throw temper tantrums

    Ⓓ compare their behavior with regard to their mothers and fathers

4. According to paragraph 3, some children display strong emotions when they are left alone because

    Ⓐ they are unused to having both parents around them

    Ⓑ they realize that overreacting gets them what they want

    Ⓒ they spend the majority of their time with one person

    Ⓓ they are upset to see both of their parents leave the home

5   ***Directions:*** Select the appropriate statements from the answer choices and match them to the reactions of children to which they relate. TWO of the answer choices will NOT be used. This question is worth 3 points.

Answer Choices	**THE REACTIONS OF CHILDREN**
1 Are prone to misbehaving when the person who cares for them departs	**Before Forming Bonds** • •
2 May be unhappy when someone they want to see is not present	
3 Are unable to differentiate between the people whom they see	**After Forming Bonds** • • •
4 Attend school and meet new people like their classmates and teachers	
5 May be tended to by someone like a grandparent or an adoptive parent	
6 Are friendly toward any individual they come into contact with	
7 Look forward to seeing a particular member of their family	

Summarizing ▷ Complete the summary by filling in the blanks.

When babies are born, they _____ their parents or others, and thus they are happy when they see anyone. However, as they age, they learn to recognize their parents and to distinguish them from others. They often then develop _____ to their parent or primary caregiver. This attachment, in which they _____ with the person, causes them to seek out the person when he or she is not around. They may even throw _____ when they cannot find their primary caregiver. As children age and begin to _____, they start to lose this attachment, so they are no longer totally dependent on one person for care.

Schema Theory

Note

1➜ Schema theory states that people have certain rules which they use to organize their knowledge and understanding of the world. These schemata rules are formed from experiences and are organized as a series of memories and images representing the way an individual views the world. By using schemata, people can understand things as they happen and can even make predictions, for instance, when they finish another person's words. Schemata rules are highly dependent on a person's cultural background and life experiences. Due to this fact, everyone interprets events in different ways. When a strange situation presents itself, people often find it difficult to assimilate this new experience because they have no schemata to help them interpret the situation.

The culture people come from plays a great role in determining their schemata. For instance, people from a technologically advanced culture will react much differently than people from a primitive culture upon seeing a new type of airplane or some kind of electronic device.

2➜ According to most accepted theories on schema, learners are actively building schemata and assimilating new knowledge all the time, and they are revising their existing schemata based on new knowledge they acquire. Some theorists believe that people have a hierarchical organization of knowledge and add new knowledge to this structure, which leads to superior intelligence. Other theorists speculate that knowledge is situation specific, which accounts for the differences between experts and novices in certain fields. In this way, simply being intelligent is not enough since one must also possess experience.

A large part of intelligence is a person's capacity to learn new information. By using schemata effectively, most people are able to learn, understand, and utilize new knowledge.

By using schemata, people do not have to put forth an **elaborate** effort to process everyday situations. A person can use experience to recognize what something is or to know how to react to a situation. For example, perhaps a person sees a brand-new car design. While the design is unfamiliar, the person knows that a car is a machine with four wheels which has an engine and carries people places. This basic knowledge enables the person easily to assimilate the new car design. Furthermore, schemata can allow a person to do or use something without having done it before. For instance, a fork is a fork no matter what its shape or design, so it can be used to eat food by anyone who has ever used one before. However, the same person may have difficulty using chopsticks. If the person has no experience with chopsticks, that individual will likely resist using them and will either ask for a fork instead or **flounder** in an attempt to use chopsticks.

By associating new knowledge with information that they already possess, people are able more easily to assimilate unfamiliar things. Those who do not already possess that particular schema must create a new one, which takes longer and slows their rate of learning.

If this new information—such as knowledge of what chopsticks are and how they are used—fits within a person's schemata, then it is much easier for the individual to assimilate a new situation into his or her existing schemata. However, if the experience is totally unfamiliar, then the initial reaction is simply to ignore this new situation. Other times, a person may be forced to adjust and assimilate a new experience. For example, a student may be assigned a

Some people simply refuse to accept anything which falls outside of their worldview. By ignoring or rejecting unfamiliar experiences or information, they are unable to create new schemata which would enable them to project on an unfamiliar subject. When reading about the topic, the student may understand the words but not the information they convey. If the assignment is required, then the student has no option but to move ahead and to try to make sense of the information, which will give the student a schema for that topic in the future. However, if the assignment is voluntary, the student is likely to abandon it because of its unfamiliarity.

process and accept the new information.

📚 **Glossary**
elaborate: extensive; complicated
flounder: to fail miserably

---

1 According to paragraph 1, which of the following is true of schema theory?
Ⓐ It concerns the way that people use knowledge to understand what is happening.
Ⓑ It focuses on using a person's culture to organize the individual's thinking process.
Ⓒ It establishes rules that are useful in determining the importance of one's memories.
Ⓓ It enables a person to interpret one event in a multitude of different ways.

2 The word "they" in the passage refers to
Ⓐ most accepted theories on schema
Ⓑ learners
Ⓒ schemata
Ⓓ some theorists

3 In paragraph 2, the author implies that intelligence
Ⓐ has nothing to do with a person's knowledge
Ⓑ might depend on the amount of experience one has
Ⓒ can only be acquired through experience
Ⓓ may arise from the formation of schemata

4 Which of the sentences below best expresses the essential information in the highlighted sentence in the passage? *Incorrect* answer choices change the meaning in important ways or leave out essential information.
Ⓐ When the student must do the work, doing so will result in the creation of a schema for that subject.
Ⓑ Unless the student is able to understand the information, it will not be possible to construct a schema.
Ⓒ One benefit of doing the assignment will be that the student gets a schema for use in the future.
Ⓓ Unless the student already has a schema, then doing the required project will require more work than is necessary.

5 ***Directions:*** An introductory sentence for a brief summary of the passage is provided below. Complete the summary by selecting the THREE answer choices that express the most important ideas of the passage. Some sentences do not belong because they express ideas that are not presented in the passage or are minor ideas in the passage. ***This question is worth 2 points.***

People construct schemata as they increase their knowledge base and assimilate what they learn.

-
-
-

Answer Choices

1. By learning how to do something new, a person can create a schema which will be useful in the future.

2. Many people dislike learning new skills because doing so can be quite difficult for them.

3. Having schemata means that people may know how to react to various situations they are faced with.

4. When people have the option of doing something new, more often than not, they will elect not to do so.

5. Schemata enable people to understand the way in which the world around them is operating.

6. Schema theorists have varying opinions on what the value of intelligence is to individual humans.

Summarizing ▶ Complete the summary by filling in the blanks.

In schema theory, people organize _____ by using certain rules. The schemata they form help them look at the world in a certain way. People are constantly learning _____, and their schemata help them greatly. They can help a person _____ new knowledge and to understand what to do in various situations that they _____. However, should a person have no schemata for a certain experience, that individual may choose to _____ the new thing rather than learn about it. But should a person investigate and learn about this new experience, that person may form a new schema that may be helpful in the future.

Possibilism and Actualism

Actualism is the philosophical idea that posits the existence only of the actual world and its inhabitants. Possibilism, on the other hand, is the philosophical position which accepts that other things can possibly exist beyond what is known actually to exist. The two positions stand in contrast to each other and thus have created a philosophical conundrum. Actualists ask how anything can exist beyond what already exists while possibilists ponder how people can know that everything which exists is all that ever will exist.

2➡ The actualists' basic tenet is that there is nothing which is not actual. The possibilists' challenge to this idea is formed on the notion of possible worlds, which is based on modal realism. The notion that other worlds exist is called a modal claim or modal belief. In the statement "It is possible that other worlds exist," the words "it is possible" indicate a mode of thinking in which a person using logical reasoning believes there is a chance that something could be true based on one's previous experiences. For instance, the statement "It is possible that it will rain tomorrow" is based on the experience of having seen or felt rain in the past coupled with the knowledge that, on any given day, it might rain again.

3➡ The main proponent of modal realism and possible worlds was American philosopher David Lewis. He argued that the word "actual" was indexical, meaning it indicated a state of being. In his mind, non-actual objects were simply just not present, but that did not mean that they did not exist somewhere else. Lewis believed in possible worlds as really existing worlds. His basic belief was that possible worlds were similar to our so-called actual world and that only their content was different. When asked what he thought they were like in more detail, he stated that he had no idea and had no way to find out and that to give the impression that he did would be using his imagination to describe something which people might wish to hear but would not be true. Lewis also argued that there were an **infinite** number of possible worlds and that they were isolated from one another in time and space.

The actualists' reaction to Lewis's theories on possible worlds and modal realism happened in two distinct ways. Some tried to embrace parts of the idea of possible worlds by conceiving possible worlds as theoretical objects that actually existed but in **abstract** form. Others attacked the theory of possible worlds mainly on the notion that the theory goes against common sense. Lewis countered by saying that ideas of common sense do not encompass all possibilities. 1 The other main argument against him was that having an infinite number of possible worlds violates the premise of Occam's razor, which states that explaining a theory is best done by reducing the elements to only what is

Note

Both actualism and positivism belong to the branch of philosophy that is known as metaphysics, which considers the nature of reality. More specifically, these two ideas are considered to be ontological problems. That is, they consider the nature of being.

When given a choice between two or more activities, whichever one the actualist chooses to do is considered the actual world. While the other choices were possible, they did not occur and thus are not a part of the actual world.

David Lewis lived from 1941 to 2001. During the course of his work, which included developing theories on counterfactuals, he came to propose that there were an infinite number of possible universes, all of which were slightly different from our own in some way. By proposing counterfactuals—if A had not happened, then B would have—he posited that these universes contained worlds virtually identical to ours.

needed. **2** In other words, arguments should be kept as simple as possible. **3** Despite criticism, Lewis never wavered in his belief in possible worlds, stating it to be true up until his death in 2001. **4**

≋ *Glossary*

infinite: having no limit; unmeasurable
abstract: being focused on the essential qualities of something

---

1 The word "conundrum" in the passage is closest in meaning to

Ⓐ query

Ⓑ puzzle

Ⓒ hypothesis

Ⓓ contradiction

2 According to paragraph 2, the possibilists disagree with the actualists because

Ⓐ they subscribe to the theory of modal realism

Ⓑ they refuse to acknowledge their past experiences

Ⓒ they believe there is no such thing as actual worlds

Ⓓ they use logic to deny what actually exists

3 In paragraph 3, the author's description of David Lewis mentions all of the following EXCEPT:

Ⓐ The reason he thought a limited number of worlds existed

Ⓑ His thoughts on the existence of possible worlds

Ⓒ The primary field of study that he was engaged in

Ⓓ What he meant when he used the word "actual"

4 Look at the four squares [■] that indicate where the following sentence could be added to the passage.

In that regard, what Lewis was postulating was deemed to be unnecessarily complicated and therefore incorrect.

Where would the sentence best fit?

5 **Directions:** Select the appropriate sentences from the answer choices and match them to the philosophical idea to which they relate. TWO of the answer choices will NOT be used. ***This question is worth 3 points.***

Answer Choices	PHILOSOPHICAL IDEA
① It is a philosophical mystery that people are still trying to solve.	**Actualism**
② Its adherents claim that all that can ever be is what exists in the real world.	•
③ It argues that it is possible for worlds to exist in other locations.	•
④ Some believe that other worlds only existed in the abstract.	**Positivism**
⑤ It argues its beliefs by trying to apply Occam's razor against its opponents.	•
⑥ It utilizes logical reasoning that is based upon prior experiences.	•
⑦ It is a relatively new theory first promulgated around 2001.	

Summarizing ▶ Complete the summary by filling in the blanks.

Two opposing philosophical ideas are _____. Actualism claims that only actual things and the world they occupy exist. Possibilism, however, disagrees, and claims that it is possible for things to exist beyond what is actually known to exist. Possibilists believe in the notion of _____. They state that by using _____, they can accept the existence of things beyond what they have experienced. _____ was a major proponent of possibilism. He was convinced that there are _____ of worlds in the universe. Actualists disagreed with Lewis's theories for a couple of reasons, but Lewis believed in his ideas all throughout his life.

Evolutionary Linguistics

¹➡ A sub-branch of linguistics is evolutionary linguistics, whose practitioners strive to discover the origins of languages. Finding the root of a language is like a **treasure hunt**, especially since most early ones have no written form. However, there are methods linguists use to trace a language's roots, including determining the presence of similar words in different languages, which they use to search for a common language that served as the basis for more modern languages. This method is not perfect, but by using disciplines such as history and archaeology, linguistic detectives can piece together where languages come from and how they developed and evolved into other languages.

²➡ One example of the intricacies involved in evolutionary linguistics can be seen in the language Proto-Indo-European, or PIE for short. This is the source for the Indo-European languages that more than half the world speaks. The Indo-European language family consists of 140 of the world's more than 5,000 languages, but many Indo-European languages have spread around the world due to the past expansion of the Europeans. Included in the Indo-European family are English, German, French, Spanish, Italian, Greek, several Baltic and Slavic languages, including Russian, and other languages spoken in Iran and India. The common words for similar things in many of these languages have led linguists to believe these languages have a similar root somewhere in the past.

³➡ For example, the number systems used in English—one, two, three—in German—*ein, zwei, drei*—and in Russian—*adin, dva, tri*—are similar. Other examples include family words such as brother in English, *bruder* in German, and *brat* in Russian. There is clearly a connection between these languages. The search for that connection began over a century ago, and it is now generally accepted among linguists that PIE is the language from which all other Indo-European languages come from. Finding exactly when and where that language was spoken is more difficult since there are no written records of PIE.

⁴➡ Evolutionary linguists managed to piece together part of the mystery of the origin of PIE by searching for the earliest-known written records of Indo-European languages. Texts of Indo-European languages found in Iran and India can be traced back to 1200 B.C. An even greater find was the discovery of a previously unknown Indo-European language and civilization in Anatolia, located in modern-day Turkey. Scholars called this language and its people Hittite. Their civilization possibly existed as far back as 1900 B.C. The next step was to find some common root words in various Indo-European languages. Oftentimes, words for numbers, family names, and animals are similar in Indo-European languages because they were common in PIE. Then, linguists looked for words in these languages that described certain human technological achievements. These were words like gun, sword, and wheel. The reason they did this was that a word like gun differs in almost all Indo-European languages because there were no guns when PIE was spoken. Therefore, by looking for similarities in words describing technological advances, evolutionary linguists established the time when PIE was spoken as somewhere around 3000 B.C.

⁵➡ Determining where PIE was spoken has been harder to prove, and scholars still disagree concerning this matter. PIE contained words for geographical features and weather-related words such as snow that have been passed on in various Indo-European languages. In addition, PIE speakers apparently

did not depend on farming for their livelihoods, which suggests they were nomadic and depended upon animals for their survival. The main theory evolutionary linguists have developed from this information is that PIE speakers came from the **steppes** of modern-day Russia that are north of the Black Sea and the Caucasus Mountains. Scholars call the people that lived there the Kurgans; the word Kurgan itself comes from a Turkish word that describes the culture's burial mounds.

1 The Kurgan culture had domesticated the horse and from this central location, expanded starting around 3000 B.C. **2** It moved west to Europe and south and east to parts of modern-day Turkey, Iran, and India. **3** This caused the Kurgan culture to overrun other cultures and languages. **4** PIE became the dominant language, and it either assimilated other languages or pushed them away. The end result was the beginning of the Indo-European language family's spread through Europe and, eventually, the world.

≋ *Glossary*
treasure hunt: an activity in which people try to find something hidden
steppe: a prairie

---

1 In paragraph 1, why does the author mention "archaeology"?

- (A) To discuss one of the branches of study that is closely related to linguistics
- (B) To compare its importance to linguists with that of the study of history
- (C) To explain how it was effective in helping linguists learn about the past
- (D) To name a field of study linguists must use in the course of their research

2 According to paragraph 2, which of the following is true of Proto-Indo-European?

- (A) At one point in time, more than half of the world's population spoke it.
- (B) It was the source of many different languages in both Europe and Asia.
- (C) It caused European languages eventually to spread throughout the world.
- (D) Many of its words were adapted by close to 5,000 of the world's languages.

3 Which of the following can be inferred from paragraph 2 about the world's languages?

- (A) Despite not evolving from PIE, many of them contain similar words and expressions.
- (B) They began to evolve in Europe and then spread to the rest of the world.
- (C) For the most part, they were uninfluenced by the Proto-Indo-European language.
- (D) Most have an equivalent number of speakers in comparison with the major ones.

4 The author discusses "number systems" in different languages in paragraph 3 in order to

- (A) develop the theory that PIE was the root language for many others
- (B) prove that several languages are essentially the same as one another
- (C) demonstrate the resemblances of some languages that evolved from PIE
- (D) use them to help explain both when and where PIE was developed

5　Which of the sentences below best expresses the essential information in the highlighted sentence in the passage? *Incorrect* answer choices change the meaning in important ways or leave out essential information.

(A) After more than one hundred years of research, the consensus among experts is that every Indo-European language has its origins in PIE.

(B) For the most part, linguists feel that they have determined how Indo-European languages came to develop from PIE.

(C) Sometime around one century ago, most linguists agreed PIE was the base language from which other Indo-European languages came.

(D) Following a century's worth of research, linguists now agree that PIE is the root language for most Indo-European languages.

6　According to paragraph 4, how did linguists determine the origin of PIE?

(A) They visited remote lands in Asia and spoke with experts in those countries.

(B) They looked for similarities in certain words in ancient written records.

(C) They made educated guesses based upon similarities in modern languages.

(D) They researched the origins of family-related words in multiple languages.

7　According to paragraph 4, words concerning human technological achievements were important to linguists because

(A) they let experts determine the rate of technological advancement in various cultures

(B) they enabled linguists to learn about PIE's origins based upon human advances

(C) they showed linguists the exact time period when humans began to use technology

(D) they proved to researchers precisely when and where PIE evolved as a language

8　According to paragraph 5, which of the following is NOT true of PIE?

(A) It contained words that let its speakers describe the climate.

(B) The people who may have first spoken it are known as the Kurgans.

(C) Some of its vocabulary was used to speak about the local geography.

(D) It is agreed that it evolved in the steppes of modern-day Russia.

9　Look at the four squares [■] that indicate where the following sentence could be added to the passage.

Thus they gradually disappeared, never to be remembered.

Where would the sentence best fit?

Click on a square [■] to add the sentence to the passage.

10 **Directions:** An introductory sentence for a brief summary of the passage is provided below. Complete the summary by selecting the THREE answer choices that express the most important ideas of the passage. Some sentences do not belong because they express ideas that are not presented in the passage or are minor ideas in the passage. **This question is worth 2 points.**

> Drag your answer choices to the spaces where they belong.
> To remove an answer choice, click on it. To review the passage, click on **View Text.**

Through extensive research, linguists have managed to determine both when and where the Proto-Indo-European language developed.

-
-
-

Answer Choices

① More than half of the people in the world speak a language which evolved from PIE.

② An area located in contemporary Russia is thought to be where PIE originated.

③ Words that describe technology have taught linguists much about languages.

④ The Kurgan culture traveled in all directions and influenced many cultures.

⑤ PIE was likely developed sometime around 5,000 years in the past.

⑥ Linguists have compared words in many languages to learn about PIE.

Children and Advertising

¹➡ The goal of every advertising firm is to find ways to help companies sell their products. One of the biggest targets of modern advertising is children as statistics show some startling facts about children and the influence they have on their parents' spending habits. In order to tap into this market, advertisers utilize clever methods to attract children to their products and to get children to convince their parents to buy them. How healthy this is for children is a matter of intense debate. Parents are on one side, and companies are on the other while children's health and billions of dollars are at stake.

²➡ The traditional advertising model of the past was directed toward parents as it sought to encourage them to buy products for their children. Now, the opposite is true, especially since the advent of the television age. In the United States, the average child watches approximately 40,000 commercials a year. Accordingly, advertising companies spend over one billion dollars a year on television commercials directed at children. The majority of these commercials are for food products and toys. Children in the four-to-twelve-year-old age group spend up to forty billion dollars a year in America, with most of this money coming from their parents in the form of allowances. In addition to this direct spending, it is estimated that children have an indirect influence on how their parents use approximately 600 billion dollars in household spending each year. With such huge amounts of income at stake, advertisers are quick to find ways to manipulate children into buying or asking their parents to purchase their products.

³➡ At the core of this success with children's advertising is the nature of how children view commercials. Many young children cannot distinguish between television programs and commercials. They often do not comprehend that the purpose of a commercial is to sell a product. Studies of children and products show that children can recognize a product brand as early as the age of three and that they may even start to form brand loyalty as early as the age of two. Advertisers and companies gear their products toward things like colorful brands, logos, and eye-catching and appealing products which will grab children's attention. Many children enjoy watching animated programs, and most of these programs have tie-ins such as character dolls or devices and machines used on the shows. ❶ Once children realize these are available for sale, what occurs next is something called the nag factor. ❷ Children will pester their parents constantly until they give in and purchase the desired product. ❸ For parents, some peace of mind is worth spending a few dollars on the toy, game, or whatever their children want. ❹

⁴➡ It is not just toys and games that advertisers attempt to influence children into buying. Children can have an effect on the food their parents buy, the toothpaste they use, and even the kind of car their parents drive. To do this, advertisers promote adult products with logos and slogans that attract children's—as well as adults'—attention. Advertisers are aided in their attempts to reach children by modern technology. Children not only watch commercials on TV but also see ads on the Internet, receive advertisements on their cell phones, and are bombarded by billboards and posters advertising everything. In addition to all of this, they also face peer pressure. Advertisers frequently use peer campaigns to increase product sales. They single out popular children or teens at a school and give them the latest sneakers, clothing, or MP3 player. The students then become part of a mobile ad campaign. Peer pressure compels other students to desire the new products, and then the nag factor begins when they harass their parents until they get what they want.

⁵➡ The end result is that children have become a __conduit__ into their parents' bank accounts. Most parents know they and their children are being manipulated, but they also want to make their children happy. Some resist and try to limit their children's access to TV and other places where they can be overwhelmed by commercials. However, it is a constant struggle, and the battle is being won by the companies and advertisers, especially since many parents are simply too weary to fight the inevitable.

📚 *Glossary*

core: the center or heart of something
conduit: a channel or passageway

---

1   The phrase "tap into" in the passage is closest in meaning to

    (A) access

    (B) increase

    (C) develop

    (D) rely upon

2   Which of the following can be inferred from paragraph 1 about modern advertising?

    (A) It spends billions of dollars annually trying to attract children.

    (B) It has had a negative effect on children's health.

    (C) It acknowledges the influence of children on their parents.

    (D) Ad campaigns consider children more important than adults.

3   Why does the author mention "the four-to-twelve-year-old age group" in the United States in paragraph 2?

    (A) To acknowledge that group's effect on convincing parents to spend their money

    (B) To show how much of their own money children in this group spend annually

    (C) To prove these children are effective at determining their parents' spending habits

    (D) To mention which group of children spends the most amount of money

4   According to paragraph 3, parents often buy products for their children because

    (A) they want their children to have new toys to play with

    (B) they want their children to stop bothering them

    (C) they feel the items are worth the money they cost

    (D) they do not think the products are overly expensive

5   Which of the sentences below best expresses the essential information in the highlighted sentence in the passage? *Incorrect* answer choices change the meaning in important ways or leave out essential information.

    (A) Children are subjected to commercial advertisements virtually everywhere they look.

    (B) Children see more commercials on TV than they do on the Internet or other media.

    (C) There are so many advertisements everywhere that children cannot avoid them.

    (D) Children prefer to see ads on TV or the Internet, not on billboards and posters.

6   The word "harass" in the passage is closest in meaning to

    (A) hassle

    (B) convince

    (C) explain to

    (D) plead with

7   According to paragraph 4, which of the following is NOT true of the peer campaigns used by advertisers?

    (A) They provide selected individuals with products for free.

    (B) They rely upon peer pressure to help sell their products.

    (C) They pay children to help them advertise their products.

    (D) They utilize popular students to make their products more popular.

8   According to paragraph 5, advertisers have an advantage over parents because

    (A) they are better able to convince children of the value of their products

    (B) many parents lack the energy not to give in to their children's constant begging

    (C) the number of commercials children hear on the radio or Internet is phenomenal

    (D) most parents are willing to spend any amount of money to please their children

9   Look at the four squares [■] that indicate where the following sentence could be added to the passage.

In many instances, the merchandising from these programs can be more valuable than the programs themselves.

Where would the sentence best fit?

                 Click on a square [■] to add the sentence to the passage.

10 *Directions:* An introductory sentence for a brief summary of the passage is provided below. Complete the summary by selecting the THREE answer choices that express the most important ideas of the passage. Some sentences do not belong because they express ideas that are not presented in the passage or are minor ideas in the passage. ***This question is worth 2 points.***

> Drag your answer choices to the spaces where they belong.
> To remove an answer choice, click on it. To review the passage, click on **View Text.**

Knowing how much influence children have over their parents' finances, advertisers have begun campaigns aimed primarily at children.

-
-
-

Answer Choices

1. Some children become loyal to particular brands at an incredibly young age.

2. Children often nag their parents until they give in and purchase something for them.

3. Peer pressure from popular children convinces other youths to buy various products.

4. Some say that parents spend up to 600 billion dollars a year because of their children.

5. Products with movie tie-ins are among the most popular with young children.

6. Children are easily manipulated by commercials and convinced to buy certain products.

1 Shyness Prevention

Some people feel uncomfortable or even afraid in situations where they must deal with others who may even be friends or colleagues. This feeling is shyness, and it affects a large number of individuals. Psychologists have devised several ways to prevent it. While some involve using medicine to alleviate feelings of nervousness or anxiety, many psychologists try to avoid this route. Instead, they may subject their patients to the very experiences which cause their shyness. For instance, a man afraid of speaking in public will be forced to do that repeatedly in order to induce him to overcome his feelings.

2 The Sociology of Trains

In the nineteenth century, railroads were expanding all across Europe. People began frequently taking trains to save on traveling expenses and time. At first, the train companies believed that members of the upper class would regularly ride their trains, so they created two separate classes: first class and coach. However, as it turned out, there were more passengers from the middle and lower classes of society, so the trains were divided into three distinct classes. This caused feelings of resentment in the people who took the two lower classes, yet it was emblematic of European society at the time, which was obsessed with class differences, especially when royalty was involved.

3 Changing Opinions

People have opinions on many subjects, ranging from deep topics like philosophical matters to minor concerns such as their favorite snacks. However, once people form an opinion, it is usually difficult for them to change it. For instance, when one person lies to another, the second person may be convinced that the liar is immoral; oftentimes, no matter what happens later, the second person will be hard-pressed to change his opinion of the liar. Likewise, when people with strong opinions—like on the death penalty or abortion—read something opposing their opinion, they are more likely to respond critically and to find holes in the logic rather than to question or change their own opinion.

4 Rote Learning

There are several learning methods that teachers use in their classrooms. One of the most common is rote learning. This requires students to memorize information so that they can regurgitate it later, usually on an examination. Rote learning has its critics, but it can be effective. For instance, students learning phonics, basic math, and scientific formulas often rely upon it. So do lawyers studying various cases. However, while students who use rote learning may know a lot of facts, they typically fail to comprehend the importance of what they have learned. Thus rote learning is less effective for complex ideas than it is for basic material.

5 Imagination

People's minds are capable of all kinds of thoughts. People can see what is around them and perceive that which exists. Additionally, they are usually able to engage in abstract thought and can therefore imagine things. That is, by using their minds, they can create images or memories that are not real but are instead made up, or imaginary. Imagination is useful in that it stimulates people's creativity and enables them to conceive of things that do not exist but which possibly could exist. Many artists, writers, and inventors possess vivid imaginations. On the other hand, some people become unable to separate their imagination from reality, so they develop psychological problems.

6 Authority

A person who holds authority over another person or group of people has a position of power over them. Most individuals will, within reason, obey a person with authority. There are many ways for someone to take authority. In the past, inherited authority was common as kings assumed their positions by virtue of their birth. Others used force to seize power and compelled people to recognize their authority. Nowadays, though, many individuals assume authority through elections when they are chosen by people to represent them. In this manner, their authority is regarded as more legitimate since the people, by voting, have given permission for the person to have authority over them.

❼ Projection

Most people possess characteristics—like greed, selfishness, or stubbornness—that are regarded as not being positive. People are often unable to recognize their own negative traits; however, they are quick to see these same traits in other people even when they do not exist. This is known as projection. For example, perhaps a selfish person eats out with a group of others. He may accuse one of them of not paying his fair share when, in fact, he did not contribute enough while the person he accused actually paid the required amount. By means of projection, he has merely repressed his own feelings and, as a defense mechanism, accused the other person of possessing his own negative characteristic.

❽ Dolphin and Human Communication

Humans use verbal and nonverbal means to communicate. Humans clearly have language, and now researchers are trying to determine if dolphins use language, too. It is obvious that dolphins communicate with each other—as do all animals in some way—and many researchers believe they actually use language like humans. For instance, dolphins communicate nonverbally. Bites, nuzzles, bubble-making, and head-nodding are just some of the myriad gestures they use. And dolphins, like humans, utilize verbal methods to communicate as well. They employ a series of clicks, squeaks, whistles, and other sounds as a sophisticated means of communication to impart all kinds of information. This, some researchers conclude, is language as humans use it.

❾ Infant Memory

Most adults have virtually no memories from before the age of two, and a large number of them cannot remember anything prior to the age of four. However, this does not mean that infants do not form memories. Even at young ages, infants can still remember certain events and can use the knowledge that they have learned and remembered. Recent research has shown that some babies as young as eight or nine weeks are able to create long-term memories lasting at least twenty-four hours. It had previously been believed that babies did not develop long-term memories until they were around nine months old.

❿ The Family System in the Industrial Revolution

As the Industrial Revolution progressed, it dramatically altered many countries' family systems. Mostly, it made family members less reliant upon one another. Previously, every family member had to help with the work to be done on the farm. However, as more families moved to cities, this was no longer the case. Instead, each family member took jobs at factories or elsewhere. Families became more individualized as young people realized they were no longer tied to the home. Subsequently, they often moved out, thereby splitting up families. Additionally, women became free to pursue work, and this, ultimately, led to the women's movement, which would dramatically alter the traditional family system.

Star Performer Topic Files **Education, Sociology, and Psychology**

- The effects of low book prices in the eighteenth century
- Various interactions between people
- Ways to improve instructors' teaching skills
- The differences in lifestyles in Northern and Southern Europe
- How the telegraph affected society
- The development of social skills in elementary school children
- How society was changed by railroads
- The changing roles of women in society
- The changes in society due to the Industrial Revolution
- How emotion affects people's behavior

absorb
academic
accommodate
accommodation
adapt
adaption
altruism
analysis
analyze
anarchy
articulate
articulation
assimilate
assimilation
attachment
authoritarian
aversion
bias
bureaucracy
bureaucratic
case study
chaotic
characterize
childhood
cognition
cognitive
colonialism
cooperate
correlation
cultural
culture
curriculum
deprive
designate
designation
discriminate
discrimination
diverse
diversity
educate
educated
education
educational
elementary
emotion
emotional
empathy
empirical
equality
equivalent
ethical
ethnic

ethnicity
ethnocentrism
examination
examine
experience
experiential
experiment
experimental
experimentation
facilitate
feminine
feminism
gender
groupthink
heritage
hierarchical
hierarchy
hypothesis
hypothesize
imagination
imagine
inequality
infancy
infant
influence
influential
inhibit
integrate
integration
integrity
intellect
intellectual
intelligence
intelligent
interact
interaction
introspection
intuition
justify
learn
learning
level
logic
masculine
maturation
mature
maturity
mechanism
memorization
memorize
memory
mental

method
methodology
modification
modify
moral
morality
multiculturalism
neocolonialism
nonverbal
norm
obedience
observation
observe
obsession
pacify
participate
participatory
pedagogical
pedagogy
peer
perceive
period
periodical
perspective
pluralism
poverty
pragmatic
pragmatism
prejudice
prejudicial
primary
process
progressive
psychoanalysis
psychoanalyze
psychosis
psychotic
punish
punishment
radical
random
rationalization
rationalize
reaction
reactionary
reasoning
reflex
reform
reformer
regressive
reinforce
reinforcement

relativism
renewal
represent
representation
repressive
role
rote
scapegoat
schema
schematic
scheme
scholar
scholastic
scholasticism
schooling
secondary
secular
segregate
segregation
self-conscious
self-esteem
sensory
sequence
sequential
social
socialize
stage
statistical
statistics
status
stereotype
stigma
stimulant
stimulate
structural
structure
subgroup
suppress
systematic
temperament
tertiary
theorize
theory
trait
transmit
transmission
university
valid
value
variable
variation
withdrawal

✑ Choose the words closest in meaning to the highlighted parts of the sentences.

1 While it is frequently believed that the terms schooling and education are synonymous, this is far from the truth.

- Ⓐ academic
- Ⓑ respectable
- Ⓒ identical
- Ⓓ advanced

2 However, if the experience is totally unfamiliar, then the initial reaction is simply to ignore this new situation.

- Ⓐ disregard
- Ⓑ postpone
- Ⓒ escape
- Ⓓ interpret

3 The age limit when children were allowed to work was raised in many lands, and governments mandated universal education for all children up to a certain age.

- Ⓐ required
- Ⓑ recommended
- Ⓒ reinstated
- Ⓓ restructured

4 Many doctors also concur that exposing children to other children at young ages and allowing them to build up their immunities to common childhood diseases will make them stronger in the future.

- Ⓐ agree
- Ⓑ postulate
- Ⓒ dispute
- Ⓓ consider

5 In some cases, however, misconceptions can have dire consequences.

- Ⓐ unexpected
- Ⓑ horrible
- Ⓒ potential
- Ⓓ advantageous

6 Inheritance passed through the male line in most cases, so sons normally waited until their father passed away to obtain land.

- Ⓐ retired
- Ⓑ moved
- Ⓒ died
- Ⓓ transferred

7 Children not only watch commercials on TV but also see ads on the Internet, receive advertisements on their cell phones, and are bombarded by billboards and posters advertising everything.

- Ⓐ destroyed
- Ⓑ assaulted
- Ⓒ invaded
- Ⓓ annihilated

8 Many children, and even caregivers, feel acute distress on the first day of school.

- Ⓐ irreparable
- Ⓑ sincere
- Ⓒ contagious
- Ⓓ severe

9 How healthy this is for children is a matter of intense debate.

- Ⓐ one-sided
- Ⓑ considerable
- Ⓒ strict
- Ⓓ passionate

10 Advertisers and companies gear their products toward things like colorful brands, logos, and eye-catching and appealing products which will grab children's attention.

- Ⓐ high-tech
- Ⓑ striking
- Ⓒ unique
- Ⓓ advanced

11 However, if the assignment is voluntary, the student is likely to abandon it because of its unfamiliarity.

(A) quit
(B) regret
(C) postpone
(D) resent

12 Colonial America was primarily a rural society with the vast majority of people dwelling on family farms.

(A) slight
(B) appropriate
(C) huge
(D) apparent

13 Despite criticism, Lewis never wavered in his belief in possible worlds, stating it to be true up until his death in 2001.

(A) trusted
(B) readjusted
(C) vacillated
(D) amplified

14 Actualists ask how anything can exist beyond what already exists while possibilists ponder how people can know that everything which exists is all that ever will exist.

(A) dispute
(B) reject
(C) assert
(D) consider

15 Essentially, schooling is limited in two ways: It covers only academic topics and is restricted in scope.

(A) usefulness
(B) range
(C) level
(D) cost

16 PIE became the dominant language, and it either assimilated other languages or pushed them away.

(A) exclusive
(B) accepted
(C) prevailing
(D) root

17 So even if children attend preschool for only a few hours each day, this gives parents time to run errands, to take care of household chores, and simply to take a break from watching over them.

(A) tasks
(B) repairs
(C) assignments
(D) requests

18 Both fears eventually diminish, and as they age, children come to be no longer totally dependent on their parents.

(A) amplify
(B) remain
(C) vanish
(D) ebb

19 This, in turn, will cause the same students to develop negative feelings toward their professor since he has no sympathy for their current situation, which was caused by them working hard.

(A) compassion
(B) regard
(C) comprehension
(D) view

20 The majority of children were educated at home by their parents while public schooling beyond the elementary level was for the rich and privileged.

(A) landed
(B) nobility
(C) advantaged
(D) gifted

Chapter 05　Economics

Economics is a social science that is concerned with the production, distribution, and consumption of both goods and services. There are two major fields in economics: microeconomics and macroeconomics. Microeconomics focuses on various minor or individual aspects of economics while macroeconomics is a more broad and general study of economics. Macroeconomics is often more concerned with economic systems on a national or even global level, and its adherents strive to comprehend how these systems act and react with one another. Some economists try to understand the various factors that either enable or prohibit the production and distribution of goods in various places. They also concern themselves with historical and political studies since both of these fields can have a tremendous effect on a country's or region's economy. Overall, economics looks at financial systems, how they developed, how they change, and how they can be improved.

Naval Power and the Republic of Venice

For hundreds of years, the Republic of Venice was a leading European power. The city-state achieved its status thanks to the enormous wealth the Venetians accumulated by cornering much of the Mediterranean seaborne trade. This wealth was then converted into military strength as powerful naval forces were constructed to protect its merchant shipping. Its power, however, eventually declined, and Venice was ultimately absorbed by the Austrians during the Napoleonic Wars, officially folding as a republic in 1797.

Venice's geographical setting at the head of the Adriatic Sea put it in a favorable position to act as a go-between for Europe and the Byzantine Empire and Arabian lands to the east. However, one threat the Venetians faced was the presence of large numbers of pirates on the multitude of islands lining the Adriatic's eastern shore. The suppression of these pirates provided the initial impetus to constructing a strong navy, but even after the pirates were eliminated and their islands occupied, Venice's navy continued to roam the seas in support of its ships. This protection served them well since as many highly sought spices from Asia passed through Venice's port, the city-state's wealth grew with each ship that arrived to unload its wares.

3➡ The Venetians also earned income from fees paid by crusaders seeking transportation to the Holy Land during the Middle Ages. In one infamous instance, in 1202, a French army agreed to pay 85,000 silver marks—an enormous sum—for transportation to the Holy Land and supplies for nine months. When the French failed to make their final payment before embarking, the wily Venetians made a new deal. They asked the French to subdue two of their rebellious colonies on islands in the Adriatic. The French quickly acquiesced, but then the Venetians displayed their ruthlessness once again. They requested that the French sack Constantinople, the capital of the Byzantine Empire, and a nominal ally of the West. In 1204, the fabled city fell, and the Venetians and the French, their quest to the Holy Land now forgotten, shared in the spoils of war.

Despite being reviled for their actions against Constantinople, Venice's trade and growth were not slowed. At the peak of its power, Venice had perhaps 3,000 merchant and naval vessels. Its navy was instrumental in many conflicts, including the landmark victory over the Ottoman Turks at Lepanto in 1571. By that time, though, Venice was in a slow but steady decline. A previous thirty-year-long war with the Turks had greatly weakened it, and it was later ravaged by plague at least twice. In the end, when the Austrians seized it in 1797, Venice was but a shadow of its former self.

📚 *Glossary*
sack: to pillage; to loot
landmark: of historical importance or value

1 Which of the sentences below best expresses the essential information in the highlighted sentence in the passage? *Incorrect* answer choices change the meaning in important ways or leave out essential information.

(A) While it was necessary to defeat the pirates and to take over their lands, the Venetian navy was primarily constructed to protect Venetian shipping interests.

(B) The presence of pirates inspired the Venetians to construct their fleet of ships, which they then used to destroy the pirates and to take over their lands.

(C) The Venetians at first built their navy to defeat the pirates, but after defeating them, their warships offered protection to other ships in their fleet.

(D) The Venetian navy was needed to watch over its merchant shipping, and it also occasionally engaged in battles where it fought and defeated pirates.

Question Type

[Sentence Simplification Question]

Sometimes the clauses in the correct answer are written in the same order in which they appear in the highlighted sentence.

2 The author discusses "Constantinople" in paragraph 3 in order to

(A) explain how the Venetians successfully plotted to conquer it

(B) mention that it was the capital city of the Byzantine Empire

(C) stress how it was allied with the West and should not have been attacked

(D) describe the manner in which the assault on it was successful

[Rhetorical Purpose Question]

Even though several of the answer choices may contain factual information, focus on the author's reason for including the information, not whether or not the answer choice is factually correct.

3 In paragraph 3, the author's description of the crusaders mentions which of the following?

(A) The amount of money one crusader army paid Venice for transportation

(B) The size of the crusader army that attacked and captured Constantinople

(C) The types of ships that the crusaders sailed on with the Venetians

(D) The amount of time it took the crusaders to sail from Venice to the Holy Land

[Factual Question]

Carefully check all of the answer choices since the three incorrect ones often have some element of truth in them.

4 *Directions:* An introductory sentence for a brief summary of the passage is provided below. Complete the summary by selecting the THREE answer choices that express the most important ideas of the passage. Some sentences do not belong because they express ideas that are not presented in the passage or are minor ideas in the passage. **This question is worth 2 points.**

Venice used its ideal location along the Adriatic Sea to transform itself into a sea power, and it became very wealthy through trade and transporting people and goods.

[Prose Summary Question]

Look for facts in the passage that back up the introductory sentence. The answer choices with this information will be the correct ones.

Answer Choices

[1] The pirates that sailed in the Adriatic Sea often gave the Venetians trouble.

[2] At one point, Venice had around 3,000 ships of a military and civilian nature.

[3] In 1204, the Venetians and the French combined forces to defeat the Byzantines.

[4] The Venetian navy sailed the seas to protect its shipping on the Mediterranean.

[5] The French paid Venice a huge amount of money for transportation to the Holy Land.

[6] The Venetians helped defeat the Ottoman Turks at the crucial Battle of Lepanto.

Single-Product Economies

All throughout history, certain regions and even entire countries have relied upon one major product as their primary source of export income. When this occurs, they are known as single-product economies. For the most part, single-product economies involve agricultural products or natural resources. While there are a few benefits to having a single-product economy, in the majority of cases, there are more disadvantages than advantages.

2➜ One of the best-known single-produce economies existed in the American South prior to the Civil War that was fought during the early 1860s. **1** In the decades leading up to the war, the South depended mostly upon cotton exports to obtain money. **2** "King Cotton," as it was called, was grown both on small farms and huge **plantations** and then exported to the northern states and to countries such as Great Britain. **3** This was to the detriment of the South, which both exhausted its soil through the constant planting of cotton and also neglected to develop other industries, one of the primary factors that led to it losing the war it fought against the technologically developed North. **4**

3➜ Today, there are some places around the world which rely upon a single crop for most of their exports. For instance, approximately ninety-five percent of the export earnings in Uganda come from coffee beans. Many regions in Southeast Asian countries rely upon rice exports as well. It is not just agricultural products that can create single-product economies. Newfoundland, a province in Canada, has an economy that depends heavily upon the fishing industry, and Zambia in Africa has its economy dominated by copper exports. In addition, numerous countries, including Venezuela, Kuwait, Iraq, and Algeria, have their economies almost entirely supported by exports of oil.

As a general rule, single-product economies exist because the products being sold command strong prices. This provides high, steady incomes for many people living in the region. Area residents can additionally focus on that one product, which lets them produce, mine, or grow it in an efficient manner so that it can become even more profitable. Nevertheless, there are many risks involved in having single-product economies. Agricultural products can be killed or damaged by drought, cold weather, or disease, which can result in a region's income shrinking dramatically. Natural resources such as **precious metals**, oil, and gas are nonrenewable, so when their supply is exhausted, the economy must transition to something else, which can be difficult and painful. Finally, as the American colonies discovered, focusing on one product results in neglecting others. This causes regions to have stunted development, so they often lag far behind other places that have more diversified economies.

≋ *Glossary*

plantation: a very large farm, often in a tropical or subtropical area, where a single cash crop is primarily grown
precious metal: a valuable metal such as gold, silver, or copper

1 In paragraph 2, the author implies that the American South

    Ⓐ became richer than the North by relying upon cotton for exports

    Ⓑ lost the Civil War in part because it was not as advanced as the North

    Ⓒ received help from Great Britain during the Civil War

    Ⓓ had more small farms than it did huge plantations before the 1860s

2 In paragraph 3, the author's description of single-product economies mentions all of the following EXCEPT:

    Ⓐ The types of products that comprise them in the present day

    Ⓑ The percentage of exports that oil provides in some countries

    Ⓒ The names of some of the countries that rely on them today

    Ⓓ The country which relies upon the export of a precious metal

3 Look at the four squares [■] that indicate where the following sentence could be added to the passage.

Following the war's conclusion, the South diversified its economy, leading it to become stronger than it had been before 1860.

Where would the sentence best fit?

4 ***Directions:*** Select the appropriate sentences from the answer choices and match them to the advantages and disadvantages of single-product economies to which they relate. TWO of the answer choices will NOT be used. ***This question is worth 3 points.***

Answer Choices	SINGLE-PRODUCT ECONOMIES
① Other countries may begin growing crops, which can affect incomes in different places.	**Advantage** • •
② Crops can be affected by forces of nature which then cause incomes to shrink.	**Disadvantage** •
③ Individuals can improve the efficiency by which they produce or develop one product.	• •
④ Prices of certain products can change whenever there are new technological developments.	
⑤ People in a certain place can receive steady incomes by depending upon a single product.	
⑥ Some places may not become as highly developed as other areas around them.	
⑦ Regions that rely upon nonrenewable resources may exhaust their supplies of them someday.	

[Inference Question]

Carefully read the sentences in the passage which concern the question as well as the important words and facts from the answer choices.

[Negative Factual Question]

Merely glimpsing at the answer choices and the paragraph in question will make it difficult to find the right answer since the correct answer often includes words that appear the passage.

[Insert Text Question]

When a sentence to be inserted has multiple clauses, be sure to read them all carefully to be able to understand precisely what the sentence is about.

[Fill in a Table Question]

Be sure to ignore answer choices that appear correct but which contain information that is not mentioned anywhere in the passage.

Raw Materials and International Trade

1→ International trade is the **lifeblood** of the global economy. Trucks, trains, airplanes, and ships transport the millions of products people desire to all points of the globe. Nations strive to export more than they import and are constantly looking for an advantage in international trade. At one point, having colonies gave a nation a great boost in trade since colonies could provide their mother country with raw materials. On the other hand, an independent nation that has a raw material that is greatly desired by other nations, such as oil, is also in an advantageous position.

In the Age of Colonialism, which lasted from the sixteenth to the twentieth century, colonies supplied much-needed raw materials to their European masters. In a sort of reciprocal trade—with most of the advantage for the mother country—the raw materials were transformed into finished products and sold back to the colonies. The colonials paid higher prices for finished products made from materials they had originally supplied. For example, during the heyday of their empire, the British imported raw materials such as timber from their colonies, particularly America. They then turned the timber into furniture, which they promptly sold back to the people in the colonies from where it had originally come.

Oil is another good example of a raw material being traded internationally. Today, there is a steady stream of tankers moving from the oil states to the rest of the world. However, when oil became a useful commodity in the mid-nineteenth century, the first sources were mainly in the United States. As the desire for oil grew, explorers found vast **untapped** oil wealth, much of it in colonies, all around the world. After gaining their independence in the twentieth century, these oil-rich lands, such as Iraq, Libya, and Kuwait, and many other already independent states, such as Venezuela, Saudi Arabia, and Iran, discovered they suddenly had the power to control a crucial part of international trade.

4→ They have used this power on several occasions, such as during the OPEC Crisis of 1973, to boost the price of oil, which has had serious economic repercussions worldwide. However, for the most part, the desire to trade their precious raw material and to make money in a stable economy has kept oil-rich states from abusing their influence too much. The global infrastructure is so dependent on the uninterrupted flow of oil that any possible disruption to it may lead to serious consequences. For instance, in 1991, a vast coalition led by the United States did not go to war to liberate Kuwait from Iraq so much as it did to protect the nearby Saudi Arabian oilfields.

🕮 *Glossary*

lifeblood: a very important aspect of something
untapped: available; unexploited

1 According to paragraph 1, nations colonized other lands because

    Ⓐ they were able to engage in trade with their colonies

    Ⓑ their colonies would purchase raw materials from them

    Ⓒ some colonies had oil, which they provided their mother country with

    Ⓓ their colonies were a source of raw materials for them

2 The word "heyday" in the passage is closest in meaning to

    Ⓐ expansion

    Ⓑ formation

    Ⓒ prime

    Ⓓ decline

3 Which of the sentences below best expresses the essential information in the highlighted sentence in the passage? *Incorrect* answer choices change the meaning in important ways or leave out essential information.

    Ⓐ By being able to control the international oil trade, some colonies were able to become free while others maintained their independence.

    Ⓑ In the twentieth century, certain former colonies and free nations learned how they could influence one aspect of international trade.

    Ⓒ Iraq, Libya, and others gained their independence in the twentieth century while other oil-rich states had already become free countries.

    Ⓓ Venezuela, Saudi Arabia, and Iran, all of which were free countries, used their oil reserves to help some colonies to become free.

4 In paragraph 4, the author uses "the OPEC Crisis of 1973" as an example of

    Ⓐ an influential and tragic occurrence that could have been avoided

    Ⓑ one of the reasons why the price of oil has increased so much

    Ⓒ an event which demonstrated the power of some oil-rich nations

    Ⓓ an oil embargo that caused problems all around the world

Taxes, Investment, and the Industrial Revolution
in Great Britain

1➡ The Industrial Revolution began in Great Britain in the late eighteenth century and continued throughout the nineteenth century. Why it occurred in Britain first and not in another nation has been the topic of endless debates. But one factor in Britain's favor was an atmosphere that encouraged business investment. Any kind of business requires **capital**, but getting people to invest their hard-earned money is frequently difficult because of the risks involved. Nevertheless, the British government's power, taxation system, and business laws promoted such investment.

Britain in the eighteenth and nineteenth centuries was a very prosperous nation. It enjoyed a long period of stable government and economic growth during this time. Its position as a maritime power— as well as its merchant fleet—was supreme. Britain had gathered many overseas colonies, and when the Industrial Revolution was in its infancy, much wealth had accumulated in Britain as a result of its colonial acquisitions. For instance, many Englishmen became extremely wealthy from the sugar trade with Caribbean sugar plantations. While comprising a mere portion of the nation's overall riches, this untapped wealth was often invested in new inventions and businesses.

3➡ In addition, although taxes overall increased in Britain in the eighteenth century, most were of an indirect nature. To get money, the British government imposed duties on common goods such as salt, candles, beer, and soap. Taxes on imported luxury goods, including tea, sugar, and coffee, were aimed at the wealthy. So were taxes on property, like the one that was determined by how many windows a house had. There was also a land tax, which required owners to pay a few **shillings** per pound of the value of their property. While most people paid indirect taxes when they bought basic goods, only the very wealthy usually paid property taxes because only they could afford land and large homes with a great number of windows. Still, these taxes, unlike modern-day income taxes, did not seriously hinder the wealthy by obligating them to pay sizable percentages of their incomes.

Limited liability laws introduced in the mid-nineteenth century also helped provide a base for the continued growth of industry in Britain by protecting investors. In limited liability companies, only those who operated the company as well as the principal owners were responsible for its debts. This meant that investors only stood to lose their original investment and did not have to pay for any debts the company acquired. This encouraged more people to open their purse strings and to provide startup capital for inventors and industrialists.

📖 *Glossary*
capital: money or funds which are often invested in some kind of venture
shilling: a monetary unit in Britain that was equal to one-twentieth of a pound

1 Which of the following can be inferred from paragraph 1 about the Industrial Revolution?

Ⓐ Some people believe that it has actually never ended.

Ⓑ People are still arguing over why it started in Great Britain.

Ⓒ The large population of Great Britain helped it begin there.

Ⓓ It was funded by investments from outside of Great Britain.

2 The word "they" in the passage refers to

Ⓐ basic goods

Ⓑ the very wealthy

Ⓒ property taxes

Ⓓ land and large homes

3 According to paragraph 3, which of the following is NOT true of taxes in Great Britain?

Ⓐ The wealthy were forced to pay large portions of their incomes in taxes.

Ⓑ They were assessed on goods that were considered necessities by people.

Ⓒ Some of them had to be paid by people who were the owners of property.

Ⓓ They were occasionally levied on certain goods exported from other countries.

4 ***Directions:*** Select the appropriate sentences from the answer choices and match them to the factor influencing investment in Great Britain to which they relate. TWO of the answer choices will NOT be used. ***This question is worth 3 points.***

Answer Choices

☐1 The prices of regular goods were increased by the levying of duties.

☐2 The British navy protected both its shipping and its colonies abroad.

☐3 These were enacted to protect investors from losing too much money.

☐4 The British had colonies in places as far away from the country as the Caribbean Sea.

☐5 The government refused to allow some people to be sued when businesses failed.

☐6 Rich individuals often had to pay the government for certain possessions they owned.

☐7 Experts are not exactly sure why Britain was the first country to become industrialized.

FACTOR INFLUENCING INVESTMENT

Limited Liability Laws
-
-

Taxes
-
-

Governmental Power
-

Economic Growth in Japan

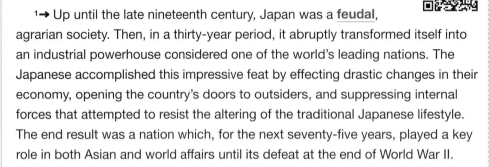

1➡ Up until the late nineteenth century, Japan was a **feudal**, agrarian society. Then, in a thirty-year period, it abruptly transformed itself into an industrial powerhouse considered one of the world's leading nations. The Japanese accomplished this impressive feat by effecting drastic changes in their economy, opening the country's doors to outsiders, and suppressing internal forces that attempted to resist the altering of the traditional Japanese lifestyle. The end result was a nation which, for the next seventy-five years, played a key role in both Asian and world affairs until its defeat at the end of World War II.

2➡ The first period of Japanese economic growth, which took place at the end of the 1800s, is usually referred to as the Meiji Period. It has that moniker because of the emperor of the same name who ruled Japan from 1868 to 1912. Prior to his reign, Japan was merely a feudal society, and the emperor was nothing more than a figurehead while the true power rested with the landed nobility. Under Emperor Meiji's leadership, however, the country initiated measures to join the modern world. The first step was to end Japan's incredibly long period of isolation from the world and to open the country to foreign trade and investment. Most of all, Japan imported knowledge. It did so in two ways: by sending Japanese students abroad to study at famous universities and by importing brainpower in the guise of foreign experts in languages, engineering, business, industrialization, warfare, and law.

The Japanese government was heavy-handed in modernizing the country's economy. It modernized the money and banking systems, created laws for commerce and taxation, and provided loans and encouraged the establishment of *zaibatsu*, or industrial conglomerates. The Japanese began importing raw materials and transformed them into finished products. One of the country's first major industries, which it established thanks to imported foreign technology, was in textiles. Simultaneously, Japan reformed its military by introducing **conscription** and updating its arsenal with modern weapons. Part of this included building a merchant fleet and advanced navy, which soon dominated the seas of East Asia. Internally, the government brooked no dissent as it abolished the militant samurai class—a remnant of its feudal society—which caused them to rebel. After much bloodshed, the national army defeated the samurais in 1877, and a way of life in Japan disappeared forever.

However, the government continued to make use of the military option in the years later. In fact, by the end of the Meiji Period, Japan had moved far down the path to military aggression, which included colonizing neighboring lands. These acts were done under the claim that they were economically necessary as Japan's leaders stated that they needed access to raw materials in colonies like

Note

Prior to the nineteenth century, Japan was almost completely isolated from the world. The Dutch were the only Europeans allowed to make port in Japan, but they could do this just once a year. It was in 1853 that American Commodore Matthew Perry brought a fleet of ships into Tokyo Harbor. His demands for Japan to open were rejected, but he returned the next year and was successful. It was after this that Japan began to open itself to the world.

During the Meiji Period, Japan underwent a tremendous about-face by rejecting isolation and subsequently becoming one of the biggest importers of knowledge and technology from all over the world.

Japan made it clear that it was a world power in the Russo-Japan War of 1904-1905. Widely expected by Westerners to win, Russia was instead defeated. Japan also proved the potency of its navy during the brief war. The war eventually ended thanks to negotiations held by American President Theodore Roosevelt. Despite receiving the Nobel Peace Prize for his efforts, Roosevelt was roundly disliked in Japan for the treaty that he negotiated. The Japanese felt that they had been treated unfairly and had been disrespected, and this would be a cause of anti-American sentiment in Japan for decades afterward.

Korea in order for Japan to maintain its position in the world order. Eventually, Japan, unsatisfied with merely colonizing Korea, invaded China in the 1930s, but its belligerent moves led to the United States and other nations to cease trading with the country. Again, hiding behind an economic pretext, Japan continued its military aggression. Needing oil, tin, rubber, and other raw materials from Southeast Asia, Japan launched a war that began with the bombing of the American Navy at Pearl Harbor in Hawaii and ended in defeat with the dropping of atomic bombs on the Japanese cities Hiroshima and Nagasaki in 1945.

📚 **Glossary**
feudal: pertaining to the feudal system
conscription: a military draft

---

1 Which of the following can be inferred from paragraph 1 about Japan?
- Ⓐ Japanese traditions were ignored in the country's race to modernize.
- Ⓑ It completed the fastest transition to modernity the world has seen.
- Ⓒ Its change into an industrial country was supported by the upper class.
- Ⓓ Prior to the nineteenth century, it was isolated from the outside world.

2 According to paragraph 2, which of the following is true of the Meiji Period?
- Ⓐ It saw the opening of world-class universities in some Japanese cities.
- Ⓑ Many Japanese emigrated and sought permanent residence elsewhere.
- Ⓒ It witnessed a change in the power that the Japanese emperor wielded.
- Ⓓ It continued until the period immediately prior to the start of World War II.

3 The word "brooked" in the passage is closest in meaning to
- Ⓐ permitted
- Ⓑ agreed to
- Ⓒ resisted
- Ⓓ banished

4 The word "them" in the passage refers to
- Ⓐ a merchant fleet and advanced navy
- Ⓑ the government
- Ⓒ its feudal society
- Ⓓ the samurais

5 **Directions:** An introductory sentence for a brief summary of the passage is provided below. Complete the summary by selecting the THREE answer choices that express the most important ideas of the passage. Some sentences do not belong because they express ideas that are not presented in the passage or are minor ideas in the passage. **This question is worth 2 points.**

During the Meiji Period in Japan, the country rapidly modernized, and it became an industrial and military powerhouse in Asia.

> -
> -
> -

Answer Choices

1. Japan was defeated at the end of World War II, and much of the country was destroyed.

2. Foreign experts in many fields were brought to the country to instruct the Japanese.

3. The samurai class resisted change, but they were defeated by the government.

4. Japanese life was based on agriculture until the country began to open to the outside.

5. Japan constructed a fleet of warships which quickly came to rule their part of the ocean.

6. The government encouraged economic expansion and helped many companies do so.

Summarizing ▶ Complete the summary by filling in the blanks.

Before _____ began in the 1800s, Japan was an agrarian culture. However, in a thirty-year period, it rapidly _____. It sent Japanese students abroad to learn about the world and imported many foreigners to provide advice and instruction in certain fields. The government also intervened in _____ and encouraged various companies to do business. It also constructed a merchant shipping fleet and navy and crushed internal dissent in the guise of _____. But Japan became militarily aggressive, and it seized _____ in Korea and China. Eventually, its actions led to World War II, where it suffered great destruction.

Cotton and the Industrial Success of Britain

1 → The Industrial Revolution started in England in the mid-eighteenth century and eventually spread around the world. One of the early successes the English had in industrialization was their development of a large cotton-weaving industry. A series of unique factors then made England ideal for developing a cotton industry. Among them were a strong financial system, overseas colonies which provided raw materials, a large merchant marine fleet, and a superior navy to protect it. England also had many creative geniuses that invented the machines and the processes which made industrialization possible. Finally, government intervention in the form of protectionism kept the cotton industry from having to deal with any competitors.

2 → Cotton became king in England during the early stages of industrialization. Financial investments enabled inventors to create machinery like the flying shuttle, the spinning jenny, and the power loom, all of which allowed wool first and cotton later to be spun and weaved at much greater rates than people could do by hand. This required enormous amounts of cotton, which were imported primarily from the Americas, India, and Egypt. The English merchant fleet shipped the cotton, and it was protected by the Royal Navy, which dominated the oceans, especially after the defeat of Napoleon's French forces at the Battle of Trafalgar in 1805. The cotton industry thus imported raw materials—cotton—to the country, turned it into useful products, and exported them overseas at great profit.

The English government **abetted** the growth of the cotton industry by passing a law overturning previous ones restricting the importation and usage of cotton. The old laws were meant to protect the country's wool industry, but by 1774, when a new law was enacted, cotton was widely regarded as the future of the country's textile industry. Indeed, by 1801, Britain was importing fifty-four million tons of cotton a year, and by 1803, it was exporting more cotton textiles than wool ones. Manchester, in northern England, became the **hub** of much of this industrial growth. Along with its rapid industrialization, the city soon became the second-most populated urban center in the entire country.

Overseas, the textile industry in India was unable to compete with English textile mills. Once the English began colonizing India in the eighteenth century, India's textile industry further declined, and it became a provider of raw materials rather than finished products. Another result of the growing industry was that many American farmers in southern states started growing cotton on immense plantations that utilized slave labor. Cotton became both a symbol of American wealth and of slavery, and it indirectly led to the American Civil War, fought partially over slavery, in the 1860s.

England was the freest and most open society in Europe at that time. With few regulations to stifle the creativity and inventiveness of its people, a number of inventions were made, all of which helped spark the Industrial Revolution.

The Royal Navy was by far the most powerful naval force on the Earth. This enabled England to be involved in and to have colonies on virtually every continent on the planet. Thanks in large part to the Royal Navy, the expression "The sun never sets on the British Empire" came into vogue.

Industrialization brought many benefits to England and the other countries that embraced it. However, it also had some negative effects. Among them were the harsh working conditions that many, including children, were subjected to. Wages were low, and there were few laws to prevent employees from being exploited by factory owners.

By the middle of the 1800s, cotton was England's leading industry. It accounted for over half of all imports and exports in the 1830s and 1840s. **1** However, in 1843, the government permitted textile machinery, which it had once jealously guarded, to be exported. **2** This led to the development of competing textile industries in Japan, Brazil, and a newly resurgent India. **3** Facing competitors who relied upon cheap labor, the English textile industry ultimately declined in the twentieth century. **4**

≋ Glossary
abet: to assist
hub: the center of something; a focal point

---

1. According to paragraph 1, which of the following is NOT true of the Industrial Revolution in England?
   - Ⓐ The supply of raw materials in England helped the English operate their factories.
   - Ⓑ It primarily centered on the textile industry when it was in its beginning stages.
   - Ⓒ England had many intelligent people whose creations enabled many changes to occur.
   - Ⓓ Actions by the government kept competition from other countries at a minimum.

2. Why does the author mention "the Battle of Trafalgar" in paragraph 2?
   - Ⓐ To provide the date when the French forces suffered an important setback
   - Ⓑ To note the time when the English navy truly came to dominate the oceans
   - Ⓒ To explain why the English fleet needed to provide protection to merchant ships
   - Ⓓ To call it the most important naval battle of the nineteenth century

3. Which of the sentences below best expresses the essential information in the highlighted sentence in the passage? *Incorrect* answer choices change the meaning in important ways or leave out essential information.
   - Ⓐ While India had once provided only raw materials, under English colonization, it changed into a producer of finished products.
   - Ⓑ India stopped producing both finished products and raw materials when the English began their takeover in the eighteenth century.
   - Ⓒ Having colonized India in the eighteenth century, the English forced them to provide raw materials for textile factories in England.
   - Ⓓ India transformed from a producer of textiles to a provider of raw materials once the English began their colonization of it in the 1700s.

4. Look at the four squares [■] that indicate where the following sentence could be added to the passage.

   Many of their secrets had already escaped, having been stolen through industrial espionage, so this was not a particularly self-destructive act by the English.

   Where would the sentence best fit?

5 ***Directions:*** Select the appropriate sentences from the answer choices and match them to the reason for the success of the cotton textile industry to which they relate. TWO of the answer choices will NOT be used. ***This question is worth 3 points.***

Answer Choices

1. Textile-making equipment was permitted to be sold to people of other nationalities.

2. African slaves were used on American plantations to raise huge amounts of cotton.

3. Laws were passed that permitted cotton to become more popular in usage than wool.

4. The power loom enabled people to create textiles at a much faster pace than before.

5. The English navy was instructed to protect English merchant shipping from predators.

6. India was transformed by the English from a textile maker into a provider of raw materials.

7. Monetary investments were made that enabled people to work on and improve machinery.

THE SUCCESS OF THE COTTON TEXTILE INDUSTRY

Government Intervention
-
-
-

Independent Actions
-
-

Summarizing ▶ Complete the summary by filling in the blanks.

The cotton textile industry was an important part of _____ in England. In the early 1800s, England dominated the cotton textile industry, but it began losing ground starting in the 1840s and continuing into _____. However, before its loss, England had come to dominate the cotton textile trade for many reasons. For example, while there were many new inventions that made creating textiles easier, there was also _____ in the industry. The Royal Navy also kept careful watch over shipments of cotton crossing the ocean. Additionally, the English government changed _____ so that cotton, not wool, had more advantages. Furthermore, India, an English colony, was transformed from a textile manufacturer into a mere supplier of _____.

Guilds

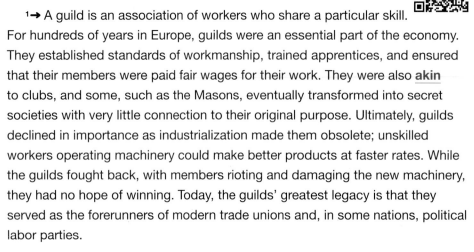

1➜ A guild is an association of workers who share a particular skill. For hundreds of years in Europe, guilds were an essential part of the economy. They established standards of workmanship, trained apprentices, and ensured that their members were paid fair wages for their work. They were also **akin** to clubs, and some, such as the Masons, eventually transformed into secret societies with very little connection to their original purpose. Ultimately, guilds declined in importance as industrialization made them obsolete; unskilled workers operating machinery could make better products at faster rates. While the guilds fought back, with members rioting and damaging the new machinery, they had no hope of winning. Today, the guilds' greatest legacy is that they served as the forerunners of modern trade unions and, in some nations, political labor parties.

Guilds originated when workers in a particular craft, such as shoemaking, baking, or carpentry, realized they could achieve more by banding together to protect their interests. They set standards of workmanship and mandated that, to become a member of a guild, a person had to work first as an apprentice, usually when he was a child. The apprentice served under a master, who would train the boy in the art of the craft for several years until the guild decided that the trainee was skilled enough first to become a journeyman and later a master craftsman. Once a person became a full-fledged member, the guild granted permission for the new master to open his own shop and to do business under the **auspices** of the guild.

3➜ Guilds had both positive and negative aspects, but, overall, they were advantageous to **those** who managed to become members. Yet, without membership, life could be difficult for nonmembers who attempted to enter particular fields of work. In many European towns, no one could establish a business without being a member of the **requisite** guild. This prevented people from competing with guild members and taking business away from them. While this early form of protectionism helped prevent local unemployment, the lack of competition was not conducive to innovation. Another drawback was that in order to qualify for a guild, a person had to spend practically his entire life—starting as a child—in one craft and then focus exclusively on it.

By the time the Industrial Revolution was beginning in the eighteenth century, guilds were an integral part of Europe's economy. However, during the industrialization of Europe, they declined rapidly, starting with the loss of their positions of power. In less than two centuries, they were relegated to positions of unimportance. They fought these changes, but the pace of industrialization did not slow. Many master craftsmen could not compete and found themselves

Guilds were not limited to Europe. There were organizations like guilds in many places in the world, including China, Africa, and India. Many of these appeared even before the rise of guilds in Europe during the Middle Ages.

During the Middle Ages in Europe, there were guilds in many different fields. Goldsmiths and doctors had their own guilds. So did stonecutters, masons, and blacksmiths.

Because they rarely innovated, members of guilds seldom made any kinds of technological advancements. It was not until the Industrial Revolution began that individuals—most of whom were not guild members—started to make new inventions.

As guilds disappeared, labor unions emerged in the nineteenth century. While they sometimes resorted to violence, labor unions still helped their members improve their working conditions.

working in factories. The trade secrets of guilds were also replaced by patent and copyright laws, which gave power to the inventor of a product or method. Guilds gradually became more like what are called trade unions today, and they focused on protecting their members' rights and setting standards of membership and work.

📚 *Glossary*

akin: similar to; resembling
requisite: mandatory

---

1 In paragraph 1, all of the following questions are answered EXCEPT:
- (A) For how long were guilds important to the European economy?
- (B) What were the primary roles of different guilds in Europe?
- (C) How did individuals manage to become members of various guilds?
- (D) What caused guilds to become less important to the economy over time?

2 The word "auspices" in the passage is closest in meaning to
- (A) patronage
- (B) tutorage
- (C) regulations
- (D) partnership

3 The word "those" in the passage refers to
- (A) guilds
- (B) both positive and negative aspects
- (C) members
- (D) nonmembers

4 Which of the following can be inferred from paragraph 3 about guilds?
- (A) They did not permit their members to quit their organizations.
- (B) Their members made few technological advances in their fields.
- (C) They required their members to pay dues on an annual basis.
- (D) They refused to allow their members to set up competing shops.

5 **Directions:** Select the appropriate sentences from the answer choices and match them with the period of time to which they relate. TWO of the answer choices will NOT be used. ***This question is worth 3 points.***

Answer Choices	PERIOD OF TIME
1 Members began departing guilds to join secret societies like the Masons.	**Before the Industrial Revolution**
2 Children were trained as apprentices to learn one particular trade.	•
3 Nonmembers were prevented from establishing businesses in certain places.	•
4 Many guilds transformed into labor unions that covered entire nations.	**During the Industrial Revolution**
5 The fees that members could charge and standards of work they did were regulated.	•
6 Guilds began to lose a certain amount of influence.	•
7 Members with particular skills were often obligated to work for other individuals.	

Summarizing ▶ Complete the summary by filling in the blanks.

Guilds were groups of craftsmen who shared a single trade. They established _____ as well as the rates their members got paid. A person who wanted to work in a trade had to begin as _____ . This was often done when the person was very young. The apprentice learned his craft over many years and eventually became _____ and could open a shop. Guild members had many advantages, but _____ were not allowed to work in some places. Guilds were powerful up until the Industrial Revolution began. Then, industrialization forced many guild members to work in _____ . Many guilds then transformed into trade unions.

The Chinese Silk Trade

Note

1➡ The ancient Romans **prized** the fine, luxurious cloth known as silk, yet they knew little about the land of its origins or how it was made. Silk originated in China, and its production remained a closely guarded secret for more than two millennia. It is not known who the first person was that recognized the potential of making cloth from the finely spun strands produced by the silkworm. However, by the time the Romans ruled the Western world, silk was being exported along the famous route which came to be called the Silk Road. The silk trade became an essential part of the Chinese economy, something which continues in modern times.

There are a number of species of silkworms—all native to China—which were used to produce silk. Over time, the Chinese domesticated them so much that they were unable to survive without assistance from humans.

The art of silk production is called sericulture, and the Chinese mastered it. Through selective breeding methods, they produced a species of silkworm that turned into a flightless moth, which, in turn, laid eggs that produced thousands of silkworms. The silkworms fed until they were ready to spin the silk cocoon they wrapped themselves into in order to transform into moths. However, if a moth emerged from the cocoon, the silk would be ruined, so preventing the moth from reaching maturity was crucial. Once the cocoons were formed, after several days, workers carefully unwound the cocoons, producing a very long thread, which they wound together with others to make a thread thick enough to be made into cloth.

Silk was primarily used to manufacture clothes, including dresses, scarves, and shirts.

3➡ In China, silk was so valuable that the Chinese used it to bribe foreign invaders, to pay the salaries of government officials, and to give as gifts during diplomatic negotiations with neighboring countries. It was also a commercial item. The silk trade from China to the West began thousands of years ago. The Silk Road, in actuality a series of trade routes from Asia to Europe, brought silk to the West while also enabling the cultures along the way to influence one another. In Rome, wearing silk became fashionable. It was incredibly expensive though, and some historians have suggested that the Roman desire for silk was partially to blame for the bankrupting of the empire in its waning years since the Romans spent tons of gold to purchase it.

The Silk Road not only transported trade goods but also knowledge. The connections between East and West enabled ideas and information to flow from Europe to China.

The Chinese maintained a monopoly on silk production by keeping its method a secret. They imposed the death penalty on anyone who revealed to others where it came from. Still, their monopoly eventually ended. **1** The Japanese were the first outsiders to begin silk production. **2** According to legend, a Japanese expedition captured some silkworms along with Chinese workers, who were forced to teach the Japanese the art of sericulture. **3** Additionally, in 552, the Byzantine Empire acquired silkworms when two monks smuggled them out of China. **4** From these small beginnings, silkworms and sericulture spread westward, first to Arabian lands and eventually to Europe.

The silk trade became an enormous money-maker for the Byzantine Empire. It was made a state monopoly, and it proved to be highly profitable for the Byzantines, who sold silk products both to their own people and to those living in Western Europe.

While the Chinese lost their monopoly and their edge as the world's largest producer of silk for centuries, today, China has **rebounded** once again to become the leader in silk production. Currently, it produces approximately 70% of the world's silk. Unfortunately, the twentieth-century development of synthetic fabrics like nylon and rayon has put a damper on the demand for silk.

≋ *Glossary*

prize: to value

rebound: to come back again; to make a recovery

1. The author discusses "the Silk Road" in paragraph 1 in order to
   - Ⓐ stress the length of the journey the silk traveled while going from China to the West
   - Ⓑ mention why that trade route had to be protected from roaming bandits
   - Ⓒ explain the reason why the Silk Road itself was formed many years ago
   - Ⓓ show the manner in which silk was brought from China to the Roman Empire

2. Which of the sentences below best expresses the essential information in the highlighted sentence in the passage? *Incorrect* answer choices change the meaning in important ways or leave out essential information.
   - Ⓐ The workers waited for some time and then unraveled the cocoons, after which they combined individual threads with one another to make cloth.
   - Ⓑ The cocoons took several days to form, and then the workers unwound them, made thread, and wound the threads together into one cloth.
   - Ⓒ In order to make clothing, the workers had to take apart the cocoons and then wrap the individual threads together into one very long strand.
   - Ⓓ Unless they had many cocoons to unwind, the workers would not be able to produce enough thread to make many articles of clothing.

3. According to paragraph 3, the Chinese treasured silk because
   - Ⓐ they were able to use it for a number of different transactions
   - Ⓑ they could utilize it to bring about the downfall of rival empires
   - Ⓒ they often used it in place of gold or silver when making purchases
   - Ⓓ they could affect other cultures and influence them with it

4. Look at the four squares [■] that indicate where the following sentence could be added to the passage.

   It was actually surprising that the secret had been kept for so long considering how pervasive the silk industry was in the country.

   Where would the sentence best fit?

5   *Directions:* An introductory sentence for a brief summary of the passage is provided below. Complete the summary by selecting the THREE answer choices that express the most important ideas of the passage. Some sentences do not belong because they express ideas that are not presented in the passage or are minor ideas in the passage. *This question is worth 2 points.*

> **The Chinese dominated the silk trade for thousands of years, and they made fabulous amounts of money by trading silk as far away as the Roman Empire.**
>
> -
> -
> -

Answer Choices

1. Sericulture, which the Chinese learned how to do, is the name used when speaking about how to produce silk.

2. While the Chinese kept the knowledge of silk's manufacture secret for centuries, foreigners eventually learned how to produce it.

3. Silk was an extremely valuable commodity in China and the rest of the world, especially in Rome, whose citizens spent exorbitant amounts on it.

4. The Chinese could not protect their silk-making secrets from either the Japanese or Byzantines.

5. China is a modern-day leader in the silk industry, but many people favor synthetic fabrics over silk, so it is not as lucrative as it once used to be.

6. The Chinese brought the production of silk to fruition through careful management of the insects that produce the threads from which it is made.

Summarizing   Complete the summary by filling in the blanks.

Silk was prized as far back as ancient times. It came from _____ , but it was traded as far away as the Roman Empire. _____ is the name for the art of silk production. The Chinese learned how to make silk from the strands of the silkworm's cocoons. Silk was valuable and had many uses, especially as a form of payment. _____ were known to have spent tons of gold purchasing it. China at first _____ on the silk trade, but both the Japanese and the _____ managed to learn the secrets of its production. Still, even today, China produces about 70% of the world's silk.

The Agricultural Revolution in Britain

1→ Since the dawn of human civilization, the vast majority of the population has been engaged in agriculture. This was true of England until the eighteenth century. Then, a series of changes in agriculture took place, the result of which was that it required less labor yet simultaneously produced a food surplus. This enabled the now well-fed population to grow rapidly, and many of these people had no ties to the land. As a result, huge numbers of people began looking for work in cities, which they found as the Industrial Revolution began. One of the main reasons the Industrial Revolution had its start in England is that the country had a large workforce available to operate the factories' machinery. Interestingly though, many historians have argued that the industrialization of England would not have been possible without the Agricultural Revolution which preceded it.

2→ The success of agriculture in England is often attributed to four factors: the enclosing of fields, a new crop rotation system, improvements in **animal husbandry**, and the mechanization of farm implements. For centuries, farmers in England had been allowed to graze their animals on common land. In actuality, these lands belonged to the British crown, yet people were permitted to use them. However, in the late eighteenth and early nineteenth centuries, laws were enacted by the government that disallowed individual farmers from using millions of acres of land that had previously been open to them. The land was, quite literally, enclosed. In some cases, farmers were permitted to continue using the land if they paid to have the fields fenced in, but the prices were too steep for most. These laws forced tens of thousands of people to abandon farming, and they subsequently moved to towns and cities to find work. Thus, England suddenly had a large number of people looking for work.

3→ Rather than reduce the amount of food produced, the enclosing of fields had the opposite effect. No longer were there many individuals inefficiently farming small strips of land. Instead, there were far fewer farmers who were more efficiently working larger pieces of land. In addition, around this time, a new system of crop rotation, which vastly improved food production, was introduced. Most farmers in Europe, including England, relied upon a three-crop system. They planted different crops in different fields while leaving some fallow to give the soil time to replenish the nutrients in it. However, Charles Townsend, an influential politician with a keen interest in agriculture, introduced a four-crop rotation system. The crops were wheat, barley, turnips, and clover. Clover, a **legume**, actually helped revitalize the soil rather than deplete it of nutrients as other crops did. It also served as fodder for livestock, increasing the farmers' food supply for their livestock by letting them graze their animals virtually all year long. Farmers also learned to take better care of their animals and to breed them more properly. This led to larger, healthier, and stronger animals which reproduced in abundance.

4→ At the same time, improvements in mechanical devices made it possible to farm with fewer people. The most important of these inventions were improved iron plows, which could dig deeper in heavier soil, especially when pulled by horses or oxen. Machines such as threshers, seed hole drillers, and mechanical steam-driven plows and harvesters significantly reduced the need for labor in the agricultural industry. Together, these factors combined to increase Britain's food production. This, in turn, helped increase Britain's population, which meant more human labor was around to work in the factories being built.

These improvements were not peacefully accomplished though. ∎ Many farmers rebelled against the enclosures, rejected the notion of machines doing what had previously been manual labor, and resented having to leave their ancestral farms for urban locales. **2** Riots occasionally flared up in protest of the enclosure acts, and blood was sometimes spilled. **3** Nor were the benefits of the Agricultural and Industrial revolutions enjoyed by all. **4** Many government officials and rich landholders reaped huge benefits from these changes while poor farmers often became poor factory workers. Undoubtedly, people suffered, lives were irrevocably changed, and a centuries-old way of life disappeared. For better or worse, Britain changed from a quiet, agrarian society into a noisy, smoky, industrial one, and the world has never been the same since.

≋ Glossary
animal husbandry: the raising and taming of animals
legume: a kind of plant that helps improve the quality of the soil

---

1   Which of the sentences below best expresses the essential information in the highlighted sentence in the passage? *Incorrect* answer choices change the meaning in important ways or leave out essential information.

    Ⓐ There were not enough people to work in the factories in England during the Industrial Revolution.

    Ⓑ Without enough people, it is doubtful the Industrial Revolution would have ever begun.

    Ⓒ England needed more people to work the machines in its numerous factories.

    Ⓓ Having enough manpower to work in factories helped England begin to industrialize.

2   Which of the following can be inferred from paragraph 1 about humans?

    Ⓐ They were more interested in farming the land than in pursuing academic endeavors.

    Ⓑ They have lacked sophisticated manufacturing ability for most of their history.

    Ⓒ They were often not able to produce enough food to feed their populations.

    Ⓓ They suffered from a lack of large cities prior to the eighteenth century.

3   According to paragraph 2, farmers could no longer use certain fields in England because

    Ⓐ the government passed laws prohibiting their usage to most people

    Ⓑ they refused to pay the fees for their use that the government demanded

    Ⓒ they were set aside as places where new industries were to be built

    Ⓓ rich landowners seized the lands for themselves and fenced them off

4   The word "fallow" in the passage is closest in meaning to

    Ⓐ fertilized

    Ⓑ blank

    Ⓒ tended for

    Ⓓ empty

5   The author discusses "Charles Townsend" in paragraph 3 in order to

     (A) credit him for a change that improved agricultural methods

     (B) mention how his power as a politician influenced others

     (C) describe the four crops that he preferred to grow in his fields

     (D) question whether or not his suggestion had an actual effect

6   According to paragraph 3, which of the following is true of clover?

     (A) It enabled the animals which ate it to become larger and healthier.

     (B) It detracted somewhat from the soil's ability to become more fertile.

     (C) It was used by people as a supplement for their daily diets.

     (D) It had a beneficial effect on the soil and improved its overall quality.

7   In paragraph 4, the author implies that farms

     (A) were able to become profitable ventures for farmers

     (B) had smaller numbers of animals thanks to some new inventions

     (C) decreased the amount of land on which they planted crops

     (D) employed smaller numbers of people than ever before after modernizing

8   The word "reaped" in the passage is closest in meaning to

     (A) gained

     (B) produced

     (C) manufactured

     (D) sustained

9   Look at the four squares [■] that indicate where the following sentence could be added to the passage.

On some occasions, people even lost their lives.

Where would the sentence best fit?

Click on a square [■] to add the sentence to the passage.

10 ***Directions:*** Select the appropriate sentences from the answer choices and match them to the reason for improvements in agriculture to which they relate. TWO of the answer choices will NOT be used. ***This question is worth 3 points.***

> Drag your answer choices to the spaces where they belong.
> To remove an answer choice, click on it. To review the passage, click on **View Text.**

Answer Choices

1. By planting clover, farmers were able to let their animals graze almost all year long.

2. Harvesters that were operated by steam permitted fewer people to work on farms.

3. Charles Townsend managed to be involved not only in politics but also in agriculture.

4. The process of raising animals changed so that animals more frequently reproduced.

5. Farmers began using a four-field crop rotation system instead of a three-field one.

6. Fewer people were working on farms, so many of them moved to find work in factories.

7. Farmers often actively resisted being forced off their lands and having to move to cities.

IMPROVEMENTS IN AGRICULTURE

Human Inventions
-
-

New Methods
-
-
-

The Industrial Revolution and the Netherlands

¹→ Economic growth does not occur everywhere at the same time. The **diffusion** of ideas and methods occurs slowly, something which has always happened throughout the history of economic development. Sometimes an entire region undergoes change at the same time while in other cases, change occurs in one location, yet next door, the same change may happen more slowly. This was the case for the spread of industrialization in Europe. Great Britain took the lead, but industrialization came slowly to the rest of Europe, especially eastern and southern Europe. In the north, though, Belgium and the German states were not far behind Britain while France slowly but steadily made industrial advances. That left one other major country—the Netherlands—to which industrialization, somewhat perplexingly, came very slowly.

²→ The Netherlands had several qualities which should have made it the leading industrial nation after Britain, but industrialization did not occur there until the mid to late nineteenth century. The Netherlands had a highly educated, literate, hardworking population that could have easily adapted to industrialization. It was one of the most highly urbanized nations in Europe, had an efficient transportation system of canals and roads, and possessed overseas colonies and a large merchant and fishing fleet. On top of all that, it had a sound financial system. Nevertheless, despite these advantages, industry arrived there much later than it should have.

³→ The first reason for this was the Netherlands' economic success prior to the eighteenth century. This era is called the Golden Age of the Netherlands. The Dutch had fought a long war to gain freedom from their Spanish colonial masters. **1** After it ended, the Dutch entered a period of prosperity, during which their country was at the cutting edge of agrarian and technological changes. **2** There is a phenomenon of progress which dictates that a people or nation that achieves great success often has a hard time following up on its accomplishments because of internal factors opposed to change. **3** The Dutch were no different, so organizations like guilds of specialized craftsmen, who had an interest in maintaining the status quo which gave them power and wealth, opposed the technologies that had the potential to erode their positions. **4** This technological conservatism was at its greatest in the late eighteenth century.

⁴→ The second reason that industrialization came late to the Netherlands was war. The Netherlands was at the center of many battles during the French Revolution and the Napoleonic Wars. Easily dominated and conquered by the French, for almost twenty-five years, the Netherlands was part of the French continental system of trade, in which the main enemy—Great Britain—was the target of economic warfare. In essence, the Dutch were prohibited from trading with the British. Furthermore, many of the Dutch overseas colonies were occupied by the British since the Dutch were a part of the French Empire. This damaged the Dutch maritime economy, and inflation and high unemployment, especially in the shipbuilding, fishing, and maritime merchant sectors, were the results. The French also imposed a large war indemnity on the Dutch and forced them to pay for a standing army of 25,000 French soldiers, thus further eroding the Dutch economy. Following the defeat of the last French armies in 1815, the Netherlands emerged to face stiff competition from the strong British economy and from neighboring Belgium, which had steadily built up its industrial base during the years of warfare.

⁵→ A third problem the Dutch had with industrialization was the high salaries Dutch workers anticipated receiving. With an already sophisticated labor market, both skilled and unskilled Dutch workers expected

high **wages**. These rates made it more difficult for businesses to compete with nations where wages were relatively lower. Businesses already had low profit margins, and thus they had less capital to reinvest to make improvements and to expand. To overcome these problems, the Dutch had to effect many changes. They began a series of economic reforms designed to lead the nation into the modern age. The guild system's power was curtailed, the government became more centralized, and the nation's internal transportation system was updated and consolidated. Eventually, the reforms made in the Netherlands brought about change, and by the mid-nineteenth century, the nation was well on its way to industrialization and renewed prosperity.

≋ *Glossary*
diffusion: transmission
wage: money paid for work done by the hour, day, or week

---

1   Which of the sentences below best expresses the essential information in the highlighted sentence in the passage? *Incorrect* answer choices change the meaning in important ways or leave out essential information.

Ⓐ   When there are changes going on in one place, the same changes may not occur at other nearby locations.

Ⓑ   The rate of change in certain places can either be sudden or take place over a long period of time.

Ⓒ   Changes can happen slowly or quickly, but it is more common for them to take place at the same rate in different locations.

Ⓓ   Sudden changes can be more disruptive than those changes which take place only in specific areas.

2   Which of the following can be inferred from paragraph 1 about industrialization in Europe?

Ⓐ   The speed with which it occurred differed from region to region.

Ⓑ   It brought more prosperity to France than it did to Germany.

Ⓒ   The countries which industrialized quickly formed open governments.

Ⓓ   The climate in each country had an effect on its rate of industrialization.

3   The word "sound" in the passage is closest in meaning to

Ⓐ   tragic

Ⓑ   transient

Ⓒ   solid

Ⓓ   aural

4   According to paragraph 2, which of the following is NOT true of the Netherlands?

Ⓐ   Few of its people were able to read in the past.

Ⓑ   The country possessed land in areas that were not found in Europe.

Ⓒ   As a general rule, much of the country's people could read and write.

Ⓓ   There was a solid infrastructure in place for travel both by land and water.

5   In paragraph 3, the author uses "guilds" as an example of

    Ⓐ one of the groups which inhibited progress for reasons related to self-interest

    Ⓑ specialists who were intimately involved in the Golden Age of the Netherlands

    Ⓒ a typical organization in the Netherlands that had become quite wealthy

    Ⓓ a faction that used its technological prowess to intervene against attempts at change

6   According to paragraph 4, the Netherlands failed to industrialize rapidly because

    Ⓐ it suffered from its involvement in a conflict between France and Britain

    Ⓑ it refused to trade with Britain, which then put an embargo on its products

    Ⓒ many of its industries were outdated and unable to compete with foreign ones

    Ⓓ it was in a state of war with France for a period lasting longer than two decades

7   The word "curtailed" in the passage is closest in meaning to

    Ⓐ diminished

    Ⓑ formalized

    Ⓒ detailed

    Ⓓ altered

8   According to paragraph 5, which of the following is true of Dutch laborers?

    Ⓐ They relied upon their membership in guilds to be paid fair wages.

    Ⓑ They expected to be paid more if they were skilled at their jobs.

    Ⓒ Their excessive rates made it hard for companies to turn a profit.

    Ⓓ They encouraged businesses to invest so as to become more competitive.

9   Look at the four squares [■] that indicate where the following sentence could be added to the passage.

    These forces often prevent a country or group from reaching its full potential because of the members' unwillingness to change the way they operate.

    Where would the sentence best fit?

    Click on a square [■] to add the sentence to the passage.

10 **_Directions:_** An introductory sentence for a brief summary of the passage is provided below. Complete the summary by selecting the THREE answer choices that express the most important ideas of the passage. Some sentences do not belong because they express ideas that are not presented in the passage or are minor ideas in the passage. **_This question is worth 2 points._**

> Drag your answer choices to the spaces where they belong.
> To remove an answer choice, click on it. To review the passage, click on **View Text.**

The Netherlands failed to industrialize as fast as other countries in Northern Europe for a number of different reasons.

-
-
-

Answer Choices

1 Dutch workers demanded high compensation for their services, thereby reducing companies' net profits.

2 The population of the Netherlands was not only educated but was also willing to work hard.

3 The countries in Northern Europe began manufacturing products faster than those in Southern and Eastern Europe.

4 The French forces were finally defeated in 1815, which ushered in an era of relative peace on the European mainland.

5 The state of war that existed for many years had a profoundly negative effect on the Dutch economy.

6 There were many agents that actively resisted changes since they were reluctant to alter methods that had made them wealthy.

1 The Black Death in Europe

From 1347 to 1351, the Bubonic Plague swept through Europe in what was known as the Black Death. In some places, entire populations were decimated virtually overnight, and many countries in Europe are thought to have lost over half of their populations. The initial economic result was that deflation set in as supplies were high while demand was low. Prices for both food and land decreased considerably. After some time, there became an acute need for labor, and given the lack of workers, day wages increased. While this improved peasants' monetary situations, it was only for the short term. Many governments intervened and reduced wages back to their pre-plague levels.

2 The Industrial Revolution in the United States

Although the Industrial Revolution started in Great Britain, it swiftly moved across the Atlantic Ocean, where it transformed the United States into the most powerful manufacturing country in the world. As in Britain, many early advances in the U.S. came in the textile industry. Inventions created in Britain were utilized—being either purchased or outright stolen—but there were also some American inventors, including Eli Whitney. In 1793, he invented the cotton gin, which could separate cotton fibers from their seeds at the speed that fifty people could do by hand. Thanks to this and other inventions, the American textile industry began reaping the benefits of industrialization.

3 Scientific Management

In the late 1800s and early 1900s, mass production was becoming prominent. Henry Ford and the Model-T automobile, which was made on the assembly line, provide one famous example of it. Frederick Taylor was an observant student of mass-production methods, and he determined that more efficient ways of making products could be done. He timed how fast it took workers to perform various skills. He did this to determine how productive workers should be and to improve manufacturing methods. He also encouraged companies actively to train their workers. And he believed that managers and workers should divide the work they did. All of his theories together were called scientific management.

4 Triangle Trade

One of the more infamous instances of international trade was what was called the triangle trade. This was trading that happened from the seventeenth to nineteenth centuries and was between Europe, West Africa, and North America. From West Africa, black slaves were transported to be sold to plantation owners on Caribbean islands or in the American South. These slaves then worked on farms that produced goods like cotton and sugar. These, and other raw materials from the Americas, were transported to Europe, where they were turned into finished products such as textiles and rum. The rum was then sold in Africa, where it was used to purchase slaves and thus completed the triangle.

5 Keynesian Economics

John Maynard Keynes was one of the most influential economists in the twentieth century. Coming from Great Britain, his ideas profoundly affected the United States during the Great Depression. Essentially, Keynes distrusted the private sector always to do what was right for the economy. He therefore advocated that it was acceptable for the government to intervene in certain situations. So, in difficult times, the government could reduce taxes or increase spending to stimulate the economy. In boom times, it could increase taxes and reduce spending to halt inflation. President Franklin Roosevelt implemented some of Keynes's ideas—with varying levels of success—in an attempt to end the Great Depression in the U.S.

6 The End of the Cottage Industry

Prior to the Industrial Revolution, there were few factories anywhere. Instead, people manufactured products on individual or small scales. For instance, people would create handicrafts in their homes, which were set up as workplaces. Clothes were items frequently made by these cottage industries. When the Industrial Revolution began, people realized that cottage industries were incredibly inefficient. In addition, the machinery often needed to be located near water, which powered the looms and other inventions. Thus, factories were born. Instead of working at home, people went to large factories, where they toiled alongside many others. The factory method was more efficient and produced cheaper goods, so it led to the demise of the cottage industry.

⑦ American Economic Expansion after World War II

When World War II ended in 1945, much of the world was shattered. Japan and Germany had been flattened by the victorious Allies. But England, Russia, France, and other victors in the war also suffered from destroyed infrastructures. Only the United States, where no battles were fought, was undamaged. This helped the U.S. undergo a tremendous economic expansion immediately following the war. Much of the expansion was in the manufacturing industry. Shipbuilding and aircraft manufacturing provided many jobs for people, and the United States became a global leader in both areas. In later years, American manufacturing dominated other fields, but these were two of the most important industries after World War II.

⑧ The Effects of New Inventions

There are always new inventions, but some have an absolutely transformative effect on society. Many of these inventions have been in transportation. For instance, in the 1800s, the horse and buggy was a common method of travel. Yet, around the turn of the century, automobiles appeared. Once Henry Ford began selling them cheaply, people abandoned the horse and buggy and purchased automobiles. The change in society was huge. People could travel farther and faster than ever before. They could live farther from their workplaces. There were many other changes. Naturally, the horse and buggy industry died, practically overnight—another example of the dramatic changes a single invention can cause.

⑨ Mercantilism

For centuries in Europe after the Middle Ages, mercantilism dominated. There were several aspects to this economic theory. Notably, countries tried to become self-sufficient so that they had no need to depend on other nations, with whom they often quarreled or fought. To be independent, they sought to establish colonies to help them attain the valuable raw materials they lacked yet required. Mercantilist countries also measured their wealth by how much bullion—specifically gold and silver—they possessed. This was another motive for acquiring colonies to exploit, and it was a main reason that countries like Spain were so rapacious in their treatment of their colonies in the Americas.

⑩ Adam Smith

Of the many economists, perhaps the greatest was Adam Smith, who lived and worked during the eighteenth century. A Scottish economic philosopher, Smith's masterpiece was the book *An Inquiry into the Nature and Causes of the Wealth of Nations*, which is often shortened to *The Wealth of Nations*. A weighty tome, his book promoted the concept of the free market and *laissez-faire* economics. He felt that the government should not involve itself in the economy in either good times or bad. He promulgated the idea of "the invisible hand," which he felt would guide markets and individuals to do what was right for the public good.

Star Performer Topic Files **Economics**

- The process of the industrialization of England
- Trade in the Mediterranean region
- The importance of raw materials to an economy
- The cottage industry in colonial America
- The influence of the Byzantine Empire on trade
- The expansion of the U.S. economy in the nineteenth century
- How government regulations affect economies
- Railroads and their effect on the American economy
- The American economy after the Civil War
- The effect of the telegraph on the American and European economies

advanced	embargo	iron	raw material
advantage	employ	ironware	recession
advantageous	employer	labor	reduce
agriculture	energy	labor union	reduction
arbitrate	enterprise	laborer	regulation
arbitration	entrepreneur	lade	regulate
bargain	expand	lend	resource
barter	expansion	levy	revolution
blockade	export	literacy	revolutionary
bond	fabric	loan	route
boycott	factor	loom	salary
business	factory	macroeconomics	scab
canal	farming	manage	sector
capital	federal	management	security
capitalism	federalism	manager	self-employed
cargo	finance	manmade	ship
centralization	financial	market	shipbuilding
centralize	finished product	marketing	shipping
ceramics	firm	material	silk
cloth	free	mediate	Silk Road
commercial	free market	mediation	socialism
commercialism	free trade	mercantilism	specialist
communism	freighter	merchant	speculate
company	generate	merchandise	speculator
compensate	generation	microeconomics	standard of living
compensation	generator	middleman	steel
consumer	goods	mine	stock
corporation	grain	monopolize	stock market
cost	growth	monopoly	strategize
cottage industry	guild	nationalize	strategy
cotton	handcrafted	opportunistic	strike
cycle	high-tech	opportunity	supply
debt	import	opportunity cost	surplus
debtor	impose	pact	system
deficit	improvement	partnership	tariff
deliver	income	plantation	tax
delivery	industrial	populate	taxation
demand	Industrial Revolution	population	technical
depression	industrialism	power	technology
deregulation	industry	price	textile
develop	inefficiency	pricing	toll
development	inefficient	primitive	trade
distribute	infrastructure	private	trade route
distribution	insurance	produce	trade union
duty	insured	production	trader
dye	interdependence	profit	transport
economical	interest	prosper	transportation
educated	international	prosperity	union
education	international trade	prosperous	wage
efficiency	invest	quality	waterway
efficient	investment	railroad	wool
electronic	investor	rate	workman

✒ Choose the words closest in meaning to the highlighted parts of the sentences.

1 While comprising a mere portion of the nation's overall riches, this untapped wealth was often invested in new inventions and businesses.

- Ⓐ imaginary
- Ⓑ fabulous
- Ⓒ explored
- Ⓓ unexploited

2 This led to the development of competing textile industries in Japan, Brazil, and a newly resurgent India.

- Ⓐ reapplied
- Ⓑ rejuvenated
- Ⓒ resentful
- Ⓓ resplendent

3 Ultimately, guilds declined in importance as industrialization made them obsolete; unskilled workers operating machinery could make better products at faster rates.

- Ⓐ extraordinary
- Ⓑ superseded
- Ⓒ retroactive
- Ⓓ passe

4 Natural resources such as precious metals, oil, and gas are nonrenewable, so when their supply is exhausted, the economy must transition to something else, which can be difficult and painful.

- Ⓐ tired
- Ⓑ decreased
- Ⓒ spent
- Ⓓ expensive

5 In some cases, farmers were permitted to continue using the land if they paid to have the fields fenced in, but the prices were too steep for most.

- Ⓐ costly
- Ⓑ outrageous
- Ⓒ nonnegotiable
- Ⓓ bothersome

6 Still, these taxes, unlike modern-day income taxes, did not seriously hinder the wealthy by obligating them to pay sizable percentages of their incomes.

- Ⓐ annoy
- Ⓑ pester
- Ⓒ hamper
- Ⓓ relieve

7 After it ended, the Dutch entered a period of prosperity, during which their country was at the cutting edge of agrarian and technological changes.

- Ⓐ affluence
- Ⓑ adaptation
- Ⓒ expansion
- Ⓓ industrialization

8 Its navy was instrumental in many conflicts, including the landmark victory over the Ottoman Turks at Lepanto in 1571.

- Ⓐ required
- Ⓑ rescued
- Ⓒ instructed
- Ⓓ crucial

9 Riots occasionally flared up in protest of the enclosure acts, and blood was sometimes spilled.

- Ⓐ shed
- Ⓑ necessary
- Ⓒ prescribed
- Ⓓ treated

10 Eventually, Japan, unsatisfied with merely colonizing Korea, invaded China in the 1930s, but its belligerent moves led to the United States and other nations to cease trading with the country.

- Ⓐ compassionate
- Ⓑ indignant
- Ⓒ aggressive
- Ⓓ unilateral

11 It was incredibly expensive though, and some historians have suggested that the Roman desire for silk was partially to blame for the bankrupting of the empire in its waning years since the Romans spent tons of gold to purchase it.

- (A) penultimate
- (B) declining
- (C) emerging
- (D) restricted

12 This was to the detriment of the South, which both exhausted its soil through the constant planting of cotton and also neglected to develop other industries, one of the primary factors that led to it losing the war it fought against the technologically developed North.

- (A) advantage
- (B) consideration
- (C) harm
- (D) use

13 Another result of the growing industry was that many American farmers in southern states started growing cotton on immense plantations that utilized slave labor.

- (A) profitable
- (B) rural
- (C) isolated
- (D) vast

14 While this early form of protectionism helped prevent local unemployment, the lack of competition was not conducive to innovation.

- (A) favorable
- (B) constrained
- (C) confined
- (D) permitted

15 In one infamous instance, in 1202, a French army agreed to pay 85,000 silver marks—an enormous sum—for transportation to the Holy Land and supplies for nine months.

- (A) notorious
- (B) legendary
- (C) actual
- (D) apocryphal

16 Following the defeat of the last French armies in 1815, the Netherlands emerged to face stiff competition from the strong British economy and from neighboring Belgium, which had steadily built up its industrial base during the years of warfare.

- (A) constant
- (B) decisive
- (C) formidable
- (D) engaging

17 They have used this power on several occasions, such as during the OPEC Crisis of 1973, to boost the price of oil, which has had serious economic repercussions worldwide.

- (A) kickbacks
- (B) penalties
- (C) consequences
- (D) retaliations

18 They planted different crops in different fields while leaving some fallow in order to give the soil time to replenish the nutrients in it.

- (A) restore
- (B) attract
- (C) congeal
- (D) influence

19 They then turned the timber into furniture, which they promptly sold back to the people in the colonies from where it had originally come.

- (A) eventually
- (B) immediately
- (C) casually
- (D) consistently

20 Internally, the government brooked no dissent as it abolished the militant samurai class—a remnant of its feudal society—which caused them to rebel.

- (A) consideration
- (B) opposition
- (C) interference
- (D) authorization

Chapter 06   Life Sciences

Life sciences are concerned with the study of living organisms. There are several fields of study in the life sciences. Most prominent among them are biology, marine biology, botany, physiology, zoology, and paleontology. Researchers in these fields study all aspects of living organisms, be they animals, plants, or creatures of another nature. They often determine organisms' characteristics, and scientists research how certain organisms interact with others. On a larger scale, scientists study entire ecosystems and note the interactions between living creatures and their environments. The enormous amount of life on the planet—both present and past—means that there are many possible fields of study for life scientists. Some concern themselves with long-extinct species such as dinosaurs. Others focus on species of plants and animals that are still alive today. Still others speculate about what kinds of organisms may live in the future or even on other worlds.

The Benefits of Earthworms

The presence of an earthworm may evoke cries of disgust when one is seen wriggling across the ground after a rainstorm, but people should be thankful for earthworms. Without this denizen of the underground world, much life could not exist as it currently does. Earthworms are a key component in fertilizing soil and keeping it intact. Without them, farmers could not grow crops in abundance, nor could the trees and plants which make the world green exist in such large quantities.

It is estimated that up to one million earthworms can reside in an **acre** of deep soil. This is fortunate for farmers because when earthworms eat, they also consume soil since the gritty earth helps them break down the food matter they have taken in. This leads to one of the major benefits earthworms provide: They serve as underground plows when they move through the ground consuming soil. As the worms tunnel through the earth, they leave open spaces where air and water can reach the lower levels of the soil and thus enrich the microorganisms that live there. If earthworms did not do this, the soil would become extremely compact, and plant roots could not grow because neither air nor water could penetrate deep enough into the soil. However, when turned over by countless earthworms, soil moves from lower levels up to the topsoil, bringing richer earth to where plants can extract vital nutrients.

Earthworms also provide for soil **cohesion**. When soil passes through earthworms and is then excreted, it emerges from their bodies with a sticky substance that is slimy to the touch. This slime helps bind particles of soil together, thereby preventing the wind and water from eroding the soil. Without earthworms performing this function, more soil would be lost to the elements, and the amount of arable land would be reduced.

⁴➡ Finally, earthworms are important as recyclers of decayed matter. Decayed matter resulting from the decomposition of organic life such as trees, plants, leaves, nuts, berries, and fruits that fall to the ground gets mixed into the soil through the actions of earthworms. This matter—and the soil around it—passes through earthworms, which break it down to produce nutrients. The soil thus becomes rich in nitrogen, calcium, magnesium, and phosphorus, all of which are important for the growth of plants and microorganisms. These various actions by earthworms combine to produce the rich, nutrient-filled soil that is vital to the growth of crops, bushes, and trees.

≋ *Glossary*
acre: an amount of land equal to 4,047 square meters
cohesion: consistency; solidity

1 Which of the sentences below best expresses the essential information in the highlighted sentence in the passage? *Incorrect* answer choices change the meaning in important ways or leave out essential information.

- Ⓐ As the earthworms go through the ground, they move soil up from the lower levels so that it may be enriched by both air and water.
- Ⓑ Microorganisms like earthworms contribute to the enrichment of the soil by enabling it to get more air and water than it normally could.
- Ⓒ Open spaces in the soil are made possible by the presence of both air and water, so earthworms are able easily to tunnel through the ground.
- Ⓓ One byproduct of earthworms' underground movements is that they enable air and water to go deep into the soil and help improve it.

| Question Type |

[Sentence Simplification Question]

Many of the key words in the highlighted sentence get replaced by synonyms in the correct answer choice.

2 The word "arable" in the passage is closest in meaning to

- Ⓐ farmable
- Ⓑ cultivated
- Ⓒ manufactured
- Ⓓ created

[Vocabulary Question]

If you do not know the meaning of a word, look at the context in which it is used. In many cases, especially when the answer choices are similar, doing this will help you find the correct answer.

3 In paragraph 4, the author uses "magnesium" as an example of

- Ⓐ a common element found in the soil of arable land
- Ⓑ a nutrient produced in soil as a direct result of earthworms
- Ⓒ a crucial nutrient needed for healthy plants to grow
- Ⓓ a product found in dead matter decaying beneath the soil

[Rhetorical Purpose Question]

Closely read the sentences in the passage before and after the one in which the subject of the question appears. They often contain hints that will enable you to find the correct answer.

4 **Directions:** An introductory sentence for a brief summary of the passage is provided below. Complete the summary by selecting the THREE answer choices that express the most important ideas of the passage. Some sentences do not belong because they express ideas that are not presented in the passage or are minor ideas in the passage. **This question is worth 2 points.**

[Prose Summary Question]

Incorrect answers may often appear as mere facts that are about the subject of the passage but which are either unimportant or contain irrelevant information.

Thanks to the actions of the numerous earthworms that live in the ground, soil can become more productive for farmers to grow their crops in.

Answer Choices

1. Decayed matter such as fruits, nuts, and berries often falls to the ground and gets buried deep in the soil.

2. A substance excreted by earthworms sticks to dirt and prevents valuable soil from being eroded.

3. Simply by moving through soil, earthworms let more air and water reach deep below the ground and make it more fertile.

4. Earthworms tend to come above the ground after it rains, so they help enrich the topsoil when this happens.

5. It is said that more than one million earthworms may live in only an acre of land in some places.

6. The breaking down of decayed matter by earthworms releases crucial nutrients into the soil.

Fossil Formation

Over several **eons**, countless numbers of plants and animals have died on the Earth. Through accidents of nature, many became fossils, some of which have been found by people and subsequently examined. Fossils are the remains of animals and plants that have been preserved to such an extent that people can recognize them as once having been living things. There are five major ways that fossils are formed: refrigeration, desiccation, carbonization, permineralization, and being trapped in asphalt or amber.

[2]→ Refrigeration is rare, yet it results in the most complete fossil finds. In these instances, animal fossils may still have their hair, skin, and even various internal organs intact. Refrigeration, as its name implies, can only take place in extremely cold climates. **[1]** To be so well preserved, an animal must have drowned in a muddy area—typically near a river bank—and then have been flash-frozen and buried before any animals had the opportunity to consume its **carcass**. **[2]** Woolly mammoths found in Russia have been some of the best-preserved fossils that paleontologists have ever discovered. **[3]** Desiccation, on the other hand, is the opposite of refrigeration. **[4]** Although it takes place in hot, arid regions such as deserts, its results are similar. Because there is so little moisture in the air in desert regions, animals' bodies become mummified, so their skin, hair, and soft tissues are preserved, albeit not as well as in the refrigeration process.

Carbonization occurs when dead plants and animals decompose, leaving only carbon behind. This carbon is impressed upon a rock, leaving an image of the dead plant or animal. Similarly, permineralization takes place when a plant or animal gets buried after dying and is then preserved as rock. Minerals filter into the dead body and crystallize as they assume the animal's or plant's shape. The dead thing then becomes rock-like, thereby creating a fossil. This is the most common form of fossilization, and all of the large, well-formed dinosaurs that have been discovered were fossilized this way.

Finally, animals or plants occasionally got trapped in asphalt or amber. Asphalt is a thick and sticky form of oil. Animals sometimes fell into asphalt pools, got trapped, and drowned. Leaves, branches, and seeds also fell into these pools and were preserved by the asphalt. Amber, however, forms when tree liquids like sap harden and fossilize. Ages ago, many small insects or invertebrates got stuck on sticky tree liquids and were eventually trapped in the oozing liquid. Over time, they became fossilized. At some point, the amber fell to the ground and was buried, only to be discovered millions of years later in amber mines.

≋ **Glossary**
eon: a period of time that may last millions or billions of years
carcass: the dead body of an animal

1 According to paragraph 2, which of the following is NOT true of refrigeration?

    (A) A number of steps must have happened for the animal to be preserved this way.

    (B) It is common for fossilized bodies of animals to be found in northern climes.

    (C) It fossilizes animals differently than desiccation, yet these fossils are somewhat alike.

    (D) Some internal body parts of animals have been found in creatures fossilized this way.

[Negative Factual Question]
Words that refer to frequency should be considered carefully when they appear in answer choices.

2 The word "This" in the passage refers to

    (A) Carbonization   (B) Carbon

    (C) Permineralization   (D) Fossil

[Reference Question]
The word which the highlighted word refers to may often not even be in the same sentence.

3 Look at the four squares [■] that indicate where the following sentence could be added to the passage.

In some rare cases, half-eaten bodies have been found fossilized, providing information not only about the prey but also about the predator.

Where would the sentence best fit?

[Insert Text Question]
Consider the subject matter of the sentence to be inserted as well as that of the sentences where it may be placed next to.

4 **Directions:** Select the appropriate sentences from the answer choices and match them to the type of fossilization to which they relate. TWO of the answer choices will NOT be used. ***This question is worth 3 points.***

[Fill in a Table Question]
These questions occasionally have three categories from which to choose. In these instances, there will be either seven or nine answer choices.

Answer Choices	TYPE OF FOSSILIZATION
① Sticky substances from trees preserve plants or animals by this method.	**Desiccation** • •
② This is the most common method of fossilization.	
③ Fossils preserved by this method look like ones that have been refrigerated.	**Permineralization** • •
④ This fossilization method results in an image of the creature being preserved.	
⑤ The plant or animal becomes crystallized, thereby creating a fossil.	**Carbonization** •
⑥ Fossils can only be preserved this way in very cold environments.	
⑦ This method can preserve parts of an animal other than just its bones.	

How Plants Recognize Seasonal Changes

[1]→ All plants have life cycles, the great majority of which are structured around the seasonal changes occurring annually wherever they grow. While there are exceptions, most plants start growing in spring when the weather becomes warmer. They produce flowers during the pleasant spring months and grow fruits during the hot summer months. As summer transitions to autumn, the fruits on plants mature while plants also lose their leaves, with those on trees frequently changing colors first. Finally, during the cold winter months, plants either die or become dormant until spring returns the following year.

For the most part, these changes in plants are activated by differences in the amount of sunlight they receive and the temperature, and botanists have long wanted to know how plants are able to recognize these differences in environmental conditions. Previously, the primary theory botanists subscribed to was that plants simply had an innate ability to recognize when seasonal changes were occurring. Some believed this recognition was based upon changes in the length of a day. During summer, days are long, but as the seasons change and winter comes, days become shorter, which means there is less sunlight during the day. Additionally, less sunlight is associated with lower temperatures, which botanists believed plants were somehow reacting to.

In the twentieth century, botanists gained access to new scientific tools and became able to investigate plants in more detail. They discovered that plants have certain **hormones**, called phytohormones, which help them regulate various metabolic processes in themselves. One type of phytohormone is called an auxin. When environmental conditions are ideal for plants to grow, large amounts of auxins are produced by plants. However, plants can detect when conditions are less than ideal, such as when there is not enough light, there is insufficient precipitation, and there are lower temperatures. In suboptimal conditions such as these, small amounts of auxins are produced. As a result, fewer auxins than normal reach the leaves of plants, resulting in fewer nutrients getting to them as well. This is one of the primary reasons that the leaves of plants change colors, die, and then fall off.

[4]→ Botanists have also determined that many plants have photoreceptors, which enable them to detect light. The types of photoreceptors that plants have tend to vary. Some can detect blue light whereas others can determine the amount of light that plants are exposed to. When seasons are changing, the photoreceptors in plants all work in conjunction to help them determine how to react. There is also a hypothetical **enzyme** called florigen that may cause plants to flower during spring and other months. Botanists believe that temperature and light conditions activate florigen, thereby enabling plants to blossom. Florigen's existence has not been verified yet, which means botanists must continue their research to determine precisely how plants recognize seasonal changes.

≋ **Glossary**
hormone: a compound that controls the growth and differentiation of plant tissue
enzyme: a protein that can induce chemical changes in organic substances

1   In paragraph 1, the author's description of seasonal changes mentions which of the following?

    (A) The time of the year when most plants' leaves fall off

    (B) The average temperature that lets plants produce flowers

    (C) The ideal type of weather for plants to grow quickly

    (D) The length of time that some plants can remain dormant

2   Which of the sentences below best expresses the essential information in the highlighted sentence in the passage? *Incorrect* answer choices change the meaning in important ways or leave out essential information.

    (A) Scientists have already determined the process through which plants recognize various changes in sunlight and temperature that they are exposed to.

    (B) Botanists believe that most changes in plants are caused by differences in the amount of sunlight received and the average temperature as well.

    (C) Environmental conditions such as exposure to sunlight and changes in temperatures are something botanists are studying with regard to their effects on plants.

    (D) Scientists have wanted to know how plants notice differences in temperature and the amount of sunlight they receive, which often activates changes in plants.

3   The word "suboptimal" in the passage is closest in meaning to

    (A) average

    (B) underestimated

    (C) extensive

    (D) poor

4   In paragraph 4, the author uses "florigen" as an example of

    (A) an enzyme that helps plants use light that they are exposed to

    (B) something that botanists used to believe in but presently no longer do

    (C) a substance that might exist and have an effect on plants

    (D) a photoreceptor that allows plants to see various colors

Pit Vipers

Snakes are among the most feared yet most fascinating of all of the members of the animal kingdom. There are many species of snakes, and virtually all are carnivorous. Some attack and disable their prey with venom while others incapacitate them by using <u>constriction</u>. Many others use bites to disable and kill their victims. Yet, as these animals lack external ears, people have long wondered how snakes sense their prey as well as approaching danger. Scientists now know that the pit viper species accomplishes this by using a unique set of sense organs in its head, which allow it to hunt, attack, and track its prey.

2→ The pit viper belongs to the *viperidae* family, which is distinguished by the long fangs that are hinged and fold back in its mouth when closed. Pit vipers comprise one of two main branches of *viperidae*, and they are common throughout the Americas and parts of Europe and Asia yet do not dwell in Africa or Australia. Pit vipers typically give live birth to their young, with the exception of the Central and South American bushmaster, which lays eggs. The pit viper family includes rattlesnakes, water moccasins, copperheads, horned desert vipers, and lance head snakes, to name but a few of the 151 members of that species.

3→ All pit vipers have a set of organs found between their eyes and nostrils called pits. The pit organ is located deep in the head and contains a system of highly sensitive nerve endings. It allows a snake to sense changes in temperature as well as to sense cool and hot areas, much like an electronic thermal imaging system. There is some evidence that the organ also allows vipers accurately to judge the distance to their prey. Since most snakes are <u>nocturnal</u> and therefore hunt at night, this ability gives pit vipers a tremendous advantage. The air is cooler at night, which makes body heat emanating from animals stand out even more.

1 Once a pit viper detects the presence of prey, it will track the animal and attack. **2** Many vipers are venomous, so they will use venom when biting their prey. **3** After a successful bite, the prey will attempt to escape; however, the viper will follow it until the animal succumbs to the venom. **4** Then, the pit viper is free to feast upon the freshly killed animal.

≋ *Glossary*
constriction: the act of squeezing or compressing something very tightly
nocturnal: active or awake at night

1 In paragraph 2, all of the following questions are answered EXCEPT:

   Ⓐ Why do most pit vipers give live birth instead of laying eggs?

   Ⓑ Where on the Earth can pit vipers often be found living?

   Ⓒ What are the names of some different types of pit vipers?

   Ⓓ What are the features of the fangs of members of the viper family?

Question Type

[Negative Factual Question]

2 In paragraph 3, the author implies that pit vipers' pit organs

   Ⓐ were the source of inspiration for electronic thermal imaging systems

   Ⓑ are the reason why pit vipers only hunt at night

   Ⓒ act in a manner similar to a piece of modern technology

   Ⓓ make them the most feared of all nocturnal predators

[Inference Question]

3 Look at the four squares [■] that indicate where the following sentence could be added to the passage.

However, should the potential prey turn out to be too large or dangerous, the snake will take evasive action and search for another victim.

Where would the sentence best fit?

[Insert Text Question]

4 ***Directions:*** Select the appropriate statements from the answer choices and match them to the specific aspect of pit vipers to which they relate. TWO of the answer choices will NOT be used. ***This question is worth 3 points.***

[Fill in a Table Question]

Answer Choices	PIT VIPERS
① Typically pursue their prey when the sun is not shining	**Characteristics**
② Use their pit organs to sense the presence of possible victims	•
③ Often use constriction methods to disable their prey	•
④ Have two long fangs which are located in the back of their mouths	**Hunting Methods**
⑤ Inject venom into their prey in order to incapacitate it	•
⑥ With one exception, give birth to live animals instead of laying eggs	•
⑦ Frequently attack prey that is much larger than they are	•

Sea Animal Defenses

1➜ All animals, no matter how big or small they may be, are in danger of being attacked by predators in any habitat. To protect themselves, many animals have developed methods of defense. Some include the ability to flee quickly, the use of warning signals when a predator approaches, the ability to blend into the background, the use of methods to disorient an attacker, and the ability to fight back with sharp claws, teeth, and poison. Sea creatures use all of these methods—with varying degrees of success—in their ongoing struggles to survive in the ocean depths.

Blending into the background is a common camouflaging defense utilized by many sea creatures. Flatfish, for example, look exactly like the ocean floor and can become virtually invisible when hiding in muddy areas. Other creatures, such as the leafy sea dragon, may resemble something that is not part of the food chain. It looks just like a green piece of seaweed, which enables it to remain hidden in plain sight of predators. In addition, its fins move very slowly, propelling the leafy sea dragon slowly along in a manner that mimics a piece of seaweed moving with the ocean currents. The final key to the leafy sea dragon's disguise is its mouth. It has a leaf-like covering and is tube shaped, giving it the appearance of being the stem of a larger piece of seaweed. In many cases, predators swim right by it without even noticing it.

Some sea creatures employ a special discharge in order to trick or **disorient** predators. Both octopus and squid use an inky discharge to elude predators. The ink is stored internally in sacs, and, when they sense danger, it is expelled, usually along with a jet of water. This produces an inky cloud in the water as the octopus or squid simultaneously either hides or swims away from the predator. This cloud has often been compared to a smokescreen used by soldiers or ships to remain hidden in battle. Some species of octopus and squid can use their inky discharge to form a more solid shape, which can fool certain predators into actually attacking the shape instead of the real creature. This again permits the creature time to escape before the predator comes to the realization that it is not attacking its intended target.

4➜ Poison as a method of defense is not particularly common among sea creatures, but a few do use it, often with deadly effect. Many species of jellyfish utilize poison; their long tentacles give extremely painful stings to any creature or person who happens to be unlucky enough to touch them. One particular species of jellyfish that lives off the coast of Australia causes stings so painful that humans who have been stung typically pass out from the pain or in some cases suffer fatal injuries. The stonefish is another sea creature that employs poison. It blends into the background and camouflages itself to look like a

Note

Most animals have a variety of defenses that they can employ and are thus not limited to one form of defense against predators.

Not all sea creatures that use camouflage are prey animals. Some, in fact, are predators. Dolphins and sharks, among many other sea creatures, have a bluish-gray color, which lets them blend in with the water when light seeps through. This makes it easier for them to approach their prey without being detected.

Starfish and sea cucumbers are two more sea creatures that can use poison that may result in fatalities. There are also various sea snakes whose bites can be toxic.

stone, but any predator that tries to eat it is in for a surprise due to the needle-like spines on its dorsal fin which contain a lethal **toxin**.

📚 *Glossary*

disorient: to confuse

toxin: a poison

1 According to paragraph 1, which of the following is true of sea creatures' defense methods?
  (A) The most common of them is the ability to respond violently to attacks.
  (B) The different methods used are not all equally effective.
  (C) Being able to flee rapidly often ensures an animal will survive an attack.
  (D) All animals have some form of defense mechanism to protect themselves.

2 The word "It" in the passage refers to
  (A) Flatfish
  (B) The leafy sea dragon
  (C) The food chain
  (D) A green piece of seaweed

3 The word "elude" in the passage is closest in meaning to
  (A) resist
  (B) avoid
  (C) escape
  (D) assault

4 According to paragraph 4, which of the following is NOT true of poisonous defense methods?
  (A) They may sometimes be strong enough to kill humans.
  (B) They are used by jellyfish as well as stonefish.
  (C) They may be used in conjunction with other defense mechanisms.
  (D) They are one of the most common defense methods for sea creatures.

5   ***Directions:*** Select the appropriate sentences from the answer choices and match them to the defense method to which they relate. TWO of the answer choices will NOT be used. ***This question is worth 3 points.***

Answer Choices	DEFENSE METHOD
① This is a method that is frequently used by jellyfish.	**Inky Discharge**
② Creatures may resemble something not considered food by others.	•
③ This gives the attacked creature time to escape predators.	•
④ The leafy sea dragon uses this to appear to be a plant.	**Camouflage**
⑤ Bottom-dwelling creatures can hide themselves in the mud this way.	•
⑥ Squid may resort to this kind of defense method.	•
⑦ This method may be used to cause physical harm to attackers.	•

Summarizing ▷ Complete the summary by filling in the blanks.

Most sea dwellers employ various _____ to protect themselves from predators. Using _____ as concealment is one such method. Flatfish may hide in the mud to disguise themselves while _____ appears to be a piece of seaweed floating in the water. Squid and octopus expel an ink-like substance to cloud the water where they are. This enables them to _____ from their attackers. Another common method of defense is poison. _____ are two such sea creatures that make use of it. In some cases, their poison may be lethal to their attackers.

Natural Selection

Within certain species of animals, there are noticeable differences, which give some of them an advantage over others, and which enable them to survive, reproduce, and pass on their genes to the next generation. This process is called natural selection. By having characteristics that allow them to survive, these animals outlive other members of their species and eventually may even become the dominant or only kind of a particular species. Some of these traits include being able to avoid predators, to find and consume certain food sources, and to reproduce more frequently with a greater chance for the offspring to survive. Whatever the case, this process may take thousands of generations, but, eventually, the fittest survive while the weaker members of a species disappear.

2➡ The principles of natural selection were first espoused by Charles Darwin in his book *On the Origin of Species* in 1859. Darwin tinkered with his notion for more than twenty years before suddenly publishing his work upon learning that a colleague working in Asia had a similar theory. Much of the basis for Darwin's theories came from his explorations while on a British naval expedition in his youth. In particular, the expedition's visit to the Galapagos Islands near South America gave Darwin the insights that led him to come up with the theory of natural selection.

On the Galapagos, Darwin noticed there were thirteen different species of finches, which are a type of bird. Each subspecies had a different-shaped **beak**, which was uniquely useful for the type of food each bird consumed. **1** Darwin found these birds on different islands in the Galapagos and surmised that all of them had come from the same species of finch in the distant past. **2** The finches' experiences on the various islands, which all provided different food sources, caused the beaks of successive generations to change their shapes and functions to suit each island's individual food source. **3** Darwin claimed that the finches whose beaks were well adapted thrived on each island while those with ill-serving beaks slowly died off. **4**

While roundly challenged and opposed during his lifetime, Darwin's theories are generally accepted today. Modern methods of observation and research into the behavior of animals have constantly proven that the strongest members of a species survive and pass on their genes to the next generation.

5➡ Not every change in animals happens naturally though. In some cases, humans may interfere with and even prompt the evolution of certain animals. For example, English settlers introduced rabbits to Australia in the mid-nineteenth century. They had no natural enemies, and, being true to their nature,

Note

Charles Darwin lived from 1809 to 1882. The publication of his famous book resulted in a controversy which continues to this day as many people still disagree with evolution. Even so, Darwin's contributions to the field of science have made him one of the most important scientists in history.

Darwin visited the Galapagos while on the *HMS Beagle*, a British ship which was on a five-year voyage. While in the Galapagos, Darwin also noticed how various tortoises and iguanas had evolved depending on factors such as which island they lived on.

Many animals have adapted to humans by evolving to live alongside and even within human settlements. It is common now for many animals to find their food sources from humans. Raccoons, for instance, often live in suburbs, where they make meals from people's garbage.

bred at prodigious rates. By the mid-twentieth century, Australian officials estimated there were around 300 million rabbits in Australia. They were eating tens of thousands of acres of vegetation and leaving deserts in their path. After much trial and error, the Australians introduced a poison that killed 99.99% of the rabbits. Unfortunately, the remaining 0.01% survived because they were immune to the poison. Their offspring, all with the same immunity, have steadily been breeding, so Australia is once again overpopulated with rabbits. While this is an extreme example of natural selection at work, it still shows how changes may take place to make some members stronger, faster, and tougher and to enable them and their offspring to survive.

📖 *Glossary*

beak: the bill of a bird; the hard part of a bird's mouth that extends from its body

breed: to reproduce; to create offspring

1 Which of the sentences below best expresses the essential information in the highlighted sentence in the passage? *Incorrect* answer choices change the meaning in important ways or leave out essential information.

Ⓐ All animals need to have some kind of characteristic that lets them dominate other species.

Ⓑ By outliving other animals, some characteristics in long-lived creatures will get passed on to others.

Ⓒ The traits of some animals enable them to dominate other members of their own species.

Ⓓ The dominant members of a species have a peculiar trait in that they live longer than other species.

2 Which of the following can be inferred from paragraph 2 about natural selection?

Ⓐ It never would have been proposed if *On the Origin of Species* had not been published.

Ⓑ The place on the Earth where it mostly takes place is the Galapagos Islands.

Ⓒ It had not actually occurred in nature until the nineteenth century.

Ⓓ Its existence in nature was visible to people other than Charles Darwin.

3 The author discusses "rabbits" in paragraph 5 in order to

Ⓐ show how natural selection can be affected by unnatural causes

Ⓑ explain why rabbits have devastated much of the land in Australia

Ⓒ mention how many rabbits currently live in Australia

Ⓓ note the difficulty involved in eliminating a species of animal

4 Look at the four squares [■] that indicate where the following sentence could be added to the passage.

This case proved to be one of the more persuasive arguments within the pages of *On the Origin of Species*.

Where would the sentence best fit?

5   **Directions:** An introductory sentence for a brief summary of the passage is provided below. Complete the summary by selecting the THREE answer choices that express the most important ideas of the passage. Some sentences do not belong because they express ideas that are not presented in the passage or are minor ideas in the passage. **This question is worth 2 points.**

Natural selection, as described in the works of Charles Darwin, occurs when certain members of a species acquire traits that allow it to dominate other members of its own species.

-
-
-

Answer Choices

1. Charles Darwin published his famous work *On the Origin of Species* in 1859.

2. The process of natural selection is slow and may take thousands of generations to manifest itself.

3. The Australians had trouble eliminating rabbits because many of them were immune to the poison they used.

4. The finches living on different islands in the Galapagos were a prime example of how the fittest members of a species survive.

5. At the same time that Darwin was doing his research, another individual was devising similar theories in Asia.

6. There are many desirable traits that may be passed on to the surviving members of a species.

Summarizing ▷ Complete the summary by filling in the blanks.

Over time, individual members of some species change, and, if the changes are beneficial, they and their offspring tend to survive while other members of the species die out. This is _____ . In 1859, Charles Darwin published *On the Origin of Species*, a work on this phenomenon, which was inspired by his observations on _____ . Darwin noticed how _____ on different islands there had developed _____ appropriate for the food they ate. However, humans may also induce natural selection. In Australia, rabbits overtaking the country were poisoned almost to eradication. Yet those that proved immune to the poison _____ exponentially, and Australia once again finds itself overpopulated by rabbits.

Trout

One of the most sought-after freshwater fish by anglers is the trout. The many varieties of trout are both delicious when eaten and also put up a tremendous fight when caught by **anglers**. Trout typically live in the waters of North America, Europe, and northern Asia; however, some species are also found in New Zealand and Australia. They are so popular that in some areas they are raised on fish farms and then released into river systems and lakes in order to be caught by sport fishermen. Unfortunately, these actions may be unwittingly contributing to the demise of some trout species.

Ichthyologists have cataloged three genera of trout comprising a total of twenty species. They may reside in virtually any body of freshwater but usually prefer cooler waters. **1** Individual species have various color patterns which suit their environments, thus enabling them to blend into the background. **2** Most trout weigh only a few pounds, and they are almost always less than a foot long. **3** However, sport fishermen have occasionally caught massive trout, with the largest on record being a lake trout that weighed over sixty-five pounds. **4** Trout consume other fish, flies, and aquatic insects and will at times eat plankton.

3→ Trout are in danger of losing many of their habitats. One of the major reasons for this in North America is acid rain, which is caused by pollution that introduces too many acidic compounds to the air, which then fall as rain. This pollution gets into the water system, making large numbers of rivers and lakes uninhabitable for many fish species, including trout. Another problem is the overuse of water by humans, which has led to decreasing water levels. A third issue is the erosion of soil caused by over-logging near lakes and rivers. When lumber companies cut down vast forests of trees, the soil becomes vulnerable to erosion. It is then washed away by rainwater only to end up in rivers and lakes, where it disrupts the delicate balance of life there.

4→ Another issue concerning trout is people's desire to breed and catch them. This is something of a double-edged sword. Although fish farms help maintain stocks of trout in lakes and rivers, they do so primarily for the benefit of sport fishermen to catch them. When a fish farm intends to stock a waterway, it typically makes an announcement so that anglers can be aware of which place will soon have abundant fish. However, a more serious issue surrounds fish farming: Wild trout are captured in great numbers by fish farms, and their eggs are taken to be hatched in relative safety until the fish are mature enough to be released into the wild. Unfortunately, this method has degraded stocks of wild trout. Furthermore, farm-raised trout lack the ability to survive as successfully as wild fish. When wild trout breed with fish-farm-raised trout in the wild, they dilute the gene pool, thereby making their offspring more vulnerable to predators,

Note

Of the many species of trout, one of the most easily identifiable is the rainbow trout, which gets its name from the multicolored stripe running down its side. Brown trout and brook trout are two more trout that are commonly fished for by anglers.

Nowadays, acid rain is less of a problem in developed countries than it was in the past due to strict environmental regulations. But in the northeast United States, particularly in New York, there are still some lakes and ponds with no life in them because of acid rain.

Fish farming is commonly used to increase the food supply in countries. The fish raised in them can be either freshwater or saltwater fish. While controversial, fish farms have managed to increase the numbers of some species of fish.

which is a contributing factor in the ongoing demise of the species.

📖 *Glossary*

angler: a fisherman

ichthyologist: a person who studies fish

---

1   The word "unwittingly" in the passage is closest in meaning to

    Ⓐ undeservingly

    Ⓑ accidentally

    Ⓒ extraordinarily

    Ⓓ possibly

2   According to paragraph 3, trout may lose some of their habitats because

    Ⓐ cutting down trees has removed shade from waterways

    Ⓑ there are not enough nutrients in a lot of places where trout live

    Ⓒ pollution has made it impossible for fish to live in some area

    Ⓓ heavy farming has made water levels low in places

3   In paragraph 4, the author implies that fish farms

    Ⓐ make a great deal of money from stocking waterways

    Ⓑ do not actually breed trout that are in captivity

    Ⓒ are causing the overall number of trout to decrease

    Ⓓ are frequently run by anglers interested in fishing for them

4   Look at the four squares [■] that indicate where the following sentence could be added to the passage.

This explains why many fishermen travel to northern regions or visit mountain streams when fishing for trout.

Where would the sentence best fit?

5   *Directions:* An introductory sentence for a brief summary of the passage is provided below. Complete the summary by selecting the THREE answer choices that express the most important ideas of the passage. Some sentences do not belong because they express ideas that are not presented in the passage or are minor ideas in the passage. ***This question is worth 2 points.***

There are many species of trout found all around the world, yet they are in some danger because of the frequency of fish farming that is occurring these days.

+--+
| • |
| |
| • |
| |
| • |
+--+

Answer Choices

1. Several species of trout are endangered due to the actions of fish farms, which do not always take good care of the trout.

2. Many fishermen enjoy the fight that trout put up when they are hooked on a fishing line, so they are a popular game fish.

3. Trout are relatively small fish, yet they can grow to weigh impressive amounts in some cases.

4. Trout live in the cool waters of at least four of the world's continents.

5. Human activities such as overlogging and the overuse of water are endangering the habitats of trout in many places.

6. Trout raised in captivity lack survival skills so are more likely to be eaten by predators when released in the wild.

Summarizing ▷ Complete the summary by filling in the blanks.

Trout are a popular fish with _____. There are many species of these freshwater fish, which prefer cool waters. They are typically a foot long and weigh a few pounds, but some may grow to bigger sizes. Unfortunately, _____ is eliminating some of their habitats by making certain waterways unlivable. Water overuse by humans and _____ of soil into waterways is making other places unlivable as well. Finally, trout are so popular that _____ raise them and later release them into public waters. However, farm-raised trout have trouble surviving on their own and produce offspring more _____ predators when they mate in the wild.

Mutualism

Note

[1]→ Mutualism occurs when two biological **entities** derive a common benefit from each other's actions. The advantage may or may not be vital to the entities' survival, yet mutualism typically increases the odds of a species surviving. There are a plethora of examples of mutualism in the plant and animal kingdoms. The interaction of bees and plants is one example. Bees extract nectar from plants' flowers while simultaneously picking up pollen from plants and spreading it to other areas. Most instances of mutualism are of that nature as both species achieve a benefit of equal value. In some cases, however, the benefit may be more one-sided, with one side deriving the majority of the benefit.

There are two main types of mutualism: obligatory and facultative. Obligatory mutualism exists when two species, like the bees and flowers, are in such close cooperation that one cannot exist without the other. Facultative mutualism is the opposite; each species can exist on its own, but they would both incur some disadvantage from the severing of the mutual relationship. In some cases, only one species may be in an obligatory relationship—it is simply unable to survive on its own—while the second could survive without the first. A mutual relationship may be symbiotic, meaning that two or more species live in a close, but not necessarily beneficial, association. In these cases, the species only connect when they need something.

Among insects, ants have a wide variety of mutual relationships with plants and other insects. Ants act as bodyguards for aphids and protect them from attacking predators like beetles. In return, the aphids allow the ants to suck the sweet honeydew nectar they produce as a byproduct of their eating sap from plants. Another mutual relationship involving ants occurs with a tropical shrub called the bull's horn acacia. **1** The ants live within hollow thorns on the plant. **2** In return, they trim away any **encroaching** plants that may cover the acacia with shade and prevent it from getting enough sunlight. **3** Furthermore, the ants go on the warpath for their acacia plant when insects or large herbivores appear and attempt to graze on its leaves. **4**

[4]→ Among plants, one of the most common forms of mutualism exists between nitrogen-producing plants and bacteria. Soil rich in nitrogen is superior for growing crops. Over thousands of years of trial and error, farmers discovered that plants such as peas, beans, clover, and alfalfa can revitalize nitrogen-poor soil. They do this through a mutual interaction with bacteria in the soil. The bacteria live in the plant and, in return, help the plant convert atmospheric nitrogen into forms of nitrogen such as various nitrates that plants need for growth. The bacteria accomplish this by causing a chemical reaction in the roots. The plant's roots respond to a chemical signal from the bacteria, and the roots then secrete chemicals that attract the bacteria, which enter the roots.

The majority of plants and animals make use of mutualism. Most are relationships that involve the sharing of resources. Pollination, on the other hand, involves one species (bees or other insects) providing a service for another while receiving a resource (nectar) from the plants that it pollinates.

Cecropia ants that live in rainforests actively protect cecropia trees. The ants live in the trees, which provide them with shelter and glucose. In return, the ants protect the trees from other animals, such as insects and herbivores, and they eliminate other plants that may try to grow on the trees.

Once in the plant, the bacteria initiate a reaction that converts atmospheric nitrogen to nitrates. This relationship between the bacteria and the plant is facultative as both are able to survive without the other.

≋ Glossary
entity: a creature; a body
encroaching: invading; intruding

---

1   According to paragraph 1, which of the following is NOT true of mutualism?

(A) It is quite a common occurrence among animals and plants.

(B) Many species attain equal benefits when engaging in mutualism.

(C) Some animals would not be able to survive without mutualism.

(D) Bees feeding on pollen from plants is an example of mutualism.

2   Which of the sentences below best expresses the essential information in the highlighted sentence in the passage? *Incorrect* answer choices change the meaning in important ways or leave out essential information.

(A) In an obligatory relationship, neither one of the species could remain alive without the other.

(B) Some species would die without their mutual relationships while their partner would still live.

(C) In some instances of mutualism, both species are able to be successful without the presence of the other.

(D) An obligatory relationship means that both species must stay with each other to survive.

3   According to paragraph 4, nitrogen-poor soil may become revitalized because

(A) farmers wait several months before harvesting certain crops

(B) the roots of some plants can convert bacteria into nitrates

(C) bacteria in some plants help create nitrates in the ground

(D) nitrates in the soil are absorbed by bacteria in the plants

4   Look at the four squares [■] that indicate where the following sentence could be added to the passage.

This, naturally, permits the acacia to grow much larger than would be possible if no ants lived in it.

Where would the sentence best fit?

5 *Directions:* Select the appropriate sentences from the answer choices and match them to the form of mutualism to which they relate. TWO of the answer choices will NOT be used. ***This question is worth 3 points.***

Answer Choices

① Without working together, one of the species would not continue living.

② Farmers plant certain vegetables in order to make their soil more productive.

③ This occurs when bacteria help introduce nitrates into plants.

④ Ants live in a wide variety of habitats that they have adapted to.

⑤ Bees and flowers have a relationship of this type.

⑥ Neither one of the species needs the other in order to continue living.

⑦ The breakup in the relationship between two species would disadvantage both of them.

FORM OF MUTUALISM

Facultative
-
-
-

Obligatory
-
-

Summarizing ▶ Complete the summary by filling in the blanks.

Two or more biological entities _____ often act together to create mutually beneficial results. This is known as mutualism. Most instances involve _____ to the partners, but that does not always happen. There are two kinds of mutualism: _____ . Obligatory mutualism means that one partner _____ without the other. This is the case for bees and plants. Bees gain nectar from plants while pollinating them. Facultative mutualism occurs when each partner can survive without the other. Ants and aphids and ants and acacia trees have facultative relationships. _____ and bacteria do as well. In every case, both partners benefit from the relationship.

Body Temperature in Animals

All living creatures are influenced by the external temperatures of their environment. The **ambient** air temperature can cause an animal's body temperature to fluctuate. The way an animal regulates its body temperature plays a vital role in its ability to survive in extreme environments as well as in its lifestyle and habitat. For the most part, animals are warm blooded or cold blooded. The vast majority of mammals and birds are warm blooded while reptiles, fish, insects, and amphibians are cold blooded. Each type of animal employs various methods to control its body temperature. However, in general, warm-blooded animals can maintain a constant internal temperature no matter what environment they are in while cold-blooded animals' body temperatures are related to the temperature of their external environment. These facts play a large role in determining where these animals live and what their lifestyles are.

²➜ Warm-blooded animals control their internal body temperature through their metabolism. This means they convert food into energy, which is then used to keep their bodies at a more-or-less constant temperature. For example, humans maintain a normal temperature of around ninety-seven degrees Fahrenheit. When the weather is too hot, warm-blooded animals sweat to cool their bodies. When the weather is too cold, they may consume more food to burn more energy or utilize shivering to increase muscle activity, which produces more heat. Some warm-blooded animals maintain constant high metabolic rates so that they can sustain their body temperatures in all environments. Additionally, warm-blooded creatures dwelling in very cold environments tend to have greater external protection. This may manifest itself as fur, hair, and feathers. Humans also wear clothing for protection; the colder the temperature, the thicker the clothing.

Cold-blooded creatures are directly affected by the ambient air temperature. When it is too hot or cold, they depend on various methods to maintain their body temperature. For example, reptiles often lie in direct sunlight when the temperature is cool. When it gets too hot, they scurry for the shade of a tree or rock or burrow underground. Some cold-blooded animals migrate to warmer climates when winter comes or go into hibernation for several months. Even some warm-blooded creatures, such as bears, hibernate in extremely cold conditions. Cold-blooded creatures cannot stay in a cold environment for too long, though, since they become **sluggish** and will eventually perish without heat to warm themselves.

⁴➜ There are both advantages and disadvantages to being warm or cold blooded. The most obvious advantage for warm-blooded creatures is that they can live in practically any environment. That does not, however, mean they can always survive in harsh environments. In extreme heat, warm-blooded creatures will sweat until they become dehydrated and will expire if they fail to drink a sufficient amount of water. In a desert, this can become a major problem, which is why most desert creatures are cold blooded. In addition, the need to consume food to sustain body temperature is a disadvantage for warm-blooded creatures. **1** Burning food and shivering to maintain body temperature require tremendous amounts of energy. **2** If there is not a large food supply, warm-blooded creatures will die in extremely cold environments. **3** Cold-blooded creatures, however, can survive on less food and endure longer periods of time without eating. **4** Their metabolism is slower than that of warm-blooded creatures since they do not depend on burning energy to maintain their body temperature.

⁵➜ Warm-blooded animals can hunt and defend themselves in a wide variety of environments whereas

cold-blooded creatures are sluggish and more easily attacked in a cold environment. However, warm-blooded creatures pay a price for these advantages. They are more prone to be hosts for bacteria and viruses, which need warmer temperatures to survive. Almost all human diseases originally started as either bacteria or a virus in warm-blooded birds or mammals. On the other hand, being hosts to these microorganisms simultaneously helps warm-blooded creatures build up immunities to them.

In the end, each type of creature has both positive and negative aspects to the way it maintains its body temperature. While being warm-blooded provides animals with the ability to operate in many environments, the need for a constant food supply partially negates this advantage. For cold-blooded creatures, the need to eat less food is certainly an advantage, but the limits on their habitats and ability to operate in all environments are a clear disadvantage.

≋ **Glossary**
ambient: concerning the immediate or surrounding area or environment
sluggish: slow-moving or lacking energy to move

---

1 Which of the sentences below best expresses the essential information in the highlighted sentence in the passage? *Incorrect* answer choices change the meaning in important ways or leave out essential information.

   Ⓐ Cold-blooded animals' temperatures may change depending on where they are, yet the body temperatures of warm-blooded animals typically remain the same.

   Ⓑ Warm-blooded animals are able to alter their body temperatures to suit their environment while cold-blooded animals cannot do so.

   Ⓒ The body temperatures of cold-blooded animals change according to the environment that they are in, and the same is true for warm-blooded creatures as well.

   Ⓓ Without being able to regulate their body temperatures like warm-blooded animals can, cold-blooded animals have to be conscious of their external environment.

2 The author discusses "shivering" in paragraph 2 in order to

   Ⓐ give an example of an activity that cold-blooded animals cannot do

   Ⓑ explain how warm-blooded animals may warm themselves in the absence of food

   Ⓒ describe a common muscle activity that all kinds of animals may engage in

   Ⓓ show how warm-blooded animals can maintain high metabolic rates in their bodies

3 In paragraph 2, the author implies that humans

   Ⓐ lack enough natural external protection to survive in extreme climates

   Ⓑ are similar to cold-blooded animals in how they are affected by heat

   Ⓒ prefer to live in weather where the outside temperature is near 100 degrees

   Ⓓ are warm-blooded animals yet cannot maintain constant body temperatures

4 The author's description of warm-blooded animals in paragraph 2 mentions all of the following EXCEPT:

    Ⓐ The way that they cool off their bodies in hot weather

    Ⓑ The manner in which they are able to keep the same body temperature

    Ⓒ Various types of external protection they have for cold environments

    Ⓓ The amount of food they must eat to stay warm on a daily basis

5 The word "scurry" in the passage is closest in meaning to

    Ⓐ meander

    Ⓑ sidle

    Ⓒ hurry

    Ⓓ wander

6 The word "expire" in the passage is closest in meaning to

    Ⓐ perish

    Ⓑ weaken

    Ⓒ faint

    Ⓓ tire

7 According to paragraph 4, which of the following is true of cold-blooded animals?

    Ⓐ They are able to survive in virtually any climate on the planet.

    Ⓑ The majority of them prefer to live in desert climates.

    Ⓒ They have been known to suffer from problems like dehydration.

    Ⓓ They require the consumption of less food than warm-blooded animals.

8 According to paragraph 5, warm-blooded creatures are more susceptible to viruses because

    Ⓐ their internal body temperatures are well suited to them

    Ⓑ the fluids in their bodies are accommodating hosts

    Ⓒ most viruses can spread easily from birds to mammals

    Ⓓ they can reproduce more easily in animals with high metabolic rates

9 Look at the four squares [■] that indicate where the following sentence could be added to the passage.

Some snakes, for instance, can go for several weeks or even months without feeding a single time.

Where would the sentence best fit?

Click on a square [■] to add the sentence to the passage.

10 **Directions:** Select the appropriate statements from the answer choices and match them to the type of animal to which they relate. TWO of the answer choices will NOT be used. ***This question is worth 3 points.***

Drag your answer choices to the spaces where they belong.
To remove an answer choice, click on it. To review the passage, click on **View Text.**

Answer Choices

① Tend to be aggressive and are primarily predatory animals

② Have trouble reacting quickly when in cold environments

③ Have a limited capacity for thought and rely mostly on instinct

④ Require large amounts of food to create energy for themselves

⑤ Are typically reptiles and insects

⑥ Are comfortable living in a wide range of different environments

⑦ Have external coverings to protect them from the cold

TYPE OF ANIMAL

Cold-Blooded Animals
-
-

Warm-Blooded Animals
-
-
-

Animal Cycles

¹→ All animals operate on cycles that control their actions. Experts use the term circadian cycle to describe the daily pattern of animals while the term circannian cycle relates to the yearly patterns of animals. These patterns are related to an animal's sleeping and feeding times and, in some animals, their hunting, breeding, hibernating, and migration times. Many of these patterns are influenced by the two fundamental necessities of life: the need for rest and a food source. Others are determined by the animals' environments as well as by the time of their periodic hibernation or migration. Finally, many animals are driven by an instinctual need to reproduce and follow a specific cycle for this purpose.

²→ Circadian rhythms are related to daily activities, which, for humans, are based on the twenty-four-hour clock people developed for the purpose of timekeeping. **1** Animals have internal clocks based on the rising and setting of the sun. **2** Most animals are either nocturnal or **diurnal**. **3** Nocturnal animals are awake during times of darkness and do their hunting, gathering, and feeding at night. **4** Nocturnal animal behavior is typically determined according to the availability of food supplies at night as well as the presence—or absence—of predators. Many nocturnal animals have developed heightened senses, such as night vision and acute hearing, to adapt to the night environment. Owls are a perfect example. They hunt at night, looking for small animals such as mice, which their superior sight enables them to locate even in the inky darkness. Diurnal animals are the opposite as they actively feed during daylight hours and fall asleep at night.

³→ Circannian cycles are patterns animals follow on a yearly basis. One driving need of all animals is to produce offspring which will carry on their genes. Some creatures have a scheduled reproductive cycle and breed only at certain times during the year. Experts call this a mating season. Alligators, for example, reproduce in the spring and early summer, laying their eggs in muddy nests they build in swamps. The spadefoot toad of the southwestern United States only reproduces during the summer rainy season when thunderstorms flood its desert habitat. Most mammals in northern lands bear young in the spring, thereby allowing their offspring time to grow before the winter cold arrives. How animals know when it is time to mate is difficult to understand. Although little is known at this point, there may be a biological factor, such as the secretion of a hormone when there are greater or lesser amounts of sunlight or changes in the temperature involved. Additionally, some animals only mate once a year, others mate two or three times annually, and a few, such as the rabbit, mate at any time.

⁴→ Other circannian patterns are related to hibernation and migration. Many cold-blooded creatures retreat underground when colder temperatures arrive. Some animals sleep for long periods during winter to use less energy. Prior to winter, when fall arrives, they begin feeding at prodigious rates and try to gain as much fat as possible so that they can survive the coming weather. The migration patterns of animals are another type of circannian pattern. The annual migration of birds is a common sight in northern lands. The birds sense the advent of winter and colder temperatures. How they do this is a matter of conjecture. Perhaps it is the angle of the sun on the horizon, the increasing cold, or the falling of leaves from trees, or maybe it is merely an instinctive urge that has been in them for generations.

⁵→ These circannian patterns can be upset because of changes in the environment. Rising temperatures in some northern areas pose one such problem. Animals that migrate or hibernate are

having their cycles disrupted by increasing temperatures. One example is the Arctic caribou, or reindeer. Herds always cross over from Arctic islands to the Canadian mainland in the spring, when the ice sheets are still thick. In recent years, however, the ice has not been thick enough, and many caribou have fallen through the ice and drowned. Despite this, the herds keep coming as their instinct to follow this migration pattern is stronger than their need to avoid death.

≋ *Glossary*
diurnal: active during the day; relating to the day
herd: a large group of land animals, such as cows, deer, or zebras

---

1   In paragraph 1, the author implies that animals
   Ⓐ have no control over their need to produce young
   Ⓑ are able to change their circadian rhythms
   Ⓒ migrate to other areas so that they may hunt for food
   Ⓓ do not get enough sleep when their circannian cycle is disrupted

2   In paragraph 2, the author uses "Owls" as an example of
   Ⓐ a species of animal that prefers to hunt mice
   Ⓑ an animal whose abilities have adapted to the night
   Ⓒ a kind of animal that has better hearing than most others
   Ⓓ an example of an animal that engages in diurnal activities

3   According to paragraph 2, which of the following is true of circadian rhythms?
   Ⓐ They always follow a twenty-four-hour-a-day pattern in humans.
   Ⓑ They help determine whether an animal is nocturnal or diurnal.
   Ⓒ They improve certain senses in nocturnal animals like owls.
   Ⓓ They concern the activities which animals engage in on a daily basis.

4   Which of the sentences below best expresses the essential information in the highlighted sentence in the passage? *Incorrect* answer choices change the meaning in important ways or leave out essential information.
   Ⓐ It is possible that something like the secreting of a hormone when the environment changes accounts for this.
   Ⓑ When the amount of sunlight or temperature changes, a hormone is secreted in some of their bodies.
   Ⓒ Biology plays an important role by prompting the release of hormones in the body due to various external factors.
   Ⓓ Scientists are not sure but believe it may be possible to secrete hormones whenever the amount of sunlight changes.

5 In paragraph 3, the author implies that the spadefoot toad

  (A) lays its eggs in rivers that are created during rainy weather

  (B) can survive by drinking water only during the rainy season

  (C) prefers to live in a climate that is primarily hot and dry

  (D) has nesting habits that are similar to those of the alligator

6 The word "prodigious" in the passage is closest in meaning to

  (A) phenomenal

  (B) rapid

  (C) exclusive

  (D) exorbitant

7 According to paragraph 4, some birds become fat before winter because

  (A) they utilize the fat when they migrate to warmer climates in the south

  (B) they know there is less food to consume during the winter months

  (C) they need to be able to survive the changes in the weather

  (D) they use the fat while they are hibernating for several months

8 According to paragraph 5, Arctic caribou continue to attempt to cross ice sheets because

  (A) they have no concept of what death means

  (B) they are fleeing from pursuing predators

  (C) they are unaware of how temperatures have decreased

  (D) they have an innate urge to cross at that time

9 Look at the four squares [■] that indicate where the following sentence could be added to the passage.

  This is not to say, however, that all people's circadian rhythms operate exactly in conjunction within this artificially created period of time.

  Where would the sentence best fit?

  Click on a square [■] to add the sentence to the passage.

10   ***Directions:*** An introductory sentence for a brief summary of the passage is provided below. Complete the summary by selecting the THREE answer choices that express the most important ideas of the passage. Some sentences do not belong because they express ideas that are not presented in the passage or are minor ideas in the passage. ***This question is worth 2 points.***

> Drag your answer choices to the spaces where they belong.
> To remove an answer choice, click on it. To review the passage, click on **View Text.**

Both circadian rhythms and circannian cycles are important determiners in how animals behave on a daily and a yearly basis.

Answer Choices

1. The owl is an animal that has heightened senses, which enable it to be a proficient night hunter.

2. Some animals' instincts to act a certain way can lead to their deaths because of external factors.

3. During winter, some animals regularly either hibernate for months or migrate to warmer climates.

4. Most animals are either nocturnal or diurnal and base their activities on one of these two habits.

5. Alligators prefer to lay their eggs in swamps, from which they can better protect their nests from marauders.

6. Nocturnal animals are typically better hunters than diurnal ones since they rely upon their instincts more.

1 Termites

Although frequently referred to as "white ants," termites are not actually related to ants. This is interesting in that both share many of the same characteristics. Like ants, termites are social creatures that live in colonies with vast numbers of inhabitants. Termites are also divided into three castes: the reproductive caste, which includes the queen and king, the soldier caste, and the worker caste. Soldiers are responsible for the protection of the colony while workers mainly provide food and work to expand the colony. Given these similarities, it is therefore rather understandable why termites are compared with ants and even occasionally mistaken for them.

2 Hatchetfish and Camouflage

One of the most common defense mechanisms in the animal kingdom is camouflage. Animals use a wide variety of ways to hide themselves from predators. One unique method is used by the deep-sea hatchetfish, which lives in the ocean depths. The hatchetfish uses something called bioluminescence to hide from predators. What it does is create light in its own body. This way, the hatchetfish can blend in with the light seeping down from the surface above. When predators look up toward the surface, they see the light coming from the hatchetfish and assume it is merely sunlight, not prey.

3 Insect Navigation

Insects employ numerous methods to navigate in their environment. Some, such as beetles that crawl on the ground, secrete a chemical substance which they use as a sort of compass to direct them to various places. However, flying insects, such as bees, rely on other navigation methods. Primarily, they use the sun to get from their food sources back to the hive. Despite the fact that the sun constantly changes location, bees and other flying insects navigate by following the sun's movement. This is one reason why bees are diurnal and not nocturnal. As for insects which come out at night, such as moths, they utilize the moon for navigation instead.

4 The Similarities between Birds and Dinosaurs

Some paleontologists have theorized that birds and dinosaurs are related. Essentially, they claim that birds evolved from dinosaurs. One of the strongest pieces of evidence is found in fossils of the Archaeopteryx, a 140-million-year-old animal that was something of a cross between a bird and a dinosaur. Indeed, many believe it was the first bird as evidence shows striking similarities between the two species. For instance, dinosaurs, like birds, frequently made nests where they laid eggs. Some even had feathers as body coverings. Finally, there is speculation that, like birds, dinosaurs were warm-blooded creatures, not cold-blooded animals, as they have long been believed to be.

5 The Rafflesia Flower

One of the most unique flowers is the *Rafflesia arnoldii*. It has the distinction of producing the largest flower in the world. When it blooms, the flower itself can be three feet—or one meter—in diameter and weigh over twenty pounds. The Rafflesia is a parasitic plant that only grows in the jungles of Indonesia and Malaysia. Its fame comes not only from the size of its flower but also from its smell. Called the "corpse flower," the Rafflesia smells like decomposing flesh when it is in bloom. This is a reproductive mechanism as the smell attracts flies, which pollinate the plant and ensure its ability to reproduce.

6 Plants and Pollination

A plant must be pollinated in order to reproduce. Flowers have both male and female parts. The male part, which produces pollen, is called the stamen. The female part is the pistil, and its top is a sticky area known as the stigma. Pollen from the stamen must come into contact with the stigma for the plant to be pollinated. Self-pollination, when a plant pollinates itself, is possible, but plants produced in this manner typically lack vigor. Cross-pollination, however, involves pollen moving from one plant to another. Usually, butterflies, bees, moths, birds, and others pollinate them when they move from plant to plant while feeding on nectar.

7 Wasps and Aggression

During the summer months, individuals may encounter many species of insects outdoors, such as the bee, the hornet, and the wasp, an insect known by its unique buzzing sound. Wasps, like bees and hornets, are some of the most aggressive of the flying insects. One reason for the wasp's aggressive tendencies is its predatory nature, which causes it to display belligerent attitudes even toward animals much bigger than itself. This is especially true when an animal approaches a wasp's nest. It will attack the intruder in an effort to protect the hive, which is one reason why humans typically avoid having wasps' nests near their dwellings.

8 Dinosaurs and Their Diets

Paleontologists have been studying dinosaurs and their fossils for well over a century, but much is still unknown about them. This is particularly true of their diets. For the most part, paleontologists can confidently divide dinosaurs into two groups: herbivores and carnivores. Basically, they can distinguish between the two by examining their fossils. For instance, carnivores are recognizable by their balanced front and back teeth, which enabled them to chew meat efficiently. However, aside from physical evidence, which is limited by the quality and number of fossils, most paleontologists must simply guess as to what exactly the dinosaurs ate.

9 The Differences between Fungi and Plants

Fungi like mushrooms are frequently assumed to be plants. This is a mistake because there are actually several differences between the two. Scientists recognize this and have categorized the two into separate animal kingdoms. For one, fungi lack chlorophyll, which is the substance in plants that gives them their green color. Second, plants rely upon photosynthesis to create energy that helps provide them with nutrition. Fungi do not undergo this process; instead, they rely upon absorption for their nutrients. This also means that while plants require sunlight to grow, fungi do not. In fact, many fungi grow in dark places, which is where mushrooms can often be found.

10 Algae

Algae are various species of plants which grow in the water. There are thousands of species, and scientists have divided them into green, red, and brown algae. Since they live in the water, part of their structure differs from that of land-based plants. The main difference is in their stems. Plants growing on land require strong, rigid stems that can support the entire plant, including its branches, flowers, and fruits. However, since water supports algae, their stems have no need for rigidity; thus the plants undulate back and forth on the water. Furthermore, algae lie flattened on the water as opposed to plants on land, which grow vertically.

Star Performer Topic Files Life Sciences

- The Cambrian explosion
- The habitats of moths
- The various species at the poles and in the tropics
- The waggle dance of bees
- How different species of birds take care of their eggs
- Bird songs
- Plant defenses
- Pinyon pines and pinyon jays
- The homes of migratory birds
- How extinction is a natural part of any ecosystem

absorb
abyss
acid
active
adhere
alga
amphibian
anatomical
anatomy
antenna
arachnid
attack
bacteria
bark
behavior
biological
biologist
biology
bioluminescence
biomass
biome
biosphere
bloom
blossom
bone
botanist
botany
breed
camouflage
carapace
carbohydrate
carbon
carbon dioxide
carnivore
cell
cellulose
characteristic
chlorophyll
chromosome
circadian rhythm
class
classify
classification
claw
climate
cold-blooded
colony
complex
consume
coral
current
defense

develop
development
dinosaur
discharge
distribute
distribution
diversity
dominant
drift
ecological
ecosystem
endangered
environment
enzyme
erode
erosion
escape
extinct
evolution
evolve
fang
feather
fitness
flock
food chain
fossil
fossilize
function
fungus
gene
generate
generation
genetic
genus
germ
germinate
grassland
growth
habitat
hatch
herbivore
hereditary
hibernate
hibernation
hive
hunt
hypothesis
inhabit
inhabitant
insect
instinct
instinctive

interact
interaction
interrelate
invade
invertebrate
lair
larva
leaf
life cycle
littoral
loam
mammal
marine
mechanism
metabolism
metamorphosis
microorganism
migrate
migration
migratory
molt
mutant
mutation
mutate
mutualism
natural selection
nectar
ocean
omnivore
offspring
organ
organism
origin
oxygen
paleontologist
paleontology
passive
petal
petrify
petrification
photosynthesis
physiological
plankton
poison
poisonous
pollen
pollinate
pollination
pollutant
pollution
populate
predator

prey
primate
protein
pupa
rainforest
reaction
rear
recessive
reef
relation
reproduce
reproduction
reptile
reptilian
root
savanna
seasonal
seaweed
seed
soil
speciation
species
stalk
stem
structure
survival
survive
symbiosis
symbiotic
talon
taproot
taxonomy
temperate
theory
tide
tissue
toxic
trait
tropical
trunk
type
variation
venomous
vertebrate
virus
vitamin
warm-blooded
wave
wing
zone
zoology
zoologist

Vocabulary **Review**

Choose the words closest in meaning to the highlighted parts of the sentences.

1 In addition, its fins move very slowly, propelling the leafy sea dragon slowly along in a manner that mimics a piece of seaweed moving with the ocean currents.

- (A) portrays
- (B) imitates
- (C) transforms
- (D) hides

2 Once in the plant, the bacteria initiate a reaction that converts atmospheric nitrogen to nitrates.

- (A) commence
- (B) repeat
- (C) prohibit
- (D) condense

3 Previously, the primary theory botanists subscribed to was that plants simply had an innate ability to recognize when seasonal changes were occurring.

- (A) extensive
- (B) apparent
- (C) inborn
- (D) impressive

4 There is some evidence that the organ also allows vipers accurately to judge the distance to their prey.

- (A) estimate
- (B) travel
- (C) increase
- (D) report

5 Some of these traits include being able to avoid predators, to find and consume certain food sources, and to reproduce more frequently with a greater chance for the offspring to survive.

- (A) progeny
- (B) relatives
- (C) ancestors
- (D) bodies

6 When the weather is too cold, they may consume more food to burn more energy or may utilize shivering to increase muscle activity, which produces more heat.

- (A) flexing
- (B) shifting
- (C) pacing
- (D) trembling

7 They had no natural enemies, and, being true to their nature, bred at prodigious rates.

- (A) respectable
- (B) exponential
- (C) phenomenal
- (D) unexpected

8 Although it takes place in hot, arid regions like deserts, its results are similar.

- (A) remote
- (B) empty
- (C) dry
- (D) humid

9 This pollution gets into the water system, making large numbers of rivers and lakes uninhabitable for many fish species, including trout.

- (A) unlivable
- (B) unpleasant
- (C) undeniable
- (D) unscrupulous

10 Darwin tinkered with his notion for more than twenty years before suddenly publishing his work upon learning that a colleague working in Asia had a similar theory.

- (A) applied
- (B) disregarded
- (C) considered
- (D) fiddled

11 Although little is known at this point, there may be a biological factor, such as the secretion of a hormone when there are greater or lesser amounts of sunlight or changes in the temperature involved.

(A) penetration
(B) compilation
(C) transfusion
(D) emission

12 These various actions by earthworms combine to produce the rich, nutrient-filled soil that is vital to the growth of crops, bushes, and trees.

(A) important
(B) customary
(C) traditional
(D) replenishing

13 Unfortunately, these actions may be unwittingly contributing to the demise of some trout species.

(A) downfall
(B) cloning
(C) migration
(D) devolution

14 Pit vipers comprise one of two main branches of *viperidae*, and they are common throughout the Americas and parts of Europe and Asia yet do not dwell in Africa or Australia.

(A) thrive
(B) migrate
(C) reside
(D) survive

15 Perhaps it is the angle of the sun on the horizon, the increasing cold, or the falling of leaves from trees, or maybe it is merely an instinctive urge that has been in them for generations.

(A) sensation
(B) desire
(C) trait
(D) retort

16 Warm-blooded animals have other advantages in that they can hunt and defend themselves in a wide variety of environments whereas cold-blooded creatures are sluggish and more easily attacked in a cold environment.

(A) lethargic
(B) unintelligent
(C) frozen
(D) transient

17 When it gets too hot, they scurry for the shade of a tree or rock, or they burrow underground.

(A) bury
(B) hide
(C) dig
(D) remain

18 Industrially, there are ongoing efforts to convert it into biofuel, but these remain in the experimental stages.

(A) create
(B) transform
(C) switch
(D) reduce

19 This again permits the creature time to escape before the predator comes to the realization that it is not attacking its intended target.

(A) hunter
(B) mate
(C) objective
(D) competitor

20 The pit organ is located deep in the head and contains a system of highly sensitive nerve endings.

(A) protruding
(B) inflamed
(C) stationary
(D) responsive

Part

B

Chapter 07 Physical Sciences

Physical sciences concentrate on the study of the characteristics, properties, and nature of nonliving things. This covers a wide range of fields, but the primary ones in this realm of study are chemistry, geology, astronomy, physics, and meteorology. Chemistry is the study of the elements, the various compounds that they can create, and the properties of both elements and compounds. Geology is the study of the Earth and everything within it, including rocks and minerals. Astronomy focuses on the study of the stars and other celestial bodies, including the moon and the other planets in the solar system. Physics is the science which examines energy, matter, force, and motion. And meteorology is the study of the weather, its causes, and its effects on the planet. Taken together, the physical sciences examine virtually everything both on and off the planet.

Comets

¹➜ Sometimes in the night sky, an object that is **bulbous** and bright in front and has a long whitish-colored tail appears. This is a comet, an icy body that orbits the sun. As the comet approaches the sun, heat emitted by the star boils the icy materials of the object, so a large head, or coma, is created. Additionally, an extended tail is usually produced when the ice melts. Comets may be small or massive; some are as big as 100,000 miles wide and a million miles long, and one has even recently been recorded with a diameter greater than the sun's. Comets have varying lifespans, and many, such as the famed Halley's Comet, regularly pass by Earth as they complete their orbit of the sun.

The existence of comets has been known since ancient times, but the fact that some are repeat visitors was not realized until the eighteenth century, when British astronomer Edmund Halley correlated different historical reports on one particular comet. Halley's Comet, for instance, visits Earth every seventy-five years and last appeared in 1986. Finding comets can create great excitement among both professional and amateur astronomers alike because they are the only celestial bodies named for their discoverers. Comets can also provide excellent opportunities for photography since some, such as the Hale-Bopp Comet, which was observed for nineteen months during the mid-1990s, remain visible for extensive periods of time.

Comets' orbits often take them far from the sun. It is thought that most of those which cross Earth's path as repeat visitors come from the Kuiper Belt, a region surrounding the solar system that is nearly fifty times farther from the sun than the Earth. Nevertheless, despite the distance, the sun's gravity is still powerful enough to **induce** comets into its orbit. Some astronomers believe more than 70,000 objects—including comets—orbit the sun in the Kuiper Belt.

Other comets may come from a more distant place—the Oort Cloud—than the Kuiper Belt. The Oort Cloud is a vast shell-like area said to **encircle** the solar system. Astronomer Jan Oort hypothesized its existence and declared that it stretches as far as 50,000 times the distance from Earth to the sun. His proposal came about as a way of explaining where comets seen only once must have come from. However, others have claimed that these comets were merely passing through the solar system and had not been captured by the sun's gravity, thus making clear why they were seen but once.

≋ *Glossary*
bulbous: rounded; spherical in shape
encircle: to surround completely; to enclose

1   In paragraph 1, the author's description of comets mentions all of the following EXCEPT:

   Ⓐ The manner in which they appear in the sky

   Ⓑ The lengths and widths some of them may attain

   Ⓒ The different parts that they are comprised of

   Ⓓ The average lifespan of most of them

Question Type

[Factual Question]

Some answer choices, upon first reading, may appear incorrect, but be sure to read the passage carefully instead of just scanning some of the words.

2   Which of the sentences below best expresses the essential information in the highlighted sentence in the passage? *Incorrect* answer choices change the meaning in important ways or leave out essential information.

   Ⓐ People learned about comets a long time ago, but Edmund Halley, who was an historian, was the first man actually to report anything about comets.

   Ⓑ Since no comets made repeat trips past Earth until the eighteenth century, it was impossible for humans to realize that many comets had regular orbits around the sun.

   Ⓒ Edmund Halley conducted research on one comet, and he realized that it had been orbiting Earth with some regularity since at least ancient times.

   Ⓓ Despite knowing about comets for centuries, it was not until much later that someone researching history recognized that some comets went by Earth with regularity.

[Sentence Simplification Question]

When a person's name is mentioned in the highlighted sentence, it does not always have to appear in the answer choice but may instead be replaced by a different word or expression.

3   The word "induce" in the passage is closest in meaning to

   Ⓐ produce   Ⓑ incite

   Ⓒ compel   Ⓓ encourage

[Vocabulary Question]

Be careful of answer choices that have similar roots or sound similar to the highlighted word. They are not necessarily correct.

4   **Directions:** An introductory sentence for a brief summary of the passage is provided below. Complete the summary by selecting the THREE answer choices that express the most important ideas of the passage. Some sentences do not belong because they express ideas that are not presented in the passage or are minor ideas in the passage. **This question is worth 2 points.**

Comets are huge, icy objects that may either orbit the sun on a regular basis or simply pass by the sun and never return.

[Prose Summary Question]

The introductory sentence may often have clauses that enable it to provide two or more ideas. Answer choices often focus on only one of these ideas. So determine what both of the ideas are and then look for answer choices which refer to only one them.

Answer Choices

☐1 The Hale-Bopp Comet appeared in the night sky for a period of several months at one point during the 1990s.

☐4 When astronomers detect a new comet, they are allowed by astronomical associations to name it after themselves.

☐2 The sun can attract objects from as far away as the Kuiper Belt, causing them to go around it every so often.

☐5 It is possible that the great distance of the Oort Cloud is the reason why some comets have only been detected once.

☐3 When the sun heats the ice of a comet, it may create a tail that stretches for millions of miles in space.

☐6 Halley's Comet is named after the astronomer who first realized exactly how often it orbited the sun.

Sunspots

On the sun's surface are many dark places, either alone or in clusters, called sunspots. They may be tens of thousands of miles in diameter and are also cooler than the surrounding surface. Sunspots have been observed since ancient times, and astronomers have meticulously cataloged them since the seventeenth century. From their studies, they have observed that sunspots appear in cycles and undergo periods of minimum and maximum activity. Sunspots also affect the brightness of the sun and the intensity of solar radiation as well as the shape and size of the sun's corona, and they are responsible for changes in the Earth's temperature and electromagnetic field.

2➡ Astronomers believe sunspots come about as a result of intense magnetic activity occurring in the sun, which reduces internal **convection** and makes the area appear to be darker than the surrounding surface of the star. Sunspots have two distinct parts: the inner umbra, which is darker, and the outer penumbra, which is lighter in color. Most can only be observed for about two weeks before they disappear from the Earth's point of view due to the sun's rotation. They commonly appear between five and thirty-five degrees north and south of the sun's **equator**.

While the sun's surface is darker and cooler in areas with sunspots, the edges of the sunspots themselves experience a higher degree of solar activity, thus making the sun produce slightly more solar radiation while making it appear brighter during periods of intense sunspot activity. Sunspots experience their minimum activity approximately every 11.3 years. Maximum activity, however, occurs irregularly between the periods of minimum activity. **1** The reasons as to why these cycles occur have thus far eluded astronomers. **2** In addition, the sun does not always strictly follow the cycles, so there have been long periods of low activity. **3** There is even a theory that a lack of sunspots over the course of sixty years in the seventeenth century may have caused what is known as the Little Ice Age, when temperatures on the Earth during this time plunged. **4**

4➡ Sunspots also have a distinct relationship with the shape of the sun's corona. The corona is the outermost layer of the sun and is the part which sends streamers of light and energy millions of miles into space. Additionally, it is observable only during eclipses or by using special instruments. When sunspot activity is low, the corona has longer streamers at the sun's equator than at the poles. During maximum sunspot activity though, the corona seems to be evenly distributed over the sun, yet it extends much farther into space. It is believed that intense sunspot activity and corona growth can interfere with radio, electrical, and magnetic fields on the Earth.

≋ *Glossary*
convection: the transfer of heat through circulation or movement
equator: a circle that divides a heavenly body into two equal parts and is equal in distance from the two poles

1 In paragraph 2, the author implies that sunspots

    Ⓐ have rarely been seen at either of the sun's two poles

    Ⓑ contribute to making the sun's entire surface darker

    Ⓒ are fairly short lived as they burn out after less than a month

    Ⓓ have two sections, both of which have different effects on the sun

2 In paragraph 4, the author discusses "the sun's corona" in order to

    Ⓐ prove that it can reduce the number of sunspots

    Ⓑ describe its relationship with sunspots

    Ⓒ point out where on the sun it is

    Ⓓ explain how it can affect the Earth's magnetic field

3 Look at the four squares [■] that indicate where the following sentence could be added to the passage.

This period is also commonly referred to as the Maunder Minimum, having been named after an astronomer who conducted research on sunspots.

Where would the sentence best fit?

4 *Directions:* Select the appropriate statements from the answer choices and match them to the feature of the sun to which they relate. TWO of the answer choices will NOT be used. *This question is worth 3 points.*

Answer Choices	FEATURE OF THE SUN
① Can appear in either large or small numbers at different periods of time	**Sunspot** • • •
② Can emit various amounts of energy from the sun and propel it into space	
③ Can be of equal size everywhere during certain conditions on the sun	**Corona** • •
④ Is most likely formed when the sun experiences some magnetic activity	
⑤ Is more likely to form on the sun during an eclipse than at any other time	
⑥ First started to appear on the sun's surface back during ancient times	
⑦ Is thought that its presence may be able to affect the temperature on the Earth	

Question Type

[Inference Question]

The correct answer choice may often have important words that do not appear in the paragraph in question.

[Rhetorical Purpose Question]

Focus on the highlighted word or words and how they are discussed in the relevant paragraph.

[Insert Text Question]

Always look for key words in the sentence to be inserted. In this case, "also" and the information following it imply that you should be looking for a name somewhere in the passage.

[Fill in a Table Question]

Be sure to review thoroughly the information on both topics in the passage. This is especially true when the two topics—sunspots and corona in this case—are mentioned in the same paragraphs rather than in separate ones.

Plate Tectonics

In the 1960s, scientists began subscribing to a theory which clarified certain perplexing mysteries on the Earth. This included explaining why sea animal fossils were found on mountaintops, why **continents** such as Africa and South America appeared practically to fit together like a jigsaw puzzle, and why earthquakes and volcanoes occurred with great frequency in certain areas. The name of the theory was plate tectonics, and it has not only been understood but has also been accepted by the scientific community as the most rational explanation for these observations.

The theory claims that the Earth's surface—its crust—is comprised of a series of interlocking plates which float on top of the planet's next lower level, the mantle. Essentially, the theory on how this works states that the less dense mantle provides a platform upon which the plates that make up the crust can float around. These plates, of which there are eight large ones and many smaller ones, float and move incredibly slowly so that, over millions of years, they have changed the shape of the Earth's surface to its present form. Eons ago, all of the Earth's continents were united in one large supercontinent, so lands like Africa and South America really were once joined together. Gradually, however, the continents separated and moved to their present locations.

³➡ The plates move against each other, and, through these actions, mountains are created, seafloors are shaped, volcanoes are born, and earthquakes are caused. When two plates meet head on, the denser one, which is usually under an ocean, dips below the lighter continental plate. Through this action, the continental land is pushed up into mountain ranges, and the seafloors are pushed down, thereby forming **trenches**. When the plates move away from each other, molten magma from below seeps up—sometimes slowly and other times violently—in a volcanic eruption. Finally, when two plates grind past one another in opposite directions, a great deal of energy is built up and suddenly released in the form of earthquakes. Certain areas, such as the entire Pacific Rim, experience frequent earthquakes and volcanic activity where plates meet, thereby indicating that they are places where plates intersect.

Plate tectonics also explained how sea animal fossils could be found located on the tops of mountains. Millions of years in the past, the mountaintops were once part of the ocean floor. However, as the continents shifted and plates collided, parts of the ocean floor were pushed up and became mountain ranges. While the theory of plate tectonics effectively answers many questions like this, geologists are still debating exactly how and why the plates themselves move.

≋ *Glossary*

continent: one of the very large landmasses found on the Earth's surface

trench: a deep area at the bottom of an ocean or sea

1 The word "perplexing" in the passage is closest in meaning to

- (A) confusing
- (B) intriguing
- (C) long-lasting
- (D) comprehensive

2 In paragraph 3, why does the author mention the "Pacific Rim"?

- (A) To note that it is one place where people are in danger of natural disasters
- (B) To provide an example of an area affected by the movement of tectonic plates
- (C) To state that two of the Earth's larger plates collide with one another there
- (D) To offer a theory on why more volcanoes than regular mountains are found in it

3 According to paragraph 3, which of the following is true of tectonic plates?

- (A) The movement of magma beneath the plates causes them to rub against one another.
- (B) Denser plates are often elevated into mountain ranges on land by lighter ones.
- (C) After an earthquake caused by two plates colliding, undersea trenches may be formed.
- (D) Their movements can release enormous amounts of energy in the form of natural disasters.

4 **_Directions:_** An introductory sentence for a brief summary of the passage is provided below. Complete the summary by selecting the THREE answer choices that express the most important ideas of the passage. Some sentences do not belong because they express ideas that are not presented in the passage or are minor ideas in the passage. **_This question is worth 2 points._**

The theory of plate tectonics explains why the Earth's surface is constantly changing as well as why some areas experience earthquakes and have many volcanoes.

Answer Choices

1. The Earth's crust comprises multiple tectonic plates that, over millions of years, have drifted apart to form the continents we know today.

2. In areas where tectonic plates meet, mountain ranges, oceanic trenches, volcanoes, and earthquakes occur due to the movements of the plates.

3. While the theory of plate tectonics answers many questions about the Earth's physical form, the mechanism behind the plates' movements is imperfectly understood.

4. When one looks at a map, it seems like Africa and South America should be able to fit together like a jigsaw puzzle.

5. Geologists have sometimes found fossils of sea creatures located on the tops of mountains, something that puzzled researchers for many years.

6. It was not until the 1960s that the theory of plate tectonics gained widespread acceptance within the scientific community.

Lightning

1→ On a hot summer day, storm clouds may build up until a light flashes and a **thunderclap** reverberates through the sky. This is a lightning storm, a common global phenomenon. Lightning is beautiful to observe; nevertheless, it is also dangerous and can kill the individuals it strikes or even spark **forest fires**. Lightning can occur within one cloud, move from one cloud to another, or travel from a cloud to the ground. On rare occasions, lightning may move from the ground to a cloud. But no matter how it travels, it is created by the same process: the separation of electrical charges due to the movement of ice particles in storm clouds.

2→ As ice particles rise and fall in a storm cloud, they collide, thereby causing the separation of their electrical charges as the positively charged particles rise and the negatively charged ones fall. These individual charges are then attracted to their opposite charges inside the cloud, in other clouds, or on the ground. For example, as a storm moves, positively charged particles on the ground follow it. The negatively charged particles at the bottom of the storm are attracted to the positively charged particles down below. Eventually, a channel is opened, the particles rush to meet one another, and the resultant electrical transfer is what people witness as lightning.

When lightning occurs, the air in the area becomes superheated to 50,000 degrees Fahrenheit. The air expands rapidly, and the ensuing sound is thunder. Since sound travels more slowly than light, the lightning is observed first, and then thunder follows it. While there are many types of lightning, cloud-to-ground lightning in its many varieties and shapes is the most common and most dangerous. Additionally, lightning has been known to occur during volcanic eruptions and forest fires. Large clouds of ash and dust in the air produce electrical charges in various parts of clouds, so lightning may flash between these differently charged areas.

Lightning is so common that an estimated twenty-five million bolts strike the ground in the United States alone every year. ■1 Lightning kills an average of sixty-two people each year in America. ■2 Most of these deaths happen in the summer, when more people are outdoors and lightning storms are more frequent. ■3 Lightning also injures an average of 250 people each year in America, some of whom get hurt quite badly. ■4 A common rule of thumb is that if thunder follows fewer than thirty seconds after lightning, then a person could be in danger of being struck by a lightning bolt.

≋ *Glossary*
thunderclap: the loud sound produced by lightning flashing
forest fire: the burning of a large amount of forested area

1   Which of the following can be inferred from paragraph 1 about lightning?

      Ⓐ   Lightning can only occur whenever the clouds are actively dropping rain.

      Ⓑ   It is more common for lightning to occur in summer than in other seasons.

      Ⓒ   Lightning moving upward from the ground is the least frequent type.

      Ⓓ   When lightning strikes people, the odds are that they will be killed.

2   In paragraph 2, the author's description of electrical charges mentions all of the following EXCEPT:

      Ⓐ   The way that they move from one place to another

      Ⓑ   The process through which they create lightning

      Ⓒ   The types of charges that they may have

      Ⓓ   The reason that some rise while others fall

3   The word "it" in the passage refers to

      Ⓐ   sound

      Ⓑ   light

      Ⓒ   lightning

      Ⓓ   thunder

4   Look at the four squares [■] that indicate where the following sentence could be added to the passage.

Of these, the greatest number of recorded hits occurs in the state of Florida.

    Where would the sentence best fit?

The Parts of the Atom

Since ancient times, great thinkers have pondered the universe and tried to understand what it is made of. The ancient Greek philosopher Aristotle, for instance, believed there were four elements: earth, air, water, and fire. Later scientists and philosophers had their own theories on **matter**. In moder times, it has been scientifically proven that matter consists of tiny particles that are called atoms. Every atom has specific characteristics that enable it to bond with other atoms to form molecules, which, in turn, form most of the matter in the entire universe. For example, every molecule of water is comprised of two hydrogen atoms and one oxygen atom that have joined together. These molecules can be found in three forms: solid, liquid, or gas. While atoms are extremely small, they are not the smallest particles in the universe. Each atom is made up of three smaller main parts called protons, neutrons, and electrons.

In the Middle Ages, alchemists believed Aristotle was right about the four elements. They also thought it was possible to combine elements to make any substance they wanted. This was one reason that so many of them tried to turn lead into gold.

Protons and neutrons comprise the center, or nucleus, of an atom while electrons orbit the nucleus in a region called the electron cloud, which, in turn, has different layers called shells. Protons have a positive electrical charge, and electrons have a negative electrical charge whereas neutrons, as their name implies, have no electrical charge. There is an electrical attraction between electrons and protons because positive and negative charges are attracted to each other; however, they never meet as electrons move rapidly around in their various shells. Due to this swift movement by electrons, which form a cloud around the nucleus, it seems as though each atom would be a solid ball; in fact, it is not.

Each shell that electrons orbit in can hold a different number of them. The shell closest to the nucleus can hold two electrons. The next can hold eight, and the one past it can hold eighteen. The more electrons in an atom, the more shells it has.

[3]→ Compared to protons and neutrons, electrons are extremely small. Protons and neutrons make up the majority of the mass of an atom with neutrons being slightly heavier than protons and electrons weighing virtually nothing. Atoms are classified according to their atomic number, which refers to the number of protons present in their nucleus. For example, carbon has an atomic number of six since that is the number of protons it has while the atomic number of gold is seventy-nine, and that of uranium is ninety-two. However, atoms can also form into isotopes, slightly different forms of the same atom created when more neutrons are added or subtracted. As an example, a carbon atom typically has six protons and six neutrons, so when combined, they form the isotope carbon-12. However, two more neutrons can be added to the nucleus, thereby creating carbon-14. In a similar manner, uranium has ninety-two protons and 146 neutrons, giving it an **atomic weight** of 238, so it is called uranium-238. Uranium-235 has 143 neutrons though while maintaining the same number of protons as uranium-238.

Every element has at least one isotope. Many of them are radioactive, which means that their nuclei are unstable and that they emit alpha, beta, or gamma rays. There are more than 1,000 radioactive isotopes, but only around fifty of them are naturally occurring. The rest are created in laboratories.

⁴➙ In most cases, an atom has the same number of protons and electrons. In addition, the outer electron cloud is vital to the stability of an atom. If there are an equal number of protons and electrons, then the atom is electrically neutral and is highly stable. However, if there are an unequal number of protons and electrons, an ion, which is unstable, is formed. Electrons move in different regions around the nucleus in shells. The shells closest to the nucleus are the strongest in attraction while those farthest away are the weakest in attraction. If any unstable electrons in an outer shell are acted upon by an outside force, such as another atom, the two atoms can combine in a chemical reaction to create a molecule.

📚 **Glossary**
matter: the substance that a physical object is made of
atomic weight: the average weight of an atom of an element

---

1   The word "bond" in the passage is closest in meaning to

    Ⓐ promise

    Ⓑ glue

    Ⓒ communicate

    Ⓓ link

2   Which of the sentences below best expresses the essential information in the highlighted sentence in the passage? *Incorrect* answer choices change the meaning in important ways or leave out essential information.

    Ⓐ Electrons are found in the electron cloud around the nucleus while protons and neutrons are in the nucleus itself.

    Ⓑ Protons are neutrons are found in various layers in the nucleus, which is being orbited by electrons in the electron cloud.

    Ⓒ The electron cloud contains layers full of electrons while the nucleus has no layers for the protons and neutrons in it.

    Ⓓ Most of the time, protons and neutrons are found in the nucleus, but electrons can move from shell to shell in the electron cloud.

3   In paragraph 3, the author uses "Uranium-235" as an example of

    Ⓐ an artificial element

    Ⓑ an isotope of uranium

    Ⓒ an element with fewer protons than gold

    Ⓓ a radioactive type of uranium

4   In paragraph 4, the author's description of atoms mentions which of the following?

  (A) The number of electrons orbiting in each shell

  (B) The ways in which chemical reactions can occur

  (C) The reason that some atoms may become unstable

  (D) The number of ions that an element may have

5   **Directions:** An introductory sentence for a brief summary of the passage is provided below. Complete the summary by selecting the THREE answer choices that express the most important ideas of the passage. Some sentences do not belong because they express ideas that are not presented in the passage or are minor ideas in the passage. **This question is worth 2 points.**

An atom is made up of protons, neutrons, and electrons, which behave in various ways.

-
-
-

Answer Choices

1. The number of protons represents an atom's atomic number while the combined number of protons and neutrons is its atomic weight.

2. The three main parts of an atom all exist in specific places inside it.

3. People have thought about atoms and their composition since before the time of the Greek Aristotle.

4. The number of protons and electrons in an atom determine whether it is neutral or an ion.

5. Elements such as uranium have different isotopes based on the number of neutrons that they have.

6. Two or more atoms can come together to create a molecule in something called a chemical reaction.

Summarizing ▷ Complete the summary by filling in the blanks.

People such as the Greek _____ have tried to understand the universe and what comprises it since ancient times. Today, scientists know that matter consists of atoms, which can bond together to _____. Protons and neutrons are in an atom's nucleus while electrons _____ in shells. The number of protons in an atom is its _____. The number of neutrons can vary, which results in isotopes being created. An equal number of protons and electrons means an atom is neutral and therefore stable. If there are _____, the atom is an ion and is unstable, so it can join with another atom to form a molecule.

Pasteurization

Pasteurization is a process used to prevent food from **spoiling**. It is commonly performed on milk and other dairy products, beer, wine, soy sauce, fruit drinks, and maple syrup in addition to a wide range of other food and beverage products. The process has two purposes: to prevent diseases from being transmitted from food to people and to increase the shelf life of a product. Milk in particular is prone to rapid spoiling and must therefore be consumed quickly when untreated. However, thanks to pasteurization, milk can be kept for a longer period of time—typically seven to sixteen days—without spoiling.

Louis Pasteur of France developed the process that is named for him in 1862 while trying to learn how to prevent wine from souring. He discovered that if wine were heated to a temperature just below its boiling point, the organisms that caused it to go sour could be killed or at least inactivated. Nowadays, this process is most commonly used in milk. Machines heat it for a certain amount of time to a temperature that will destroy *Coxelliae burnettii*, the pathogen in milk most resistant to heat and which is responsible for Q fever. This microorganism causes pneumonialike symptoms and passes from animals to humans through milk, meat, and animal skin. To kill it, the machines heat milk to sixty-three degrees Celsius for at least thirty minutes or seventy-two degrees Celsius for sixteen seconds. Milk is considered pasteurized if inspectors fail to find the presence of alkaline phosphatase in it.

3➡ There are several ways that milk and other dairy products may be pasteurized. The two most common are the batch method and the continuous method. In the batch method, the product is placed in a vat surrounded by circulating water, steam, or coils with water or steam inside of them. The vat is then shaken or mixed so that there is uniform heating throughout the product. This method is more commonly used for cream and other non-milk dairy products. The continuous method, meanwhile, is considered more efficient and faster. A machine forces the milk through a system of heated plates that have a temperature of seventy-two degrees Celsius, and the milk then passes through a cooling system where the temperature is reduced to four degrees Celsius. This process is called high-temperature short-time (HTST) pasteurization.

4➡ A third type is ultra-high temperature (UHT) pasteurization, in which milk is **zapped** for a fraction of a second at 138 degrees Celsius. Yet another, newer, method is called extended shelf-life pasteurization, or ESL. It uses HTST pasteurization but also passes the milk through microfiber filters designed to catch any pathogens which somehow survive the pasteurization process. **1** Thanks to ESL, the shelf life of milk can be further extended by many days. **2**

Note

Louis Pasteur lived from 1822 to 1895. Aside from his work on pasteurization, he helped create the field of microbiology. He also developed the first vaccine for rabies and did work in chemistry.

A number of diseases can spread through liquids that have not been pasteurized. Tuberculosis, diphtheria, and brucellosis can all spread through untreated milk. Other beverages, including beer and wine, can be carriers of fatal diseases if they are left untreated.

Liquids are not the only foods that can be pasteurized. Fish and certain shellfish, including clams and crabs, can all be pasteurized both to prevent spoilage and to kill bacteria.

Pasteurized milk and milk products are standard in most advanced nations, and no milk can qualify for the pasteurized label unless it is government approved. **3** While there is no accurate data, it has been suggested that pasteurization has helped improve health standards in countries where it is used. **4**

📚 *Glossary*
spoil: to go bad; to rot
zap: to heat very quickly and for a short period of time

1 The word "it" in the passage refers to
(A) microorganism
(B) milk
(C) meat
(D) animal skin

2 According to paragraph 3, which of the following is NOT true of pasteurization?
(A) The batch method puts the milk in a vat where it can be pasteurized.
(B) Cream is often treated by one of the main types of pasteurization.
(C) The continuous method heats and then subsequently cools the liquid.
(D) The batch method heats the liquid up to seventy-two degrees Celsius.

3 According to paragraph 4, which of the following can be inferred about extended shelf-life pasteurization?
(A) It makes milk last longer than any other kind of pasteurization.
(B) It is the most expensive type of pasteurization used on milk.
(C) It is used more often than ultra-high temperature pasteurization.
(D) There are four steps involved in pasteurizing milk that way.

4 Look at the four squares [■] that indicate where the following sentence could be added to the passage.

However, one drawback is that the milk slightly changes color, which has made it less appealing in some markets, particularly the American one.

Where would the sentence best fit?

5 **Directions:** Select the appropriate sentences from the answer choices and match them to the pasteurization method to which they relate. TWO of the answer choices will NOT be used. **This question is worth 3 points.**

Answer Choices	PASTEURIZATION METHOD
① It takes less than a second for the process to be complete.	**Batch Method** • •
② The container the milk is in must be shaken to ensure the process is complete.	
③ It uses microfiber filters to catch various pathogens in the liquid.	**Continuous Method** • •
④ It can be responsible for the presence of Q fever in a substance.	
⑤ It involves both heating and cooling the liquid as it goes through a container.	**Ultra-High Temperature Method** •
⑥ Dairy products that are not milk are typically pasteurized this way.	
⑦ This is the faster of the two main methods of pasteurizing milk.	

Summarizing ▷ Complete the summary by filling in the blanks.

Pasteurization is the process by which certain liquids are treated to keep them from _____.
It is commonly used on milk. It was first discovered by _____ in 1862. The two most
common methods are the batch method and _____. They both involve heating the liquid to
preserve it. However, the continuous method uses higher heat, so it must also _____ the
liquid. Ultra-high heat pasteurization is another type, but it uses extremely high heat for a very brief time. Finally,
_____ is a new method that can help products like milk stay fresh for many more days than
conventionally treated milk.

Note

Types of Planets

[1]➡ Within the solar system, there are three main types of planets orbiting the sun: gas giants, terrestrial planets, and dwarf planets. Each planet has characteristics common to the others in its group as well as its own unique properties. Jupiter, Saturn, Uranus, and Neptune comprise the solar system's gas giants while Mercury, Venus, Earth, and Mars are its terrestrial planets. Pluto was once considered a terrestrial planet, yet in 2006, the International Astronomical Union changed its designation to that of a dwarf planet. There are several others, including Ceres, which orbits the sun from the asteroid belt between Mars and Jupiter, and Eris.

The gas giants are frequently referred to as the Jovian planets, having been named after Jupiter, which is the largest planet in this group. Essentially, these planets are huge balls of glowing, heaving gases, most of which are hydrogen and helium. The surfaces of these planets have low-density clouds, but they become much denser closer to the core; however, being gaseous in nature, the Jovian planets lack solid surfaces. Additionally, the compositions of the gas giants are so **toxic** that carbon-based life forms could definitely not exist on them.

There are two more characteristics the Jovian planets share: They all have rings and numerous satellites. While Saturn is the only planet to have rings easily visible, the other four possess thin rings that are believed to be **transient**. **1** As for moons, as of 2023, each planet has many: Jupiter has ninety-two, Saturn has eighty-three, Uranus has twenty-seven, and Neptune has fourteen, and more may be discovered in the future. **2** The moons themselves vary in composition; some are gaseous while others are rocky and icy. **3** Finally, the gas giants are extremely distant from the sun, requiring Jupiter, the closest to the sun of them, almost a dozen years to complete one orbit while Neptune does the same in around 165 years. **4**

[4]➡ Meanwhile, the terrestrial planets form the solar system's inner core, which is conveniently separated from the outer core by the asteroid belt. This places the terrestrial planets closer to the sun, with Mercury being nearest and Mars being farthest away. Unlike the Jovian planets, these four have solid, rocky surfaces composed of numerous kinds of minerals. Despite Venus being covered by a dense cloud of gas, it is not a gas giant. Its cloud cover does, however, make observing the planet extremely difficult. Still, the four planets are known not only to have similar compositions but also to have other characteristics in common. They orbit the sun much more quickly than the Jovian planets, and they have a much smaller number of satellites. Mercury and Venus have none, Earth has one, and Mars has two.

The terrestrial planets are closest to the sun. Next come the asteroid belt and the four gas giants. The dwarf planets, excepting Ceres, orbit the sun from beyond Neptune.

Jupiter is by far the largest planet in the solar system.

Saturn is mostly known for its large number of rings.

Uranus is the third-largest planet and is often called an ice planet because of its composition.

Neptune is the farthest planet in the solar system from the sun and takes almost 165 years to orbit it.

Mercury is the smallest planet in the solar system.

Venus is known as Earth's "sister planet" because of its many similarities to Earth.

Earth is the third planet in the solar system and the only one known to have any life on it.

As for dwarf planets, they are a newly named group, and their best-known member is Pluto. Essentially, they are large bodies orbiting the sun that have enough gravity to form themselves into somewhat rounded bodies yet which lack the power to clear their orbits of other objects. With the exception of Ceres, the other four—including Pluto—that are classified as dwarf planets are incredibly distant from Earth, so little is known of their composition, structure, or general characteristics.

≋ *Glossary*

toxic: poisonous

transient: fleeting; temporary

Mars is called the "red planet" because of the red color that the iron oxide on the planet gives it.

---

1 In paragraph 1, why does the author mention "Eris"?

(A) To note that it orbits the sun from within the asteroid belt

(B) To contrast its composition with that of the terrestrial planets

(C) To provide an example of a dwarf planet other than Pluto

(D) To argue that it should be considered a terrestrial planet

2 The word "them" in the passage refers to

(A) solid surfaces

(B) compositions

(C) gas giants

(D) carbon-based life forms

3 According to paragraph 4, which of the following is NOT true of the terrestrial planets?

(A) They all orbit the sun from positions closer to it than the asteroid belt.

(B) They have a vastly smaller number of satellites than the gas giants.

(C) There are four of them, with Mercury being the closest of them to the sun.

(D) Their surfaces, with the exception of Venus, are all rocky and full of minerals.

4 Look at the four squares [■] that indicate where the following sentence could be added to the passage.

In addition, astronomers believe that some of their moons, particularly Jupiter's Io and Europa, could possibly harbor some forms of life.

Where would the sentence best fit?

5   ***Directions:*** Select the appropriate sentences from the answer choices and match them to the type of planet to which they relate. TWO of the answer choices will NOT be used. ***This question is worth 3 points.***

Answer Choices

1 Their entire bodies, not just their cores, are composed of solid rocks.

1 They are the largest of all the bodies in the solar system except for the sun.

1 These bodies lack the gravitational strength to clear other objects from their paths.

3 They have no more than two natural satellites which orbit them.

5 They take a minimum of a dozen years to complete one orbit of the sun.

6 Pluto and Ceres, both of which are rocky, belong to this group.

7 They are hostile to life because of their surface compositions.

TYPE OF PLANET

Jovian Planets
-
-
-

Terrestrial Planets
-
-

Summarizing ▷   Complete the summary by filling in the blanks.

The planets orbiting the sun belong to three groups: gas giants, terrestrial planets, and dwarf planets. The gas giants are _____ , Saturn, Uranus, and Neptune; they orbit the sun from afar. They are huge balls of gas with conditions _____ to humans. They also have rings and large numbers of _____ and take years to orbit the sun. _____ are Mercury, Venus, Earth, and Mars. They are all rocky, have minerals, have few moons, and take a short period of time to orbit the sun. The dwarf planets are Pluto, Ceres, and three others. Most of them are _____ from the sun, so little is known about them.

Mastering the Subject

Stephen Hales

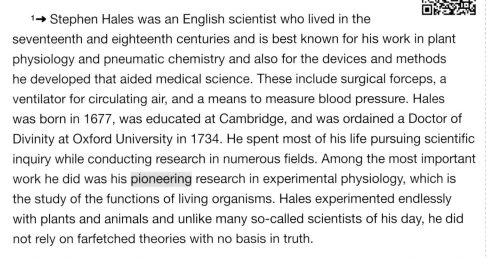

Note

One common field of study during Hales' lifetime was alchemy, whose practitioners tried to transmute lead into gold. A pseudoscience, alchemy often involved the study of magic and other arcane arts.

1➔ Stephen Hales was an English scientist who lived in the seventeenth and eighteenth centuries and is best known for his work in plant physiology and pneumatic chemistry and also for the devices and methods he developed that aided medical science. These include surgical forceps, a ventilator for circulating air, and a means to measure blood pressure. Hales was born in 1677, was educated at Cambridge, and was ordained a Doctor of Divinity at Oxford University in 1734. He spent most of his life pursuing scientific inquiry while conducting research in numerous fields. Among the most important work he did was his pioneering research in experimental physiology, which is the study of the functions of living organisms. Hales experimented endlessly with plants and animals and unlike many so-called scientists of his day, he did not rely on farfetched theories with no basis in truth.

One of Hales' true loves was his work with plants. His greatest written work is *Statical Essays*, which dealt with various aspects of plant physiology. His experiments on plants included work on their growth rates, how they lose water through evaporation, and the nature of their roots. Hales is often noted for his work in pneumatic chemistry, which he conducted essentially as an offshoot of his work with plants. This was a branch of chemistry that no longer exists but had numerous **adherents** between the sixteenth and nineteenth centuries. Important discoveries, including numerous gases like oxygen, hydrogen, helium, and nitrogen and the identification of the physical properties of some of them, were made by the followers of pneumatic chemistry during this period. Among the great scientists who **delved** into pneumatic chemistry were Robert Boyle, Antoine Lavoisier, Daniel Rutherford, Joseph Priestley, and Henry Cavendish. Much modern-day work in chemistry could never have been accomplished without their initial research.

Hales began his work right at the end of the Scientific Revolution, which lasted from roughly 1500 to 1700. During this period and after, great advances were made in both scientific discoveries and the methods used to make them. Both Galileo Galilei and Johannes Kepler were major figures in the Scientific Revolution.

Hales' work in pneumatic chemistry covered two seemingly unconnected topics: how plants receive some of their nourishment from the air and the properties of the atmosphere. Hales surmised that perhaps something in the air was responsible for how plants grew. This led him to study the atmosphere, about which he hypothesized that certain gases present in the atmosphere were responsible. Hales never learned what gases were responsible for plant growth during his experiments as the discovery of these gases was left to chemists who came in later years. However, he did manage to develop a device similar to a pneumatic trough, an instrument which is still used in laboratories to collect gases.

Stagnant air allows bacteria and fungi more easily to grow. These can both be harmful to people and explain why individuals in dark, confined spaces often lived for a short amount of time.

4➔ Hales is also remembered for his examination of the properties of fresh and stale air. Something he had noticed was that in areas with a lack of fresh air—prisons, ship holds, and other confined spaces—there was an increase in the mortality rate of the occupants. Prisons of his day were notorious for being dank, dark dungeons, and an extended prison term was virtually an automatic death sentence. However, Hales contrived a device similar to the bellows system used to operate an organ which could circulate air. When used in Savoy Prison in England, the mortality rate dropped considerably. His idea was quickly copied and used in ships, hospitals, and other places with similar results.

📖 **Glossary**

adherent: a follower; a supporter
delve: to look into; to examine

---

1 The word "pioneering" in the passage is closest in meaning to

Ⓐ exotic

Ⓑ original

Ⓒ scientific

Ⓓ tentative

2 According to paragraph 1, which of the following is true of Stephen Hales?

Ⓐ Rather than conduct research, he was content to obtain his learning from books.

Ⓑ He was ordained a minister prior to beginning his work as a scientist.

Ⓒ He invented several important tools crucial to the study of pneumatic chemistry.

Ⓓ The theories he relied on often differed from those of other contemporary scientists.

3 Which of the sentences below best expresses the essential information in the highlighted sentence in the passage? *Incorrect* answer choices change the meaning in important ways or leave out essential information.

Ⓐ The discoveries of many gases were made by pneumatic chemists during that time.

Ⓑ Scientists of that age not only found new gases but also learned much about them.

Ⓒ The properties of certain gases were identified by some famous researchers.

Ⓓ First, gases were discovered, and then their properties had to be examined carefully.

4 In paragraph 4, the author implies that Stephen Hales

Ⓐ used his invention that circulated air to make himself wealthy

Ⓑ improved the bellows system upon which organs operated

Ⓒ hoped his inventions would increase the mortality rates of jails

Ⓓ was directly responsible for saving many people's lives

5 **Directions:** An introductory sentence for a brief summary of the passage is provided below. Complete the summary by selecting the THREE answer choices that express the most important ideas of the passage. Some sentences do not belong because they express ideas that are not presented in the passage or are minor ideas in the passage. ***This question is worth 2 points.***

Stephen Hales was a scientist who studied plants and pneumatic chemistry and who also invented several important tools that improved medical science.

-
-
-

Answer Choices

1. Hales made connections between his two major fields of interest to learn much about the composition of the atmosphere.

2. Hales did much of his work in the eighteenth century, which was a time when not everyone was dedicated to the scientific method.

3. Hales learned about the root systems of plants as well as the process by which plants lose water due to evaporation.

4. Before Hales' air circulation device was implemented, people who spent long terms in jail often died before their terms were complete.

5. Scientists such as Robert Boyle, Antoine Lavoisier, and Joseph Priestley were all contemporaries of Stephen Hales.

6. A major part of Hales' legacy was the air circulation machine that he developed to help ventilate confined and enclosed places.

Summarizing ▷ Complete the summary by filling in the blanks.

Stephen Hales was a scientist who lived during _____ centuries. He conducted work on plants and in chemistry and also was responsible for inventions in the field of _____ . Hales conducted many experiments on plants, which led him to do work in pneumatic chemistry, a branch of chemistry that no longer exists but which, during his lifetime, had _____ and was responsible for much groundbreaking work on gases. Hales also investigated the contents of _____ because of his interest in plants. Finally, he invented _____ for closed places that helped save many lives.

Predicting Volcanic Eruptions

1➜ As a result of the instability of the Earth's interior, volcanoes have been erupting since the planet was formed. The layer located immediately beneath the upper crust is the mantle, and it is constantly in motion and extremely hot. In fact, the high temperatures there melt rock, thereby forming molten rock, otherwise known as magma. When there is enough magma below a weak point in the crust, the pressure increases until there is a volcanic eruption. If people are living nearby, this may result in disaster. On account of the acute danger people face from volcanoes, since ancient times, humans have tried predicting volcanic eruptions. Yet despite the technical advances of modern science, experts still cannot predict eruptions with one-hundred-percent accuracy.

2➜ There are three main types of volcanoes: active, dormant, and extinct. Active volcanoes exhibit current signs of being alive, dormant volcanoes have erupted during recorded history but may not have done so for centuries, and extinct volcanoes have erupted in the past but did so long before there were any humans around to record the event. The problems that volcanologists face are that dormant volcanoes can rapidly move to an active state while active volcanoes can literally blow their tops at virtually any time. Of course, there are some obvious signs that a volcano will soon erupt, and volcanologists are constantly on the lookout for them. Most of these signs are connected to seismic activity, magma, and certain gases commonly associated with volcanoes.

3➜ Seismic activity means tremors in the ground—earthquakes. Long before most volcanoes erupt, the earth begins shaking. This is frequently the first obvious sign of growing instability. As the region becomes more unstable, the number of tremors grows while the intervals between them shorten. Secondly, gases and magma are vented from small cracks that appear in the sides or top of the volcano. Scientists examine these gases and magma to detect any changes in composition that may indicate an impending eruption. For example, the release of increasing amounts of sulfur dioxide is a sign an eruption is imminent. Additionally, when taken over a period of many days or weeks, photographs and instrument readings of a volcano's surface can indicate whether the volcano is beginning to swell from an internal buildup of magma.

4➜ Despite many successes in volcanic eruption prediction, it remains an imperfect science facing several major obstacles. The first is that despite signs of a looming eruption, sometimes nothing may happen. The magma may cool off, the seismic activity may end, and the volcano may become less active or even enter a dormant stage. Other issues are of the manmade variety and are related to the funding of volcanic research and monitoring. Most volcanoes have lain dormant for thousands or even tens of thousands of years. Monitoring all of them is both impossible and too expensive. Scientists' salaries, their equipment, and supporting the monitoring teams cost enormous sums of money. Thus, choices—not all of which are right—must be made as to which volcanoes to observe. Additionally, when experts predict a volcanic eruption that never occurs, their sponsors tend to be displeased by their error.

Another problem which may arise is the reaction of those living near a volcano upon hearing news of a possible eruption. The land around volcanoes is typically quite attractive to humans due to the rich volcanic soil that produces bumper crops. ▮ In cases where a volcano lies dormant for a long time, settlements may be established, and tens of thousands—or even millions—of people may live in the volcano's vicinity. **2** Despite the dire warnings and the pleas of scientists, many denizens are reluctant to leave their homes, farms, and businesses. **3** Some stubbornly refuse to evacuate under the misguided opinion that they can protect their property. **4** Police and military forces must often compel them to leave to save their lives.

⁶→ Ultimately, once a volcano is set to erupt, nothing in its path can be saved. However, given enough warning, if the eruption is of the nonviolent type that frequently occurs in Hawaii, barriers can be built and property sometimes saved. When time is lacking, only lives can be saved. And when there is no warning or not enough signs to predict an eruption, the results may be catastrophic.

≋ Glossary
volcanologist: a person who studies volcanoes
tremor: the shaking of the earth, as in an earthquake

1   The word "acute" in the passage is closest in meaning to

    Ⓐ sharp

    Ⓑ potential

    Ⓒ deathly

    Ⓓ serious

2   In paragraph 1, which of the following can be inferred about volcanoes?

    Ⓐ They are among the most destructive of all of nature's forces.

    Ⓑ People in the past predicted their eruptions better than people do today.

    Ⓒ They may cause so much destruction that they injure people in the vicinity.

    Ⓓ The magma that they release may be expelled in the form of lava or ash.

3   Which of the sentences below best expresses the essential information in the highlighted sentence in the passage? *Incorrect* answer choices change the meaning in important ways or leave out essential information.

    Ⓐ Scientists face the problem that some volcanoes erupt at any time while other dormant ones remain inactive for long periods of time.

    Ⓑ Volcanologists so far fail to understand what makes some dormant volcanoes become active while other volcanoes suddenly erupt.

    Ⓒ Volcanoes can quickly change their status, with some suddenly erupting and others which were previously inactive coming back to life.

    Ⓓ While a dormant volcano may change to an active stage, it is also possible for an active volcano to fall into a period of dormancy.

4 According to paragraph 2, which of the following is NOT true of volcanoes?

    &Ⓐ Some dormant volcanoes come to life and erupt for centuries at a time.

    Ⓑ Dormant volcanoes might not have erupted for several hundred years.

    Ⓒ Scientists are often able to detect when a volcano is preparing to erupt.

    Ⓓ Volcanologists have categorized them into several different groups.

5 According to paragraph 3, earthquakes happen before an eruption because

    Ⓐ the gases being released by the volcano contribute to the shaking

    Ⓑ magma building up inside the volcano causes them to occur

    Ⓒ gas and magma beneath the surface are making the ground move

    Ⓓ the volcano is becoming unstable and is preparing to erupt

6 The author discusses "volcanic eruption prediction" in paragraph 4 in order to

    Ⓐ state that governments should not be involved in doing it at all

    Ⓑ argue that more money needs to be spent to help experts engaged in it

    Ⓒ point out some problems those engaged in it have to deal with

    Ⓓ claim that volcanologists have a nearly perfect record of doing it

7 The word "bumper" in the passage is closest in meaning to

    Ⓐ nutritious

    Ⓑ fast-growing

    Ⓒ gigantic

    Ⓓ abundant

8 In paragraph 6, why does the author mention volcanic eruptions in Hawaii?

    Ⓐ To demonstrate that people can be protected from volcanic eruptions

    Ⓑ To note that volcanic eruptions occur there on a regular basis

    Ⓒ To imply that those eruptions lack large amounts of magma

    Ⓓ To show that it is possible for people's lives to be saved after eruptions

9 Look at the four squares [■] that indicate where the following sentence could be added to the passage.

Yet this obstinacy often results in their deaths, as fifty-seven people found out in 1980 when they were caught in the eruption of Mt. St. Helens in Washington in the USA.

Where would the sentence best fit?

Click on a square [■] to add the sentence to the passage.

10   ***Directions:*** An introductory sentence for a brief summary of the passage is provided below. Complete the summary by selecting the THREE answer choices that express the most important ideas of the passage. Some sentences do not belong because they express ideas that are not presented in the passage or are minor ideas in the passage. ***This question is worth 2 points.***

> Drag your answer choices to the spaces where they belong.
> To remove an answer choice, click on it. To review the passage, click on **View Text.**

While people have a great interest in predicting the eruptions of volcanoes, it is difficult to do so and does not always end in success.

-
-
-

Answer Choices

1   Sometimes barriers can be erected that are able to prevent a volcanic eruption from being too destructive.

2   Even when all of the signs of a volcanic eruption are present, it does not mean that one is imminent.

3   It costs a tremendous amount of money to monitor volcanoes, so only a few can be watched at all times.

4   Some active volcanoes can instantly erupt, which makes it difficult for scientists to predict this occurrence.

5   There are three major categories of volcanoes, all of which denote the frequency with which they erupt.

6   People have been trying to predict eruptions for thousands of years because of the havoc they can wreak on people and land.

The Life of a Star

1 → The universe is so filled with stars that an exact estimate of their numbers is impossible to make. In the Milky Way Galaxy, to which Earth belongs, there are approximately 100 billion stars, and astronomers believe there are almost ten billion galaxies in the universe. Unsurprisingly, given such an enormous sampling, there are many different types of stars, all of which are at various stages in their life cycles. However, all stars form in a similar fashion, progress through specific stages, and eventually die. The majority of information astronomers have about stars comes from the sun, which is the closest star to Earth. Based on its size, astronomers theorize it has roughly three to four more billion years of life. During this period, it will expand, contract, and, ultimately, perish.

2 → Most scientists agree with the theory that eons ago, the **big bang** created the universe. From a small point in whatever existed prior to the presence of the universe, all energy and matter exploded and expanded outward. This big bang, as it is called, produced atoms, and these subsequently formed elements, with hydrogen and helium being the two most common. Condensing clouds of these elements combined with one another to form galaxies. Within the galaxies themselves, dense clouds of gases called nebulae were established, marking the first stage in the formation of a star. Over a period lasting millions of years, gravity contracted the gases in individual nebulae and forced them to assume more regular shapes. As these gases started to contract, the nebulae's centers began heating up, and nuclear reactions that turned hydrogen into helium began to occur, thereby giving birth to stars.

3 → At first, a new star is quite stable and has a constant energy output due to the contained nuclear reactions ongoing in its interior. Astronomers refer to this period of a star's life as the yellow dwarf stage. Most stars in the known universe are somewhere in the middle of this stage. However, over a period of billions of years, a star eventually exhausts its supply of hydrogen, and the nuclear reactions lessen until they come to a halt. This causes the star to undergo cooling, and its core contracts. Simultaneously, its surface area begins expanding. At some point, the helium extant in the star starts burning, so the star heats up again; however, this time, it expands tremendously, becoming what astronomers call a red giant. Eventually, it may transform into a massive blue star 400 times its original size.

4 → This is when the death stage of the star is initiated. Once its supply of helium is depleted, the star once again begins to collapse, yet this time the end really is near. The star shrinks dramatically, becoming smaller than it was as a yellow dwarf, and it becomes a tiny white dwarf. After more time **elapses**, the star loses its ability to produce heat and light, so it transforms into a black dwarf. In this stage, only the heavy, dense core of material in the star remains. Still, its death can take millions or even billions of years to transpire. Each stage in a star's life also includes many sub-stages, and there are also several classes of yellow, red, blue, and white stars.

5 → It should be noted that stars do not all begin their lives having identical sizes, for some are gargantuan when formed and are considered giant stars. These stars rapidly deplete their hydrogen and helium supply and therefore have shorter lifespans than yellow dwarves like the sun. Some of these stars may not actually collapse but instead explode in what is called a supernova. When this occurs, there are two possible results: One is the creation of a neutron star, which is a remnant of the giant star. Neutron stars emit pulsars, which are pulses of electromagnetic radiation that can be noticed on the Earth. **1** The other is that a black hole, a phenomenon with extremely strong gravity from which not even light may escape, is formed. **2** In opposition to giant stars, very tiny stars reddish in color—so astronomers call them red dwarves—are also sometimes formed. **3** Paradoxically, they burn their hydrogen and helium quite slowly, so they last longer than their much larger cousins do. **4**

≋ Glossary

big bang: the explosion of a small, hot, dense ball of matter billions of years ago that created the universe
elapse: to pass by

---

1 In paragraph 1, why does the author mention "the Milky Way Galaxy"?

 Ⓐ To show which galaxy Earth belongs to

 Ⓑ To demonstrate how small it is compared to the entire universe

 Ⓒ To explain its relation to the other galaxies in the universe

 Ⓓ To emphasize the huge number of stars that lie within it

2 According to paragraph 1, which of the following is true of stars?

 Ⓐ A sizable percentage of them may be found in the Milky Way Galaxy.

 Ⓑ Despite their many types, their life cycles all resemble one another.

 Ⓒ Most of the stars in the galaxy are older than Earth's sun.

 Ⓓ They frequently live for fewer than three or four billion years.

3 Which of the following can be inferred about the big bang in paragraph 2?

 Ⓐ The fact that it occurred has been verified by astronomers.

 Ⓑ Astronomers know roughly when it took place.

 Ⓒ The location in the universe where it happened is known.

 Ⓓ No one knows what actually existed before it happened.

4 The word "exhausts" in the passage is closest in meaning to

 Ⓐ expends

 Ⓑ extols

 Ⓒ exudes

 Ⓓ excerpts

5 According to paragraph 3, a red giant forms because

    (A) the star is burning the hydrogen that remains in its core

    (B) the star expands once it starts to cool off

    (C) the helium left in the star begins to be consumed

    (D) there is not enough energy remaining for it to use

6 In paragraph 4, all of the following questions are answered EXCEPT:

    (A) How long can it take a star to die?

    (B) What are some of the sub-stages in the life of a star?

    (C) What is the process through which a star becomes a white dwarf?

    (D) What happens when a star uses up its supply of helium?

7 The word "Paradoxically" in the passage is closest in meaning to

    (A) Ironically

    (B) Uniquely

    (C) Individually

    (D) Sardonically

8 In paragraph 5, the author implies that supernovas

    (A) are what may happen to dying yellow dwarves

    (B) produce enough energy to destroy a black hole

    (C) are able to be seen from the Earth when they happen

    (D) can only happen during the death of a giant star

9 Look at the four squares [■] that indicate where the following sentence could be added to the passage.

In fact, they are so powerful that they can theoretically consume planets and even stars.

Where would the sentence best fit?

Click on a square [■] to add the sentence to the passage.

10 *Directions:* Select the appropriate sentences from the answer choices and match them to the type of star to which they relate. TWO of the answer choices will NOT be used. ***This question is worth 3 points.***

> Drag your answer choices to the spaces where they belong.
> To remove an answer choice, click on it. To review the passage, click on **View Text.**

Answer Choices

1. When the star leaves this stage, it begins to shrink.

2. This kind of star no longer burns hydrogen since it lacks that element.

3. This is the most common type of star in the galaxy.

4. It can explode with such force that it becomes a supernova.

5. This star produces neither heat nor light as it is about to die.

6. Earth's star belongs to this category.

7. It may become hundreds of times bigger than its original size.

TYPE OF STAR

Yellow Dwarf
-
-
-

Red Giant
-
-

❶ Jupiter's Moon Io

Of Jupiter's ninety-two known moons, Io is the third largest, being slightly greater in size than Earth's moon. It was also one of the first to be identified, having been discovered in the year 1610 by Galileo Galilei, the noted astronomer. Io is the most volcanically active body in the entire solar system, and the smoke plumes from its constantly erupting volcanoes can reach almost 190 miles above its surface. Due to its elliptical orbit around Jupiter, caused in part by two other large moons—Europa and Ganymede—Io is subjected to strong tidal forces. These forces cause its surface to crest up and down by as much as 330 feet.

❷ The Formation of the Solar System

The formation of the solar system is believed by astronomers to have taken place several billion years ago. Essentially, the area that is now the solar system was initially a huge cloud of gas and dust. Because of some outside stimulus—possibly the exploding of a supernova—the gas and the dust were tightly compressed into a ball by the force of gravity. The ball began to spin, heating up on the inside while remaining cooler on the outside. In places, particles came together to form planets and moons. They broke off as the inside part of the ball transformed into a star. The planets eventually cooled off and began orbiting the sun.

❸ Nitrogen

Nitrogen is element number seven on the periodic table of the elements and is a colorless, odorless gas. It is the most prevalent gas in the Earth's atmosphere, comprising around 78% of it. Nitrogen is found in the tissues of all living creatures, be they animals or plants. It is also commonly used for commercial purposes for two main reasons. The first is that it is an inert gas, which means that it does not easily react with other elements, so it can often prevent combustion or oxidation from occurring in certain situations. Additionally, nitrogen in its liquid form is incredibly cold, so it is ideal for use as a chilling agent.

❹ Determining the Distances of Stars

When observed from the Earth, all stars have varying levels of brightness. However, their distance is not the only factor that determines their brightness. The amount of energy emitted from the star is integral as well. Therefore, some stars close to Earth may be dim because they are weak while others far away may be bright because of their strength. By using the method called parallax, astronomers have long been able to estimate how far away stars are. Parallax involves calculating distance by using Earth's rotation to determine where in the sky a star is at certain times of the year. Today, though, advanced telescopes such as the Hubble Space Telescope can accomplish these calculations more easily and accurately.

❺ Signs of Water on Mars

The question as to whether there is life on Mars has long intrigued humans. The presence of liquid water on Mars would make it a more likely possibility. That there is ice at Mars's polar caps is well known. There are also various patches of ice in frigid places around the planet, and some water exists in vapor form, too. However, recently, probes sent to Mars have taken pictures of the same places at different periods of time. The pictures show that the terrain has changed in ways that suggest the presence of liquid water running on the surface. More research needs to be done, but it appears liquid water may exist on the planet's surface.

❻ The Earth's Inner and Outer Cores

The Earth is divided into three main parts: the outer crust, the mantle, and the core, which is the innermost part of the planet. However, the core itself has two parts: the inner core and the outer core. Both parts are comprised mainly of iron, yet the outer core has some nickel. However, while the inner core is solid iron, the iron and the nickel in the outer core are in their liquid forms. The outer core is also responsible for the Earth's magnetic field. Interestingly, it is believed that the inner core rotates slightly faster than the rest of the planet, which may influence the Earth's magnetic field.

7 Comets and Asteroids

Aside from the sun, planets, and moons, other objects exist in the solar system. Two are comets and asteroids. Comets are huge balls of mostly ice that orbit the sun. There may be large numbers of them, yet most never leave the solar system's outer regions. When they near the sun, some of their ice melts, giving them a tail, or coma, that can be millions of miles long. Asteroids, however, are solid rocks orbiting the sun from within the solar system. They may be a few yards or several hundred miles in diameter. They also typically orbit the sun from the asteroid belt between Mars and Jupiter. Some, however, have orbits that take them near Earth.

8 Crustal Uplift

The Earth has an incredibly diverse geology. There are mountains, hills, valleys, trenches, and many other kinds of natural structures. However, people have often theorized on how they were formed. As for mountains and hills, there is a theory called crustal uplift which explains it. The crust is comprised of many different plates, which are all constantly moving. Occasionally, these plates crash into one another. This causes an uplift in various parts of the crust. In some cases, this can be dramatic. The Himalaya and Rocky mountains were formed from a violent clashing of plates. Resultantly, the mountains rose high above the ground.

9 Alfred Wegener

One of the most influential of all geologists was Alfred Wegener. He was one of the first to propose that there was once a giant supercontinent, which he called Pangaea, millions of years ago. At first, his ideas were widely ridiculed by other scientists. Nevertheless, Wegener constantly promoted this hypothesis, along with the theory of continental drift. He first published his ideas in 1912, and he expanded upon them in later volumes. When he died in 1930, his theories were still mostly unaccepted. However, decades later, as more evidence was accumulated, Wegener's theories began to be reconsidered. Today, continental drift is widely accepted as truth in the geological community.

10 Magma

Deep in the Earth's mantle, the temperature is so intense, and the heat is so great that much of the rock melts. There, in its molten form, it is known as magma. However, magma is not entirely liquid. It is comprised of different minerals, and all of them have their own melting points. Therefore, magma is a combination of solids, liquids, and gases that are fluid, thereby allowing it to move. While magma usually remains underground, it may rush to the planet's surface when a volcano erupts. There, it comes out of the volcano as lava, and it seeps down the sides of the mountain, where it eventually cools and hardens.

Star Performer Topic Files — **Physical Sciences**

- The surface of Mars
- Various methods of sea navigation
- The process by which Jupiter was formed
- The mapping of the oceans
- Earth's environment after its formation
- Seismic waves
- The effects of plate tectonics on California
- Crystals
- The inner structure of the Earth
- Nitrogen fixation

alkaline
amino acid
anthracite
apogee
aquifer
arroyo
asteroid
asthenosphere
astronomer
astronomy
atmosphere
atmospheric
atoll
atom
atomic mass
atomic weight
axis
basalt
base
binary compound
bituminous
black hole
bolt
brightness
buffer
butte
carbonate
celestial
circulate
circulation
clay
coagulate
collapse
coma
combust
combustion
comet
composition
conduct
conduction
conjunction
continent
continental
continental drift
core
cosmic
covalent bond
critical mass
crust
crystallization
crystallize
delta

diameter
diffusion
distill
drainage
dwarf planet
earthquake
ebb tide
eclipse
electromagnetic
electron
element
entropy
eon
epicenter
epoch
era
erosion
evaporation
evaporate
experiment
experimentation
fault
fission
flood
formation
fossil
fusion
galactic
galaxy
gas giant
geyser
glacier
granite
gravitation
gravity
half-life
helium
hydrogen
hydrothermal
igneous
inhibit
inhibitor
ion
isotope
Jovian
karst
kinetic
landform
lava
land bridge
landslide
light year

lightning
lithosphere
lunar
magma
magnetic
magnetism
mantle
metamorphic
meteor
meteorite
Milky Way
mineral
molecular
molecule
neap tide
neutron
nova
nuclear
nuclear reaction
obsidian
orbit
orbital
organic
output
oxidation
oxidize
oxygen
ozone
Pangaea
parallax
parsec
particle
pasteurization
pasteurize
perigee
periodic
permeable
petrification
petrify
petroleum
planet
planetary
polarity
polymer
pressure
property
proton
quarry
radiation
react
reaction
regression

revolution
revolve
rotate
rotation
runoff
satellite
saturate
saturated
sediment
sedimentary
seism
seismograph
shale
sinkhole
solar
solar flare
solar system
solute
solvent
space shuttle
space station
spectrum
sphere
spontaneous
stratosphere
striation
sublimate
sublimation
sunspot
surface
supernova
tectonic plate
terrestrial
theoretical
theory
thermodynamics
thunder
tremor
trench
troposphere
universe
unsaturated
vapor
vaporize
viscosity
volatile
volcanic
volcano
watershed
wave
weather
weathered

📝 Choose the words closest in meaning to the highlighted parts of the sentences.

1   Hales experimented endlessly with plants and animals and unlike many so-called scientists of his day, he did not rely on farfetched theories with no basis in truth.

   Ⓐ particularly
   Ⓑ regularly
   Ⓒ constantly
   Ⓓ potentially

2   Finding a comet can create great excitement among both professional and amateur astronomers alike because they are the only celestial bodies named for their discoverers.

   Ⓐ extraterrestrial
   Ⓑ manmade
   Ⓒ natural
   Ⓓ gigantic

3   This causes the star to undergo cooling, and its core contracts.

   Ⓐ center
   Ⓑ importance
   Ⓒ material
   Ⓓ mass

4   However, atoms can also form into isotopes, slightly different forms of the same atom created when more neutrons are added or subtracted.

   Ⓐ activated
   Ⓑ attracted
   Ⓒ departed
   Ⓓ removed

5   In the batch method, the product is placed in a vat surrounded by circulating water, steam, or coils with water or steam inside of them.

   Ⓐ bowl
   Ⓑ container
   Ⓒ bottle
   Ⓓ glass

6   Sunspots have been observed since ancient times, and astronomers have meticulously cataloged them since the seventeenth century.

   Ⓐ witnessed
   Ⓑ researched
   Ⓒ recorded
   Ⓓ studied

7   For example, the release of increasing amounts of sulfur dioxide is a sign an eruption is imminent.

   Ⓐ ominous
   Ⓑ possible
   Ⓒ complete
   Ⓓ impending

8   Something he had noticed was that in areas with a lack of fresh air—prisons, ship holds, and other confined spaces—there was an increase in the mortality rate of the occupants.

   Ⓐ depressing
   Ⓑ cramped
   Ⓒ degraded
   Ⓓ captive

9   This is a lightning storm, a common global phenomenon.

   Ⓐ interest
   Ⓑ occurrence
   Ⓒ fear
   Ⓓ problem

10 Essentially, these planets are huge balls of glowing, heaving gases, most of which are hydrogen and helium.

   Ⓐ pulsing
   Ⓑ shining
   Ⓒ emitting
   Ⓓ warming

11 When this occurs, there are two possible results: One is the creation of a neutron star, which is a remnant of the giant star.

- (A) relative
- (B) mirror image
- (C) signal
- (D) vestige

12 As a result of the instability of the Earth's interior, volcanoes have been erupting ever since the planet was formed.

- (A) volatility
- (B) weakness
- (C) composition
- (D) formation

13 It is believed that intense sunspot activity and corona growth can interfere with radio, electrical, and magnetic fields on the Earth.

- (A) coincide
- (B) exemplify
- (C) obstruct
- (D) transmit

14 Still, its death can take millions or even billions of years to transpire.

- (A) begin
- (B) stop
- (C) instigate
- (D) happen

15 Despite Venus being covered by a dense cloud of gas, it is not a gas giant.

- (A) thick
- (B) transparent
- (C) hazy
- (D) obtuse

16 Eventually, a channel is opened, the particles rush to meet one another, and the resultant electrical transfer is what people witness as lightning.

- (A) ensuing
- (B) final
- (C) powerful
- (D) conclusive

17 Astronomer Jan Oort hypothesized its existence and declared that it stretches as far as 50,000 times the distance from Earth to the sun.

- (A) announced
- (B) guaranteed
- (C) proved
- (D) proposed

18 Despite many successes in volcanic eruption prediction, it remains an imperfect science that faces several major obstacles.

- (A) possibilities
- (B) barriers
- (C) questions
- (D) theories

19 In addition, the outer electron cloud is vital to the stability of an atom.

- (A) crucial
- (B) repeated
- (C) portrayed
- (D) replicated

20 The name of the theory was plate tectonics, and it has not only been understood but has also been accepted by the scientific community as the most rational explanation for these observations.

- (A) serious
- (B) literate
- (C) logical
- (D) comprehensive

Chapter 08 Environmental Sciences

Environmental sciences focus on the study of the environment. There are many different fields of study in the environmental sciences. Its practitioners are typically are involved in interdisciplinary studies, so they are frequently competent in fields such as biology, chemistry, geology, physics, meteorology, and other sciences. In environmental studies, researchers focus on how the environment operates as a whole and in various smaller ecosystems. In addition, they often look at the effects the environment has on the organisms—including humans—that live in it while also examining the effects that organisms—especially humans—have on it. Others concentrate on how to preserve the environment as well as how to conserve the Earth's natural resources. And some researchers focus on climate studies as they explore various issues in both global warming and cooling. Overall, experts in this field are students of the Earth, everything that lives on it, and everything that affects it.

Rainforest Reforestation

Rainforests comprise around seven percent of the Earth's land surface, yet they are one of the most important biomes on the planet. The towering trees and other vegetation produce around twenty percent of the oxygen in the atmosphere. Approximately one-quarter of all medicines come from rainforests, and there are countless undiscovered plant and animal species living in them. Today, <u>slash-and-burn agriculture</u>, logging, and mining have led to large parts of the world's rainforests to be cut down. Deforestation is a gigantic problem yet one that can be overcome through various reforestation methods.

2→ Both governments and nongovernmental organizations (NGOs) around the world are making an effort to reforest areas. One common method is to make cutting down trees illegal without permission. This has been somewhat successful, yet illegal loggers working deep in the forests are still able to evade law enforcement while practicing their trade. There are also NGOs in many countries that focus on planting new trees. Groups in Indonesia, Brazil, and the Congo, among other places, have planted millions of trees in recent years. Their efforts have led to parts of many rainforests making speedy recoveries while also maintaining the biodiversity of the forests. This has also prevented the extinction of numerous animal species, which were rapidly losing their homes due to deforestation.

One major success story regarding rainforest reforestation is Costa Rica. In the 1940s, roughly seventy-five percent of the entire country was rainforest. Over the next few decades, loggers devastated the rainforests so much that by the late 1980s, around half of all the rainforests in Costa Rica had been destroyed. The government stepped in and made logging illegal. It also introduced the PES (payments for ecosystem services) project. It encouraged local farmers both to protect the local environment and to engage in sustainable forestry practices. Those who joined the program were paid for their efforts. PES payments, in conjunction with the money they earned from farming, enabled their work to be profitable, which improved their level of desire to participate in the program.

The PES program has been incredibly successful. Today, Costa Rica's rainforests have returned as around sixty-percent of the country is covered with rainforests, and the number keeps rising annually. Now that local citizens have an economic incentive to protect the rainforest and to encourage its growth, the recovery will likely be permanent. Biologists estimate that at least half a million plant and animal species, including numerous endangered ones such as macaws, now reside in the country's forests. Costa Rica presently serves as a <u>role model</u> for other countries on how to restore their lost forests and proves that it is possible for rainforests to come back in a relatively short period of time.

📚 *Glossary*

slash-and-burn agriculture: the act of burning forested areas to clear land for farming
role model: someone or something whose behavior or actions can be imitated by others in a positive way

1   The word "overcome" in the passage is closest in meaning to

     (A) contemplated   (B) proposed

     (C) defeated   (D) challenged

Question Type

[Vocabulary Question]

For difficult vocabulary words, use the context of the sentence and the ones around it to eliminate incorrect answer choices.

2   In paragraph 2, why does the author mention "Indonesia, Brazil, and the Congo"?

     (A) To claim that they have passed laws in an effort to fight illegal logging

     (B) To complain that people cutting down their rainforests are evading law enforcement

     (C) To name some places where successful reforestation efforts have been occurring

     (D) To point out that their NGOs are helping save various endangered animal species

[Rhetorical Purpose Question]

Always take the topic of the paragraph into consideration when looking for the reason why the author includes information.

3   Which of the sentences below best expresses the essential information in the highlighted sentence in the passage? *Incorrect* answer choices change the meaning in important ways or leave out essential information.

     (A) Costa Rica is a positive example for countries and shows that rainforests can be restored fairly quickly.

     (B) Many countries are trying to imitate the methods that Costa Rica is using to restore its rainforests.

     (C) One role model is Costa Rica, which is attempting to bring back rainforests to the entire country.

     (D) Some countries such as Costa Rica have been successful at planting trees to help their rainforests recover.

[Sentence Simplification Question]

Eliminate answer choices by looking at individual phrases and determining whether or not they have information which disagrees with what is included in the highlighted sentence.

4   ***Directions:*** An introductory sentence for a brief summary of the passage is provided below. Complete the summary by selecting the THREE answer choices that express the most important ideas of the passage. Some sentences do not belong because they express ideas that are not presented in the passage or are minor ideas in the passage. ***This question is worth 2 points.***

Many countries around the world are making an effort to restore rainforests that had previously been destroyed.

Answer Choices

   ☐1   Costa Rica has succeeded in restoring more forested areas than any other country in the world has.

   ☐2   Both governments and NGOs are trying to fight deforestation by passing laws and by planting trees.

   ☐3   Illegal loggers are not only cutting down rainforest trees but are also evading law enforcement.

   ☐4   The PES program in Costa Rica has helped the country get over its deforestation problems.

   ☐5   Rainforests in some countries have recovered, thereby saving endangered plant and animal life.

   ☐6   Rainforests produce not only large amounts of oxygen but also many of the world's medicines.

[Prose Summary Question]

Introductory sentences provide an overall summary of the passage, and the answer choices should also summarize parts of the passage.

The Process of Desertification

1→ A tremendous amount of the Earth's surface is covered by deserts; however, not all deserts are identical to one another as some are extremely hot while other deserts are actually quite cold. The one feature that all deserts—no matter where on the planet they exist or how they were formed—have in common is that they receive a **miniscule** amount of annual rainfall. Since the Earth has several types of deserts, it is only natural that the process of desertification, which involves the actual conversion of fertile land into uncultivable desert, can take place in several different ways. Two of the more unique types of deserts are rain shadow deserts and coastal deserts. Coincidentally, both form in areas where individuals would not normally expect that a desert could be; however, due to various meteorological phenomena, they exist.

Rain shadow deserts form on the **leeward** side of mountain ranges. In addition, they typically form relatively close to oceans or other large bodies of water. First, moisture in the air is pushed up when it reaches the mountain ranges. As the moist air rises, it becomes cool, condenses, and consequently falls as precipitation in storms, some of which are heavy, in the form of rain, ice, or snow. As a result, the air being blown across the mountains by the wind is entirely void of moisture. The land immediately adjacent to the mountains accordingly gets no or very little water, so it transforms into a desert. The Atacama Desert in South America was formed this way as was the Gobi Desert in Asia, which lies in the rain shadow of the Himalaya Mountains.

3→ Coastal deserts, meanwhile, are geographical entities which, upon first glance, are difficult to account for. They exist right next to large bodies of water—oceans or seas—yet receive little rainfall themselves. The reason for this is currents in the ocean. Ocean currents can move either warm or cold water. In cases where the water is warm, there tends to be a large amount of moisture in the air, which results in a region receiving a large amount of rainfall. Florida, which is alongside the Gulf Stream, is a prime example. However, if a current transports cold water, then the air above it will have a small amount of moisture, so very little rain will fall there. This explains how certain regions, such as Baja California in Mexico and the Namib Desert in South Africa, were formed.

≋ *Glossary*

miniscule: very tiny
leeward: toward the direction the wind is blowing

1 According to paragraph 1, which of the following is NOT true of deserts?

   (A) There are several reasons why they have been created.

   (B) They sometimes exist in somewhat unlikely locations.

   (C) The range of temperatures they experience is rather wide.

   (D) In some cases, they are known to have fertile land.

Question Type

[Negative Factual Question]

Do not be distracted by words or phrases that mention a possibility which is contradicted by information that appears in the passage.

2 The word "it" in the passage refers to

   (A) moisture

   (B) land

   (C) water

   (D) desert

[Reference Question]

Sometimes answer choices appear that are found after the highlighted word in the passage. While rare, they may occasionally be correct answers.

3 Which of the following can be inferred from paragraph 3 about coastal deserts?

   (A) They do not appear next to places with stagnant water.

   (B) Their existence has yet to be explained by experts.

   (C) The temperature is typically cold where they exist.

   (D) They have few winds blowing across them.

[Inference Question]

Use the process of elimination to get rid of answer choices that you know have false information. This will make finding the correct answer easier.

4 ***Directions:*** Select the appropriate statements from the answer choices and match them to the type of desert to which they relate. TWO of the answer choices will NOT be used. ***This question is worth 3 points.***

[Fill in a Table Question]

Be careful of adverbs when trying to determine which answer choices should not be used.

Answer Choices	TYPE OF DESERT
1 Undergo temperature fluctuations on occasion	**Rain Shadow Desert**
	•
2 Are caused by the current in a body of water	•
	•
3 Are created because of the wind blowing dry air above the land	
4 Can exist virtually anywhere on the entire planet	**Coastal Desert**
	•
5 Are found both in South Africa and also in Mexico	•
6 Are always found next to a mountain range	
7 May see the land near them get large amounts of rain	

Climate Change and Species Distribution

1→ One constant on the Earth is that the climate is continually undergoing various changes. At certain times during the Earth's history, the planet has witnessed hot, cold, wet, and dry weather both at extreme and moderate levels. In addition, parts of the planet—no matter how far north or south they may be—have seen varying types of weather, particularly with regard to temperature. While these changes frequently affect the topology of the planet, they always have an effect on the types of species—both flora and fauna—that exist in certain areas.

In some cases, the consequences of climate change can be quite dramatic as it can have devastating results on the plant and animal populations. For instance, over the years, the Earth has been struck repeatedly by asteroids and meteors. Most of the time, they are **incinerated** in the atmosphere and never reach the ground. However, every so often—once in several million years—one of these celestial bodies strikes the Earth with such force that countless species of plants and animals become extinct almost instantly. This is what scientists believe caused the dinosaurs to die out, and previous strikes may have been responsible for other mass extinctions as well.

3→ In addition, volcanic eruptions—while confined to a local area—can still have a global influence. Some, such as Krakatoa, an Indonesian volcano that violently erupted in 1883, may cause the entire planet's weather to change. Powerful volcanic eruptions similar to Krakatoa and the Yellowstone **supervolcano** have happened on other occasions in the past. Not only volcanoes, but glaciers that rapidly expand during sudden ice ages can also cause the extinction of species simply by destroying their habitats.

Fortunately, many of the changes in climate are not so dramatic but occur more gradually. Warm areas slowly transform into tropical regions, or cold areas gradually warm up or perhaps become slightly colder. When any of these changes—either sudden or measured—occur, they affect the plants and animals living in an area. In general, the animals, depending upon which type of climate they prefer, begin migrating either to warmer or cooler lands. However, not all are successful, so many succumb during their journey. Similarly, much of the plant life growing in an area changes, too. A major reason for this is the availability of water, which often changes along with the weather. When the water supply increases or decreases, various plant species die out while others become dominant. Whatever the case, changes in the climate can have the end result of radically changing the living conditions of the plants and animals inhabiting a region.

🗢 **Glossary**
incinerate: to burn completely
supervolcano: a volcano that erupts with a tremendous amount of power

1 According to paragraph 1, the physical appearance of the Earth changes because

[Factual Question]

- Ⓐ the Earth is constantly evolving
- Ⓑ the planet's weather always varies
- Ⓒ sometimes the Earth becomes too hot
- Ⓓ there are many species of flora and fauna on the Earth

2 Which of the sentences below best expresses the essential information in the highlighted sentence in the passage? *Incorrect* answer choices change the meaning in important ways or leave out essential information.

[Sentence Simplification Question]

- Ⓐ On rare occasions, many organisms are wiped out entirely when something from outer space hits the planet.
- Ⓑ Several times each million-year period, plants and animals are made extinct when something strikes the Earth.
- Ⓒ The last time that there was a mass extinction on the planet from an outside force was millions of years ago.
- Ⓓ Without celestial bodies hitting the planet, there would be more species of plants and animals today.

3 The author discusses "Krakatoa" in paragraph 3 in order to

[Rhetorical Purpose Question]

- Ⓐ compare its power with that of the Yellowstone supervolcano
- Ⓑ give the name of a glacier that once expanded rapidly
- Ⓒ show how a single event can have global consequences
- Ⓓ prove that volcanoes have more destructive power than glaciers

4 *Directions:* An introductory sentence for a brief summary of the passage is provided below. Complete the summary by selecting the THREE answer choices that express the most important ideas of the passage. Some sentences do not belong because they express ideas that are not presented in the passage or are minor ideas in the passage. *This question is worth 2 points.*

[Prose Summary Question]

When the planet's climate changes for whatever reason, it often causes species either to die out or to move to other regions to live.

Answer Choices

① Without access to water, animals will not be able to live and thus will quickly die.	④ An asteroid strike can disrupt the Earth's weather so much that many species may go extinct.
② Krakatoa's eruption caused the temperature of the entire planet to change for a while.	⑤ The Yellowstone supervolcano exploded with a force that has never been equaled.
③ Animals will migrate to warmer places if their current habitat suddenly becomes cooler.	⑥ Volcanic eruptions can have a huge effect on the planet's weather patterns and climate.

Erosion and Its Causes

The Earth's surface is constantly undergoing changes. While these changes may not be obvious to the naked eye since they frequently take thousands or even millions of years to occur, they are still happening all the time. Mainly, they are caused by the forces of erosion. Erosion is the gradual movement of the soil, rocks, and other __inanimate__ matter across the Earth's surface. There are many factors that can cause erosion, but the primary ones are water, wind, gravity, and ice.

² → Water is the most important of all the forms of erosion and is arguably the most powerful force. Water erosion typically occurs because of running water in the guise of streams and rivers. The water basically moves particles of earth from one place to another. It can also wear down riverbeds and even carve out the sides of mountains, as one can see clearly happened in the Grand Canyon in the United States. **1** While the Colorado River took millions of years to create the Grand Canyon, the effects of water erosion manifest themselves more quickly in other places. **2** The Mississippi River Delta in the Gulf of Mexico is one such place. **3** Tons of sediment are annually carried by the river to the gulf, where it is deposited in various places, thereby actively altering the landscape of the Mississippi area. **4**

³ → Wind and gravity are two more powerful erosive forces; however, their effects are usually limited to particular geographical areas. Wind erosion mostly takes place in deserts, where the winds quickly whip sand around. They can also contribute to desertification. For instance, in the 1930s, the Dust Bowl in Oklahoma, Texas, and other Western states was caused primarily by wind removing much of the fertile topsoil from the land and leaving nothing but sandy, useless soil. Gravity erosion, on the other hand, typically takes place in mountainous or hilly areas. Basically, it occurs through avalanches, rockslides, and mudslides when materials at high elevations fall and are deposited at areas with lower elevations, often in a very rapid manner.

Much like gravity erosion, ice erosion can be both incredibly dramatic in its effects and also extremely quick acting. In some instances, water __seeps__ into cracks in rocks and boulders. When the temperature drops, the water turns to ice, and it is often strong enough to break huge chunks of the rocks off literally overnight. In other cases, glaciers—frozen ice sheets—can scrape off and radically alter the landscape as they expand and recede over time.

≋ *Glossary*
inanimate: lifeless; inorganic
seep: to ooze; to creep

1   According to paragraph 2, which of the following is NOT true of water erosion?

     Ⓐ Its effects may not be seen for a long period of time.

     Ⓑ Some believe it is more powerful than other forms of erosion.

     Ⓒ It is somewhat less dominant than other forms of erosion.

     Ⓓ It requires running water in order for it to be effective.

2   In paragraph 3, the author implies that the Dust Bowl

     Ⓐ destroyed some land that was once being farmed on

     Ⓑ happened over a very short period of time

     Ⓒ was confined to land that was already mostly desert

     Ⓓ could have been prevented by the people living there

3   Look at the four squares [■] that indicate where the following sentence could be added to the passage.

In fact, maps covering the area must constantly be updated on account of the changes being wrought.

Where would the sentence best fit?

4   **_Directions:_** Select the appropriate sentences from the answer choices and match them to the type of erosion to which they relate. TWO of the answer choices will NOT be used. **_This question is worth 3 points._**

          Answer Choices   **TYPE OF EROSION**

① It may happen at the same rate of speed as ice erosion.

② It occurs when very low temperatures break apart rocks.

③ It typically only occurs in areas that are deserts.

④ The Grand Canyon was created by this kind of erosion.

⑤ It requires the movement of earth from one altitude to another.

⑥ A number of rocks falling down at once is an example of this erosion.

⑦ It may sometimes move earth by making use of rivers.

Water
-
-

Gravity
-
-
-

Savanna Fires

1→ Savannas are tropical grasslands replete with various kinds of grasses, shrubs, and even a few trees and cover approximately one-fifth of the Earth's entire land surface. However, the trees found on savannas are spaced far enough apart from one another so as not to be able to create forested areas. Savannas comprise around half of the land in Africa and are also commonplace in Australia, India, and South America. In fact, wherever on the planet there is either warm or hot weather, there are likely to be savannas. One crucial feature they all share is that they have two important seasons: a rainy season and a dry season.

In parts of Africa, the rainy season typically peaks in October, resulting in numerous thunderstorms and the land being drenched with water. However, by January, the dry season is well underway; therefore, the land becomes extremely parched during this month. **1** This is exactly when many of the seasonal fires sweep through the savannas. **2** Some of these fires may be attributed to **arson**, but the vast majority of them are simply acts of nature. **3** Contrary to what many people think, these fires are not actually harmful to the savanna, but in fact, they are integral to it; for without the fires, life on the savanna would be much different. **4**

3→ To begin with, most of the animals that perish in the flames are those with short lifespans, namely, insects. Yet even their deaths provide life for others as numerous birds flock to the fires after they are extinguished to feast upon the grasshoppers, crickets, and other insects that died. As for larger animals, they either hide from the fires or flee. Savannas typically have holes or crevices in which animals can retreat to avoid the fast-moving flames. In other cases, many large mammals that live on the savannas simply outrun the fires and seek safe **havens**.

4→ In addition, while many grasses burn in the fires, their roots run extremely deep in the ground. While the roots evolved that way in order to maximize their ability to extract water from the parched soil, they serve another purpose: Their deepness ensures that they are protected from the fires, so although their aboveground parts burn, they survive. This means that the plants will grow again once the rains return, which typically happens in March. The few trees which live on the grasslands have their own survival mechanisms as many have fire-resistant bark which keeps them alive. Furthermore, other trees frequently retain certain amounts of moisture in their aboveground parts—their trunk, branches, and leaves—which provides them with some modicum of protection as well.

Finally, the annual fires also assist in replenishing the soil. By burning the grasses and other organic material, which then combine with the soil, the savanna fires provide more nutrients for the earth. This, in turn, enables grasses, shrubs, and trees to grow more quickly and to reproduce in abundance, which allows life once again to thrive on the savannas.

≋ **Glossary**
arson: the intentional starting of a fire for harmful purposes
haven: a place of safety

1   According to paragraph 1, which of the following is true of savannas?
   Ⓐ They are only rarely found on continents such as the Americas.
   Ⓑ They experience temperatures slightly less hot than that of deserts.
   Ⓒ They cover around twenty percent of the Earth's entire surface area.
   Ⓓ They have vegetation larger than plants but not in sizable numbers.

2   Why does the author mention "grasshoppers" in paragraph 3?
   Ⓐ To note how they are hunted by numerous birds living on the savannas
   Ⓑ To provide an example of animals which often die in savanna fires
   Ⓒ To show that they are not clever enough to know to hide from the fires
   Ⓓ To prove that their deaths in great numbers have no effect on savannas

3   In paragraph 4, all of the following questions are answered EXCEPT:
   Ⓐ How does the bark of some trees keep them alive during fires?
   Ⓑ Why did some plants evolve to have roots that grow deep underground?
   Ⓒ What are some of the trees that retain moisture in their trunk, branches, and leaves?
   Ⓓ When does it usually start to rain again on savannas?

4   Look at the four squares [■] that indicate where the following sentence could be added to the passage.

   For instance, lightning strikes may provide the sparks necessary to begin a great conflagration.

   Where would the sentence best fit?

5 ***Directions:*** An introductory sentence for a brief summary of the passage is provided below. Complete the summary by selecting the THREE answer choices that express the most important ideas of the passage. Some sentences do not belong because they express ideas that are not presented in the passage or are minor ideas in the passage. ***This question is worth 2 points.***

The fires that occur annually on savannas are part of a natural cycle and are even somewhat beneficial to the land and organisms living there.

-
-
-

Answer Choices

1. Many trees are able to stay alive during the fires because they have evolved to be able to resist flames in certain ways.

2. The ashes of burned grasses and plants make the soil more nutrient rich, which lets new plant life grow much faster.

3. Few animals wind up being killed by the fires, and those which do succumb to the flames are typically eaten by others.

4. After the rainy season ends, the dry season quickly arrives, so fires on the savannas begin to occur.

5. Some of the fires are caused by human beings intentionally starting them in order to destroy parts of the savannas.

6. Savannas are found in areas where the weather is rather hot and are present on many of the Earth's continents.

Summarizing ▶ Complete the summary by filling in the blanks.

Savannas are hot, dry areas found in many places. They endure both _____ season. During the dry season, they experience fires, almost all of which break out naturally. These fires are actually _____ to the savannas. First, the few animals that die are typically just _____, and their bodies serve as food for many animals. Next, _____ survive and immediately grow back once the rains return. Trees also have natural protections to help them survive the fires. And the burned vegetation helps _____, giving it more nutrients to let plants grow better and faster.

Variations in the Sea Level

The term "sea level" is used to describe the height of the sea compared to a fixed mark on the local land. It is frequently difficult to measure since there are many factors, such as tides, winds, wave motion, currents, water temperature and salinity, precipitation, and evaporation, involved. Over long periods of time, other issues, such as the movement of the continents and periodic ice ages, may also come into play. For instance, in the past, when the Arctic and Greenland ice caps expanded, vast amounts of seawater became ice, which lowered the levels of the world's oceans.

There is no average sea level on the Earth. The sea level actually varies from place to place in all of the world's oceans.

2→ During the last great ice age about 18,000 years ago, the enormous amount of frozen water reduced sea levels everywhere by as many as 130 meters. Much of this reduction was the result of water evaporating and falling as snow, which then froze on the Arctic and Greenland ice caps. In some instances, natural bridges between landmasses emerged as parts of the ocean floor were exposed. For example, there was once a land bridge between Asia and North America, which may have been the route humans took to reach the Americas. Once the ice melted and the ice caps and glaciers receded, sea levels rose, and the land bridges disappeared beneath the waves.

In the time between the last great ice age and the present, there have been numerous minor ice ages. One is called the Maunder Minimum. It occurred from 1645 to 1715 and is also known as the Little Ice Age.

3→ Rather than being concerned with low sea levels, many people today are focused on the possibility of the ice caps melting to the point that sea levels will instead begin to rise. Scientists measure the rate that the ice caps at the poles and in Greenland melt with something called the mass balance. This is the difference between the amount of ice that melts into the oceans and the amount which returns from the oceans to the ice caps in the form of frozen precipitation. When the mass balance tips towards more ice melting than precipitation returning, sea levels may rise. For example, if the entire Greenland ice shelf melted and no water returned, worldwide sea levels could rise by as much as seven meters.

Changes in the Earth's temperature could be sudden or occur more slowly. Sudden changes, such as those connected with a lack of sunspots, could result in the rapid return of cold weather and possibly even a new ice age.

The good news is that, despite the obvious shrinkage of the polar ice caps and Greenland's ice cap, worldwide sea levels have not significantly changed. At most, measurements taken in a wide number of places have registered a rise of only a few millimeters. This may not just be the result of ice caps melting, but it could be a combination of reasons. The reality is that measuring the world's sea level is such a complex task involving so many factors that no one really knows why such small increases are occurring.

From the human perspective, the bad news is that the Earth is overdue for a rise in sea levels. The geologic record shows that the planet has undergone major fluctuations in sea levels throughout its history. Part of this was a result of the continents shifting due to plate tectonics. When more continental land mass was located near the poles, more snow could accumulate on land, and more ice could build up, thereby reducing sea levels. At the moment, global sea levels are near historically low levels. Perhaps it will not occur during the current population's lifetime, but a massive rise in sea levels is surely inevitable.

≋ *Glossary*
salinity: the level of salt in a substance, typically water
fluctuation: constant change, often involving both rising and falling

1   In stating that other issues may "come into play," the author means that some other factors may
   Ⓐ be responsible
   Ⓑ be involved
   Ⓒ need considering
   Ⓓ be researched

2   According to paragraph 2, which of the following is true of the last great ice age?
   Ⓐ It happened because of the expansion of glaciers past where they normally are.
   Ⓑ It resulted in a tremendous lowering of sea levels around the world.
   Ⓒ The people living at the time constructed land bridges between continents.
   Ⓓ It occurred mostly in the Northern Hemisphere around the year 1800.

3   In paragraph 3, the author implies that Greenland
   Ⓐ has enough ice on it that it could affect the world were it to melt
   Ⓑ has seen a climate much warmer in the past than it has today
   Ⓒ is where glaciers stopped receding at the end of the last ice age
   Ⓓ caused the level of the oceans to drop by more than seven meters

4   The word "it" in the passage refers to
   Ⓐ more snow
   Ⓑ more ice
   Ⓒ the current population's lifetime
   Ⓓ a massive rise in sea levels

5   **_Directions:_** An introductory sentence for a brief summary of the passage is provided below. Complete the summary by selecting the THREE answer choices that express the most important ideas of the passage. Some sentences do not belong because they express ideas that are not presented in the passage or are minor ideas in the passage. **_This question is worth 2 points._**

There are many factors which can affect global sea levels, but the most important is how much water has been frozen in various parts of the world.

-
-
-

Answer Choices

[1] The amount of ice at the polar caps and in Greenland can greatly affect how high or low the oceans are.

[2] The amount of rain as well as the evaporation of water can help affect the level of the sea in some places.

[3] The last ice age happened around 18,000 years ago, so temperatures were much colder at that time.

[4] Since the levels of the world's oceans are so low nowadays, it is guaranteed that they will rise sometime in the future.

[5] Even the movement of the continents can have an effect on the level of the seas throughout the Earth.

[6] When the level of the sea was lower in the past, land bridges between landmasses allowed people to migrate easily.

Summarizing ▶ Complete the summary by filling in the blanks.

The sea levels of the Earth's oceans are difficult to _____ for a variety of reasons. In addition, they are constantly rising and falling depending on certain factors. In the last great ice age around _____ , sea levels were up to 130 meters lower than they are today. Much of the Earth's water was _____ , which changed the way many landmasses looked. However, today, people are concerned more about sea levels rising, not falling. Yet while _____ are smaller, the sea level has not risen much for reasons no one is sure about. However, the Earth is likely to experience _____ sometime in the future.

Energy from the Ocean

[1]→ Renewable energy sources account for only a small percentage of worldwide energy consumption. The most common types of renewable energy are wind, solar, geothermal, and hydroelectric power. They are called renewable because, while producing electricity, they do not consume their energy source, unlike fossil-fuel-fired electric plants or nuclear power plants. Another potential renewable energy source is the power of the oceans. Scientists and engineers are working on using both wave and tidal power to produce electricity, but tidal power appears to have the greatest potential.

Tidal power as an energy source has both positive and negative aspects. First, on the plus side, the tides are constant—occurring twice every day— so the supply of energy is **inexhaustible**. **1** Secondly, the use of tidal power causes virtually no pollution. **2** On the negative side, tidal power can only be cost efficient in areas with tides strong enough to justify the construction of a tidal power system. **3** In addition, depending on the type of tidal power system built, there may be some level of environmental impact on the marine life in the area. **4**

[3]→ There are two basic types of tidal power systems: barrage and tidal turbines. Barrage systems are built across a narrow estuary or inlet where the tides are usually very high. The barrage has sluice gates, which open when the tide is rising and allow massive amounts of water to flow past them. Once the tide begins receding, the sluice gates are closed, trapping the water. Operators slowly release it over turbines, which spin and then generate electricity. Tidal turbine power systems, meanwhile, utilize individual turbines or small combinations of turbines that are built in the water and anchored to the seabed floor. Water enters the system and flows over the internal turbines to generate electricity. There are many varieties of this type of tidal power system.

The barrage system may disrupt local marine life and is also quite expensive to build and maintain. Additionally, there are relatively few places where barrage systems can be built. La Rance, France, is one such place and is also the site of the biggest and oldest barrage system. Due to these **drawbacks**, not many barrage tidal power systems have been built. The tidal turbine type is cheaper, but it can also cause problems for marine life. Sometimes fish enter the turbines and may be killed if they are spinning fast enough. Because of this danger, the turbines typically have fences to prevent sea life from entering. However, even with these safety measures, smaller fish may still be sucked into turbines and killed.

In the end, the amount of power generated by tidal power systems is

Fossil fuels such as coal, natural gas, and oil are nonrenewable resources that, once expended, cannot be replaced.

The most common type of hydroelectric power utilized today is created by dams. Many of the planet's major and minor rivers have multiple dams on them to harness their power and to utilize it to create electricity.

Because of the negative effects on the environment that barrage systems may cause, some governments are reluctant to build any of these types of power systems.

miniscule compared to the world's requirements. Overall, renewable energy production usually amounts to less than 5% of energy requirements even in nations with advanced renewable energy programs. While it is acknowledged that tidal energy has unlimited potential and causes no pollution, the difficulties in constructing and maintaining tidal power systems, plus their impact on local marine ecosystems, mean that few tidal power systems will likely be built.

≋ **Glossary**

inexhaustible: without end

drawback: a disadvantage

1 According to paragraph 1, which of the following is NOT true of various energy sources?

Ⓐ Using the tides to create energy is something that is still being worked on.

Ⓑ The attaining of energy from heat in the Earth is a renewable resource.

Ⓒ Fossil-fuel-fired power plants rely upon renewable energy to make electricity.

Ⓓ Wind and solar power are two renewable energy sources frequently used.

2 The author discusses "sluice gates" in paragraph 3 in order to

Ⓐ show why barrage systems must be built in estuaries

Ⓑ compare them with the turbines used in another type of power plant

Ⓒ explain how much water they can actually let flow through them

Ⓓ mention what captures the water to help create energy

3 The word "they" in the passage refers to

Ⓐ barrage tidal power systems

Ⓑ problems

Ⓒ fish

Ⓓ the turbines

4 Look at the four squares [■] that indicate where the following sentence could be added to the passage.

Unfortunately, this automatically eliminates a number of potential sites where the building of tidal power plants would be ideal.

Where would the sentence best fit?

5 **Directions:** Select the appropriate sentences from the answer choices and match them to the type of tidal power system to which they relate. TWO of the answer choices will NOT be used. ***This question is worth 3 points.***

Answer Choices

1. It may frequently have a very negative effect on the marine life in the area.

2. The electricity-creating part of the system is fixed on the bottom of the water.

3. Various protections can be used to cause less loss of life to fish and other creatures.

4. It is similar to a fossil-fuel-fired power plant in its method of operation.

5. The power plant at La Rance, France, makes use of this system.

6. It relies upon using nuclear power in order to get the plant to function.

7. This system does not require a tremendous expenditure of funds.

TIDAL POWER SYSTEM

Barrage
-
-

Tidal Turbine
-
-
-

Summarizing ▷ Complete the summary by filling in the blanks.

There are many forms of _____ , but they are not used nearly as much as fossil fuels are. One promising form of renewable energy is using _____ . Tidal power is an _____ energy source that creates almost no pollution. Yet it cannot be used everywhere, and it can harm marine life. Both _____ are in use. Barrage systems are expensive and can only be located in a few places. Turbine systems are _____ but can also kill many fish. There are many issues with tidal power, so it is likely not to be used very much in the future.

Evidence for Ice Ages

Even though humans were alive during the time of the last great ice age, approximately 18,000 years ago, there were no writing systems then, so, consequently, no records of it exist. Yet by using certain methods, scientists know that it occurred. By examining geological, ice core, and fossil evidence, scientists have pieced together the story of the last ice age and have postulated that it was not the only one in the Earth's history. When these theories were first proposed in Europe during the middle of the nineteenth century, most of the scientific community was **skeptical**. Today, however, it is accepted that, during many periods in the past, great sheets of ice expanded from the polar ice caps, Greenland, and mountain ranges like the Alps and Himalayas and covered much of the Northern Hemisphere in an icy wintry embrace.

Much of the geological evidence for ice ages comes from North America and Europe. In places today that lack glaciers, certain geological features commonly associated with them exist over wide swaths of land on these two continents. For example, large stones sitting on an open plain must have had some force push them there. Land formations like glacial moraines—deposits of dirt and rock scraped by the leading edge and sides of a glacier—formed where massive glaciers stopped their forward movement and began retreating. In addition, the northern areas of Canada and Scandinavia have many deep-cut valleys and fjords, both of which are associated with glacial activity. First noticed by Alpine experts in Europe in the early nineteenth century, these odd geological features helped initiate the debate over whether ice once covered the Northern Hemisphere.

3➜ Other evidence for ice ages comes from ice cores. By drilling deep into the ice caps in Greenland and the Arctic, scientists have recovered ice samples from past ages. Careful study of the trapped air bubbles in this ice can reveal the temperature, the quantity of carbon dioxide in the air, and other factors that indicate to scientists the climatic conditions of certain time periods. Through an examination of these climatic changes, scientists have estimated that there were at least four great ice ages in the Earth's history with many smaller ones in between. The ice core records show that about 18,000 years ago, there was a great cooling period. This most recent ice age is often called the Little Ice Age because it was not as severe as previous ones.

4➜ Finally, scientists look for evidence of ice ages in fossils. Animals that **favored** warmer climates migrated south when the ice began expanding. If large numbers of fossils of a species are found further south than they usually are, this may indicate that an ice age was occurring. There are two explanations as to how certain species traveled southward. Perhaps the animals migrated south,

Note

During the last major ice age, enormous sheets of ice covered much of the Northern Hemisphere. In some places, the sheets of ice were several kilometers thick.

The Great Lakes in the United States are believed to have been gouged out by receding glaciers. In addition, the Great Plains area in the U.S. is so flat because the movement of glaciers reduced any mountains once there to nothingness.

Fossils are the remains of dead animals or plants. They may be the calcified bones of the animals, or they may be imprints on rock. The studying of fossils has taught scientists much about many periods in the past.

died, and were fossilized there. Or the animals died in the north and became fossilized, but then massive ice sheets scraped them up and carried them to more southerly regions. Unfortunately, this method of determining if and when ice ages occurred depends on finding these fossils in the first place, which is not particularly easy.

📚 **Glossary**

skeptical: doubtful

favor: to prefer

1   The word "postulated" in the passage is closest in meaning to

     Ⓐ theorized

     Ⓑ considered

     Ⓒ believed

     Ⓓ rejected

2   Which of the sentences below best expresses the essential information in the highlighted sentence in the passage? *Incorrect* answer choices change the meaning in important ways or leave out essential information.

     Ⓐ Places on two continents that have no glaciers might have had them in small areas sometime in the past.

     Ⓑ There are many glaciers on two separate continents, and they also used to exist in other places.

     Ⓒ There is evidence of the prior existence of glaciers where there are none today on certain landmasses.

     Ⓓ Without glaciers on certain areas of land, large parts of certain continents would look different than they do today.

3   In paragraph 3, the author implies that past ice ages

     Ⓐ lasted roughly for about the same amount of time

     Ⓑ were more severe in the past than the most recent ones were

     Ⓒ had a traumatic effect on the people who lived through them

     Ⓓ tended to vary in the degree of their cold temperatures

4   According to paragraph 4, using fossils to obtain information on past ice ages is difficult because

     Ⓐ the glaciers that moved the fossils frequently destroyed them

     Ⓑ it is somewhat hard actually to unearth the fossils themselves

     Ⓒ the fossils are often found encased in the ice of massive glaciers

     Ⓓ scientists are not quite sure where to look for these fossils

5 ***Directions:*** Select the appropriate sentences from the answer choices and match them to the method of studying past ice ages to which they relate. TWO of the answer choices will NOT be used. ***This question is worth 3 points.***

Answer Choices	METHOD OF STUDYING PAST ICE AGES
① Scientists can also learn about certain animals that moved south with this method.	**Geological Features**
	•
② Scientists might travel to the Arctic to conduct studies with this method.	•
③ With this method, scientists look for rocks in places where they do not usually exist.	**Ice Cores**
	•
④ This method involves drilling holes deep in certain parts of the Earth.	•
⑤ This method is somewhat difficult due to the lack of evidence scientists have found.	•
⑥ Scientists have learned about the number of major ice ages with this method.	
⑦ Scientists look for evidence of glaciers cutting out valleys in the land.	

Summarizing ▶ Complete the summary by filling in the blanks.

There are no _____ of the last ice age, which took place around 18,000 years ago. So scientists must examine _____, ice core, and fossil evidence to learn about it. The geological evidence in North America and Europe comes from the changes that _____ made as they receded toward the north. For ice core evidence, scientists examine ice from the Arctic and _____ to examine its quality. This can tell them many things about the past. They can also _____ to learn different things about the animals that once lived during the ice age.

Coral Reefs

1➙ One of the Earth's largest living organisms is neither the elephant nor the blue whale but the coral reef called the Great Barrier Reef, which lies off Australia's eastern coast. Coral is a living organism plant-like in appearance and is composed of thousands of polyps of coral grouped together. Coral reefs are found in most of the world's oceans, but they exist predominately in tropical waters, with the largest and most widespread reefs being in the southwest Pacific Ocean. They are home to abundant undersea plant and animal life and comprise unique ecosystems of their own. However, in many places, coral reefs are in danger as pollution and other manmade problems threaten their existence.

2➙ There are a wide variety of coral species, but those responsible for reef building secrete calcium carbonate, which hardens into a rock-like substance. As the coral die, their skeletons become cemented together, providing an anchoring point for the new living coral to rest on. When in shallow water fewer than fifty meters deep, coral can interact with sunlight and reproduce, thereby increasing the reef's size. It can reproduce either asexually or sexually. In sexual reproduction, a coral emits thousands of eggs and sperm, which undergo reproduction and begin forming new coral. After a short time spent near the surface of the water to gain energy, a new coral swims to the bottom and attaches itself to the reef's surface. Sometimes, an entire colony reproduces at the same time, giving itself a much greater chance to increase in size. In asexual reproduction, a coral grows new polyps, which expand the size of the coral colony. Sometimes these polyps detach and establish their own colonies in different areas.

Some coral species feed on small fish and plankton, but the majority depend on the single-cell zooxanthellae algae. This organism lives within the coral, which serves as its home. In return, the coral gets nutrients when the algae go through photosynthesis in sunlight and in water warmer than eighteen degrees Celsius. This absorption of nutrients allows the coral to grow, reproduce, and expand, making reefs larger. Therefore, most coral reefs only form in shallow tropical waters that receive plenty of sunlight. In addition, coral reefs generally do not form in areas where there is plenty of freshwater runoff, as in the case of those near the coastline where large rivers such as the Amazon flow into the ocean. Coral reefs are highly sensitive to changes in the temperature and salinity of the water and may die if these change even slightly.

4➙ There are several types of coral reefs. Some circle an island or atoll, others, such as the Great Barrier Reef, form long, continuous lines out in the ocean far from land, and some are attached to shores and fringe the coastline. They have been both boons and **banes** to sailors throughout the ages. They can provide shelter from the forces of the treacherous ocean so long as a ship can find passageways through them. Otherwise, a coral reef may be the instrument of a ship's destruction, ripping a ship apart, sinking it, and drowning its crew.

5➙ Coral reefs attract large numbers of tourists, who come to observe the **kaleidoscope** of life that is attracted to the reef. Some, like Hanauma Bay in Hawaii, witness hordes of visitors each year. Thousands of species of fish, mollusks, crustaceans, and larger creatures are found in and around coral reefs. Unfortunately, human intruders often disrupt the ecosystem there, taking chunks of coral for their aquariums or to make jewelry with. In addition, sport fishermen can alter the balance of life on the reefs by overfishing them.

However, by far the greatest danger to the continued existence of coral reefs is environmental factors. Polluted water is the primary problem. **1** When water becomes over-polluted from human sewage, garbage, or chemical waste, algae grow in enormous quantities. **2** They overwhelm the sensitive coral, which then expels the zooxanthellae. **3** Since they are what give the coral their various colors, the coral then become white in a process called coral bleaching. **4** Once bleached, coral take time to recover. If the water conditions return to their previous state, the zooxanthellae return. Often, however, the bleached coral die, and entire reefs may be destroyed in such an event.

≋ *Glossary*
bane: a curse; an annoyance
kaleidoscope: a changing pattern of both shapes and colors

---

1 According to paragraph 1, which of the following is NOT true of coral reefs?
- (A) Their numbers are greater in one ocean than in the others.
- (B) A wide range of animals may make their homes in them.
- (C) A coral reef is comprised of a single enormous organism.
- (D) Coral grow better when they are in fairly warm waters.

2 In paragraph 1, the author implies that coral reefs
- (A) are typically the same size as a large whale
- (B) may be found completely encircling Australia
- (C) will only exist when they are in tropical waters
- (D) are able to be killed by outside forces

3 The word "secrete" in the passage is closest in meaning to
- (A) emit
- (B) manufacture
- (C) use
- (D) require

4 According to paragraph 2, which of the following is true of polyps?
- (A) They may only be created through asexual reproduction.
- (B) They can help a coral reef double in size in a short period of time.
- (C) They cannot reproduce when they are in water more than fifty meters deep.
- (D) They are capable of migrating from one place to another.

5 Which of the sentences below best expresses the essential information in the highlighted sentence in the passage? *Incorrect* answer choices change the meaning in important ways or leave out essential information.

    Ⓐ Coral reefs are seldom seen in areas where sizeable rivers such as the Amazon release their freshwater into the ocean.

    Ⓑ Freshwater will kill coral reefs, which is why they are not located anywhere near rivers' ending points in the world's oceans.

    Ⓒ The Amazon is well known for not having any coral reefs because of all the freshwater that it brings to the ocean.

    Ⓓ The coasts of rivers such as the Amazon do not have any coral reefs because of their relationship with the ocean.

6 The word "fringe" in the passage is closest in meaning to

    Ⓐ border

    Ⓑ near

    Ⓒ approach

    Ⓓ reveal

7 Which of the following can be inferred from paragraph 4 about coral reefs?

    Ⓐ They have caused more shipwrecks than any other natural features.

    Ⓑ Sailors have attempted to map some of the bigger reefs.

    Ⓒ They are most commonly found circling islands.

    Ⓓ There can be gaps in them that allow some ships to pass.

8 In paragraph 5, why does the author mention "Hanauma Bay"?

    Ⓐ To name some of the sea creatures that live in reefs like it

    Ⓑ To describe how large it is compared to the Great Barrier Reef

    Ⓒ To give an example of a reef that is popular with tourists

    Ⓓ To emphasize the need to protect it from human invaders

9 Look at the four squares [■] that indicate where the following sentence could be added to the passage.

The result of this growth is a number of problems.

Where would the sentence best fit?

Click on a square [■] to add the sentence to the passage.

10 *Directions:* An introductory sentence for a brief summary of the passage is provided below. Complete the summary by selecting the THREE answer choices that express the most important ideas of the passage. Some sentences do not belong because they express ideas that are not presented in the passage or are minor ideas in the passage. *This question is worth 2 points.*

> Drag your answer choices to the spaces where they belong.
> To remove an answer choice, click on it. To review the passage, click on **View Text.**

Coral reefs are unique ecosystems that support a wide variety of life, but they are in danger of dying because of the actions of humans.

-
-
-

Answer Choices

1. Some people take pieces of coral home with them or even go fishing in the reefs.

2. Some coral reefs have been made protected areas by various countries' governments.

3. Coral are able to reproduce both sexually as well as asexually.

4. When people dump garbage into waters with coral reefs, they can kill coral.

5. While coral prefer to live in tropical waters, they may be found in numerous places.

6. Thousands of species of fish and other animals may live around a coral reef.

Soil Formation and Preservation

1➡ Soil formation is the result of various factors related to the actions of water, the atmosphere, and plant and animal life. Most soil is originally created by the weathering of rock into small particles, but soil composition and changes in the soil itself can result from the other factors mentioned. Soil is crucial to all life on the Earth because without it, not much life could exist on land. Soil has many layers, and there are many types of soil in different climates. Within each soil type are unique ecosystems vital to the continued fertility of the soil.

2➡ Most soil originated as rock, yet over time, wind and water wore it down into progressively smaller particles. Depending upon which abrasives are nearby, the effects of the wind's actions can proceed either extremely slowly or quite rapidly. In places with strong abrasives such as sand, the wind can pick up these particles and utilize them to shape and wear away rock swiftly. Water can also act in the same manner as wind. In warmer climates, it takes a considerable amount of time to erode rock whereas in colder climates, it can literally happen overnight. As water filters through cracks in rocks, night comes, the temperature drops, and the water freezes and subsequently expands, thereby cracking the rocks and breaking off enormous pieces. Another way soil can be created is through the actions of glaciers. During the last great ice age, while retreating northward, massive glaciers scraped and wore away rocks, leaving behind rich soil. Finally, volcanoes can also produce soil, which is good for agriculture, from the ash that their eruptions spew across the land.

3➡ After soil is formed, chemical changes in it attract bacteria, fungi, and plants. Plant roots bind the soil together to prevent further erosion, trees prevent rain from washing it away, and bacteria and fungi decompose the decaying matter of plants, animals, and animal feces. The final result is humus, a dark, extremely fertile soil ideal for growing crops. Soil scientists, or pedologists, typically divide soil into four layers of what they call horizons. At the top is horizon A, the humus-rich topsoil and the most important part. Below that is horizon B, which is filled with minerals washed down from horizon A. Although it is more compact and lighter, it is less fertile than layer A. Under horizon B is horizon C, which is rocky, infertile soil. Finally, horizon D is solid bedrock, which lies under the upper soil levels. Depending on the part of the world, the depth of the soil ranges from a few centimeters to several meters. Naturally, not all soil follows this layer chart, and the chemical composition of all soil differs, with much of it depending on the climate and the plants growing in it.

4➡ One thing all soil has in common is that it can disappear much faster than it was formed. Soil preservation is a constant battle against the elements and man's mistakes. Some things help preserve soil: The ecosystem of animals, fungi, and bacteria helps maintain soil's fertility and preserves it; earthworms are additionally considered essential to this. They tunnel into the soil and leave behind secretions frequently called slime. These secretions are nitrogen rich, which helps create fertile soil, and therefore enable abundant plant growth. In addition, the sticky slime assists in holding the soil together. Furthermore, tree and plant roots play vital roles in soil cohesion by anchoring it to the ground.

5➡ Water poses the biggest threat to soil, and its already formidable powers can be further augmented by humans. Rainfall washes away soil from hills and brings it to lower areas or into river systems. If no plants or trees are anchoring the soil, it will be too loose and will simply wash away. Deforestation is, essentially, the bane of soil and when combined with water, can devastate the land. The overcutting of forests was a major reason for the decline of several civilizations throughout history. **1** With no trees, the soil lost the precious humus-rich topsoil vital for farming. **2** This led to declines in food stocks, followed by massive famines, the breakdown of order, warfare, anarchy, and, eventually, the death of civilization. **3** To prevent modern-day occurrences, societies must wisely manage their land to ensure it remains fertile. **4**

≋ *Glossary*
abrasive: something which is coarse or rough
secretion: a substance that is discharged or emitted from a body

---

1   The word "weathering" in the passage is closest in meaning to

      Ⓐ aging

      Ⓑ modification

      Ⓒ expelling

      Ⓓ disintegrating

2   According to paragraph 1, which of the following is NOT true of soil?

      Ⓐ Depending on where a person is, the type of soil might be different.

      Ⓑ All life on the Earth exists because of the presence of soil.

      Ⓒ There are many different ways in which it can be created.

      Ⓓ Most soil is formed when rocks are broken down to become it.

3   The word "rich" in the passage is closest in meaning to

      Ⓐ prosperous

      Ⓑ productive

      Ⓒ balanced

      Ⓓ prodigious

4   In paragraph 2, the author uses "volcanoes" as an example of

      Ⓐ a way that soil can be created quickly

      Ⓑ things that are able to make fertile soil

      Ⓒ competitors with glaciers in soil creation

      Ⓓ a kind of abrasive that can create soil

5 According to paragraph 3, humus is created because

Ⓐ farmers have a need for rich, fertile soil

Ⓑ plants are able to decompose dead material to make it

Ⓒ a number of factors help soil transform into it

Ⓓ plant roots prevent the soil from being washed away

6 The word "anchoring" in the passage is closest in meaning to

Ⓐ securing

Ⓑ resorting

Ⓒ portraying

Ⓓ growing

7 In paragraph 4, the author implies that earthworms

Ⓐ can only live in areas that have soil that is very fertile

Ⓑ can secrete slime because of the nutrients they take from the soil

Ⓒ are more important to soil preservation than other animals

Ⓓ are in competition with bacteria and fungi when living in the soil ecosystem

8 According to paragraph 5, which of the following is true of deforestation?

Ⓐ It is a more powerful destroyer of soil than water is.

Ⓑ It has caused more civilizations to decline than wars have.

Ⓒ It enables rich soil easily to be washed away by the elements.

Ⓓ It is often caused when a region begins to get less rainfall.

9 Look at the four squares [■] that indicate where the following sentence could be added to the passage.

The Maya in Central America were one such group of people whose downfall may have been brought about in this manner.

Where would the sentence best fit?

Click on a square [■] to add the sentence to the passage.

10 **Directions:** Select the appropriate sentences from the answer choices and match them to the cause and effect of soil formation to which they relate. TWO of the answer choices will NOT be used. ***This question is worth 3 points.***

> Drag your answer choices to the spaces where they belong.
> To remove an answer choice, click on it. To review the passage, click on **View Text.**

Answer Choices	SOIL FORMATION
1 The roots of trees anchor the soil to the ground, so it is not blown away.	**Cause**
	•
2 Rocks are broken down by the elements over a certain amount of time.	•
3 People cut down trees in certain areas, so deforestation begins to take place.	**Effect**
	•
4 Bacteria and fungi act in concert, which permits the creation of humus.	•
5 The land may become fertile enough for farmers to grow crops on it.	•
6 Some civilizations have met their end because their soil was swept away.	
7 Water may freeze in rocks, causing them to crumble into small pieces.	

1 Desertification in the Southwestern United States

In the United States, the Southwest has long been an arid, desert land. However, for several reasons, these regions are expanding because of desertification. One is that large numbers of cattle ranchers live there. Their cattle graze on the grasslands, thereby consuming much of the vegetation. Cattle also compact the ground, making it extremely hard. This makes it difficult for grass to grow and therefore leads to the creating of deserts. Additionally, the lack of trees in the Southwest means there are no roots to help keep topsoil in place. The wind and other elements sweep away the best soil, making the land infertile and more susceptible to desertification.

2 Prairie Plants and Water

A prairie is a large, flat land in a temperate climate that receives little water. However, it does not lack vegetation. While prairies have few trees, many species of grasses and wildflowers grow in places such as the Great Plains, a Midwestern American prairie. One reason the grasses there survive so well is that they maximize their use of water. The leaves of the grasses and other plants are often shaped to let them retain water well. They also have deep roots ideal for absorbing water. It is often these factors that prevent desertification from occurring on prairies and converting them into barren, dry lands.

3 Urban Heat Island

People have long been aware that temperatures in urban areas tend to be greater than temperatures in nearby rural areas. This phenomenon has come to be known as urban heat island. Essentially, the reason why the urban areas are hotter—by several degrees in some cases—is that the landscape of the cities has been altered much more than the rural areas have. Particularly, the large amount of concrete and asphalt used to construct buildings and roads is responsible for the urban heat island effect. Concrete and asphalt both have heat-retaining properties; therefore, the cities, especially at night, tend to retain heat better, which causes them to have higher temperatures.

4 Weather Seeding

Men have long desired to control the weather, particularly rain. Scientists have accordingly developed weather seeding, or cloud seeding, as it is also known. Weather seeding induces clouds to release rain by the dropping of either dry ice, which is frozen carbon dioxide, or silver iodide in clouds. The science is still in the developmental stages, but it appears to be effective at times. In recent years, the Chinese government has made use of weather seeding. It was very interested in it prior to the 2008 Summer Olympics, where it was hoping that rain would help reduce the smog and air pollution surrounding Beijing, where the Olympics were held.

5 The Sun's Effects on the Earth's Climate

If the sun were suddenly to disappear, the Earth's temperature would rapidly reach absolute zero, and all life on the planet would cease to exist. However, the sun's relationship with the Earth is perfect enough that it allows for the existence of life. Fortunately, the distance between the sun and Earth is ideal. If the Earth were merely 5% closer to the sun, the polar caps would melt, and sea levels would rise considerably, flooding most coastal areas. If the Earth were slightly further away from the sun, the planet would be much colder, the polar caps would expand, and there would be virtually a permanent ice age on much of the planet.

6 The Extinction of the Dinosaurs

When the dinosaurs lived on the Earth, the planet's climate was much different than it is today. It was a much warmer place, which enabled enormous creatures much larger than any that exist today to live. However, around sixty-five million years ago, the dinosaurs—and much of the rest of the Earth's life—suddenly died. Most scientists agree it was an asteroid strike which caused this extinction event. When the asteroid hit, huge amounts of debris were cast into the air. This essentially blocked much of the sun's rays from reaching the Earth for several years. The temperature dropped considerably, plant matter died, and so too did the animals when their food sources disappeared.

7 Types of Soil

There are several types of soil: sandy, silty, clay, loamy, peaty, and chalky. Sandy soil is composed of disintegrated and weathered rocks and can be fairly fertile. Silty soil is quite fertile as it has many nutrients and retains water well, too. Clay soil is heavy, compact soil that is hard for farmers to work with. Loamy soil is considered the best soil to grow crops in and is the most fertile. While peaty soil is organic, having been formed by the decomposition of living matter, it is highly acidic and has few nutrients. Chalky soil has numerous rocks and is the least fertile and worst soil to grow anything in.

8 Insecticides

In the twentieth century, global agricultural production increased exponentially. One reason for this was the use of insecticides, which killed insects and other pests harmful to crops. Among the most famous of these was DDT. However, in recent decades, many people have opposed the use of insecticides, and DDT has been banned in some countries. People claim that insecticides harm animals and plants other than the insects it is supposed to kill. DDT, which had previously killed malaria-carrying mosquitoes, is no longer used in many places in Africa, thereby permitting malaria, a disease that was once practically eliminated, to spread again, so that it kills around one million Africans annually today.

9 Inuit Homes

The Inuit are the natives of northern Canada and Alaska. The land there is frigid, but they still built homes that could retain what little heat there was. In the summer, their homes were simple tents covered with animal hides. However, when winter came, the temperature dropped, so they constructed igloos, which were homes made of ice and snow. Igloos were rounded huts with very narrow entrances. The snow and the ice froze together, which let the insides retain heat well. With a small oil lamp and body heat, the temperature inside an igloo could be forty degrees Celsius warmer than the outside, thus enabling the Inuit to defeat their environment and survive.

10 Glacier Formation

A glacier is an extended sheet of ice that either descends from a mountain or runs from a place with a heavy accumulation of snow. Glaciers can take hundreds of years to form. They only develop in areas where there is snow all year long. The snow, since it does not melt, continues to accumulate and subsequently turns into ice. As more and more snow falls, the snow compresses and becomes denser. This eventually leads to the snow becoming very firm. Over time, the ice becomes so dense that a glacier is formed. Some glaciers may be just hundreds of feet long, but others can stretch for hundreds of miles.

Star Performer Topic Files **Environmental Sciences** —

- The effects of past ice ages
- Different types of pollution
- The processing of forming sand dunes
- Paleogeology
- Soil dispersion
- The changes in the water layers according to the seasons
- Groundwater
- The similarities between the world's rainforests
- How humans can change the environment
- The effects of floods in China

acclimatize	electrical	habituate	prey
acid rain	electricity	host	protect
aerosol	encase	hydroelectric	protected
air stream	endanger	ice age	radioactive
arctic	endangered	iceberg	reactor
ash	endangerment	imbalance	recede
atmosphere	engulf	impact	reclaim
atmospheric	enrich	industrial	reclamation
avalanche	environment	industrialization	recyclable
bacteria	environmental	inorganic	recycle
balance	erode	insecticide	renewable
ban	erosion	irrigate	resource
banned	erupt	irrigation	rich
bedrock	eruption	landmass	rise
biodiversity	estuary	lava	rockslide
biosphere	exhaust	license	sample
break down	expand	littoral	sand
carbon dating	expansion	lower	savanna
carbon dioxide	expend	magma	sea level
carbon monoxide	extinct	marine	seasonal
climate	extinction	melt	silt
coastal	evaporate	methane	smog
conduct	evaporation	microbe	smoke
conflagration	evolution	moisture	soil
congestion	evolve	mudslide	solar
conservation	famine	natural	solar flare
conserve	fauna	nature	sunspot
consume	feature	nuclear	species
consumption	fertile	nutrient	subsoil
continent	fertilizer	ocean	supervolcano
continental	fjord	oceanic	survival
conversion	flame	over-polluted	temperate
coral	flood	organic	temperature
coral reef	flora	organism	thermal
current	flow	oxygen	tidal
decline	fossil fuel	ozone	tide
deforestation	formation	ozone layer	topsoil
decompose	fracture	parasite	transform
deposit	freeze	particle	tree ring
desert	frozen	pesticide	tropical
desertification	fumes	pestilent	tsunami
destroy	fungus	poacher	ultraviolet rays
destruction	generate	polar cap	urban heat island
distribution	generation	pollutant	variable
dominant	geology	pollute	variation
drill	geological	pollution	volcanic
drought	geothermal	power plant	volcano
dump	geyser	prairie	waste
dune	glacier	predator	weather
earthquake	greenhouse effect	presence	weathered
ecosystem	groundwater	preservation	weathering
electric	habitat	preserve	wildlife

Vocabulary *Review*

📝 Choose the words closest in meaning to the highlighted parts of the sentences.

1 In parts of Africa, the rainy season typically peaks in October, resulting in numerous thunderstorms and the land being drenched with water.

Ⓐ overcome
Ⓑ touched
Ⓒ covered
Ⓓ soaked

2 Some circle an island or atoll, others, such as the Great Barrier Reef, form long, continuous lines out in the ocean far from land, and some are attached to shores and fringe the coastline.

Ⓐ surround
Ⓑ approach
Ⓒ enter
Ⓓ bypass

3 Part of this was a result of the continents shifting due to plate tectonics.

Ⓐ moving
Ⓑ growing
Ⓒ amending
Ⓓ transforming

4 Finally, volcanoes can also produce soil, which is quite good for agriculture, from the ash that their eruptions spew across a land.

Ⓐ eject
Ⓑ transport
Ⓒ carry
Ⓓ push

5 This has been somewhat successful, yet illegal loggers working deep in the forests are still able to evade law enforcement while practicing their trade.

Ⓐ fight
Ⓑ dodge
Ⓒ negotiate with
Ⓓ find

6 Unfortunately, human intruders often disrupt the ecosystem there, taking chunks of coral for their aquariums or to make jewelry with.

Ⓐ plants
Ⓑ stems
Ⓒ lumps
Ⓓ trunks

7 Savannas are tropical grasslands replete with various kinds of grasses, shrubs, and even a few trees and which cover approximately one-fifth of the Earth's entire land surface.

Ⓐ filled
Ⓑ sated
Ⓒ overrun
Ⓓ limited

8 Tidal turbine power systems, meanwhile, utilize individual turbines or small combinations of turbines that are built in the water and anchored to the seabed floor.

Ⓐ snared
Ⓑ trapped
Ⓒ crouched
Ⓓ attached

9 It encouraged local farmers both to protect the local environment and to engage in sustainable forestry practices.

Ⓐ recyclable
Ⓑ supportable
Ⓒ consistent
Ⓓ helpful

10 Naturally, not all soil follows this layer chart, and the chemical composition of all soil differs, with much of it depending on climate and the plants growing in it.

Ⓐ reaction
Ⓑ production
Ⓒ makeup
Ⓓ value

11 In some instances, natural bridges between landmasses emerged as parts of the ocean floor were exposed.

(A) portrayed
(B) established
(C) revealed
(D) constructed

12 Water erosion typically occurs because of running water in the guise of streams and rivers.

(A) notion
(B) form
(C) organization
(D) disguise

13 In some cases, the consequences of climate change can be quite dramatic as it can have devastating results on the plant and animal populations.

(A) forces
(B) causes
(C) effects
(D) determinations

14 Coastal deserts, meanwhile, are geographical entities which, upon first glance, are difficult to account for.

(A) corpuses
(B) beings
(C) regions
(D) organisms

15 Careful study of the trapped air bubbles in this ice can reveal the temperature, the quantity of carbon dioxide in the air, and other factors that indicate to scientists the climatic conditions of certain time periods.

(A) obscure
(B) influence
(C) reduce
(D) divulge

16 While the roots evolved that way in order to maximize their ability to extract water from the parched soil, they serve another purpose: Their deepness ensures that they are protected from the fires, so, although their above-ground parts burn, they survive.

(A) arid
(B) fertile
(C) untilled
(D) hard

17 They are home to abundant undersea plant and animal life and comprise a unique ecosystem of their own.

(A) plentiful
(B) considerate
(C) several
(D) unique

18 Tons of sediment are annually carried by the river to the gulf, where it is deposited in various places, thereby actively altering the landscape of the Mississippi area.

(A) improving
(B) abandoning
(C) changing
(D) containing

19 On the negative side, tidal power can only be cost efficient in areas with tides strong enough to justify the construction of a tidal power system.

(A) validate
(B) determine
(C) organize
(D) manage

20 As a result, the air being blown across the mountains by the wind is entirely void of moisture.

(A) deserving
(B) exacting
(C) conducive
(D) empty

Part

C

Experiencing the TOEFL iBT Actual Tests

CONTINUE

Reading Section Directions

This section measures your ability to understand academic passages in English. You will have **72 minutes** to read and answer questions about **4 passages**. A clock at the top of the screen will show you how much time is remaining.

Most questions are worth 1 point but the last question for each passage is worth more than 1 point. The directions for the last question indicate how many points you may receive.

Some passages include a word or phrase that is <u>underlined</u> in blue. Click on the word or phrase to see a definition or an explanation.

When you want to move to the next question, click on **Next**. You may skip questions and go back to them later. If you want to return to previous questions, click on **Back**. You can click on **Review** at any time, and the review screen will show you which questions you have answered and which you have not answered. From this review screen, you may go directly to any question you have already seen in the Reading section.

Click on **Continue** to go on.

The Battle of Lepanto

A painting of the Battle of Lepanto

There are few instances throughout history when truly significant events with long-lasting effects occur. One took place on October 7, 1571. This is the date of the Battle of Lepanto, which was fought by a cobbled-together group of European Christians against their Muslim Turkish opponents from the Ottoman Empire. For centuries, the Turks had been encroaching on European lands. More than a century earlier, in 1453, they had conquered Constantinople, the capital of the Byzantine Empire, and they were making significant inroads in the Balkans in Southeastern Europe and in other areas around the Mediterranean Sea. The Europeans were frightened of the Ottomans and considered them invincible. This changed after Lepanto.

The Byzantine Empire had long served as a **buffer zone** between the Ottoman Empire and the European states. However, with its destruction, the Turks began to move against the Europeans. The Europeans, meanwhile, were frequently busy squabbling to establish a cohesive front against the Turks. They were therefore easy targets for the Turks to pick off one by one. But once Cyprus, an island strategically located in the eastern Mediterranean, was captured by the Turks, Pope Pius V organized the Holy League to oppose the Turks. The pope convinced the Hapsburg Empire, its main possessions of Austria and Spain, and several Italian city-states, most significantly Venice, to join the league. Venice had previously owned Cyprus and had been agitating for its invasion and recapture. The league determined to fight the Turks on the sea, so a fleet of more than 200 ships was organized under the leadership of the Spaniard Don Juan.

The two fleets, both comprised mostly of **galleys**, encountered each other near Lepanto off the Greek coast, and there they formed their battle lines. Lacking sails, the galleys required hundreds of sailors to man the oars. The Turks were notorious for using convicted prisoners and captured

Europeans and Africans as slaves to row their galleys whereas the rowers on the Holy League's ships were frequently volunteers. Each galley carried a contingent of armed men, who used both rudimentary firearms and edged weapons like swords in battle. As for tactics, the Turkish navy favored ramming its opponents' ships, boarding them, and then engaging in hand-to-hand combat. The Europeans, however, had armed their ships with cannons and preferred to fire broadsides before engaging their opponents more closely. They also had six galleasses, which were towed ships armed with numerous cannons.

The galleasses were the key to the battle. They poured an enormous amount of firepower into the Turkish ships and caused significant damage. Still, there was a tremendous amount of hand-to-hand fighting, and the battle's climax came when Don Juan's flagship fought directly with the flagship of Ali Pasha, the Turkish admiral. After receiving reinforcements, the soldiers from Don Juan's ship overwhelmed Ali Pasha's, and Ali Pasha himself was killed in the subsequent carnage. Five hours after it started, the Turkish navy was utterly destroyed. Somewhere around 200 ships were either sunk or captured, and approximately 30,000 Turks were dead while only fifteen Holy League galleys and a few thousand of its men were lost.

The victory at Lepanto inspired virtually the entire European continent. It was the first time in around 200 years that the Turks had suffered a major defeat. This encouraged demoralized Europeans not to give up hope. The Holy League, however, proved to be ephemeral and disbanded in 1573, one year following the death of the pope, the primary force in its establishment. Each member of the league once again began acting independently. The Spanish focused on protecting the western Mediterranean while the Venetians, who were much closer to the Ottoman Empire, were left to fend for themselves. With their treasury exhausted, the Venetians had no choice but to make peace with the Turks in 1574, so they formally ceded Cyprus to the Turks. The Turks swiftly rebuilt their fleet yet never again dominated the seas as they once had. In fact, new naval powers—primarily England and France—quickly arose in Western Europe, and while the Ottoman Empire managed to last until the twentieth century, it no longer inspired fear and dread in the hearts of Europeans like it once had.

≋ Glossary

buffer zone: a neutral zone between two hostile countries
galley: a ship powered by oars and sails that was used in ancient and medieval times

1   According to paragraph 1, which of the following is true of the Ottoman Empire?

   (A) It was established in 1453 when the Turks conquered the Byzantine Empire.

   (B) It had expanded its territory in the time leading up to the Battle of Lepanto.

   (C) It had conquered the Balkans by the time the Battle of Lepanto was fought.

   (D) It once controlled all of the land on every side of the Mediterranean Sea.

2   The phrase "agitating for" in the passage is closest in meaning to

   (A) planning

   (B) asking about

   (C) pleading for

   (D) insisting upon

3   Which of the following can be inferred from paragraph 2 about Don Juan?

   (A) He was the most experienced seaman in the Holy League.

   (B) He had some kind of a connection with the Hapsburg Empire.

   (C) He was selected by the pope to lead the Holy League's fleet.

   (D) He helped finance some of the ships in the Holy League's fleet.

The Battle of Lepanto

1 ➡ There are few instances throughout history when truly significant events with long-lasting effects occur. One took place on October 7, 1571. This is the date of the Battle of Lepanto, which was fought by a cobbled-together group of European Christians against their Muslim Turkish opponents from the Ottoman Empire. For centuries, the Turks had been encroaching on European lands. More than a century earlier, in 1453, they had conquered Constantinople, the capital of the Byzantine Empire, and they were making significant inroads in the Balkans in Southeastern Europe and in other areas around the Mediterranean Sea. The Europeans were frightened of the Ottomans and considered them invincible. This changed after Lepanto.

2 ➡ The Byzantine Empire had long served as a **buffer zone** between the Ottoman Empire and the European states. However, with its destruction, the Turks began to move against the Europeans. The Europeans, meanwhile, were frequently busy squabbling to establish a cohesive front against the Turks. They were therefore easy targets for the Turks to pick off one by one. But once Cyprus, an island strategically located in the eastern Mediterranean, was captured by the Turks, Pope Pius V organized the Holy League to oppose the Turks. The pope convinced the Hapsburg Empire, its main possessions of Austria and Spain, and several Italian city-states, most significantly Venice, to join the league. Venice had previously owned Cyprus and had been agitating for its invasion and recapture. The league determined to fight the Turks on the sea, so a fleet of more than 200 ships was organized under the leadership of the Spaniard Don Juan.

📚 *Glossary*

buffer zone: a neutral zone between two hostile countries

4 Which of the sentences below best expresses the essential information in the highlighted sentence in the passage? *Incorrect* answer choices change the meaning in important ways or leave out essential information.

Ⓐ The Holy League hired rowers for their galleys, which the Turks also did in addition to employing slave labor on their ships at times.

Ⓑ It was well known that captured sailors would be forced to row Turkish galleys, but this was not true for the Holy League's galleys.

Ⓒ While the Holy League used sailors who were free men, the Turks relied upon both prisoners and slaves to row their galleys.

Ⓓ The Turks had prisoners row their ships, but both sides relied upon slave labor to do the majority of the work on the galleys.

5 The word "climax" in the passage is closest in meaning to

Ⓐ end

Ⓑ accomplishment

Ⓒ success

Ⓓ apex

6 In paragraph 4, why does the author mention the tactics used by the Turks and Europeans?

Ⓐ To contrast the way in which the two opposing sides made battle

Ⓑ To emphasize why the Turks needed to use slave labor on their ships

Ⓒ To explain why the Holy League emerged victorious from the battle

Ⓓ To stress the superiority of the Holy League's weapons over those of the Turks

⫸ *Glossary*

galley: a ship powered by oars and sails that was used in ancient and medieval times

The two fleets, both comprised mostly of **galleys**, encountered each other near Lepanto off the Greek coast, and there they formed their battle lines. Lacking sails, the galleys required hundreds of sailors to man the oars. The Turks were notorious for using convicted prisoners and captured Europeans and Africans as slaves to row their galleys whereas the rowers on the Holy League's ships were frequently volunteers. Each galley carried a contingent of armed men, who used both rudimentary firearms and edged weapons like swords in battle. As for tactics, the Turkish navy favored ramming its opponents' ships, boarding them, and then engaging in hand-to-hand combat. The Europeans, however, had armed their ships with cannons and preferred to fire broadsides before engaging their opponents more closely. They also had six galleasses, which were towed ships armed with numerous cannons.

[4]➡ The galleasses were the key to the battle. They poured an enormous amount of firepower into the Turkish ships and caused significant damage. Still, there was a tremendous amount of hand-to-hand fighting, and the battle's climax came when Don Juan's flagship fought directly with the flagship of Ali Pasha, the Turkish admiral. After receiving reinforcements, the soldiers from Don Juan's ship overwhelmed Ali Pasha's, and Ali Pasha himself was killed in the subsequent carnage. Five hours after it started, the Turkish navy was utterly destroyed. Somewhere around 200 ships were either sunk or captured, and approximately 30,000 Turks were dead while only fifteen Holy League galleys and a few thousand of its men were lost.

7 According to paragraph 4, which of the following is NOT true of the Battle of Lepanto?

Ⓐ The Holy League's galleasses were crucial to its victory against the Turks.

Ⓑ Don Juan and Ali Pasha engaged in hand-to-hand combat with each other.

Ⓒ The Turks suffered losses several times greater than the Europeans' losses.

Ⓓ The head of the Turkish armada was killed in the middle of the battle.

8 According to paragraph 5, what happened after the Holy League disbanded?

Ⓐ The Turks quit building ships and focused more on their army.

Ⓑ Many people throughout Europe became demoralized.

Ⓒ The Venetians were forced to give up territory to the Turks.

Ⓓ The pope tried to reorganize the countries of Europe into another group.

9 Look at the four squares [■] that indicate where the following sentence could be added to the passage.

In addition, the Holy League caught the Turks by surprise since they had not encountered galleasses in battle before.

Where would the sentence best fit?

Click on a square [■] to add the sentence to the passage.

---

⁴→ The galleasses were the key to the battle. **1** They poured an enormous amount of firepower into the Turkish ships and caused significant damage. **2** Still, there was a tremendous amount of hand-to-hand fighting, and the battle's climax came when Don Juan's flagship fought directly with the flagship of Ali Pasha, the Turkish admiral. **3** After receiving reinforcements, the soldiers from Don Juan's ship overwhelmed Ali Pasha's, and Ali Pasha himself was killed in the subsequent carnage. **4** Five hours after it started, the Turkish navy was utterly destroyed. Somewhere around 200 ships were either sunk or captured, and approximately 30,000 Turks were dead while only fifteen Holy League galleys and a few thousand of its men were lost.

⁵→ The victory at Lepanto inspired virtually the entire European continent. It was the first time in around 200 years that the Turks had suffered a major defeat. This encouraged demoralized Europeans not to give up hope. The Holy League, however, proved to be ephemeral and disbanded in 1573, one year following the death of the pope, the primary force in its establishment. Each member of the league once again began acting independently. The Spanish focused on protecting the western Mediterranean while the Venetians, who were much closer to the Ottoman Empire, were left to fend for themselves. With their treasury exhausted, the Venetians had no choice but to make peace with the Turks in 1574, so they formally ceded Cyprus to the Turks. The Turks swiftly rebuilt their fleet yet never again dominated the seas as they once had. In fact, new naval powers—primarily England and France—quickly arose in Western Europe, and while the Ottoman Empire managed to last until the twentieth century, it no longer inspired fear and dread in the hearts of Europeans like it once had.

10 *Directions:* An introductory sentence for a brief summary of the passage is provided below. Complete the summary by selecting the THREE answer choices that express the most important ideas of the passage. Some sentences do not belong because they express ideas that are not presented in the passage or are minor ideas in the passage. *This question is worth 2 points.*

> Drag your answer choices to the spaces where they belong.
> To remove an answer choice, click on it. To review the passage, click on **View Text**.

The victory at Lepanto was a turning point in the European struggle against the Ottoman Empire as it showed the Europeans that the Turks could be defeated.

-
-
-

Answer Choices

1. The Turks lost huge amounts of treasure during the battle when the Europeans captured their ships.

2. The Europeans were encouraged by their victory and refused to give in to the Ottoman Empire.

3. Pope Pius V organized the Holy League, but it quickly broke up in the year after his death.

4. The victory at Lepanto was the first time the Ottoman Empire had been defeated in years.

5. The Byzantine Empire had once helped defend the Europeans against the Ottoman Empire.

6. The Turkish navy was annihilated during the battle thanks to the Holy League's galleasses.

Autochrome Photography

Photography has existed for more than 150 years, and during this period, it has captured precious moments for people to look back on and to recall. In the early days of photography, black and white photographs were all that could be produced, and the only successful attempts to make color photography resulted from the use of multiple cameras with different filters related to the spectrums of light. Then, in 1903, two French brothers, Auguste and Louis Lumiere, pioneered a process which radically simplified color photography and permitted the use of a single camera. This breakthrough, which became the standard for color photography for the next thirty years, depended on the use of a surprising product: the potato.

The Lumiere brothers grew up with cameras since they worked in their father's successful photography business in Lyon, France. After he retired, the brothers took over and set off in a new direction: motion pictures. The Lumieres are often credited with being among the first to develop motion pictures in the late nineteenth century. Yet photography remained their primary business. Then, in 1903, they developed the process known as autochrome photography. There had been many previous attempts to produce color photographs, but most were unsuccessful. The only triumph required the use of a process in which the subject was photographed with three cameras, each of which had different-colored filters. The three images were then superimposed on one another to form a single color photograph. However, this process was time consuming and had severe limitations.

In a burst of inspiration, the Lumieres decided to use potato grains to act as a color filter. They ground some potatoes into extremely fine grains, divided them into three batches, and dyed each one a separate major color index of the spectrum. One was dyed red-orange, another violet, and the last green. The colored potato grounds were then mixed together. From there, a glass photographic plate was varnished, and the colored potato grains were attached to it before it dried so that they stuck to the plate. Extreme pressure was then applied to the plate by using rollers so that the grains remained firmly attached. Black carbon was applied to fill in the gaps in the potato grains, and finally, silver bromide emulsion was added to complete the ready-to-use colored photographic plate. Once the plate was put in the camera, the shutter was opened, light filtered through the colored potato grains, and the image was imprinted on the silver bromide emulsion. After the negative was developed, it produced a **muted**, toned photograph with vivid colors unlike anything ever produced before.

The Lumieres patented the process in 1903 but labored to perfect it for four years; thus, they did not reveal their technique until 1907. It was an instant success, and within a few years, the autochrome process was so popular that the Lumiere's factory in Lyon had difficulty keeping up with the demand for photographic plates. Much of their success was due to the quality of the photographs as seemingly vibrant colors were composed with the dreamlike qualities of a painting done by a master. A surge of interest in photography accompanied the unveiling of the autochrome process, and more than one would-be painter abandoned his brush and palette and to pick up a camera and photographic plate. For the following three decades, the autochrome process dominated the field of colored photography.

It was not to last though. Other better, faster methods overtook the autochrome process. One problem with the technique was that the camera lens needed to stay open for at least one minute, requiring the subject to remain absolutely still for a perfect photograph. Some experts claim this was the reason for the quality of the photos; they note the calm serenity of stillness ingrained in many lasting images. Yet stillness was not what every photo enthusiast desired. In addition, the bulky camera and photo plates imposed limits on photographers. By the 1930s, smaller cameras using rolls of 35mm film were in vogue. Coupled with new photo processing methods developed by the Kodak and Agfa companies, autochrome photography as an art died out. However, images taken in those few decades have a **sublime** quality and richness many consider superior to the most modern photographic techniques today.

📚 *Glossary*
muted: subdued
sublime: transcendent

11 According to paragraph 1, which of the following is true of the early years of photography?

Ⓐ They were dominated by a small number of European companies.

Ⓑ Inventors never tried to develop a way to make color photographs.

Ⓒ People were able to take both black and white as well as color pictures.

Ⓓ The Lumiere brothers played a crucial role in photograph's creation.

12 According to paragraph 2, autochrome photography before 1903 was rare because

Ⓐ few people were engaged in experiments to develop it

Ⓑ the public preferred black and white photographs instead

Ⓒ taking color photographs was a complicated procedure

Ⓓ people could not afford the three cameras that it required

Autochrome Photography

1 ➜ Photography has existed for more than 150 years, and during this period, it has captured precious moments for people to look back on and to recall. In the early days of photography, black and white photographs were all that could be produced, and the only successful attempts to make color photography resulted from the use of multiple cameras with different filters related to the spectrums of light. Then, in 1903, two French brothers, Auguste and Louis Lumiere, pioneered a process which radically simplified color photography and permitted the use of a single camera. This breakthrough, which became the standard for color photography for the next thirty years, depended on the use of a surprising product: the potato.

2 ➜ The Lumiere brothers grew up with cameras since they worked in their father's successful photography business in Lyon, France. After he retired, the brothers took over and set off in a new direction: motion pictures. The Lumieres are often credited with being among the first to develop motion pictures in the late nineteenth century. Yet photography remained their primary business. Then, in 1903, they developed the process known as autochrome photography. There had been many previous attempts to produce color photographs, but most were unsuccessful. The only triumph required the use of a process in which the subject was photographed with three cameras, each of which had different-colored filters. The three images were then superimposed on one another to form a single color photograph. However, this process was time consuming and had severe limitations.

13 According to paragraph 3, which of the following is NOT true of the Lumiere brothers' autochrome photography method?

- Ⓐ Light emitted by the lens traveled through the grains on the glass plate.
- Ⓑ It was necessary to mix the potato grains with the silver bromide emulsion.
- Ⓒ It made use of potato grains which had been dyed various colors.
- Ⓓ It required silver bromide emulsion in order to create a negative.

14 Which of the sentences below best expresses the essential information in the highlighted sentence in the passage? *Incorrect* answer choices change the meaning in important ways or leave out essential information.

- Ⓐ People became so interested in taking pictures in color that painting as an art form rapidly decreased in popularity in favor of photography.
- Ⓑ Many people chose to take photographs that resembled pictures which had been painted once they were able to make use of autochrome photography.
- Ⓒ Painters often took snapshots in color and then tried to replicate these pictures by painting the images which they had captured in color.
- Ⓓ Once color photography became simplified, people became more interested in it, which often led to painters quitting art to become photographers.

15 According to paragraph 4, the Lumiere's factory was often behind on the production of photographic plates because

- Ⓐ it was overwhelmed by the large number of orders that it was receiving
- Ⓑ it employed inefficient machinery that could not produce plates fast enough
- Ⓒ it took a long time for the Lumieres to perfect their production method
- Ⓓ making plates that took high-quality pictures was a time-consuming process

³➜ In a burst of inspiration, the Lumieres decided to use potato grains to act as a color filter. They ground some potatoes into extremely fine grains, divided them into three batches, and dyed each one a separate major color index of the spectrum. One was dyed red-orange, another violet, and the last green. The colored potato grounds were then mixed together. From there, a glass photographic plate was varnished, and the colored potato grains were attached to it before it dried so that they stuck to the plate. Extreme pressure was then applied to the plate by using rollers so that the grains remained firmly attached. Black carbon was applied to fill in the gaps in the potato grains, and finally, silver bromide emulsion was added to complete the ready-to-use colored photographic plate. Once the plate was put in the camera, the shutter was opened, light filtered through the colored potato grains, and the image was imprinted on the silver bromide emulsion. After the negative was developed, it produced a **muted**, toned photograph with vivid colors unlike anything ever produced before.

⁴➜ The Lumieres patented the process in 1903 but labored to perfect it for four years; thus, they did not reveal their technique until 1907. It was an instant success, and within a few years, the autochrome process was so popular that the Lumiere's factory in Lyon had difficulty keeping up with the demand for photographic plates. Much of their success was due to the quality of the photographs as seemingly vibrant colors were composed with the dreamlike qualities of a painting done by a master. A surge of interest in photography accompanied the unveiling of the autochrome process, and more than one would-be painter abandoned his brush and palette and to pick up a camera and photographic plate. For the following three decades, the autochrome process dominated the field of colored photography.

📖 **Glossary**
muted: subdued

16 In stating that smaller cameras using rolls of 35mm film were "in vogue," the author means that these cameras were

- Ⓐ cheaper than others
- Ⓑ abundant
- Ⓒ fashionable
- Ⓓ more compatible than others

17 In paragraph 5, the author mentions "the Kodak and Agfa companies" as an example of

- Ⓐ two companies that helped develop 35mm photography
- Ⓑ two firms which came up with new ways to make photographs
- Ⓒ two companies which made improvements to the autochrome process
- Ⓓ two firms that were responsible for running the Lumiere brothers out of business

18 Which of the following can be inferred from paragraph 5 about autochrome photography?

- Ⓐ It was ideal for taking photographs of landscapes.
- Ⓑ It took a long time to develop photographs taken using it.
- Ⓒ It was able to take clear photos from a considerable distance.
- Ⓓ Photographers came to dislike it because of its expensive nature.

⁵➡ It was not to last though. Other better, faster methods overtook the autochrome process. One problem with the technique was that the camera lens needed to stay open for at least one minute, requiring the subject to remain absolutely still for a perfect photograph. Some experts claim this was the reason for the quality of the photos; they note the calm serenity of stillness ingrained in many lasting images. Yet stillness was not what every photo enthusiast desired. In addition, the bulky camera and photo plates imposed limits on photographers. By the 1930s, smaller cameras using rolls of 35mm film were in vogue. Coupled with new photo processing methods developed by the Kodak and Agfa companies, autochrome photography as an art died out. However, images taken in those few decades have a sublime quality and richness many consider superior to the most modern photographic techniques today.

≋ *Glossary*
sublime: transcendent

19 Look at the four squares [■] that indicate where the following sentence could be added to the passage.

They believed there was more potential in this field than the one in which they had been working with their father.

Where would the sentence best fit?

Click on a square [■] to add the sentence to the passage.

■ The Lumiere brothers grew up with cameras since they worked in their father's successful photography business in Lyon, France. ■ After he retired, the brothers took over and set off in a new direction: motion pictures. ■ The Lumieres are often credited with being among the first to develop motion pictures in the late nineteenth century. ■ Yet photography remained their primary business. Then, in 1903, they developed the process known as autochrome photography. There had been many previous attempts to produce color photographs, but most were unsuccessful. The only triumph required the use of a process in which the subject was photographed with three cameras, each of which had different-colored filters. The three images were then superimposed on one another to form a single color photograph. However, this process was time consuming and had severe limitations.

20 **Directions:** An introductory sentence for a brief summary of the passage is provided below. Complete the summary by selecting the THREE answer choices that express the most important ideas of the passage. Some sentences do not belong because they express ideas that are not presented in the passage or are minor ideas in the passage. **This question is worth 2 points.**

Drag your answer choices to the spaces where they belong.
To remove an answer choice, click on it. To review the passage, click on **View Text**.

The autochrome photography method created by the Lumiere brothers greatly simplified color photography and remained popular for several decades.

-
-
-

Answer Choices

1. Instead of using three cameras, the Lumiere's color photography method needed just one.

2. The photographs that could be taken with the new method inspired many artists to become photographers instead.

3. The Lumiere brothers inherited their father's photography company and then went into the motion picture business.

4. When 35mm film began to be developed, the autochrome photography method fell out of favor.

5. The Lumieres utilized potato grains on a glass plate to enable them to take color photographs.

6. The early years of photography were dominated by black and white photographs rather than color ones.

Aquaculture

Marine aquaculture farms in the Atlantic Ocean

Aquaculture, otherwise referred to as fish farming, refers to the breeding, raising, and harvesting of marine life, including fish, shellfish, <u>crustaceans</u>, and algae, for various purposes. Among these purposes are to provide food for people, to replenish stocks of fish in the wild, to restore damaged ecosystems, and to prevent threatened and endangered species from going extinct. Aquaculture has been practiced for at least 2,500 years as tilapia is known to have been farmed by the ancient Egyptians. Since then, it was practiced at times at various places around the world until it became much more prominent during the twentieth century. Today, aquaculture accounts for more than fifty percent of all the seafood consumed by humans around the world, and that number is likely to rise in the future.

Both freshwater and marine aquaculture are practiced by people today. Some of the most common freshwater species which are farmed are catfish, tilapia, trout, carp, and bass. Marine aquaculture deals with a more diverse range of creatures, including salmon, sea bass, yellowtail, shrimp, clams, oysters, algae, and several types of seaweed. Freshwater aquaculture is frequently practiced in small ponds or tanks. It can be practiced by regular people who stock their ponds with an assortment of fish to catch and eat as well as individuals who raise fish, especially trout, to release into the wild. There are also large <u>fisheries</u> that also raise great numbers of fish to sell commercially.

Marine aquaculture can be accomplished in a number of different manners. Creating artificial saltwater environments is economically unfeasible for many practitioners of aquaculture, so marine fish farming is almost always done in the ocean or sea itself. Saltwater tanks are used at times, but it is much easier and more inexpensive to raise fish in pens in a saltwater environment. Cages for fish may be floating ones or those set up on the ocean floor. Shellfish are often seeded on the ocean floor or raised in cages as well.

Freshwater aquaculture has the advantage of being a closed environment. Farmers can therefore protect their fish in ponds and lakes from predators simply by not introducing them to the ecosystem. Food intake can be easily monitored, and farmers can keep the water clean and algae-free by introducing filtration systems. Yet another advantage is that harvesting the fish being raised is often as simple as putting a net into the water. Fish farmers need to be wary of diseases that may affect fish since they can kill huge numbers of fish living close together in a microenvironment. In addition, algae blooms can swiftly remove the oxygen from small bodies of water, which can cause many fish to die.

One of the drawbacks to marine aquaculture is that farmed fish can sometimes escape into the ocean. As genetically modified fish are being raised by some farmers, there are worries by environmentalists that these fish will escape and then interbreed with wild fish. Pollutants in the ocean are also impossible to keep away from farmed marine fish since the fish are merely kept in pens. However, farmed marine fish can develop much more quickly than fish in the wild on account of them being fed regularly by fish farmers. This enables farmers to bring fish to the market at a relatively fast rate.

As standards of living around the globe continue to rise, more and more people are demanding meat in their diets and can afford to pay for it as well. Fish and seafood are acceptable foodstuffs to them, especially to those individuals living near the ocean. Because demand will surely rise alongside the increasing global population, aquaculture will be more frequently practiced. Some individuals have even begun engaging in aquaponics, which combines raising fish and growing vegetables in the same tanks. Waste from the fish is utilized as nutrients by the growing plants. Creative solutions such as aquaponics indicate that fish farmers will be able to satisfy the needs of the global population. Additionally, because people will rely less upon fish caught in the wild, stocks of fish in the world's oceans may be able to recover, which will have an overall beneficial effect on the world's marine ecosystems.

≋ *Glossary*
crustacean: a sea creature with a hard shell or crust, including lobsters, crabs, and shrimp
fishery: a place where fish are bred and raised

21 According to paragraph 1, which of the following is NOT true of aquaculture?

Ⓐ It can be used to increase the number of endangered species in the wild.

Ⓑ More than half of all the seafood consumed today is produced by using this method.

Ⓒ People have been doing it since the time when the ancient Egyptians were alive.

Ⓓ It can only be used to raise animals such as fish and shellfish.

22 In paragraph 1, the author implies that aquaculture

Ⓐ is practiced more often today than it ever was in the past

Ⓑ costs less money to engage in than does fishing on the ocean

Ⓒ has saved species such as the tilapia from becoming extinct

Ⓓ is done by people in nearly all of the countries in the world

23 According to paragraph 2, which of the following is true of freshwater aquaculture?

Ⓐ It can be done by people in ponds, rivers, and lakes.

Ⓑ People can engage in it on both small and large scales.

Ⓒ More freshwater species are farmed than saltwater ones.

Ⓓ Most people who raise trout do it in order to consume them.

Aquaculture

1 ➜ Aquaculture, otherwise referred to as fish farming, refers to the breeding, raising, and harvesting of marine life, including fish, shellfish, crustaceans, and algae, for various purposes. Among these purposes are to provide food for people, to replenish stocks of fish in the wild, to restore damaged ecosystems, and to prevent threatened and endangered species from going extinct. Aquaculture has been practiced for at least 2,500 years as tilapia is known to have been farmed by the ancient Egyptians. Since then, it was practiced at times at various places around the world until it became much more prominent during the twentieth century. Today, aquaculture accounts for more than fifty percent of all the seafood consumed by humans around the world, and that number is likely to rise in the future.

2 ➜ Both freshwater and marine aquaculture are practiced by people today. Some of the most common freshwater species which are farmed are catfish, tilapia, trout, carp, and bass. Marine aquaculture deals with a more diverse range of creatures, including salmon, sea bass, yellowtail, shrimp, clams, oysters, algae, and several types of seaweed. Freshwater aquaculture is frequently practiced in small ponds or tanks. It can be practiced by regular people who stock their ponds with an assortment of fish to catch and eat as well as individuals who raise fish, especially trout, to release into the wild. There are also large fisheries that also raise great numbers of fish to sell commercially.

≋ *Glossary*

crustacean: a sea creature with a hard shell or crust, including lobsters, crabs, and shrimp
fishery: a place where fish are bred and raised

24 The word "unfeasible" in the passage is closest in meaning to

Ⓐ unaware

Ⓑ unbelievable

Ⓒ illegitimate

Ⓓ impractical

25 In paragraph 4, why does the author mention "filtration systems"?

Ⓐ To claim that they can be used to keep predators away from fish

Ⓑ To stress that most of the ones used today rely on advanced technology

Ⓒ To name them as one of the most expensive aspects of aquaculture

Ⓓ To point out some equipment necessary to keeping water clean

26 The phrase "wary of" in the passage is closest in meaning to

Ⓐ knowledgeable about

Ⓑ cautious of

Ⓒ interested in

Ⓓ prepared for

27 According to paragraph 5, people are concerned about genetically modified fish because

Ⓐ they are highly likely to pass on diseases to fish that have not been modified

Ⓑ they develop much too fast so they may be unhealthy for people to consume

Ⓒ they are usually unable to survive in the wild after they escape from their pens

Ⓓ they might get out of their pens and produce offspring with wild fish

Marine aquaculture can be accomplished in a number of different manners. Creating artificial saltwater environments is economically unfeasible for many practitioners of aquaculture, so marine fish farming is almost always done in the ocean or sea itself. Saltwater tanks are used at times, but it is much easier and more inexpensive to raise fish in pens in a saltwater environment. Cages for fish may be floating ones or those set up on the ocean floor. Shellfish are often seeded on the ocean floor or raised in cages as well.

4➜ Freshwater aquaculture has the advantage of being a closed environment. Farmers can therefore protect their fish in ponds and lakes from predators simply by not introducing them to the ecosystem. Food intake can be easily monitored, and farmers can keep the water clean and algae-free by introducing filtration systems. Yet another advantage is that harvesting the fish being raised is often as simple as putting a net into the water. Fish farmers need to be wary of diseases that may affect fish since they can kill huge numbers of fish living close together in a microenvironment. In addition, algae blooms can swiftly remove the oxygen from small bodies of water, which can cause many fish to die.

5➜ One of the drawbacks to marine aquaculture is that farmed fish can sometimes escape into the ocean. As genetically modified fish are being raised by some farmers, there are worries by environmentalists that these fish will escape and then interbreed with wild fish. Pollutants in the ocean are also impossible to keep away from farmed marine fish since the fish are merely kept in pens. However, farmed marine fish can develop much more quickly than fish in the wild on account of them being fed regularly by fish farmers. This enables farmers to bring fish to the market at a relatively fast rate.

28 The author discusses "aquaponics" in paragraph 6 in order to

(A) point out that it is a somewhat new and untested process people use to raise fish

(B) argue that more farmers should engage in it rather than just do aquaculture

(C) describe the process through which it helps raise fish and grow vegetables

(D) state that it costs less than traditional aquaculture while also producing healthier fish

6 → As standards of living around the globe continue to rise, more and more people are demanding meat in their diets and can afford to pay for it as well. Fish and seafood are acceptable foodstuffs to them, especially to those individuals living near the ocean. Because demand will surely rise alongside the increasing global population, aquaculture will be more frequently practiced. Some individuals have even begun engaging in aquaponics, which combines raising fish and growing vegetables in the same tanks. Waste from the fish is utilized as nutrients by the growing plants. Creative solutions such as aquaponics indicate that fish farmers will be able to satisfy the needs of the global population. Additionally, because people will rely less upon fish caught in the wild, stocks of fish in the world's oceans may be able to recover, which will have an overall beneficial effect on the world's marine ecosystems.

29 Look at the four squares [■] that indicate where the following sentence could be added to the passage.

These cages are usually found close to shore in relatively shallow water to permit easy access to them.

Where would the sentence best fit?

Click on a square [■] to add the sentence to the passage.

Marine aquaculture can be accomplished in a number of different manners. **1** Creating artificial saltwater environments is economically unfeasible for many practitioners of aquaculture, so marine fish farming is almost always done in the ocean or sea itself. **2** Saltwater tanks are used at times, but it is much easier and more inexpensive to raise fish in pens in a saltwater environment. **3** Cages for fish may be floating ones or those set up on the ocean floor. **4** Shellfish are often seeded on the ocean floor or raised in cages as well.

30 **_Directions:_** Select the appropriate statements from the answer choices and match them to the type of aquaculture to which they relate. TWO of the answer choices will NOT be used. **_This question is worth 3 points._**

> Drag your answer choices to the spaces where they belong.
> To remove an answer choice, click on it. To review the passage, click on **View Text**.

Answer Choices	**TYPE OF AQUACULTURE**
① May require the usage of cages that float on the water	**Freshwater**
② Costs a lot of money and can be difficult to practice at times	•
③ Is easy to keep track of the amount of food the fish eat	•
④ Raises a wide variety of fish and other aquatic creatures	**Marine**
⑤ Was practiced thousands of years ago by the Egyptians	•
⑥ Often takes place in a closed environment	•
⑦ Can expose fish to a variety of pollutants in the water	•

The African Sahel

The Sahel region near the Niger River

The Sahara is the world's largest desert and occupies an immense area of land in North Africa. Its barrenness contrasts sharply with the savannas and the jungles in the continent's southern part. The boundary between these two geographical features is called the Sahel by the North African people. The Sahel is a zone roughly 120 to 240 miles wide that corresponds to the thirteenth **parallel of latitude** as it runs across the entire breadth of Africa from Senegal on the Atlantic coast to Sudan on the Red Sea coast. Sahel means "shore" in Arabic, and the word suggests a place where something begins and where something ends.

The north-south boundaries of the Sahel are not set in stone though; instead, they are determined by the amount of rainfall the region gets. Over the last eight decades, the Sahel has been gradually shifting south. Its northern boundary is determined by an isohyet that is around six inches. An isohyet is an imaginary line connecting areas that receive equal amounts of annual rainfall. The southern boundary of the Sahel, meanwhile, is determined by an approximately twenty-four-inch isohyet. Between 1931 and 1960, the southern boundary was about sixty miles further north than it was between 1966 and 1997. This shifting of lesser amounts of rainfall to the south is the result of rising ocean temperatures causing changes in African rainfall patterns. As less rainfall occurred, vegetation died, the soil came loose, and the sand and the desert moved further south, thereby disrupting the lives of the roughly fifty million people living in this area of bleak nothingness.

The decrease in vegetation has been exacerbated by the overcutting of trees and overgrazing by herd animals owned by local residents. However, some studies of vegetation growth show a different pattern as the people of the region are fighting to regain control of their land from the encroaching desert. While ground surveys show vegetation in the Sahel has deteriorated over the past fifty years, in some areas, fertile land has been making a comeback at a faster rate than in the past. Niger is one such example: The country's northern lands are mostly desert whereas its southern part is a long, wide plain of vegetation. In addition, it has almost 20,000 square miles more land with vegetation than it did a mere two decades ago. The reasons for this apparent miracle are disputed. It has been suggested that incessant regional warfare has reduced the human population so greatly that the land, now mostly uninhabited, is regenerating after centuries of abuse. Another suggestion is that some regions are undergoing climate change, causing them to receive more rainfall than before.

The people of the Sahel are a mix of Arabs and Africans. They are mostly Muslims, but some Christians live there. Low-intensity conflicts have **scarred** the Sahel for the past several decades. In Mali, Chad, Niger, and especially the Sudan, hundreds of thousands of people have been killed and millions more displaced by the war and the shifting deserts. In the Darfur region of Sudan in the center of the Sahel, almost 200,000 people have perished in recent years, and more than two million have been made homeless. These factors combine to make the Sahel one of the most dangerous areas of the world, and people do not lightly enter this conflict zone without good reason.

Yet the region is not without its history and charms. The famed city of Timbuktu in Mali lies near its northern border. Once a famous town of scholars centuries ago, Timbuktu is now a tourist destination and a civilized area in the almost featureless desert lands surrounding it. Timbuktu houses many libraries devoted to the collection and preservation of Arabic manuscripts, some of which are over 1,000 years old and date back to the time when Muslim Arabs first swept across North Africa. Nowadays, the people of Timbuktu and the other cities, towns, and villages of the Sahel persevere in some of the most trying circumstances any humans face. Expanding desert, endemic warfare, poverty, unemployment, and famine are curses of the Sahel. Yet people remain and try to eke out an existence in the "shore" between the deserts of the north and the jungles of the south.

≋ *Glossary*
parallel of latitude: an imaginary circle on the Earth moving east-west and measured by its distance from the equator
scar: to disfigure

31 The word "barrenness" in the passage is closest in meaning to

   Ⓐ deterioration

   Ⓑ desolateness

   Ⓒ description

   Ⓓ denigration

32 According to paragraph 1, which of the following is NOT true of the Sahel?

   Ⓐ It runs from one side of the African continent to the other.

   Ⓑ It is located directly north of the Sahara Desert in Africa.

   Ⓒ It either widens or narrows depending upon where it is.

   Ⓓ It divides two extremely different geographical areas in Africa.

33 In paragraph 2, the author implies that the Sahel

   Ⓐ is one of the most fertile places in Africa

   Ⓑ has a smaller population than it is capable of handling

   Ⓒ lacks an exact location as it is always changing

   Ⓓ is being developed more than the rest of Africa is

34 According to paragraph 2, which of the following is true of the Sahel?

   Ⓐ Its presence was acknowledged for the first time in the twentieth century.

   Ⓑ It began to expand greatly during the time around 1931 to 1997.

   Ⓒ It has shifted southward in recent years for climate-related reasons.

   Ⓓ It transformed desert land into rainforest during the twentieth century.

The African Sahel

[1]➙ The Sahara is the world's largest desert and occupies an immense area of land in North Africa. Its barrenness contrasts sharply with the savannas and the jungles in the continent's southern part. The boundary between these two geographical features is called the Sahel by the North African people. The Sahel is a zone roughly 120 to 240 miles wide that corresponds to the thirteenth **parallel of latitude** as it runs across the entire breadth of Africa from Senegal on the Atlantic coast to Sudan on the Red Sea coast. Sahel means "shore" in Arabic, and the word suggests a place where something begins and where something ends.

[2]➙ The north-south boundaries of the Sahel are not set in stone though; instead, they are determined by the amount of rainfall the region gets. Over the last eight decades, the Sahel has been gradually shifting south. Its northern boundary is determined by an isohyet that is around six inches. An isohyet is an imaginary line connecting areas that receive equal amounts of annual rainfall. The southern boundary of the Sahel, meanwhile, is determined by an approximately twenty-four-inch isohyet. Between 1931 and 1960, the southern boundary was about sixty miles further north than it was between 1966 and 1997. This shifting of lesser amounts of rainfall to the south is the result of rising ocean temperatures causing changes in African rainfall patterns. As less rainfall occurred, vegetation died, the soil came loose, and the sand and the desert moved further south, thereby disrupting the lives of the roughly fifty million people living in this area of bleak nothingness.

≋ *Glossary*

parallel of latitude: an imaginary circle on the Earth moving east-west and measured by its distance from the equator

35 The word "encroaching" in the passage is closest in meaning to

  Ⓐ expanding

  Ⓑ trespassing

  Ⓒ appropriating

  Ⓓ invading

36 According to paragraph 3, which of the following is true of Niger?

  Ⓐ It has been in a state of war for much of the past century.

  Ⓑ The changes in the Sahel have affected it in a positive manner.

  Ⓒ Its population has decreased because of recent warfare.

  Ⓓ Its citizens have deforested much of its land that lies in the Sahel.

37 In paragraph 4, why does the author mention "the Darfur region"?

  Ⓐ To compare the number of dead there with the number of dead elsewhere

  Ⓑ To explain why people fear for their lives when they are in that part of Africa

  Ⓒ To emphasize how destructive the wars in the Sahel region have been

  Ⓓ To mention the number of people who have become refugees there

³➡ The decrease in vegetation has been exacerbated by the overcutting of trees and overgrazing by herd animals owned by local residents. However, some studies of vegetation growth show a different pattern as the people of the region are fighting to regain control of their land from the encroaching desert. While ground surveys show vegetation in the Sahel has deteriorated over the past fifty years, in some areas, fertile land has been making a comeback at a faster rate than in the past. Niger is one such example: The country's northern lands are mostly desert whereas its southern part is a long, wide plain of vegetation. In addition, it has almost 20,000 square miles more land with vegetation than it did a mere two decades ago. The reasons for this apparent miracle are disputed. It has been suggested that incessant regional warfare has reduced the human population so greatly that the land, now mostly uninhabited, is regenerating after centuries of abuse. Another suggestion is that some regions are undergoing climate change, causing them to receive more rainfall than before.

⁴➡ The people of the Sahel are a mix of Arabs and Africans. They are mostly Muslims, but some Christians live there. Low-intensity conflicts have scarred the Sahel for the past several decades. In Mali, Chad, Niger, and especially the Sudan, hundreds of thousands of people have been killed and millions more displaced by the war and the shifting deserts. In the Darfur region of Sudan in the center of the Sahel, almost 200,000 people have perished in recent years, and more than two million have been made homeless. These factors combine to make the Sahel one of the most dangerous areas of the world, and people do not lightly enter this conflict zone without good reason.

📚 *Glossary*

scar: to disfigure

38 According to paragraph 5, Timbuktu is a notable city because

(A) it is the most famous city that is still populated in the entire region of the Sahel

(B) it serves as a center for academics doing research on ancient Arabic history

(C) it is one of the few places in the Sahel with some semblance of development

(D) it was one of the only places that withstood attacks by Muslim Arabs centuries ago

[5] → Yet the region is not without its history and charms. The famed city of Timbuktu in Mali lies near its northern border. Once a famous town of scholars centuries ago, Timbuktu is now a tourist destination and a civilized area in the almost featureless desert lands surrounding it. Timbuktu houses many libraries devoted to the collection and preservation of Arabic manuscripts, some of which are over 1,000 years old and date back to the time when Muslim Arabs first swept across North Africa. Nowadays, the people of Timbuktu and the other cities, towns, and villages of the Sahel persevere in some of the most trying circumstances any humans face. Expanding desert, endemic warfare, poverty, unemployment, and famine are curses of the Sahel. Yet people remain and try to eke out an existence in the "shore" between the deserts of the north and the jungles of the south.

39 Look at the four squares [■] that indicate where the following sentence could be added to the passage.

More experts believe that the latter theory is more likely to be true than the former one.

Where would the sentence best fit?

Click on a square [■] to add the sentence to the passage.

The decrease in vegetation has been exacerbated by the overcutting of trees and overgrazing by herd animals owned by local residents. However, some studies of vegetation growth show a different pattern as the people of the region are fighting to regain control of their land from the encroaching desert. While ground surveys show vegetation in the Sahel has deteriorated over the past fifty years, in some areas, fertile land has been making a comeback at a faster rate than in the past. Niger is one such example: The country's northern lands are mostly desert whereas its southern part is a long, wide plain of vegetation. In addition, it has almost 20,000 square miles more land with vegetation than it did a mere two decades ago. **1** The reasons for this apparent miracle are disputed. **2** It has been suggested that incessant regional warfare has reduced the human population so greatly that the land, now mostly uninhabited, is regenerating after centuries of abuse. **3** Another suggestion is that some regions are undergoing climate change, causing them to receive more rainfall than before. **4**

40 ***Directions:*** An introductory sentence for a brief summary of the passage is provided below. Complete the summary by selecting the THREE answer choices that express the most important ideas of the passage. Some sentences do not belong because they express ideas that are not presented in the passage or are minor ideas in the passage. ***This question is worth 2 points.***

> Drag your answer choices to the spaces where they belong.
> To remove an answer choice, click on it. To review the passage, click on **View Text**.

The Sahel lies in Africa between the Sahara Desert and the southern rainforests and is a region that has suffered much, especially recently.

-
-
-

Answer Choices

1. Tourists visit Timbuktu because of its well-known history and ancient manuscripts.

2. For years, there has been a state of continual warfare in many parts of the Sahel.

3. The Sahel runs from coast to coast and divides the country into two separate regions.

4. There are both Christians and Muslims residing in different parts of the Sahel.

5. The constant changes in the Sahel have forced millions of people to move to other places.

6. Some countries, such as Niger, have seen their amount of infertile land expand in recent years.

CONTINUE

Reading Section Directions

This section measures your ability to understand academic passages in English. You will have **54 minutes** to read and answer questions about **3 passages**. A clock at the top of the screen will show you how much time is remaining.

Most questions are worth 1 point but the last question for each passage is worth more than 1 point. The directions for the last question indicate how many points you may receive.

Some passages include a word or phrase that is <u>underlined</u> in blue. Click on the word or phrase to see a definition or an explanation.

When you want to move to the next question, click on **Next**. You may skip questions and go back to them later. If you want to return to previous questions, click on **Back**. You can click on **Review** at any time, and the review screen will show you which questions you have answered and which you have not answered. From this review screen, you may go directly to any question you have already seen in the Reading section.

Click on **Continue** to go on.

Animal Communication

In the animal kingdom, communication is just as important as it is for humans. Animals communicate to warn others of danger, to mark their territory, to attract mates, to indicate where food sources are located, to show aggressive intent, and to convey many other messages. However, animals do not communicate in the same manner humans mainly do: by using speech. Instead, they rely upon various nonverbal and verbal means of communication. Not all animals use every method of communication though; what they use depend on the species.

While animals do not speak like humans, many are capable of vocalization: Birds sing, frogs croak, dogs bark, and monkeys screech. These are forms of vocalization that can express a plethora of meanings. Birds, whose songs are imprinted at birth, may use them as part of their mating <u>rituals</u> or to warn others of the presence of a predator. Dogs may bark to show happiness or hunger while they may growl to express anger or fear. Monkeys and other primates are capable of communicating a large number of expressions and emotions through vocalization.

Many animals rely upon pheromones—chemical signals created by their bodies that are exclusively used with members of their own species—to communicate, letting them avoid vocalizing to some extent. For the most part, animals detect pheromones as scents. They are often capable of releasing a number of pheromones, all of which have different purposes. For instance, one might signal the approach of a predator, thereby prompting other members of the species to hide or flee. The same animal might also release another pheromone after detecting a food source since it desires to share it with others. The most common use of pheromones is for reproductive purposes. Females of various species typically release pheromones indicating their readiness to breed. Female lions can emit powerful pheromones that indicate to any male within range—which is often a great distance— that they are ready for copulation. Pheromones are also common in the insect world as ants and bumblebees, for example, both use trail pheromones, which provide directions to their anthill or beehive. Another pheromone they release indicates to members of the colony that a particular ant or bee belongs there and is not an interloper.

Some animals communicate by <u>urinating</u>. In general, an animal urinates in certain areas to mark its territory and to signal to other members of its species that they are entering an area that does not belong to them. Hyenas, leopards, rabbits, and members of the canine family, among others, are known to do this. Meanwhile, instead of using urine, other animals, including some species of cats, secrete different substances, such as sweat, to mark their territory.

Much like humans use body language when speaking with others, animals may also utilize body movements to communicate. Probably the most famous example in nature is the bee dance, or waggle dance, as it is sometimes called. When a bee locates a food source, it returns to the hive and performs a series of movements; in doing so, it indicates to the other members of its hive the location of a food source and how much food is available. There are many effective though less colorful examples as well. For instance, animals may indicate their preparedness to fight by baring their teeth, assuming a low, crouching position, flattening their ears, or using other methods native to their species.

A final nonverbal method of communication by animals is perhaps one of the most unusual. It is color, and the animal kingdom is replete with examples of it. The herring gull has a red spot on its beak that its young peck to encourage their mother to regurgitate food from her body for them to eat. This action is purely instinctive since the chicks peck at anything brightly colored. Color can be used in mating rituals, such as the one employed by the bowerbird of New Guinea. These birds spend a tremendous amount of effort making displays of colorful objects and plants in an effort to attract a mate. Other animals can change the color of parts of their bodies to send messages to other members of their species.

≋ *Glossary*
ritual: a pattern or behavior performed in a set manner
urinate: to expel liquid waste from the body

1   In stating that animals communicate to "show aggressive intent," the author means that the animals are

Ⓐ preparing to defend themselves

Ⓑ willing to attack

Ⓒ looking for prey

Ⓓ searching for shelter

2   According to paragraph 1, which of the following is NOT true of animal communication?

Ⓐ It is dissimilar from the way humans most often communicate with each other.

Ⓑ Animals rely upon one primary and many secondary forms of communication.

Ⓒ The messages that animals convey through communicating are various.

Ⓓ Animals depend upon many different ways to communicate with one another.

3   According to paragraph 2, vocalization is important to birds because

Ⓐ it enables them to find a partner with whom they can reproduce

Ⓑ they are instinctively aware of how to do so as soon as they hatch

Ⓒ it helps them imitate the sounds of other animals in their ecosystem

Ⓓ they are able to exhibit a wide range of emotions through their songs

Animal Communication

¹➜ In the animal kingdom, communication is just as important as it is for humans. Animals communicate to warn others of danger, to mark their territory, to attract mates, to indicate where food sources are located, to show aggressive intent, and to convey many other messages. However, animals do not communicate in the same manner humans mainly do: by using speech. Instead, they rely upon various nonverbal and verbal means of communication. Not all animals use every method of communication though; what they use depend on the species.

²➜ While animals do not speak like humans, many are capable of vocalization: Birds sing, frogs croak, dogs bark, and monkeys screech. These are forms of vocalization that can express a plethora of meanings. Birds, whose songs are imprinted at birth, may use them as part of their mating **rituals** or to warn others of the presence of a predator. Dogs may bark to show happiness or hunger while they may growl to express anger or fear. Monkeys and other primates are capable of communicating a large number of expressions and emotions through vocalization.

≋ *Glossary*

ritual: a pattern or behavior performed in a set manner

4 The word "it" in the passage refers to

(A) a predator

(B) the same animal

(C) another pheromone

(D) a food source

5 In paragraph 3, the author implies that the emitting of pheromones by female lions

(A) may cause multiple males to respond

(B) frequently happens during the spring

(C) is part of the lions' mating ritual

(D) is detectable by other large cats like tigers

6 In paragraph 4, why does the author mention "Hyenas, leopards, rabbits, and members of the canine family"?

(A) To compare their method of communication with that of cats

(B) To name some animals which communicate through urination

(C) To show that mostly mammals use urine to mark their territory

(D) To explain how these animals avoid using pheromones to communicate

³→ Many animals rely upon pheromones—chemical signals created by their bodies that are exclusively used with members of their own species—to communicate, letting them avoid vocalizing to some extent. For the most part, animals detect pheromones as scents. They are often capable of releasing a number of pheromones, all of which have different purposes. For instance, one might signal the approach of a predator, thereby prompting other members of the species to hide or flee. The same animal might also release another pheromone after detecting a food source since it desires to share it with others. The most common use of pheromones is for reproductive purposes. Females of various species typically release pheromones indicating their readiness to breed. Female lions can emit powerful pheromones that indicate to any male within range—which is often a great distance—that they are ready for copulation. Pheromones are also common in the insect world as ants and bumblebees, for example, both use trail pheromones, which provide directions to their anthill or beehive. Another pheromone they release indicates to members of the colony that a particular ant or bee belongs there and is not an interloper.

⁴→ Some animals communicate by urinating. In general, an animal urinates in certain areas to mark its territory and to signal to other members of its species that they are entering an area that does not belong to them. Hyenas, leopards, rabbits, and members of the canine family, among others, are known to do this. Meanwhile, instead of using urine, other animals, including some species of cats, secrete different substances, such as sweat, to mark their territory.

≋ *Glossary*

urinate: to expel liquid waste from the body

7   Which of the sentences below best expresses the essential information in the highlighted sentence in the passage? *Incorrect* answer choices change the meaning in important ways or leave out essential information.

   (A) Bees return to their hive to perform the waggle dance, which requests that the other bees begin searching for food.

   (B) After successfully locating a large amount of food, bees will perform movements in front of the hive to show where it is.

   (C) Without the benefit of their intricate movements, bees would not be able to locate large numbers of food sources.

   (D) Bees will do a dance in front of other members of the hive to show the amount of food they have found and its location.

8   According to paragraph 6, which of the following is true of color as a means of animal communication?

   (A) Birds are the animals that make the most frequent use of it.

   (B) It can involve the animal physically changing hues.

   (C) Brighter colors have more important meanings to animals.

   (D) It is the rarest form of communication by animals.

Much like humans use body language when speaking with others, animals may also utilize body movements to communicate. Probably the most famous example in nature is the bee dance, or waggle dance, as it is sometimes called. When a bee locates a food source, it returns to the hive and performs a series of movements; in doing so, it indicates to the other members of its hive the location of a food source and how much food is available. There are many effective though less colorful examples as well. For instance, animals may indicate their preparedness to fight by baring their teeth, assuming a low, crouching position, flattening their ears, or using other methods native to their species.

⁶➔ A final nonverbal method of communication by animals is perhaps one of the most unusual. It is color, and the animal kingdom is replete with examples of it. The herring gull has a red spot on its beak that its young peck to encourage their mother to regurgitate food from her body for them to eat. This action is purely instinctive since the chicks peck at anything brightly colored. Color can be used in mating rituals, such as the one employed by the bowerbird of New Guinea. These birds spend a tremendous amount of effort making displays of colorful objects and plants in an effort to attract a mate. Other animals can change the color of parts of their bodies to send messages to other members of their species.

9   Look at the four squares [■] that indicate where the following sentence could be added to the passage.

The newcomers then realize that maintaining their present course may result in an attack on them.

Where would the sentence best fit?

Click on a square [■] to add the sentence to the passage.

Some animals communicate by **urinating**. **1** In general, an animal urinates in certain areas to mark its territory and to signal to other members of its species that they are entering an area that does not belong to them. **2** Hyenas, leopards, rabbits, and members of the canine family, among others, are known to do this. **3** Meanwhile, instead of using urine, other animals, including some species of cats, secrete different substances, such as sweat, to mark their territory. **4**

≋ *Glossary*

urinate: to expel liquid waste from the body

10 **Directions:** An introductory sentence for a brief summary of the passage is provided below. Complete the summary by selecting the THREE answer choices that express the most important ideas of the passage. Some sentences do not belong because they express ideas that are not presented in the passage or are minor ideas in the passage. **This question is worth 2 points.**

> Drag your answer choices to the spaces where they belong.
> To remove an answer choice, click on it. To review the passage, click on **View Text**.

The members of the animal kingdom rely upon a wide variety of methods to communicate with one another despite not using speech as humans do.

-
-
-

Answer Choices

1. Humans are mostly unable to detect pheromones, but this is typically not a problem for members of the animal kingdom.

2. There is a bird that lives in New Guinea that communicates with colors when it is trying to find a mate for itself.

3. Some animals release scents that can be detected and interpreted by members of their own species.

4. Many animals are able to vocalize to some extent, so they can express meaning through barks, chirps, squeaks, and other sounds.

5. One nonverbal method of communication between animals involves the use of colors to convey meaning.

6. Humans have successfully taught some animals, particularly primates, how to communicate in various human languages such as English.

Planetary Object Strikes

Hoba, the largest known meteorite on the Earth

In outer space, there are a seemingly infinite number of rocks and pieces of ice floating around. Occasionally, they strike other bodies, including Earth and the other planets in the solar system. When an impact occurs, the magnitude depends on the size of the object and the planet. For instance, a massive object striking Jupiter, the largest planet, will have a marginal effect on it. Likewise, a small object colliding with Earth will cause a minimal amount of damage. The primary threat is that of large objects striking the smaller <u>terrestrial planets</u>—Mercury, Venus, Earth, and Mars—as well as the various moons orbiting the solar system's planets. Large-magnitude impacts on Earth have happened several times, most famously sixty-five million years ago when an asteroid hit Earth and, according to many scientists, resulted in the demise of the dinosaurs. Evidence from this event and others on Earth and throughout the solar system provides some clues as to what could happen if another large object were to collide with Earth in the future.

The most common objects floating in space are comets, asteroids, and meteoroids. While they vary in size and composition, they can all be deadly if they are of sufficient size and their orbits cause them to crash into the Earth. In recorded history, comets and large asteroids have passed close to Earth, but none has impacted the planet. Meteoroids, on the other hand, do so regularly. Meteoroids that enter Earth's atmosphere are called meteors, and should they survive the intense heat and strike the planet, they are called meteorites. Most are quite small, but the largest intact meteorite ever found on the Earth weighs fifty-five metric tons and is located in Namibia in Africa. Additionally, visible impact craters around the planet provide ample evidence that much larger meteorites have struck in the past.

Scientists have managed to reconstruct the possible course of events that resulted from a major strike. The initial impact would have caused massive fires and earthquakes while also throwing up enormous clouds of dust and ash from the impact and the burning forests. In the case of an ocean strike, enormous tsunamis would have raced literally around the world and wreaked havoc on coastal regions. In addition, the destructive power of the impact would have boiled away much of the seawater at the point of impact, thereby exposing the seafloor and thus casting both dust and rock in the air. After either a land or sea impact, the dust would have reached high into the atmosphere and lingered there for years as it blocked the sun's heat and light and reduced temperatures to the point that most vegetation would have quickly died. Lacking plants, herbivores would have quickly succumbed, and so too would the carnivores that depended on the herbivores as their food sources.

While no major strikes on the Earth have happened in millions of years, this is not true for the rest of the solar system. In July 1994, the Shoemaker-Levy 9 comet slammed into Jupiter. Astronomers had predicted the collision before it happened, so they watched the resulting impact as it actually occurred. Prior to the collision, Jupiter's gravity had broken the comet into a number of fragments, which all crashed into the planet. The impacts were powerful enough to leave visible scars on the planet for months. The largest impact site measured 12,000 kilometers in diameter, which is roughly the size of the Earth. Years later in July 2009, Jupiter was again struck by an unknown object, leaving a highly visible scar.

Had either of the objects that struck Jupiter hit Earth, the planet, and all life on it, would have been obliterated. In fact, Jupiter has likely saved Earth—and the other terrestrial planets—from similar impacts in the past and will undoubtedly do so in the future, too. Some astronomers theorize that Jupiter acts like a cosmic vacuum: Its powerful gravity sucks in objects that could strike other planets. Still, Jupiter has clearly not stopped impacts from occurring elsewhere. All it would take is just one fragment from a comet such as Shoemaker-Levy 9 to hit Earth for most life to die and for the planet to be irrevocably changed.

≋ *Glossary*
terrestrial planet: a planet made mostly of rocks and silica
obliterate: to destroy completely

11 The author discusses "the smaller terrestrial planets" in paragraph 1 in order to

Ⓐ note that fewer asteroids and comets hit them than they do moons

Ⓑ compare the damage done by celestial objects striking each of them

Ⓒ describe how often they are hit by objects coming from outer space

Ⓓ state that they are in danger of being struck by celestial objects

12 Which of the sentences below best expresses the essential information in the highlighted sentence in the passage? *Incorrect* answer choices change the meaning in important ways or leave out essential information.

Ⓐ The last time Earth was hit by an asteroid came many millions of years ago when an asteroid struck the planet and wiped out the dinosaurs.

Ⓑ The dinosaurs likely became extinct millions of years ago because of an asteroid strike, one of the many powerful impacts of Earth by extraplanetary objects.

Ⓒ On the rare occasions when a large enough object impacts the planet, entire species of creatures, like the dinosaurs, can be killed instantly.

Ⓓ Asteroids sometimes hit Earth, and when this happens, the resulting impact can lead to the deaths of millions of animals such as the dinosaurs.

Planetary Object Strikes

[1]➡ In outer space, there are a seemingly infinite number of rocks and pieces of ice floating around. Occasionally, they strike other bodies, including Earth and the other planets in the solar system. When an impact occurs, the magnitude depends on the size of the object and the planet. For instance, a massive object striking Jupiter, the largest planet, will have a marginal effect on it. Likewise, a small object colliding with Earth will cause a minimal amount of damage. The primary threat is that of large objects striking the smaller terrestrial planets—Mercury, Venus, Earth, and Mars—as well as the various moons orbiting the solar system's planets. Large-magnitude impacts on Earth have happened several times, most famously sixty-five million years ago when an asteroid hit Earth and, according to many scientists, resulted in the demise of the dinosaurs. Evidence from this event and others on Earth and throughout the solar system provides some clues as to what could happen if another large object were to collide with Earth in the future.

≋ *Glossary*

terrestrial planet: a planet made mostly of rocks and silica

13 According to paragraph 2, which of the following is true of comets?

    (A) They are much larger in size than both asteroids and meteoroids.

    (B) There is no evidence of them hitting the Earth at any time in human history.

    (C) One of them was responsible for a mass extinction on the Earth millions of years ago.

    (D) Their orbits have caused some to crash into the Earth in recent times.

14 According to paragraph 2, it is known that large meteorites have impacted the Earth because

    (A) they do so on a regular basis all throughout the year

    (B) large craters exist on the moon, which indicates the Earth was also struck

    (C) there is physical evidence of meteor strikes on the planet

    (D) a meteor weighing many tons has been found in Africa

15 The word "lingered" in the passage is closest in meaning to

    (A) remained

    (B) infested

    (C) dissipated

    (D) vaporized

16 In paragraph 3, the author's description of the events following a major impact on the Earth mentions all of the following EXCEPT:

    (A) The amount of time that massive fires on the Earth would burn for

    (B) The places from where dust and rock would be cast into the atmosphere

    (C) The order in which various forms of life would perish

    (D) The effects that the lack of sunlight on the planet would have

2→ The most common objects floating in space are comets, asteroids, and meteoroids. While they vary in size and composition, they can all be deadly if they are of sufficient size and their orbits cause them to crash into the Earth. In recorded history, comets and large asteroids have passed close to Earth, but none has impacted the planet. Meteoroids, on the other hand, do so regularly. Meteoroids that enter Earth's atmosphere are called meteors, and should they survive the intense heat and strike the planet, they are called meteorites. Most are quite small, but the largest intact meteorite ever found on the Earth weighs fifty-five metric tons and is located in Namibia in Africa. Additionally, visible impact craters around the planet provide ample evidence that much larger meteorites have struck in the past.

3→ Scientists have managed to reconstruct the possible course of events that resulted from a major strike. The initial impact would have caused massive fires and earthquakes while also throwing up enormous clouds of dust and ash from the impact and the burning forests. In the case of an ocean strike, enormous tsunamis would have raced literally around the world and wreaked havoc on coastal regions. In addition, the destructive power of the impact would have boiled away much of the seawater at the point of impact, thereby exposing the seafloor and thus casting both dust and rock in the air. After either a land or sea impact, the dust would have reached high into the atmosphere and lingered there for years as it blocked the sun's heat and light and reduced temperatures to the point that most vegetation would have quickly died. Lacking plants, herbivores would have quickly succumbed, and so too would the carnivores that depended on the herbivores as their food sources.

17 Which of the following can be inferred from paragraph 4 about the Shoemaker-Levy 9 comet?

    Ⓐ Its impact on Jupiter was less powerful than the most recent strike on the planet.

    Ⓑ Its crashing into Jupiter upset the gravitational effects of the planet.

    Ⓒ It was the first celestial object to impact a non-terrestrial planet.

    Ⓓ Its orbit was known to astronomers before it crashed into Jupiter.

18 According to paragraph 5, which of the following is true of Jupiter?

    Ⓐ Its presence has enabled all of the terrestrial planets to suffer fewer impacts.

    Ⓑ Any life that once existed on the planet was likely destroyed by Shoemaker-Levy 9.

    Ⓒ Its gravitational force prevents objects in the asteroid belt from leaving their orbits.

    Ⓓ It only stops the largest celestial objects from entering the inner solar system.

19 Look at the four squares [■] that indicate where the following sentence could be added to the passage.

One only needs to look at the large number of impact craters on the moon to see proof of that.

Where would the sentence best fit?

> Click on a square [■] to add the sentence to the passage.

⁴➡ While no major strikes on the Earth have happened in millions of years, this is not true for the rest of the solar system. **1** In July 1994, the Shoemaker-Levy 9 comet slammed into Jupiter. **2** Astronomers had predicted the collision before it happened, so they watched the resulting impact as it actually occurred. **3** Prior to the collision, Jupiter's gravity had broken the comet into a number of fragments, which all crashed into the planet. **4** The impacts were powerful enough to leave visible scars on the planet for months. The largest impact site measured 12,000 kilometers in diameter, which is roughly the size of the Earth. Years later in July 2009, Jupiter was again struck by an unknown object, leaving a highly visible scar.

⁵➡ Had either of the objects that struck Jupiter hit Earth, the planet, and all life on it, would have been <u>obliterated</u>. In fact, Jupiter has likely saved Earth—and the other terrestrial planets—from similar impacts in the past and will undoubtedly do so in the future, too. Some astronomers theorize that Jupiter acts like a cosmic vacuum: Its powerful gravity sucks in objects that could strike other planets. Still, Jupiter has clearly not stopped impacts from occurring elsewhere. All it would take is just one fragment from a comet such as Shoemaker-Levy 9 to hit Earth for most life to die and for the planet to be irrevocably changed.

≋ *Glossary*

obliterate: to destroy completely

20 **Directions:** Select the appropriate statements from the answer choices and match them to the aspect of a planetary strike to which they relate. TWO of the answer choices will NOT be used. **This question is worth 3 points.**

> Drag your answer choices to the spaces where they belong.
> To remove an answer choice, click on it. To review the passage, click on **View Text**.

Answer Choices	**PLANETARY STRIKE**
① The altering of the condition of the atmosphere	**Cause**
② The vanquishing of entire species of animals	•
③ The gravitational pull of a large object	•
④ The intersecting of the orbits of two celestial objects	**Effect**
⑤ The casting of debris into outer space	•
⑥ The changing of a planet's orbit around the sun	•
⑦ The creation of a crater on a surface	•

Floods

Floods occur when so much water accumulates in an area that it inundates land where it normally does not flow. They may be caused by many factors, the most common of which are excessive rainfall, rapid snowmelt, and oceanic surges accompanying storm systems such as hurricanes, typhoons, and cyclones. In rarer situations, the collapse of a dam or the sudden blocking of a river with ice or debris from landslides can result in flooding. All floods, no matter how they occur, are potentially dangerous and frequently result in the loss of human life, the destruction of property, and changes in the landscape. Additionally, the desire of many people to live in close proximity to water has increased the impact floods have had on humanity as a whole.

Because water is necessary to sustain life, provides a source of irrigation for farmland, and enables quick and easy transportation, it is no surprise that large numbers of humans reside near water. In fact, the world's four original civilizations—Mesopotamia, Egypt, the Indus River Valley, and the Yellow River in China—developed around river systems, all of which flooded at various times. Rather than dreading the floods, people welcomed them since they brought nutrient-rich silt that settled on fields, allowing farmers to grow surplus food. These civilizations still recognized how perilous floods were, so they took measures, including building high walls around cities, to protect themselves. Even today, despite recognizing—and living through—the horrors of floods, humans still predominantly live near rivers, lakes, and oceans since, to many, the benefits of living close to water outweigh the possible dangers.

Floods happen in two ways: slowly or quickly. Slow-moving floods are often seasonal. They may occur every spring as snow begins melting or during a region's rainy season, when it may get a large amount of rainfall in a short period of time. When slow-moving floods occur, people usually have time to shore up riverbanks or to construct temporary levees to hold back the water. If the water fails to recede, there is still time to evacuate the population, thereby avoiding any loss of life. Nevertheless, property will still be damaged by the ensuing flood. Water will enter homes and businesses, where it will damage people's belongings, vehicles will be washed away, and small trees and other vegetation will be **uprooted**. Once the water level recedes, enormous amounts of silt and debris such as rocks and even garbage will remain until people remove it to make the region livable once again.

Fast-moving floods are much more dangerous. They may occur when there is a sudden thunderstorm, when a dam bursts, or when a river is blocked. In these cases, the water rises so quickly that it has nowhere to go but over its banks. These floods may wash away bridges, roads, and buildings, cause landslides, **drown** people and livestock, and uproot large trees. Tropical storms often cause these floods. They can move inland and drop several inches or even feet of rain in a twenty-four-hour period, and upon making landfall, they are accompanied by a storm surge. This is a massive wall of water—at levels higher than the tides—that can crash into the shore with the power of a tsunami. Anyone caught in a storm surge is in danger of being swept out to sea. Additionally, the shoreline itself can change as cliffs may be eroded and beaches altered. In 2005, Hurricane Katrina's storm surge caused water to breach the levees of New Orleans, which caused much of the city to be flooded and resulted in more than one thousand deaths.

The effects of floods do not end when the water recedes. Floods may bring unclean water to the underground water table, ponds, and lakes comprising an area's fresh water supply and thus contaminate drinking water. Dead bodies—both human and animal—can decompose and spread diseases in the water if they are not quickly removed. If crops are still in fields when floods strike, they may be washed away while farmland is made unsuitable for agriculture. This is especially true when oceanic storm surges bring water with a high saline content. Floods also disrupt services and the production of goods, making businesses struggle to recover. New Orleans, which was devastated by Katrina in 2005, required several years to recover after the water retreated.

≋ *Glossary*
uproot: to pull up by the roots, often referring to trees or other forms of vegetation
drown: to die from being suffocated by water

21 According to paragraph 1, which of the following is true of floods?

Ⓐ Those caused by landslides are more destructive than other types of floods.

Ⓑ They typically occur during the spring and summer months in many places.

Ⓒ They are caused by storms more frequently than because of faulty engineering.

Ⓓ They increase in power when they happen near large bodies of water such as oceans.

22 The word "dreading" in the passage is closest in meaning to

Ⓐ relishing

Ⓑ cursing

Ⓒ avoiding

Ⓓ fearing

Floods

¹➤ Floods occur when so much water accumulates in an area that it inundates land where it normally does not flow. They may be caused by many factors, the most common of which are excessive rainfall, rapid snowmelt, and oceanic surges accompanying storm systems such as hurricanes, typhoons, and cyclones. In rarer situations, the collapse of a dam or the sudden blocking of a river with ice or debris from landslides can result in flooding. All floods, no matter how they occur, are potentially dangerous and frequently result in the loss of human life, the destruction of property, and changes in the landscape. Additionally, the desire of many people to live in close proximity to water has increased the impact floods have had on humanity as a whole.

Because water is necessary to sustain life, provides a source of irrigation for farmland, and enables quick and easy transportation, it is no surprise that large numbers of humans reside near water. In fact, the world's four original civilizations—Mesopotamia, Egypt, the Indus River Valley, and the Yellow River in China—developed around river systems, all of which flooded at various times. Rather than dreading the floods, people welcomed them since they brought nutrient-rich silt that settled on fields, allowing farmers to grow surplus food. These civilizations still recognized how perilous floods were, so they took measures, including building high walls around cities, to protect themselves. Even today, despite recognizing—and living through—the horrors of floods, humans still predominantly live near rivers, lakes, and oceans since, to many, the benefits of living close to water outweigh the possible dangers.

23 The author's description of slow-moving floods in paragraph 3 mentions all of the following EXCEPT:

(A) The amount of time it takes to clean up after them

(B) The types of events that can cause them to occur

(C) The reason people are usually not killed in them

(D) The type of damage that they tend to cause

24 In paragraph 4, the author uses "a tsunami" as an example of

(A) a force of nature that is more powerful than a flood is

(B) what a storm surge hitting the coastline is similar to

(C) one of the reasons for inland flooding caused by hurricanes

(D) a wave that can be caused by a tropical storm

25 In paragraph 4, all of the following questions are answered EXCEPT:

(A) Why are tropical storms often the causes of fast-moving floods?

(B) How powerful was the hurricane that damaged New Orleans in 2005?

(C) How can fast-moving floods cause the shoreline to be altered?

(D) What are the primary causes of fast-moving floods?

³➡ Floods happen in two ways: slowly or quickly. Slow-moving floods are often seasonal. They may occur every spring as snow begins melting or during a region's rainy season, when it may get a large amount of rainfall in a short period of time. When slow-moving floods occur, people usually have time to shore up riverbanks or to construct temporary levees to hold back the water. If the water fails to recede, there is still time to evacuate the population, thereby avoiding any loss of life. Nevertheless, property will still be damaged by the ensuing flood. Water will enter homes and businesses, where it will damage people's belongings, vehicles will be washed away, and small trees and other vegetation will be **uprooted**. Once the water level recedes, enormous amounts of silt and debris such as rocks and even garbage will remain until people remove it to make the region livable once again.

⁴➡ Fast-moving floods are much more dangerous. They may occur when there is a sudden thunderstorm, when a dam bursts, or when a river is blocked. In these cases, the water rises so quickly that it has nowhere to go but over its banks. These floods may wash away bridges, roads, and buildings, cause landslides, **drown** people and livestock, and uproot large trees. Tropical storms often cause these floods. They can move inland and drop several inches or even feet of rain in a twenty-four-hour period, and upon making landfall, they are accompanied by a storm surge. This is a massive wall of water—at levels higher than the tides—that can crash into the shore with the power of a tsunami. Anyone caught in a storm surge is in danger of being swept out to sea. Additionally, the shoreline itself can change as cliffs may be eroded and beaches altered. In 2005, Hurricane Katrina's storm surge caused water to breach the levees of New Orleans, which caused much of the city to be flooded and resulted in more than one thousand deaths.

≋ *Glossary*

uproot: to pull up by the roots, often referring to trees or other forms of vegetation

drown: to die from being suffocated by water

26 According to paragraph 4, Hurricane Katrina was a deadly storm because

    Ⓐ the people living in the region where it struck were unprepared

    Ⓑ it was accompanied by a tsunami that hit the area around New Orleans

    Ⓒ the city's defenses were overwhelmed by an incoming wave of water

    Ⓓ the levees were located in the wrong places to withstand the storm surge

27 The word "contaminate" in the passage is closest in meaning to

    Ⓐ infect

    Ⓑ decay

    Ⓒ fertilize

    Ⓓ degrade

28 Which of the following can be inferred from paragraph 5 about farmland?

    Ⓐ It reacts poorly when salt is added to it.

    Ⓑ It is the most fertile when located near oceans.

    Ⓒ It requires constant care to yield the most crops.

    Ⓓ It can be irrigated to some extent by floodwaters.

---

⁴→ Fast-moving floods are much more dangerous. They may occur when there is a sudden thunderstorm, when a dam bursts, or when a river is blocked. In these cases, the water rises so quickly that it has nowhere to go but over its banks. These floods may wash away bridges, roads, and buildings, cause landslides, **drown** people and livestock, and uproot large trees. Tropical storms often cause these floods. They can move inland and drop several inches or even feet of rain in a twenty-four-hour period, and upon making landfall, they are accompanied by a storm surge. This is a massive wall of water—at levels higher than the tides—that can crash into the shore with the power of a tsunami. Anyone caught in a storm surge is in danger of being swept out to sea. Additionally, the shoreline itself can change as cliffs may be eroded and beaches altered. In 2005, Hurricane Katrina's storm surge caused water to breach the levees of New Orleans, which caused much of the city to be flooded and resulted in more than one thousand deaths.

⁵→ The effects of floods do not end when the water recedes. Floods may bring unclean water to the underground water table, ponds, and lakes comprising an area's fresh water supply and thus contaminate drinking water. Dead bodies—both human and animal—can decompose and spread diseases in the water if they are not quickly removed. If crops are still in fields when floods strike, they may be washed away while farmland is made unsuitable for agriculture. This is especially true when oceanic storm surges bring water with a high saline content. Floods also disrupt services and the production of goods, making businesses struggle to recover. New Orleans, which was devastated by Katrina in 2005, required several years to recover after the water retreated.

≋ *Glossary*

drown: to die from being suffocated by water

29 Look at the four squares [■] that indicate where the following sentence could be added to the passage.

This, in turn, enabled some farming communities to have more leisure time, so they pursued other ventures, permitting civilization further to develop.

Where would the sentence best fit?

Click on a square [■] to add the sentence to the passage.

Because water is necessary to sustain life, provides a source of irrigation for farmland, and enables quick and easy transportation, it is no surprise that large numbers of humans reside near water. **1** In fact, the world's four original civilizations—Mesopotamia, Egypt, the Indus River Valley, and the Yellow River in China—developed around river systems, all of which flooded at various times. **2** Rather than dreading the floods, people welcomed them since they brought nutrient-rich silt that settled on fields, allowing farmers to grow surplus food. **3** These civilizations still recognized how perilous floods were, so they took measures, including building high walls around cities, to protect themselves. **4** Even today, despite recognizing—and living through—the horrors of floods, humans still predominantly live near rivers, lakes, and oceans since, to many, the benefits of living close to water outweigh the possible dangers.

30 ***Directions:*** An introductory sentence for a brief summary of the passage is provided below. Complete the summary by selecting the THREE answer choices that express the most important ideas of the passage. Some sentences do not belong because they express ideas that are not presented in the passage or are minor ideas in the passage. ***This question is worth 2 points.***

> Drag your answer choices to the spaces where they belong.
> To remove an answer choice, click on it. To review the passage, click on **View Text**.

Floods occur for a wide number of reasons, and in places that suffer from them, there may often be widespread death and destruction.

-
-
-

Answer Choices

1. Human settlements often flood because people tend to construct them close to water because of the many advantages it offers.

2. Floods may happen either gradually or rapidly, and while many people can escape gradual flooding, rapid flooding can cause disasters.

3. In 2005, Hurricane Katrina singlehandedly caused so much destruction to New Orleans that the city took years to recover.

4. Despite knowing how dangerous floods can be, many people still choose to settle in areas that see frequent or periodic flooding.

5. The first human civilizations, such as those in Egypt and Mesopotamia, arose in areas which experience annual flooding.

6. Flooding can continue to have a negative effect after floodwaters recede as diseases may spread, drinking water may be polluted, and crops may be destroyed.

TOEFL® MAP
Reading

New TOEFL® Edition

Advanced

Answers and Explanations

 DARAKWON

TOEFL® MAP

Reading

New TOEFL® Edition

Advanced

Answers and Explanations

DARAKWON

Part B
Building Background Knowledge of TOEFL Topics

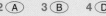 Chapter 01 | History

Mastering Question Types A1 — p.40

1 ⒞   2 ⒜   3 ⒝   4 ⒟

1 [Sentence Simplification Question]

The highlighted sentence notes that lots of people understood how the colonists felt but did not want to fight England and that these people did not choose sides. These ideas are best expressed in answer choice ⒞.

2 [Vocabulary Question]

When someone has a grievance, that person makes a complaint.

3 [Factual Question]

The author writes, "The colonists had their own legislatures as well as some measure of autonomy," which shows that the colonists were permitted to rule themselves, but only in part.

4 [Rhetorical Purpose Question]

The sentence that mentions the Seven Years' War notes that the break between England and America was the result of the debt that England amassed because of the war, which explains why the Americans rebelled against England.

Mastering Question Types A2 — p.42

1 ⒞   2 ⒜   3 ❸   4 First Punic War: ②, ⑦
Second Punic War: ③, ⑤, ⑨   Third Punic War: ④, ⑧

1 [Negative Factual Question]

There is no mention anywhere in the passage of the type of government that ruled over Carthage.

2 [Reference Question]

The "it" that once again became bellicose was Carthage.

3 [Insert Text Question]

The sentence before the third square notes that the Battle of Cannae was a terrible defeat for Rome since so many soldiers died, and the sentence to be inserted points out that Cannae, along with another battle, were among the worst defeats in Roman history.

4 [Fill in a Table Question]

According to the passage, the First Punic War involved the father of Hannibal Barca and took place because of some incidents that happened at sea. The Second Punic War started when Carthage attacked a Roman ally, included a great defeat of Roman Forces at Cannae, and involved some warfare using elephants. As for the Third Punic War, it involved the complete destruction of Carthage and happened after reparations to Rome ceased.

Mastering Question Types B1 — p.44

1 ⒝   2 ⒞   3 ⒜   4 ①, ③, ⑥

1 [Factual Question]

The passage reads, "Rome's leaders often used the promise of citizenship to attract allies to their side," and it also notes how new citizens were often conquered people, thereby proving that they had been enemies.

2 [Vocabulary Question]

When you confer something upon someone, you bestow something to that person.

3 [Rhetorical Purpose Question]

The author points out that only Roman citizens could be sued, which shows how citizens and noncitizens had different rights.

4 [Prose Summary Question]

According to the passage, enemy tribes could be turned into allies if all of the males in the tribe were given citizenship. In addition, the Romans assimilated barbarians into the empire by giving them citizenship. And citizens enjoyed certain rights that noncitizens did not have.

Mastering Question Types B2 — p.46

1 ⒜   2 ⒝   3 ⒝   4 ❸

1 [Inference Question]

The author writes, "The vast majority of the continent never truly opened to human habitation until the nineteenth century advent of railroads," which implies that much of North America was unsettled in the eighteenth century.

2 [Negative Factual Question]

Railroads began operating in the United States in 1830, but the passage does not mention when and where they were invented.

3 [Reference Question]

The previous sentence mentions that Chicago became a "major urban and manufacturing center," so when the next sentence refers to a "meatpacking hub," it is about Chicago.

4 [Insert Text Question]

The sentence before the third square mentions that people could travel from coast to coast in a few days, and the sentence to be inserted begins with "despite the speed of the journey" as it notes that the journey west was still dangerous.

Mastering the Subject A

p.48

1 Ⓑ   2 Ⓓ   3 Ⓒ   4 Ⓒ   5 Before the Civil War: ③, ④   After the Civil War: ②, ⑥, ⑦

1 [Vocabulary Question]

A denizen is a person who lives in a certain place, which makes that individual a resident of that place.

2 [Inference Question]

The author writes, "The land was empty except for the natives and a few white hunters and trappers," which implies that Lewis and Clark met few people on their trip.

3 [Factual Question]

The author writes, "Some people who moved west came from the east and south to seek better, more fertile farmland," which shows they wanted to raise crops.

4 [Sentence Simplification Question]

The highlighted sentence notes that certain people were interested in farming in order to make money. This is best described in answer choice Ⓒ.

5 [Fill in a Table Question]

According to the passage, before the Civil War, a very small number of people lived in the west, and, since there was no transcontinental railroad, it took a long time to get there. After the Civil War, many European immigrants started moving to the west. In addition, the transcontinental railroad was finished, which let a greater number of people move to the west to live.

Summarizing ▶

The American population in the western part of the country increased between 1830 and 1870. In the early 1800s, the land was mostly empty of settlers. However, several events happened to change this. In 1848, gold was discovered in California, so many people moved there. Additionally, after the Civil War, a transcontinental railroad connecting east and west was finished. This opened cheap farmland to people. Both Americans and immigrants moved west to farm and to start new lives. In addition, as transportation methods improved, it became easier to make money, so even more people moved west to take up farming.

Mastering the Subject B

p.51

1 Ⓒ   2 Ⓐ   3 Ⓓ   4 Ⓒ   5 ②, ⑤, ⑥

1 [Inference Question]

When the author writes about Europe's increased population, it is written that the higher population "enabled Europe to begin a revival that has never really stopped," which implies that Europe has prospered for centuries.

2 [Rhetorical Purpose Question]

In the sentence mentioning oats, the author notes how the peasants had better diets because they ate oats.

3 [Factual Question]

It is written, "With more mouths to feed, farmers are forced to find ways to produce more food. They either increase their own labor or become more willing to try unproven ideas to produce more food." This explains why farmers had to try unproven methods.

4 [Negative Factual Question]

There is no mention in the passage of how the Europeans were able to dominate the world in the years after the medieval period ended.

5 [Prose Summary Question]

According to the passage, improved agricultural methods let farmers produce more food. Farmers also had to produce more food because of the increasing population. And the agricultural revolution was what first enabled Europe to increase its population and thus begin to become powerful throughout the world.

Summarizing ▶

From the fifth to tenth centuries, the European population was rather small. However, in the tenth and eleventh centuries, it began to increase. Historians note that the Europeans began producing more agricultural products, which let them live healthier lives. One reason the farmers became more successful was that they made good use of animals to till their fields. They also grew better and more nutritious crops like oats and used crop rotation methods to avoid wearing out the soil. As the population began growing, towns appeared, and people engaged in trade. Ultimately, Europe's greater population helped it become a world power.

Mastering the Subject C

1 (D) 2 (D) 3 (B) 4 (A) 5 2, 3, 4

1 [Sentence Simplification Question]

The highlighted sentence notes that Watt's invention helped transform the world from an agrarian society to an industrialized one. This thought is best expressed in answer choice (D).

2 [Factual Question]

The passage notes that Watt worked on other people's designs of the steam engine and that the one he made was four time more efficient than existing ones.

3 [Reference Question]

The "them" in which numerous problems such as crime and pollution occur are crowded cities.

4 [Vocabulary Question]

A person who is tinkering with something is fiddling around with it.

5 [Prose Summary Question]

According to the passage, many parts of the world, such as the U.S. and Western Europe, became industrialized. England became an industrialized country after having been mostly agrarian. And the engine Watts made was better than Newcomen's, so it helped spark the Industrial Revolution.

Summarizing ▶

While James Watt did not invent the steam engine, he improved it greatly. This helped spark the Industrial Revolution and change the world into a technologically based society. Watt was fascinated by using steam as power, so he worked with Newcomen's engine to make a much more efficient one. He then installed his engine in factories, thereby increasing their productivity. As a result, factories sprang up everywhere as England became an industrial powerhouse. Other places, such as the U.S. and Western Europe, also became more industrialized during this period.

Mastering the Subject D

p.57

1 (C) 2 (D) 3 (B) 4 **4** 5 Athens: 1, 6
Sparta: 4, 5, 7

1 [Inference Question]

The passage reads, "Sparta was the preeminent land power in Greece in the fifth century B.C.," which implies that its navy was not as good as its army since the author also writes, "Athens was more accomplished in

naval warfare, and it was at sea that the Athenians were usually the masters of the Spartans."

2 [Vocabulary Question]

The helots were slaves and were often eager to rebel because of their abject poverty, so this means they were living in wretched conditions.

3 [Negative Factual Question]

The author notes, "Spartan women were considered equals with men," so they could not have been on the same level as slaves.

4 [Insert Text Question]

The sentence to be inserted mentions Athens's "potent naval forces," and the sentence prior to the fourth square also notes how the Athenians were accomplished in naval warfare.

5 [Fill in a Table Question]

According to the passage, Athens lacked a fulltime army while it also did not let its women participate in politics since only certain men did that. As for Sparta, it had the preeminent land army in Greece. It also relied on its helots—slaves—to grow crops and was known mostly for its military accomplishments.

Summarizing ▶

Athens and Sparta were ancient Greece's two greatest city-states. However, they were quite different from one another. The Spartans had a very militaristic society. They kept a standing army and even used their women to help train young warriors. The Spartans also enslaved large numbers of helots and forced them to raise their crops. Athens, meanwhile, was the birthplace of democracy. Ironically, though, Athenian women were less free than Spartan women. While its navy was strong, Athens is known more for its people's accomplishments in fields like architecture, literature, philosophy, science, and history.

TOEFL Practice Tests A

p.60

1 (B) 2 (A) 3 (C) 4 (D) 5 (C)
6 (A) 7 (C) 8 (B) 9 **3**
10 Native Americans: 1, 2, 5 Jamestown Colonists:
4, 6

1 [Vocabulary Question]

An indigenous person is one who is native to a certain area.

2 [Inference Question]

The author writes, "Unwittingly, the colonists would wreak havoc on the native population and the land they lived on," which implies that they did not mean to harm the Native Americans despite doing so.

3 [Factual Question]

The passage notes that sometimes there was saltwater from Chesapeake Bay in the area where Jamestown was located.

4 [Sentence Simplification Question]

The highlighted sentence mentions that land was fenced in, which kept the natives off of it and caused problems between them and the colonists. This is best described in answer choice Ⓓ.

5 [Factual Question]

About the natives' farming practices, the author writes, "Corn, squash, and beans were cultivated together, and the nitrogen-replenishing beans kept the soil fertile and moist," thereby showing that the crops "helped improve the soil."

6 [Rhetorical Purpose Question]

The Europeans did not purposely introduce the worms to the land, but since the worms harmed the natives, this was an indirect method of how the Europeans negatively affected the Native Americans.

7 [Vocabulary Question]

A harbinger of change is a portent or an omen.

8 [Factual Question]

The author notes, "Tobacco sucks the life out of the soil in just a few years, so new lands were constantly being sought and forests cut down," which explains why the colonists had to clear new land for farming.

9 [Insert Text Question]

The use of the word "despite" in the sentence to be inserted means that it is countering a point made in the sentence before it, which should therefore be the one before the third square.

10 [Fill in a Table Question]

According to the passage, the Native Americans did not mark their territory with fences, and they were also affected by many imported diseases. They also did not attack the colonists when they could have. The Jamestown colonists raised many domesticated animals and also wanted to profit from the land.

TOEFL Practice Tests B

p.64

1 Ⓐ 2 Ⓓ 3 Ⓑ 4 Ⓒ 5 Ⓒ
6 Ⓑ 7 Ⓐ 8 Ⓓ 9 **2**
10 **2**, **3**, **5**

1 [Factual Question]

It is written, "Most of the historical record is lost," which means that there is little written evidence of this time period.

2 [Rhetorical Purpose Question]

The author points out that Julius Caesar was the first Roman to invade Britain.

3 [Vocabulary Question]

When something flares up, it starts or begins.

4 [Inference Question]

It is written, "Rebellions constantly flared up," which implies that there was no continual state of peace in Britain.

5 [Factual Question]

The author writes, "The road system was vital for ensuring the speedy transportation of troops and supplies across the island," which shows why the Romans built such good roads in Britain.

6 [Sentence Simplification Question]

The highlighted sentence notes that the Romans needed to pay their soldiers, encourage trade, and make purchases, so they imported lots of money. This is best described in answer choice Ⓑ.

7 [Factual Question]

The author notes that historians disagree about why Roman rule in Britain ended by writing, "Some historians blame economic decline and a decrease in the amount of circulating funds. Others place the blame on increasing barbarian attacks and the Roman administration's inability to deal with them."

8 [Inference Question]

When the author writes, "Roads fell into disrepair, currency disappeared, and trade returned to a primitive barter system," it is implied that Britain became less civilized than it had been during Roman times.

9 [Insert Text Question]

The sentence next to the second square notes that Rome's rulers refused to send any more troops to Britain while the sentence to be inserted explains what they did with their troops instead.

10 [Prose Summary Question]

According to the passage, the construction of infrastructure by the Romans led to the people in Britain building towns in places where the infrastructure was strong, and some of these places are still populated. The roads the Romans built were also a part of the invaluable infrastructure they established. One great effect of the Romans on the people in Britain was that they introduced Roman laws and customs to the country.

p.71

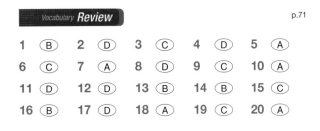

1	Ⓑ	2	Ⓓ	3	Ⓒ	4	Ⓓ	5	Ⓐ
6	Ⓒ	7	Ⓐ	8	Ⓓ	9	Ⓒ	10	Ⓐ
11	Ⓓ	12	Ⓓ	13	Ⓑ	14	Ⓑ	15	Ⓒ
16	Ⓑ	17	Ⓓ	18	Ⓐ	19	Ⓒ	20	Ⓐ

Chapter **02** | The Arts

Mastering Question Types A1
p.74

1Ⓐ   2Ⓓ   3Ⓑ   4⬜1,⬜2,⬜5

1   [Vocabulary Question]

When something makes a comeback, it is said to make a reappearance.

2   [Factual Question]

The paragraph emphasizes how much people disliked actors and treated them badly by writing, "In sixteenth-century Britain, actors—who were always men—were considered among the lowest members of society. They were frequently called 'rogues' or 'scoundrels' by the populace, and they performed under constant threat of punishment by the law."

3   [Sentence Simplification Question]

The highlighted sentence notes that actors who got carried away on stage while improvising could be punished by officials. This is best expressed in answer choice Ⓑ.

4   [Prose Summary Question]

According to the passage, the first acting troupe to be created was called Leicester's Men. Additionally, touring troupes frequently performed in the yards of inns. And it was the sponsorship of nobles that gave them more rights than they had previously possessed.

Mastering Question Types A2
p.76

1Ⓐ   2Ⓒ   3Ⓐ   4 Calligraphy: ⬜2,⬜4,⬜6
Zen Buddhism: ⬜5,⬜7

1   [Reference Question]

The "they" who are highly praised when their works come close to resembling the originals are the artists.

2   [Negative Factual Question]

While calligraphy is important in Chinese traditional paintings, nothing is mentioned about how people who excel at it also produce Chinese traditional paintings.

3   [Inference Question]

It is written that Chinese traditional paintings have "a distinctive appearance that is unmatched by any other style of painting," which implies that it looks different from art created by Western artists.

4   [Fill in a Table Question]

According to the passage, calligraphy involves the painstaking application of the brush to the paper or silk and uses a stylistic manner. The artists also look at each brushstroke as a work of art. Zen Buddhism requires the artists to focus very much while they also think about their work prior to starting it.

Mastering Question Types B1
p.78

1Ⓒ   2Ⓑ   3Ⓓ   4⬜1,⬜2,⬜4

1   [Rhetorical Purpose Question]

The author spends much of paragraph 2 describing the influence that Greek artists had on the development of Roman sculpture art.

2   [Sentence Simplification Question]

The highlighted sentence notes that the colors of the statue, which is very detailed, have faded and that this has happened to many Greek and Roman sculptures. These thoughts are best expressed in answer choice Ⓑ.

3   [Factual Question]

The author writes, "Bas-reliefs had an advantage over portrait statues and busts in that they could portray a wide variety of subjects in great detail."

4   [Prose Summary Question]

According to the passage, the Romans used bas-reliefs to show events in great detail. In addition, works such as Augustus at Prima Porta and Trajan's Column, were impressive. Finally, many creators of Roman sculptures were Greek, but they used the style that the Romans preferred.

Mastering Question Types B2
p.80

1Ⓐ   2Ⓐ   3**2**   4 Gothic: ⬜2,⬜6   Renaissance: ⬜1,⬜4,⬜7

1 [Reference Question]

The "it" that is coming to an end is the Gothic Age of art and architecture.

2 [Inference Question]

The author writes, "It was almost as if the ordered Renaissance were a response to the irregularity that was common during Gothic times," which implies that the Renaissance architecture was intentionally the opposite of Gothic architecture.

3 [Insert Text Question]

The sentence before the second square names several buildings constructed during the Renaissance, and the sentence to be inserted includes the phrase "there were, of course, a large number of other buildings."

4 [Fill in a Table Question]

According to the passage, Gothic architecture was often dark and shadowy as well as constructed very high. Renaissance architecture was inspired by past styles, was very precise, and focused more on appearance than size.

Mastering the Subject A
p.82

1 [Vocabulary Question]

If a person embraces a movement, it means that the person accepts it.

2 [Sentence Simplification Question]

The highlighted sentence defines Realism as being art that depicts regular people doing typical activities. This is best described in answer choice ⓒ.

3 [Factual Question]

It is written that Courbet "claimed to be independent of any artistic movement," but he was "influenced by the school of landscape artists that used the countryside near Paris as their subject and also by a trend toward using more rural settings in works of art."

4 [Reference Question]

The "them" who could pain their personal visions were artists.

5 [Prose Summary Question]

According to the passage, Courbet was a Realist painter who tried to paint reality as he saw it. Realists also tried to paint the lives of regular people. And photography greatly influenced Realism by showing life as it actually was.

Summarizing ▶

In the mid-nineteenth century, the Realism movement began. It was a reaction against Romanticism in that it tried to represent everyday scenes and people as they actually were. One reason Realism developed was that photography showed people exactly as they appeared. So the artists sought to imitate the pictures. Gustave Courbet was the man who came up with the term "Realism." He and his followers created the art movement after being influenced by certain landscape artists. Realism did not just affect the world of art; its followers became involved in politics and also influenced other art movements such as Naturalism and Impressionism.

Mastering the Subject B
p.85

1 [Inference Question]

The author mentions the "dancer's guttural utterances, which were in no recognizable language," and notes that a translator was needed. Both of these imply that most people could not understand the dancer's words.

2 [Negative Factual Question]

The passage reads, "Today, African tribes use the masks and the costumes in religious and social ceremonies."

3 [Rhetorical Purpose Question]

The author mentions that "the importance of African masks began to wane" when the European colonial masters arrived in Africa.

4 [Insert Text Question]

The sentence prior to the first square states that feathers appear in the plume; feathers come from birds, which are mentioned in the sentence to be inserted.

5 [Fill in a Table Question]

According to the passage, people held mask dances to prepare for the gathering of crops and before coming-of-age ceremonies. The effects of the mask dances were that people were given advice, interpreters were needed for the dances, and people believed the dancers were possessed by spirits.

Summarizing ▶

In parts of Africa south of the Sahara Desert, tribes used to wear masks when they held various rituals or ceremonies, but the practice ended when the colonialism period began. The shapes, the sizes, and the materials of the masks depended upon the tribes that made them, so they all looked different. But there were four basic types of masks: the headdress, the facemask, the horizontal plank mask, and the helmet mask. Each was different from the others. Mask dances are making a comeback in Africa these days and are used in ceremonies held for various reasons.

Mastering the Subject C
p.88

1 D   2 B   3 D   4 A   5 Medieval Art: 2, 5   Renaissance Art: 1, 4, 6

1 [Reference Question]

The "it" that heavily affected all artistic endeavors following the fall of the Roman Empire was Christianity.

2 [Sentence Simplification Question]

The highlighted sentence notes that the human body was God's symbol of perfection and also that nudes were themes in Renaissance art. These two ideas are best described in answer choice B.

3 [Rhetorical Purpose Question]

About *David*, it is written "*David* is often said to have been influenced by a Greek statue known as *The Spear Bearer*, yet David's face has more expression in it."

4 [Factual Question]

The author writes that masters during this period "employed notions of human perfection to their work but added a new element—human emotion—to make them superior to their Greek and Roman forbearers."

5 [Fill in a Table Question]

According to the passage, medieval art lacked depth and cared little about how humans looked. Renaissance art used foreshortening, imitated past art, and employed humanlike expressions.

Summarizing ▶

Life in Europe during the Renaissance changed in many ways. It even affected the type of art that was created. Before the Renaissance, medieval artists painted in two dimensions, did not use light well, and did not depict anatomically correct humans. But thanks to the influence of the Greeks and Romans, Renaissance artists painted in a new style. They used depth in their paintings and also accurately depicted the human body. The greatest art was created during the High Renaissance. Masters such as Michelangelo, Leonardo da Vinci, and Raphael incorporated human emotions into their works to make them masterpieces. This was true of both the paintings and the sculptures that they made.

Mastering the Subject D
p.91

1 A   2 C   3 D   4 ❶   5 3, 5, 6

1 [Vocabulary Question]

When a person speaks in an impromptu manner, what he or she says is unrehearsed.

2 [Inference Question]

Since commedia dell'arte "employed some common themes," it is implied that the performances were related to one another.

3 [Negative Factual Question]

Only the Captain and Punch changed from play to play.

4 [Insert Text Question]

The sentence before the first square reads, "There were some stock gestures, phrases, and situations that a commedia dell'arte audience expected during each performance," and the sentence to be inserted begins with "yet," indicating that despite the audience knowing what to expect, the people watching still wanted to see how the performance would turn out.

5 [Prose Summary Question]

According to the passage, Shakespeare wrote plays in this genre, thereby showing how popular it was. Harlequin acted the same way in every performance, which exemplified the basic theme. And the theme of jealousy was also shared in many performances.

Summarizing ▶

In fourteenth-century Italy, commedia dell'arte was created as a new form of stage presentation. It remained popular for 400 years but is no longer practiced today. It had common themes like love, jealousy, and mistaken identities, but it had no set dialog. The actors would discuss roughly how the play would go and would then give impromptu performances. There were a number of stock characters in the form, and they always had certain features which defined them. There were also certain gestures, phrases, and situations that always occurred in each performance. Writers such as Shakespeare created works in this genre, and characters like Harlequin are still imitated in literary forms today.

TOEFL Practice Tests A
p.94

1 C   2 D   3 D   4 D   5 A
6 C   7 B   8 D   9 ❸
10 Cause: 4, 5   Effect: 3, 6, 7

1 [Vocabulary Question]

Something ephemeral is brief or only lasts a short time.

2 [Rhetorical Purpose Question]

When mentioning Surrealism, the author writes that it was the movement to which many Dadaists turned.

3 [Sentence Simplification Question]

The highlighted sentence notes the disillusionment the Dadaists felt because of the war and their desire to show people how stupid it was. These two ideas are best exemplified by answer choice Ⓓ.

4 [Inference Question]

When the author mentions "neutral Switzerland," it is implied that Switzerland was not involved in World War I.

5 [Negative Factual Question]

Dada was rambling and nonsensical, and its artists followed no particular method.

6 [Factual Question]

The journal was printed to "spread the word about Dada."

7 [Vocabulary Question]

When something is belied, it is contradicted.

8 [Inference Question]

The passage mentions that Dada's disappearance was hastened by the appearance of Surrealism since the members of the Paris Dada movement began turning to it.

9 [Insert Text Question]

Surrealism is an art movement, and it is identified as such in the sentence to be inserted when it is written "this was yet another movement."

10 [Fill in a Table Question]

According to the passage, Dada formed because artists wanted to show the absurdity of present times and because people were protesting the war. Its effects were that more artists began protesting, Surrealism was eventually founded by former Dadaists, and people came to believe that Dadaists did not really make real art.

TOEFL Practice Tests B

p.98

1 Ⓐ	2 Ⓓ	3 Ⓐ	4 Ⓑ	5 Ⓒ
6 Ⓓ	7 Ⓑ	8 Ⓓ	9 **3**	
10 **2**, **3**, **4**				

1 [Rhetorical Purpose Question]

When discussing the Renaissance, the author explains that, except for the piano, the instruments in the orchestra were developed then.

2 [Inference Question]

Since the Renaissance ended in the sixteenth century and the Baroque Period came after it, it is implied that the Baroque Period started sometime after the beginning of the sixteenth century.

3 [Rhetorical Purpose Question]

The author notes that the harpsichord was the ancestor of the piano.

4 [Sentence Simplification Question]

The highlighted sentence describes the improvement to the piano that Cristofori made. This is best described in answer choice Ⓑ.

5 [Negative Factual Question]

There is no mention as to whether or not there are more woodwinds than string instruments in the orchestra.

6 [Factual Question]

It is written, "The music of the Classical Era was based on the sonata form."

7 [Factual Question]

While covering symphonies, the author mentions the many musical instruments in them but also writes, "Stringed instruments were the dominant instruments in classical music, and the violin was the prime instrument in symphonies."

8 [Vocabulary Question]

Something with a profound influence has a considerable effect on other things.

9 [Insert Text Question]

The sentence before the third square mentions the "many variations" of the sonata, and the sentence to be inserted explains why these variations made "the Classical Era such a rich source of all kinds of musical sounds."

10 [Prose Summary Question]

According to the passage, the sonata was a new kind of music that was created, and so was the music played by only four musicians. In addition, many new instruments, including drums and the piano, were created, which influenced the type of music.

Vocabulary *Review*

1 Ⓒ 2 Ⓐ 3 Ⓐ 4 Ⓑ 5 Ⓓ
6 Ⓒ 7 Ⓐ 8 Ⓓ 9 Ⓐ 10 Ⓑ
11 Ⓐ 12 Ⓒ 13 Ⓑ 14 Ⓑ 15 Ⓐ
16 Ⓓ 17 Ⓓ 18 Ⓑ 19 Ⓒ 20 Ⓐ

Chapter 03 | Archaeology and Anthropology

Mastering Question Types A1
p.108

1 Ⓑ 2 Ⓑ 3 Ⓓ 4 ③, ④, ⑤

1 [Vocabulary Question]

Something done for the sake of creating music is done for the purpose of creating it.

2 [Factual Question]

The author writes, "Percussion instruments were possibly the first type of musical instruments as they can be essentially anything that is beaten or beaten together and therefore require little work to produce."

3 [Rhetorical Purpose Question]

The author mentions Hohle Fels Cave in order to name one of the places where one of the oldest known musical instruments was found.

4 [Prose Summary Question]

According to the passage, wind instruments were made from various materials. In addition, flutes are the oldest known prehistoric instruments, and the earliest humans made percussion instruments from things such as stones.

Mastering Question Types A2
p.110

1 Ⓒ 2 Ⓓ 3 ❹ 4 Cuneiform: ④, ⑦ Proto-Writing: ①, ②, ⑥

1 [Reference Question]

The "They" that desired to keep accurate counts of certain things were bureaucracies.

2 [Negative Factual Question]

The passage reads, "Scholars believe [proto-writing] developed between the eighth and sixth millennium B.C. How and when proto-writing became cuneiform are unknown, but around the fourth millennium B.C., an early form of it was in use in Mesopotamia.

3 [Insert Text Question]

The sentence before the fourth square reads, "Most of the extant clay tablets with cuneiform on them deal with bureaucratic matters such as the amount of grain produced somewhere." The sentence to be inserted begins with "in other instances, however," and then it describes another type of writing that was recorded in cuneiform.

4 [Fill in a Table Question]

According to the passage, cuneiform was created in Mesopotamia because bureaucrats wanted to keep better records. In addition, proto-writing was developed sometime between the eighth and sixth millennium B.C., relied upon symbols, and has been found to have been used in various cultures.

Mastering Question Types B1
p.112

1 Ⓐ 2 Ⓑ 3 Ⓓ 4 ②, ⑤, ⑥

1 [Factual Question]

The passage reads, "Domesticated animals are tame and do not lash out and attack humans or flee in their presence."

2 [Rhetorical Purpose Question]

In the passage, it is written, "History is replete with stories of wolves suckling abandoned human infants," and in the next sentence, the author mentions the story of Romulus and Remus and how they were raised by a wolf.

3 [Sentence Simplification Question]

The highlighted sentence states that a wolf did not give into its instincts to fear humans since it sensed no danger from them, so it felt a sense of companionship with them. These thoughts are best expressed in answer choice Ⓓ.

4 [Prose Summary Question]

According to the passage, horses are some of the animals that must overcome their fear of humans and be broken before they can be domesticated. In addition, wolves were tamed when abandoned wolves overcame their fear of humans. Finally, many animals have not been tamed since they remain afraid of humans.

Mastering Question Types B2
p.114

1 Ⓒ 2 Ⓐ 3 Ⓓ 4 Cause: ③, ⑤, ⑥ Effect: ②, ④

1 [Reference Question]

The "them" that include population pressures, quests for food and fodder, and in the case of the Mongols, the desire for conquest, were the reasons for migrating.

2 [Negative Factual Question]

The Botai were the first to tame the horse, and while they "lived in what is Kazakhstan today," they were not the "Kazakhstani people."

3 [Inference Question]

The author notes that when tribes migrated elsewhere, there were often battles, which resulted in "a certain amount of bloodshed."

4 [Fill in a Table Question]

According to the passage, the causes of mass migrations include there not being enough food, battles for resources between tribes, and the interest in conquest of some tribes. The effects include battles between the tribes and people as far away as Europe and also the defeat of civilizations such as Rome.

Mastering the Subject A
p.116

1 [Negative Factual Question]

The passage reads, "Finally, archaeologists must deal with modern-day governments and their frequent desire to prohibit the removal of artifacts," so it is not true that artifacts are removed from sites by governments.

2 [Vocabulary Question]

Something that is daunting can wind up being discouraging to an individual.

3 [Inference Question]

The author first writes, "Some sites have been occupied continuously for thousands of years," and then later mentions, "This is a common problem that archaeologists face when examining ruins from the Roman Empire and ancient Middle Eastern societies." These sentences imply that the land once occupied by the Roman Empire has been continuously inhabited.

4 [Insert Text Question]

The sentence before the second square mentions archaeologists going through garbage pits to see what people ate while the sentence to be inserted includes information about determining "ancient people's diets."

5 [Prose Summary Question]

According to the passage, among the problems archaeologists encounter are government interference, a lack of written records, and people living in areas

erasing traces of past civilizations.

Summarizing ▶

For many reasons, archaeology is not an exact science, so its practitioners often have problems conducting it. There were no written records in the past, so archaeologists cannot rely on them for their research. Instead, they must carefully inspect ancient sites as they excavate them and unearth buildings and artifacts to analyze. In addition, many modern-day cultures have built on ancient sites, so remains from the past are hard to get at or have even been destroyed. Finally, many governments are reluctant to let some people dig in places. They are concerned about looting and that their carefully crafted national myths may be disproven.

Mastering the Subject B
p.119

1 [Sentence Simplification Question]

The highlighted sentence states that people probably began preserving their food by burying it underground after the last ice age. This sentiment is best described in answer choice Ⓑ.

2 [Vocabulary Question]

When farmers experience lean years, it means that they are unproductive and produce few crops.

3 [Reference Question]

The "it" that people wanted to prevent animals and insects from consuming was grain. Since "consume" implies to eat, a look at the answer choices will show that only one of them is edible.

4 [Factual Question]

People began putting food in caves since they were cool, which enabled them to preserve their food in the same way that burial pits did.

5 [Fill in a Table Question]

According to the passage, people began to use food burial pits since farmers grew more food than could be eaten quickly and since they needed to preserve grain to plant the next year. Its effects were that food took longer to spoil, people developed pottery to store their food in, and people could eat enough food despite insufficient harvests.

Summarizing ▶

Humans have always been concerned about preserving their food, so they have sought ways to keep bacteria and other microorganisms from spoiling it. Mostly, they used burial pits to do this. They kept their food underground since the cooler temperatures there help food remain edible longer. Once agriculture was learned, having burial pits became imperative since people could keep their surplus food and the next year's grain for planting in them. Other cultures used caves to keep their food in since they were cool. This also led to the invention of pottery because people needed containers to keep their food in before burying them.

Mastering the Subject C

1 Ⓑ 2 Ⓐ 3 Ⓒ 4 Ⓒ 5 The Land Bridge
Theory: ②, ④, ⑥ The Sailing Theory: ①, ⑤

1 [Factual Question]

When referring to migration to Asia and Europe, the author writes, "There were no real obstacles since all three continents are interconnected." But when referring to the Americas, it is written, "However, how humans reached the Americas, which are unconnected to other landmasses, is a matter of conjecture."

2 [Reference Question]

The "it" that is the more logical of the two and has a plethora of evidence to defend is the land bridge theory.

3 [Rhetorical Purpose Question]

The author includes Easter Island to show how far east across the Pacific Ocean the Polynesian islanders reached. In the paragraph, the northern and southern extents of the Polynesians' journeys are also noted.

4 [Sentence Simplification Question]

The highlighted sentence states that due to current higher water levels, former coastal settlements are hard to excavate because they are now underwater. These facts are best described in answer choice Ⓒ.

5 [Fill in a Table Question]

According to the passage, the land bridge theory is the more likely explanation for how people migrated to the Americas, and it happened while people were following herds of animals. In addition, the land bridge is now unavailable for people to cross over. As for the sailing theory, is states that the Polynesians were the first to visit the Americas and that there is also little archaeological evidence to support it.

Summarizing ▶

The Americas were the last continents that humans settled. There are two competing theories on how this happened. The first is that lower sea levels exposed a land bridge between modern-day Siberia and Alaska. People

from Asia followed herds of animals across the bridge and migrated to the two continents. Some archaeological evidence supports this theory. The other theory is that people sailed to the Americas. Some claim Pacific Polynesian islanders sailed to the Americas. Others say that sailors went up the coast of Asia, past the Aleutian Islands, and down into the Americas. Finding coastal settlements has been hard because any possible sites are beneath the ocean now.

Mastering the Subject D

1 Ⓒ 2 Ⓒ 3 Ⓑ 4 ② 5 ③, ④, ⑤

1 [Negative Factual Question]

There is no mention in the paragraph of the kinds of excavations that archaeologists have done at Stonehenge.

2 [Factual Question]

The author writes, "Originally, the circular monument was built of wood, but it was later replaced with stones," so the stones were not a part of its original construction.

3 [Inference Question]

The passage notes that the Druids were "ancient" and thus implies that they were in England prior to the Romans and Saxons.

4 [Insert Text Question]

The sentence before the second square begins with "some" while the sentence to be inserted starts with "others." The two sentences have a relationship in style and in content, which means that they belong together.

5 [Prose Summary Question]

According to the passage, Stonehenge's purpose is not known, but it could have been used to look at the stars and may have been sacred to its builders as well. There is some mystery about the stones used in its construction, and it is thought to have been erected 5,000 years ago although no one is sure about that.

Summarizing ▶

One of the oldest and most mysterious ancient sites is Stonehenge in southwest England. Very little is known about it. It is a monument made of dozens of stones sitting upright in a circle. No one knows how the stones got there or who erected them. Some think supernatural forces were responsible, but this is highly unlikely. People have proposed that the ancient Druids, Romans, and Saxons were all responsible, but no one is certain. Nevertheless, it appears to be at least 5,000 years old. Some believe Stonehenge was an astronomical observatory, and others claim it was a sacred spot for worshippers.

TOEFL Practice Tests A

p.128

1 [Inference Question]

The passage reads, "The Mayans once numbered in the millions, but by 1839, they had all but disappeared, in the process becoming one of the great mysteries of history," which implies that some Mayans were still alive during the nineteenth century.

2 [Factual Information Question]

The paragraph includes several different reasons as to why the small kingdoms could never unite into one large kingdom.

3 [Negative Factual Question]

Kings and dynasties began to appear around 250 A.D., but Mayan society already existed by then.

4 [Reference Question]

The "them" who were promised rain to grow their crops were the peasants.

5 [Rhetorical Purpose Question]

The Mayans believed "the annual rainfall was a divine gift" and that "the kings' and priests' prayers brought rain." Both statements show the importance of religion to the Mayans.

6 [Sentence Simplification Question]

The highlighted sentence gives two reasons why the Mayans could not be united: The farmers could not produce enough food for the kings' armies, and the armies were relatively immobile. Both of these reasons are best explained in answer choice Ⓒ.

7 [Vocabulary Question]

A yield from a crop is the amount of that crop which is harvested.

8 [Factual Information Question]

The paragraph notes that the Spanish decimated the Mayans, so, in killing many of them, the Spaniards contributed to the disappearance of Mayan civilization.

9 [Insert Text Question]

The sentence prior to the second square includes the phrase "even civil warfare among the peasantry broke out." The sentence to be inserted notes that there is evidence of rebellions by farmers, so these sentences

should be placed next to one another.

10 [Prose Summary Question]

According to the passage, the Mayans disappeared slowly over the course of several hundred years. In addition, their deforesting of the jungle was caused by their inefficient farming practices. And they were primarily an agricultural people who built cities later in their history.

TOEFL Practice Tests B

p.132

1 [Factual Question]

The passage reads, "Early humans were nomads by necessity, not by choice. The first humans to walk the Earth were constantly moving in search of food." These sentences indicate that nomads had to wander in order to survive.

2 [Vocabulary Question]

Sustenance is provided by food and drink, both of which provide nourishment.

3 [Inference Question]

The author notes, "One constant theme throughout human history is the clash of nomads with more civilized people," which implies that nomads made war against people living in cities and other settlements.

4 [Rhetorical Purpose Question]

It is written, "An occasional strong leader, like Attila the Hun or Genghis Khan, could unite many tribes for a common purpose such as military conquest," so the author mentions Attila the Hun to show how he once united several tribes.

5 [Inference Question]

The author writes, "The nomadic way of war was to strike fast and damage the enemy but to flee if necessary," which implies that they would not fight to the death in battle but would instead retreat when they realized they were losing.

6 [Factual Question]

The paragraph mentions, "Women were expected to learn to ride a horse and to fight if necessary. Fathers raised their sons to be warriors, to use spears, swords, and bows and arrows to hunt animals and to kill men from horseback." Thus men, women, and children were involved in fighting wars.

7 [Vocabulary Question]

A city that contains teeming hordes of people is packed with them.

8 [Negative Factual Question]

There is no mention of cities being established in nomads' lands, so there is no way to know how they felt about that.

9 [Insert Text Question]

The sentence before the fourth square states that there were constantly clashes between nomads and civilized humans, and the sentence to be inserted mentions that there was a lot of bloodshed "when unfortunate events like this occurred."

10 [Prose Summary Question]

According to the passage, nomads had a dislike of cities, so they preferred to avoid them. In addition, their migrations and wanderings were made easier thanks to their having domesticated animals, and since they disliked urban areas, they refused to abandon their wandering ways.

Vocabulary *Review*									p.139
1	Ⓒ	2	Ⓑ	3	Ⓐ	4	Ⓑ	5	Ⓓ
6	Ⓓ	7	Ⓐ	8	Ⓑ	9	Ⓒ	10	Ⓒ
11	Ⓑ	12	Ⓓ	13	Ⓐ	14	Ⓑ	15	Ⓐ
16	Ⓒ	17	Ⓐ	18	Ⓓ	19	Ⓑ	20	Ⓒ

Chapter 04 | Education, Sociology, and Psychology

Mastering Question Types A1

p.142

1 Ⓒ   2 Ⓒ   3 Ⓐ   4 **2**, **5**, **6**

1 [Vocabulary Question]

Surpluses that farmers might have to trade with are excesses of crops.

2 [Rhetorical Purpose Question]

It is written, "Mothers taught their daughters to sew, to cook, and to run a household while fathers taught their sons about farming, hunting, fishing, and conducting business."

3 [Factual Question]

The author writes, "Most children did not receive much of an education beyond learning reading, writing, and arithmetic."

4 [Prose Summary Question]

According to the passage, fathers and sons did manual labor while mothers and daughters took care of domestic chores. In addition, sons and daughters learned different skills while families had many children to share in the work and since so many children died in infancy.

Mastering Question Types A2

p.144

1 Ⓐ   2 Ⓑ   3 Ⓐ   4 **2**

1 [Reference Question]

The "them" that the parents are taking a break from watching is their children.

2 [Negative Factual Question]

The passage reads, "Many doctors also concur that exposing children to other children at young ages and allowing them to build up their immunities to common childhood diseases will make them stronger in the future."

3 [Inference Question]

The author notes, "In some cases, they also play games, engage in artistic endeavors, and even learn to play musical instruments," which implies that music is not in the standard curriculum at most preschools.

4 [Insert Text Question]

The sentence before the second square states that some people disagree with having children attend preschool. The sentence to be inserted begins with "instead" and presents a part of these people's justification for keeping children out of preschool.

Mastering Question Types B1

p.146

1 Ⓐ   2 Ⓐ   3 Ⓑ   4 **1**, **2**, **3**

1 [Sentence Simplification Question]

The highlighted sentence mentions that students graduating from high school attend classes for twelve years and will go to school even longer if they attend college. These two thoughts are best expressed in answer choice Ⓐ.

2 [Rhetorical Purpose Question]

In the paragraph, the author notes that home economics is typically an elective, which means that students do not have to take it.

3 [Vocabulary Question]

When a person mentors another, that individual

instructs that person how to do something.

4 [Prose Summary Question]

According to the passage, education can occur either at a person's home or office. In addition, people can educate their relatives on how to act and to live properly. Finally, while schooling takes place at school, there is a limit to how much a student can learn there.

Mastering Question Types B2

p.148

1 Ⓑ   2 Ⓑ   3 **3**   4 Before the Industrial Revolution: **3**, **6**   During the Industrial Revolution: **2**, **4**, **7**

1 [Inference Question]

The passage reads, "At the end of the eighteenth century, most European families lived together in rural agrarian settings," which implies that a minority of Europeans were living and working in cities.

2 [Reference Question]

The them who were going off to seek their fortunes were the sons.

3 [Insert Text Question]

The sentence before the third square mentions some of the hardships people faced when working during the Industrial Revolution. The sentence to be inserted notes that Dickens wrote about these and other hardships during the period; thus, the two sentences belong together.

4 [Fill in a Table Question]

According to the passage, before the Industrial Revolution, people usually stayed in the areas where they were born, and the men and boys ran the family farms. During the Industrial Revolution, family members spent less time together, children were required to attend school, and people could spend more than half the day working in their factories.

Mastering the Subject A

p.150

1 Ⓓ   2 Ⓑ   3 Ⓓ   4 **4**   5 **3**, **4**, **5**

1 [Negative Factual Question]

The passage reads, "Misconceptions are false ideas people can have about virtually anything."

2 [Inference Question]

The passage notes that the professor "may react negatively to those students who are yawning," which implies that he feels the students are disrespecting him

by yawning.

3 [Vocabulary Question]

Someone who is shabbily dressed is dressed poorly.

4 [Insert Text Question]

The sentence before the fourth square states that there is a misconception "which may prevent the two of them from ever getting together," and the sentence to be inserted follows up by beginning with "essentially" and then noting what the final result is going to be.

5 [Prose Summary Question]

According to the passage, people can have misconceptions about others because of their feelings about themselves, a particular experience in the past, and a lack of information.

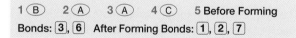

When people have false ideas about others, they are said to have misconceptions. While they are typically not harmful, misconceptions can arise because of a variety of internal and external factors. People's self-image—how they look at themselves—is one factor that often creates misconceptions. This happens because others cannot know exactly what another person is thinking. Likewise, some misconceptions can result from how people react to another individual. And some misconceptions may last a long time and may be difficult for a person to change without the presence of new information that could possibly change a person's opinion about a preconceived notion.

Mastering the Subject B

p.153

1 Ⓑ   2 Ⓐ   3 Ⓐ   4 Ⓒ   5 Before Forming Bonds: **3**, **6**   After Forming Bonds: **1**, **2**, **7**

1 [Sentence Simplification Question]

The highlighted sentence states that as babies' cognitive abilities develop, they can a) recognize their parents and b) recognize that other people are not their parents. These two ideas are best expressed in answer choice Ⓑ.

2 [Reference Question]

The "them" who are developing a fear of strangers are the babies, which are the main subject of the entire paragraph.

3 [Rhetorical Purpose Question]

The author explains, "This attachment is related to their need to be taken care of and to feel secure," which are two reasons why babies become attached to their caregivers.

4 [Factual Question]

The paragraph notes, "Children who spend all of their time with one primary caregiver will display strong emotions when that caregiver departs."

5 [Fill in a Table Question]

According to the passage, before babies form bonds, they cannot differentiate between people and are friendly with anyone with whom they come into contact. After babies form bonds, they may misbehave when their caregiver departs and may be unhappy when a person they want to see is not around. They also often look forward to seeing a certain member of their family, typically the person with whom they have bonded.

Summarizing ▶

When babies are born, they cannot recognize their parents or others, and thus they are happy when they see anyone. However, as they age, they learn to recognize their parents and to distinguish them from others. They often then develop an attachment to their parent or primary caregiver. This attachment, in which they bond with the person, causes them to seek out the person when he or she is not around. They may even throw temper tantrums when they cannot find their primary caregiver. As children age and begin to attend school, they start to lose this attachment, so they are no longer totally dependent on one person for care.

Mastering the Subject C   p.156

| 1 Ⓐ | 2 Ⓑ | 3 Ⓓ | 4 Ⓐ | 5 ⓵, ⓷, ⓹ |

1 [Factual Question]

The first sentence in the paragraph notes, "Schema theory states that people have certain rules which they use to organize their knowledge and understanding of the world."

2 [Reference Question]

The "they" in the sentence refers to learners, who are "revising their existing schemata based on new knowledge they acquire."

3 [Inference Question]

The author writes, "Some theorists believe that people have a hierarchical organization of knowledge and add new knowledge to this structure, which leads to superior intelligence," which implies that intelligence may arise after schemata have been formed.

4 [Sentence Simplification Question]

The highlighted sentence notes that when students have to do the required assignments, then they will have to form a schema for that topic. This notion is best expressed in answer choice Ⓐ.

5 [Prose Summary Question]

According to the passage, people can create a useful schema when they learn something new. They can also know what to do in certain situations if they have many schemata. And their schemata enable them to understand how the world works.

Summarizing ▶

In schema theory, people organize their knowledge by using certain rules. The schemata they form help them look at the world in a certain way. People are constantly learning new information, and their schemata help them greatly. They can help a person assimilate new knowledge and to understand what to do in various situations that they have never experienced before. However, should a person have no schemata for a certain experience, that individual may choose to ignore the new thing rather than learn about it. But should a person investigate and learn about this new experience, that person may form a new schema that may be helpful in the future.

Mastering the Subject D   p.159

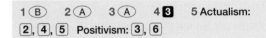

| 1 Ⓑ | 2 Ⓐ | 3 Ⓐ | 4 ❸ | 5 Actualism: |
| ⓶, ⓸, ⓹ | Positivism: ⓷, ⓺ |

1 [Vocabulary Question]

A conundrum is another word for a puzzle.

2 [Factual Question]

The paragraph includes the following sentence: "The possibilists' challenge to this idea is formed on the notion of possible worlds, which is based on modal realism."

3 [Negative Factual Question]

According to the paragraph, Lewis said, "Lewis also argued that there were an infinite number of possible worlds and that they were isolated from one another in time and space," which is the opposite of answer choice Ⓐ.

4 [Insert Text Question]

The sentence to be inserted begins with the phrase "in that regard," which indicates that the sentence will expand upon a point that has just been mentioned.

5 [Fill in a Table Question]

According to the passage, the actualists thought that everything which can exist already does, and they also often tried to use Occam's razor. Yet some thought other worlds could exist, but only in the abstract. The positivists, meanwhile, thought other worlds existed elsewhere and used logical reasoning based on prior experiences.

Summarizing ▶

Two opposing philosophical ideas are actualism and possibilism. Actualism claims that only actual things and the world they occupy exist. Possibilism, however, disagrees, and claims that it is possible for things to exist beyond what is actually known to exist. Possibilists believe in the notion of other worlds. They state that by using logical reasoning, they can accept the existence of things beyond what they have experienced. David Lewis was a major proponent of possibilism. He was convinced that there are an infinite number of worlds in the universe. Actualists disagreed with Lewis's theories for a couple of reasons, but Lewis believed in his ideas all throughout his life.

TOEFL Practice Tests A

p.162

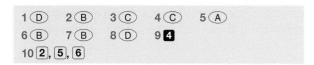

1 Ⓓ 2 Ⓑ 3 Ⓒ 4 Ⓒ 5 Ⓐ
6 Ⓑ 7 Ⓑ 8 Ⓓ 9 **4**
10 **2**, **5**, **6**

1 [Rhetorical Purpose Question]

Archaeology is mentioned along with history as a discipline that linguists need to study.

2 [Factual Question]

The author writes, "Included in the Indo-European family are English, German, French, Spanish, Italian, Greek, several Baltic and Slavic languages, including Russian, and some other languages spoken as far east of Europe as Iran and India," which shows that Proto-Indo-European was the source of languages in both Europe and Asia.

3 [Inference Question]

The paragraph notes that "the Indo-European language family consists of only 140 of the world's more than 5,000 languages," which implies that most of the world's languages were uninfluenced by PIE.

4 [Rhetorical Purpose Question]

The author mentions the number systems of some languages in order to show they "are quite similar."

5 [Sentence Simplification Question]

In the highlighted sentence, it is noted that after one hundred years, most linguists say that the Indo-European languages all evolved from PIE. This thought is best expressed in answer choice Ⓐ.

6 [Factual Question]

The writer mentions that some linguists tried to "find

some common root words in various Indo-European languages," and the writer also notes that these linguists looked for the words in ancient texts.

7 [Factual Question]

It is written, "The reason they did this was that a word like gun differs in almost all Indo-European languages because there were no guns when PIE was spoken. Therefore, by looking for similarities in words that described technological advances, evolutionary linguists established the time when PIE was spoken as being somewhere around 3000 B.C." Thus human advances helped linguists learn about PIE's origins.

8 [Negative Factual Question]

The author writes, "Determining where PIE was spoken has been harder to prove, and there is still disagreement among scholars concerning this matter." Therefore, the matter of PIE's evolution is not agreed on.

9 [Insert Text Question]

The sentence before the fourth square mentions that the Kurgan culture overran other cultures and languages. The sentence to be inserted mentions that they disappeared and would not be remembered in the future.

10 [Prose Summary Question]

According to the passage, linguists believe PIE originated in an area in contemporary Russia sometime around 5,000 years ago. They have also compared languages to one another to learn about PIE.

TOEFL Practice Tests B

p.166

1 Ⓐ 2 Ⓒ 3 Ⓑ 4 Ⓐ 5 Ⓑ
6 Ⓐ 7 Ⓒ 8 Ⓑ 9 **1**
10 **2**, **4**, **6**

1 [Vocabulary Question]

By tapping into a market, a person can gain access to it.

2 [Inference Question]

The paragraph notes, "Advertisers utilize clever methods to attract children to their products and to get children to convince their parents to buy them," which implies that modern advertisers recognize the influence of children on their parents.

3 [Rhetorical Purpose Question]

Immediately after mentioning this age group, the author writes that they "spend up to 40 billion dollars a year in America."

4 [Sentence Simplification Question]

The highlighted sentence names many of the places where children are subjected to commercial advertisements, and this is best represented in answer choice (A).

5 [Factual Question]

The author writes, "Children will pester their parents constantly until they give in and purchase the desired product. For parents, some peace of mind is worth spending a few dollars on the toy, game, or whatever it is their children want."

6 [Vocabulary Question]

When children harass their parents, they hassle them.

7 [Negative Factual Question]

Advertisers may give gifts to children, but they do not pay children to help advertise products.

8 [Factual Question]

The final sentence in the paragraph reads, "However, it is a constant struggle, and the battle is being won by the companies and advertisers, especially since many parents are simply too weary to fight the inevitable."

9 [Insert Text Question]

The key expression is "in many instances," which is referring to the animated programs mentioned in the sentence before the first square.

10 [Prose Summary Question]

According to the passage, children can influence their parents' purchases by nagging them. In addition, parents spend hundreds of billions of dollars a year because of their children, who are easily manipulated by commercials.

Vocabulary **Review**   p.173

1	Ⓒ	2	Ⓐ	3	Ⓐ	4	Ⓐ	5	Ⓑ
6	Ⓒ	7	Ⓑ	8	Ⓓ	9	Ⓓ	10	Ⓑ
11	Ⓐ	12	Ⓒ	13	Ⓒ	14	Ⓓ	15	Ⓑ
16	Ⓒ	17	Ⓐ	18	Ⓓ	19	Ⓐ	20	Ⓒ

Chapter **05** | Economics

Mastering Question Types A1   p.176

1 Ⓒ   2 Ⓐ   3 Ⓐ   4 **4**, **5**, **6**

1 [Sentence Simplification Question]

The highlighted sentence notes that the Venetians built their navy to suppress pirates, and they later used it to protect their merchant fleet. These two thoughts are best expressed in answer choice Ⓒ.

2 [Rhetorical Purpose Question]

The paragraph emphasizes the ruthlessness of the Venetians and how they plotted to get the French to attack Constantinople and to help them conquer it.

3 [Factual Question]

The passage reads, "In one infamous instance, in 1202, a French army agreed to pay 85,000 silver marks—an enormous sum—for transportation to the Holy Land and supplies for nine months."

4 [Prose Summary Question]

According to the passage, Venice was such a great sea power that its navy protected its ships in the Mediterranean Sea, they were paid money by French crusaders going to the Holy Land, and they helped defeat the Ottoman Turks at the Battle of Lepanto.

Mastering Question Types A2   p.178

1 Ⓑ   2 Ⓑ   3 **4**   4 Advantage: **3**, **5**
Disadvantage: **2**, **6**, **7**

1 [Inference Question]

The author writes, "This was to the detriment of the South, which both exhausted its soil through the constant planting of cotton and also neglected to develop other industries, one of the primary factors that led to it losing the war it fought against the technologically developed North," which implies that one reason the South lost the war is that it was not as advanced as the North.

2 [Negative Factual Question]

There is no mention in the passage of the percentage of exports that oil provides in some countries.

3 [Insert Text Question]

The sentence between the fourth square describes what happened during the Civil War. The sentence to be inserted focuses on the events that happened after the war ended. Thus, the two sentences go well together.

4 [Fill in a Table Question]

According to the passage, the advantages of single-product economies are that individuals can produce or develop them more efficiently and that people can make steady incomes from individual products. As for the disadvantages, nature can affect crops and make incomes shrink, some places may not develop as much as others, and nonrenewable resources may be exhausted.

Mastering Question Types B1
p.180

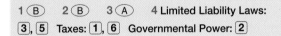
1 (D) 2 (C) 3 (B) 4 (C)

1 [Factual Question]

The passage reads, "At one point, having colonies gave a nation a great boost in trade since colonies could provide their mother country with raw materials."

2 [Vocabulary Question]

When the British Empire was in its heyday, it was in its prime.

3 [Sentence Simplification Question]

The highlighted sentence notes that oil-rich states that were already independent and those that gained their independence in the twentieth century learned how they could influence international trade. This idea is best described in answer choice (B).

4 [Rhetorical Purpose Question]

The author writes, "They have used this power on several occasions, such as during the OPEC Crisis of 1973, to boost the price of oil, which has had serious economic repercussions worldwide," which shows the power of the oil-rich nations.

Mastering Question Types B2
p.182

1 (B) 2 (B) 3 (A) 4 Limited Liability Laws:
[3], [5] Taxes: [1], [6] Governmental Power: [2]

1 [Inference Question]

When the author writes, "Why it occurred in Britain first and not in another nation has been the topic of endless debates," the implication is that people are still arguing about this aspect of the Industrial Revolution.

2 [Reference Question]

The "they" who can "afford land and large homes with a great number of windows" refers to the very wealthy.

3 [Negative Factual Question]

The author writes, "These taxes, unlike modern-day income taxes, did not seriously hinder the wealthy by obligating them to pay sizable percentages of their incomes," which is the exact opposite of answer choice (A).

4 [Fill in a Table Question]

According to the passage, limited liability laws kept

investors from losing too much money and prevented them from being sued when businesses failed. Taxes increased the prices of goods, and they were often levied on the rich to pay for certain possessions of theirs. Governmental power was exemplified by the British navy protecting both the country's shipping fleet and its colonies.

Mastering the Subject A
p.184

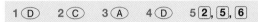
1 (D) 2 (C) 3 (A) 4 (D) 5 [2], [5], [6]

1 [Inference Question]

The passage notes that it was during the nineteenth century that Japan began "opening the country's doors to outsiders," which implies that it had been isolated prior to this time.

2 [Factual Question]

The paragraph reads, "Prior to his reign, Japan was merely a feudal society, and the emperor was nothing more than a figurehead while the true power rested with the landed nobility. Under Emperor Meiji's leadership, however, the country initiated measures to join the modern world."

3 [Vocabulary Question]

When the government brooked no dissent to its policies, it permitted no one to disagree with it.

4 [Reference Question]

The "them" who rebelled were the samurais, who were resisting the changes being brought about by Emperor Meiji.

5 [Prose Summary Question]

According to the passage, during the Meiji Period, foreign experts were brought to Japan, the country constructed warships that dominated the seas around Japan, and the government helped companies expand Japan's economy.

Summarizing ▶

Before the Meiji Period began in the 1800s, Japan was an agrarian culture. However, in a thirty-year period, it rapidly modernized. It sent Japanese students abroad to learn about the world and imported many foreigners to provide advice and instruction in certain fields. The government also intervened in the economy and encouraged various companies to do business. It also constructed a merchant shipping fleet and navy and crushed internal dissent in the guise of the samurais. But Japan became militarily aggressive, and it seized colonies in Korea and China. Eventually, its actions led to World War II, where it suffered great destruction.

Mastering the Subject B

p.187

1 Ⓐ 2 Ⓑ 3 Ⓓ 4 **2** 5 Government
Intervention: ③, ⑤, ⑥ Independent Actions: ④, ⑦

1 [Negative Factual Question]

It is not true that the supply of raw materials in England helped the English operate their factories.

2 [Rhetorical Purpose Question]

The author writes, "The English merchant fleet shipped the cotton, and it was protected by the Royal Navy, which dominated the oceans, especially after the defeat of Napoleon's French forces at the Battle of Trafalgar in 1805," which indicates exactly when the English navy really started to rule the oceans.

3 [Sentence Simplification Question]

The highlighted sentence describes the transformation of India from being a producer of textiles to a mere provider of raw materials once England colonized it. This fact is best expressed in answer choice Ⓓ.

4 [Insert Text Question]

The sentence before the second square notes that the government allowed once-guarded secrets to be exported, and the sentence to be inserted continues this line of thought by describing how some of those secrets had already been stolen.

5 [Fill in a Table Question]

According to the passage, government intervention involved passing laws that made cotton more popular than wool. It also involved using the English navy to protect the English merchant fleet, and it changed India into a producer of raw materials. Independent actions were connected with the invention of the power loom and monetary investments into developing better machinery.

Summarizing ▶

The cotton textile industry was an important part of the Industrial Revolution in England. In the early 1800s, England dominated the cotton textile industry, but it began losing ground starting in the 1840s and continuing into the twentieth century. However, before its loss, England had come to dominate the cotton textile trade for many reasons. For example, while there were many new inventions that made creating textiles easier, there was also much investment in the industry. The Royal Navy also kept careful watch over shipments of cotton crossing the ocean. Additionally, the English government changed the country's laws so that cotton, not wool, had more advantages. Furthermore, India, an English colony, was transformed from a textile manufacturer into a mere supplier of raw materials.

Mastering the Subject C

p.190

1 Ⓒ 2 Ⓐ 3 Ⓒ 4 Ⓑ 5 Before the
Industrial Revolution: ②, ③, ⑤ During the Industrial
Revolution: ⑥, ⑦

1 [Negative Factual Question]

There is no mention in the paragraph of how individuals managed to become members of various guilds.

2 [Vocabulary Question]

The people under the auspices of the guilds were under their patronage.

3 [Reference Question]

"Those" in the passage refers to the members of the guilds themselves.

4 [Inference Question]

In writing about guilds, the author mentions that "the lack of competition was not conducive to innovation," which implies that guild members made few technological advances in their fields.

5 [Fill in a Table Question]

According to the passage, before the Industrial Revolution, guilds began training children to become apprentices, and they prevented nonmembers from setting up businesses in certain places. They also determined the fees that could be charged and the standards of work to be met. During the Industrial Revolution, guilds started to lose influence, and guild members even had to go to work for other individuals, such as at factories.

Summarizing ▶

Guilds were groups of craftsmen who shared a single trade. They established standards of workmanship as well as the rates their members got paid. A person who wanted to work in a trade had to begin as an apprentice. This was often done when the person was very young. The apprentice learned his craft over many years and eventually became a master craftsman and could open a shop. Guild members had many advantages, but nonmembers were not allowed to work in some places. Guilds were powerful up until the Industrial Revolution began. Then, industrialization forced many guild members to work in factories. Many guilds then transformed into trade unions.

Mastering the Subject D

p.193

1 Ⓓ 2 Ⓐ 3 Ⓐ 4 **1** 5 ②, ③, ⑥

1 [Rhetorical Purpose Question]

The passage reads, "By the time the Romans ruled the Western world, silk was being exported along the famous route which came to be called the Silk Road," which shows how silk got from China to Rome.

2 [Sentence Simplification Question]

The highlighted sentence notes the process by which the cocoons were unwound and individual threads were spun together to make cloth. This method is best expressed in answer choice Ⓐ.

3 [Factual Question]

The passage reads, "In China, silk was so valuable that the Chinese used it to bribe foreign invaders, to pay the salaries of government officials, and to give as gifts during diplomatic negotiations with neighboring countries. It was also a commercial item."

4 [Insert Text Question]

The sentence before the first square notes that the Chinese monopoly on silk eventually ended, and the sentence to be inserted claims that it was surprising that the Chinese had kept their monopoly for so long.

5 [Prose Summary Question]

According to the passage, despite the fact that the Chinese dominated the silk trade for centuries, foreigners eventually learned the secret of how to make silk. Silk was also valuable in China, Rome, and other places. And the Chinese produced silk by managing the insects that produced the threads.

Summarizing ▶

Silk was prized as far back as ancient times. It came from China, but it was traded as far away as the Roman Empire. Sericulture is the name for the art of silk production. The Chinese learned how to make silk from the strands of the silkworm's cocoons. Silk was valuable and had many uses, especially as a form of payment. The Romans were known to have spent tons of gold purchasing it. China at first had a monopoly on the silk trade, but both the Japanese and the Byzantine Empire managed to learn the secrets of its production. Still, even today, China produces about 70% of the world's silk.

TOEFL Practice Tests A

p.196

1 Ⓓ   2 Ⓑ   3 Ⓐ   4 Ⓓ   5 Ⓐ
6 Ⓓ   7 Ⓓ   8 Ⓐ   9 **3**
10 Human Inventions: **2**, **6**   New Methods: **1**, **4**, **5**

1 [Sentence Simplification Question]

The highlighted sentence notes that England had a

large workforce that could work in the factories, which helped it industrialize. This thought is best expressed in answer choice Ⓓ.

2 [Inference Question]

The first sentence reads, "Since the dawn of human civilization, the vast majority of the population has been engaged in agriculture," and, along with the rest of the paragraph, it implies that humans have lacked manufacturing ability for most of their history.

3 [Factual Question]

The author writes, "In the late eighteenth and early nineteenth centuries, laws were enacted by the government that disallowed individual farmers from using millions of acres of land that had previously been open to them."

4 [Vocabulary Question]

When a field is left fallow, nothing is planted in it, so it is empty.

5 [Rhetorical Purpose Question]

It is written, "Charles Townsend, an influential politician with a keen interest in agriculture, introduced a four-crop rotation system," which shows how he was responsible for a change in improving agricultural methods.

6 [Factual Question]

The author writes, "Clover, a legume, actually helped revitalize the soil rather than deplete it of nutrients as other crops did."

7 [Inference Question]

The passage reads, "At the same time, improvements in mechanical devices made it possible to farm with fewer people."

8 [Vocabulary Question]

When the landowners reaped huge benefits, they gained these benefits.

9 [Insert Text Question]

The sentence before the third square mentions that there were riots and bloodshed, and the sentence to be inserted claims that some people were even killed in these incidents.

10 [Fill in a Table Question]

According to the passage, human inventions resulted in harvesters being operated, but industrialization also led to many people moving off farms to work in factories. As for new methods, famers planted clover to improve the soil, they raised animals more efficiently, and they used the four-field crop rotation system as well.

TOEFL Practice Tests B

p.200

1 (B) 2 (A) 3 (C) 4 (A) 5 (A)
6 (A) 7 (A) 8 (C) 9 **3**
10 **1**, **5**, **6**

1 [Sentence Simplification Question]

The highlighted sentence notes that changes can happen very quickly in some places yet can be very slow to occur in others. This is best described in answer choice (B).

2 [Inference Question]

The paragraph reads, "This was the case for the spread of industrialization in Europe. Great Britain took the lead, but industrialization came slowly to the rest of Europe, especially eastern and southern Europe," which implies that the speed of industrialization was different throughout Europe.

3 [Vocabulary Question]

A sound financial system is one that is solid and not in danger of collapsing.

4 [Negative Factual Question]

The passage reads, "The Netherlands had a highly educated, literate, hardworking population that could have easily adapted to industrialization," so it is not true that few of the people in the Netherlands could not read.

5 [Rhetorical Purpose Question]

Concerning guilds, the author writes, "Organizations like guilds of specialized craftsmen, who had an interest in maintaining the status quo which gave them power and wealth, opposed the technologies that had the potential to erode their positions."

6 [Factual Question]

The passage reads, "The second reason that industrialization came late to the Netherlands was war. The Netherlands was at the center of many battles during the French Revolution and the Napoleonic Wars. Easily dominated and conquered by the French, for almost twenty-five years, the Netherlands was part of the French continental system of trade, in which the main enemy—Great Britain—was the target of economic warfare."

7 [Vocabulary Question]

When the power of the guild system was curtailed, its influence diminished.

8 [Factual Question]

The passage reads, "A third problem the Dutch had with industrialization was the high salaries Dutch

workers anticipated receiving," and, "These rates made it more difficult for businesses to compete with nations where wages were relatively lower. Businesses already had low profit margins, and thus they had less capital to reinvest to make improvements and to expand."

9 [Insert Text Question]

The sentence before the third square notes that some forces are often "opposed to change," and the sentence to be inserted proceeds to describe the actions of "these forces."

10 [Prose Summary Question]

According to the passage, the Netherlands industrialized slowly because of the high compensation Dutch workers demanded, the state of war that existed in the country for many years, and the groups of people that resisted changes in the economy.

Vocabulary *Review*

p.207

1 (D) 2 (B) 3 (B) 4 (C) 5 (A)
6 (C) 7 (A) 8 (D) 9 (A) 10 (C)
11 (B) 12 (C) 13 (D) 14 (A) 15 (A)
16 (C) 17 (C) 18 (A) 19 (B) 20 (B)

Chapter **06** | Life Sciences

Mastering Question Types A1

p.210

1 (D) 2 (A) 3 (B) 4 **2**, **3**, **6**

1 [Sentence Simplification Question]

The highlighted sentence describes the manner in which earthworms help improve the quality of the soil. This is best described in answer choice (D).

2 [Vocabulary Question]

Land that is arable is fertile, so it is therefore farmable.

3 [Rhetorical Purpose Question]

The author writes, "The soil thus becomes rich in nitrogen, calcium, magnesium, and phosphorus, all of which are important for the growth of plants and microorganisms." All of these minerals are broken down by earthworms.

4 [Prose Summary Question]

According to the passage, earthworms help prevent the soil from eroding, and they also make the soil more fertile through their movements. In addition, they break down decayed matter to release nutrients into the soil.

Mastering Question Types A2

p.212

1 (B)　　2 (C)　　3 **2**　　4 Desiccation: [3], [7]
Permineralization: [2], [5]　Carbonization: [4]

1　[Negative Factual Question]

The passage does not mention anything about where fossilized bodies of animals are typically found.

2　[Reference Question]

The method of fossilization that is being described is permineralization.

3　[Insert Text Question]

The sentence before the second square notes that the bodies of some animals that were not consumed by predators have been found while the sentence to be inserted notes that sometimes half-eaten bodies are found instead. Thus, the two sentences go together.

4　[Fill in a Table Question]

According to the passage, desiccation results in preserved animals looking as though they have been refrigerated, and it can also preserve many parts of an animal's body, not just its bones. Permineralization is the most common method of fossilization, and it happens when the specimen becomes crystallized. Carbonization occurs when an image of the specimen is preserved.

Mastering Question Types B1

p.214

1 (A)　　2 (D)　　3 (D)　　4 (C)

1　[Factual Question]

The author writes, "As summer transitions to autumn, the fruits on plants mature while plants also lose their leaves."

2　[Sentence Simplification Question]

The highlighted sentence notes that botanists want to know how differences in environmental conditions, which cause changes in plants, are recognized by them. This thought is best expressed in answer choice (D).

3　[Vocabulary Question]

Suboptimal conditions are poor ones.

4　[Rhetorical Purpose Question]

The author writes, "There is also a hypothetical enzyme called florigen that may cause plants to flower during spring and other months. Botanists believe that temperature and light conditions activate florigen, thereby enabling plants to blossom. Florigen's

existence has not been verified yet."

Mastering Question Types B2

p.216

1 (A)　　2 (C)　　3 **2**　　4 Characteristics: [4], [6]
Hunting Methods: [1], [2], [5]

1　[Negative Factual Question]

There is no mention in the paragraph of why pit vipers normally give live birth instead of laying eggs.

2　[Inference Question]

In describing the viper's pit organ, it is written, "It allows a snake to sense changes in temperature as well as to sense cool and hot areas, much like an electronic thermal imaging system," which implies that the pit organ acts similarly to a piece of modern technology.

3　[Insert Text Question]

The word "however" indicates that the sentence to be inserted will be in opposition to the one in the passage. It best fits after the sentence before the second square, which concerns how the viper uses venom to attack its prey.

4　[Fill in a Table Question]

According to the passage, pit vipers have two long fangs in the back of their mouths, and they typically give birth to live animals. Concerning their hunting methods, they do not hunt while the sun is up, they sense potential victims with their pit organs, and they inject venom to incapacitate their prey.

Mastering the Subject A

p.218

1 (B)　　2 (B)　　3 (C)　　4 (D)　　5 Inky Discharge:
[3], [6]　Camouflage: [2], [4], [5]

1　[Factual Question]

The author notes, "Sea creatures use all of these methods—with varying degrees of success—in their ongoing struggles to survive in the ocean depths."

2　[Reference Question]

The "It" that looks like a green piece of seaweed is the leafy sea dragon, which uses that disguise as a form of camouflage.

3　[Vocabulary Question]

When an octopus or squid uses ink to elude predators, it escapes from them.

4　[Negative Factual Question]

The passage reads, "Poison as a method of defense

is not particularly common among sea creatures, but a few do use it, often with deadly effect."

5 [Fill in a Table Question]

According to the passage, the inky discharge gives attacked creatures time to escape and is something used by squid. As for camouflage, some creatures may use it to resemble other things not considered food, it is used by the leafy sea dragon, and bottom dwellers may hide in the mud as another form of it.

Most sea dwellers employ various defense mechanisms to protect themselves from predators. Using camouflage as concealment is one such method. Flatfish may hide in the mud to disguise themselves while the leafy sea dragon appears to be a piece of seaweed floating in the water. Squid and octopus expel an ink-like substance to cloud the water where they are. This enables them to flee or hide from their attackers. Another common method of defense is poison. The jellyfish and stonefish are two such sea creatures that make use of it. In some cases, their poison may be lethal to their attackers.

Mastering the Subject B

p.221

1 Ⓒ   2 Ⓓ   3 Ⓐ   4 **4**   5 ②, ④, ⑥

1 [Sentence Simplification Question]

The highlighted sentence mentions that animals can use their characteristics to dominate other members of their species. This thought is best expressed in answer choice Ⓒ.

2 [Inference Question]

The author writes, "Darwin tinkered with his notion for more than twenty years before suddenly publishing his work upon learning that a colleague working in Asia had a similar theory," which implies that he was not the only person who recognized natural selection in nature.

3 [Rhetorical Purpose Question]

The author notes, "Not every change in animals happens naturally though. In some cases, humans may interfere with and even prompt the evolution of certain animals," and then provides the example of the rabbits in Australia, thereby showing how unnatural causes can affect natural selection.

4 [Insert Text Question]

The sentence in front of the fourth square explains why some finches thrived while others died, and the sentence to be inserted explains the importance of this in *On the Origin of Species*.

5 [Prose Summary Question]

According to the passage, natural selection can take years to produce results, one example of it is the finches that lived on the Galapagos Islands, and it results from members of a species passing on desirable traits to others.

Over time, individual members of some species change, and, if the changes are beneficial, they and their offspring tend to survive while other members of the species die out. This is natural selection. In 1859, Charles Darwin published *On the Origin of Species*, a work on this phenomenon, which was inspired by his observations on the Galapagos Islands. Darwin noticed how finches on different islands there had developed specialized beaks appropriate for the food they ate. However, humans may also induce natural selection. In Australia, rabbits overtaking the country were poisoned almost to eradication. Yet those that proved immune to the poison have reproduced exponentially, and Australia once again finds itself overpopulated by rabbits.

Mastering the Subject C

p.224

1 Ⓑ   2 Ⓒ   3 Ⓑ   4 **1**   5 ④, ⑤, ⑥

1 [Vocabulary Question]

When people unwittingly do something, they accidentally do it.

2 [Factual Question]

The author notes, "One of the major reasons for this in North America is acid rain, which is caused by pollution that introduces too many acidic compounds to the air, which then fall as rain. This pollution gets into the water system, making large numbers of rivers and lakes uninhabitable for many fish species, including trout."

3 [Inference Question]

The paragraph reads, "However, a more serious issue surrounds fish farming: Wild trout are captured in great numbers by fish farms, and their eggs are taken to be hatched in relative safety until the fish are mature enough to be released into the wild," which implies that captive trout are not actually bred with one another.

4 [Insert Text Question]

The sentence located before the first square notes that trout prefer cool water, and the sentence to be inserted then states where fishermen must go to find places with cool water.

5 [Prose Summary Question]

According to the passage, trout live in many places

around the world, their habitats are endangered because of human activities, and trout raised on fish farms lack the survival skills of wild trout.

Summarizing ▶

Trout are a popular fish with anglers. There are many species of these freshwater fish, which prefer cool waters. They are typically a foot long and weigh a few pounds, but some may grow to bigger sizes. Unfortunately, acid rain is eliminating some of their habitats by making certain waterways unlivable. Water overuse by humans and the eroding of soil into waterways is making other places unlivable as well. Finally, trout are so popular that many fish farms raise them and later release them into public waters. However, farm-raised trout have trouble surviving on their own and produce offspring more vulnerable to predators when they mate in the wild.

Mastering the Subject D

p.227

1 Ⓓ   2 Ⓑ   3 Ⓒ   4 **❸**   5 Facultative:
3, **6**, **7** Obligatory: **1**, **5**

1 [Negative Factual Question]

The author writes, "Bees extract nectar from plants' flowers while simultaneously picking up pollen from plants and spreading it to other areas."

2 [Sentence Simplification Question]

The highlighted sentence notes that in some relationships, one member would die without the other while the other member would survive. This is best expressed in answer choice Ⓑ.

3 [Factual Question]

The paragraph reads, "Plants such as peas, beans, clover, and alfalfa can revitalize nitrogen-poor soil. They do this through a mutual interaction with bacteria in the soil. The bacteria live in the plant and, in return, help the plant convert atmospheric nitrogen into forms of nitrogen such as various nitrates that plants need for growth."

4 [Insert Text Question]

The sentence before the third square explains how ants enable the acacia to get more sunlight, and the sentence to be inserted shows the effect of the ants' actions.

5 [Fill in a Table Question]

According to the passage, facultative mutualism occurs when bacteria introduce nitrogen to the soil. In addition, while neither needs the other to survive, a breakup in their relationship would disadvantage both of them. As for obligatory mutualism, one species could not live

without the other, and the bee-flower relationship is an example of it.

Summarizing ▶

Two or more biological entities like plants and animals often act together to create mutually beneficial results. This is known as mutualism. Most instances involve equal benefit to the partners, but that does not always happen. There are two kinds of mutualism: obligatory and facultative. Obligatory mutualism means that one partner could not survive without the other. This is the case for bees and plants. Bees gain nectar from plants while pollinating them. Facultative mutualism occurs when each partner can survive without the other. Ants and aphids and ants and acacia trees have facultative relationships. Nitrogen-producing plants and bacteria do as well. In every case, both partners benefit from the relationship.

TOEFL Practice Tests A

p.230

1 Ⓐ   2 Ⓑ   3 Ⓐ   4 Ⓓ   5 Ⓒ
6 Ⓐ   7 Ⓓ   8 Ⓐ   9 **❹**
10 Cold-Blooded Animals: **2**, **5** Warm-Blooded
Animals: **4**, **6**, **7**

1 [Sentence Simplification Question]

The highlighted sentence claims that a) warm-blooded animals' body temperatures often stay the same while b) cold-blooded animals' body temperatures may change. These two points are best expressed in answer choice Ⓐ.

2 [Rhetorical Purpose Question]

The author notes, "When the weather is too cold, they may consume more food to burn more energy or utilize shivering to increase muscle activity, which produces more heat," which shows that shivering can warm animals in the absence of food.

3 [Inference Question]

The paragraph mentions, "Humans also wear clothing for protection; the colder the temperature, the thicker the clothing," which implies that humans need extra protection to survive in extreme climates.

4 [Negative Factual Question]

There is no mention in the paragraph of how much food warm-blooded animals must eat to stay warm each day.

5 [Vocabulary Question]

An animal that scurries away is hurrying.

6 [Vocabulary Question]

Expire means to die or to perish.

7 [Factual Question]

It is written, "If there is not a large food supply, warm-blooded creatures will die in extremely cold environments. Cold-blooded creatures, however, can survive on less food and endure longer periods of time without eating."

8 [Factual Question]

Concerning viruses, the author writes that warm-blooded creatures "are more prone to be hosts for bacteria and viruses, which need warmer temperatures to survive."

9 [Insert Text Question]

The sentence in front of the fourth square mentions that cold-blooded animals can "endure longer periods of time without eating," and the sentence to be inserted gives an example of how long some snakes, which are cold blooded, can go without eating.

10 [Fill in a Table Question]

According to the passage, cold-blooded animals react poorly in cold environments, and they are often reptiles and insects. As for warm-blooded animals, they need to eat a lot of food, can live in many different environments, and have external coverings to protect them from the cold.

TOEFL Practice Tests B

p.234

1 Ⓐ	2 Ⓑ	3 Ⓓ	4 Ⓐ	5 Ⓒ
6 Ⓐ	7 Ⓒ	8 Ⓓ	9 **1**	
10 ②, ③, ④				

1 [Inference Question]

The author writes, "Finally, many animals are driven by an instinctual need to reproduce and follow a specific cycle for this purpose," which implies that, since the need to reproduce is instinctual, animals have no control over it.

2 [Rhetorical Purpose Question]

The author writes, "Many nocturnal animals have developed heightened senses, such as night vision and acute hearing, to adapt to the night environment. Owls are a perfect example of this." This shows how owls have adapted to the night.

3 [Factual Question]

The passage reads, "Circadian rhythms are related to daily activities."

4 [Sentence Simplification Question]

The highlighted sentence states that a secreted hormone may be the reason why animals know when to mate, but scientists are not sure. This is best expressed in answer choice Ⓐ.

5 [Inference Question]

The author notes that the spadefoot toad lives in a "desert environment," which therefore implies that it prefers a climate that is primarily hot and dry.

6 [Vocabulary Question]

Animals that feed at prodigious rates are eating a phenomenal amount of food.

7 [Factual Question]

The author points out, "Prior to winter, when fall arrives, they begin feeding at prodigious rates and try to gain as much fat as possible so that they can survive the coming weather."

8 [Factual Question]

About the Arctic caribou attempting to cross the ice sheets, the author writes, "The herds keep coming as their instinct to follow this migration pattern is stronger than their need to avoid death."

9 [Insert Text Question]

The sentence in front of the first square notes that humans usually operate on a twenty-four-hour internal clock; however, the sentence to be inserted claims that not everyone's body operates that way.

10 [Prose Summary Question]

According to the passage, animals' instincts can actually lead them to their deaths. In addition, some animals hibernate or migrate during winter. And nocturnal and diurnal animals have developed activities based on when they are active.

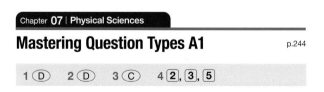

Vocabulary **Review**   p.241

1 Ⓑ	2 Ⓐ	3 Ⓒ	4 Ⓐ	5 Ⓐ
6 Ⓓ	7 Ⓒ	8 Ⓒ	9 Ⓐ	10 Ⓓ
11 Ⓓ	12 Ⓐ	13 Ⓐ	14 Ⓒ	15 Ⓑ
16 Ⓐ	17 Ⓒ	18 Ⓑ	19 Ⓒ	20 Ⓓ

Chapter 07 | Physical Sciences

Mastering Question Types A1

p.244

1 Ⓓ	2 Ⓓ	3 Ⓒ	4 ②, ③, ⑤

1 [Factual Question]

There is no mention in the passage about the average

lifespan of most comets.

2 [Sentence Simplification Question]

The highlighted passage notes that despite people knowing about comets in ancient times, it was not until Edmund Halley in the eighteenth century that people realized they went by Earth regularly. This is best expressed in answer choice Ⓓ.

3 [Vocabulary Question]

When comets are induced into the sun's orbit, they are compelled to go around it.

4 [Prose Summary Question]

According to the passage, comets can be attracted by the sun even out in the Kuiper Belt. They may form tails that extend for millions of miles. And some may have only been seen once because the Oort Cloud is so far away.

Mastering Question Types A2   p.246

1 Ⓐ   2 Ⓑ   3 **4**   4 Sunspot: 1, 4, 7 Corona: 2, 3

1 [Inference Question]

The author writes that sunspots "commonly appear between five and thirty-five degrees north and south of the sun's equator," which implies that they rarely appear at the sun's poles.

2 [Rhetorical Purpose Question]

The author writes, "Sunspots also have a distinct relationship with the shape of the sun's corona," and then describes that relationship in the paragraph.

3 [Insert Text Question]

The sentence before the fourth square is about the Little Ice Age, which is also known as the Maunder Minimum.

4 [Fill in a Table Question]

According to the passage, sunspots may appear in large or small numbers, may form when the sun experiences some magnetic activity, and may affect the temperature on the Earth. As for the corona, it can emit energy and propel it into space and may be of equal size everywhere on the sun.

Mastering Question Types B1   p.248

1 Ⓐ   2 Ⓑ   3 Ⓓ   4 1, 2, 3

1 [Vocabulary Question]

A perplexing mystery is one that is confusing.

2 [Rhetorical Purpose Question]

Concerning the Pacific Rim, the author mentions that they "are places where plates intersect," and thus they are affected by the movement of plates.

3 [Factual Question]

The passage notes that volcanic eruptions and earthquakes can result from the movements of tectonic plates.

4 [Prose Summary Question]

According to the passage, the Earth's tectonic plates have moved to create the continents. In places where they meet, landforms may be created while natural disasters may also occur. However, geologists still know little about how the plates actually move.

Mastering Question Types B2   p.250

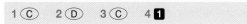
1 Ⓒ   2 Ⓓ   3 Ⓒ   4 **1**

1 [Inference Question]

The passage reads, "On rare occasions, lightning may move from the ground to a cloud," which implies that this form of lightning is the least frequent type.

2 [Negative Factual Question]

The paragraph reads, "As ice particles rise and fall in a storm cloud, they collide, thereby causing the separation of their electrical charges as the positively charged particles rise and the negatively charged ones fall," but it does not explain why positive particles rise while negative ones fall.

3 [Reference Question]

The "it" that thunder follows is lightning.

4 [Insert Text Question]

The sentence before the first square mentions the number of lightning strikes in the United States each year, and the sentence to be inserted follows up by noting that the state of Florida receives the greatest number of hits.

Mastering the Subject A   p.252

1 Ⓓ   2 Ⓐ   3 Ⓑ   4 Ⓒ   5 1, 2, 4

1 [Vocabulary Question]

When one atom bonds with another, it links to the other atom.

2 [Sentence Simplification Question]

The highlighted sentence notes that electrons orbit

the nucleus in the electron cloud while protons and neutrons stay in the nucleus. This is best expressed in answer choice Ⓐ.

3 [Rhetorical Purpose Question]

The author writes, "However, atoms can also form into isotopes, slightly different forms of the same atom created when more neutrons are added or subtracted." Then, it is written, "Uranium-235 has 143 neutrons though while maintaining the same number of protons as uranium-238," so the author uses uranium-235 as an example of an isotope of uranium.

4 [Factual Question]

The paragraph reads, "However, if there are an unequal number of protons and electrons, an ion, which is unstable, is formed."

5 [Prose Summary Question]

According to the paragraph, the atomic number of an atom is the number of protons it has while its atomic weight is the number of protons and neutrons combined. In addition, the three main parts of an atom are in specific places inside it. and the number of protons and neutrons in an atom determine whether it is neutral or an ion.

Summarizing ▷

People such as the Greek philosopher Aristotle have tried to understand the universe and what comprises it since ancient times. Today, scientists know that matter consists of atoms, which can bond together to form molecules. Protons and neutrons are in an atom's nucleus while electrons orbit the nucleus in shells. The number of protons in an atom is its atomic number. The number of neutrons can vary, which results in isotopes being created. An equal number of protons and electrons means an atom is neutral and therefore stable. If there are an unequal number, the atom is an ion and is unstable, so it can join with another atom to form a molecule.

Mastering the Subject B p.255

1 Ⓐ   2 Ⓓ   3 Ⓐ   4 **2**   5 Batch Method:
2, **6** Continuous Method: **5**, **7** Ultra High
Temperature Method: **1**

1 [Reference Question]

The "it" that needs to be killed is the microorganism.

2 [Negative Factual Question]

The heated plates have a temperature of seventy-two degrees Celsius, but there is no mention of how hot the liquid becomes.

3 [Inference Question]

When the author writes, "Thanks to ESL, the shelf life of milk can be further extended by many days," it is implied that ESL milk lasts longer than milk pasteurized in any other way.

4 [Insert Text Question]

The sentence in front of the second square notes a positive feature—the extended shelf life—but the sentence to be inserted begins with "however" and then describes a negative feature. Thus, the two sentences go together.

5 [Fill in a Table Question]

According to the passage, the batch method requires that the milk be shaken, and it is often used on non-milk dairy products. The continuous method uses both heating and cooling and is the faster of the two primary pasteurization methods. The ultra-high temperature method takes less than one second to complete.

Summarizing ▷

Pasteurization is the process by which certain liquids are treated to keep them from spoiling. It is commonly used on milk. It was first discovered by Louis Pasteur in 1862. The two most common methods are the batch method and the continuous method. They both involve heating the liquid to preserve it. However, the continuous method uses higher heat, so it must also cool the liquid. Ultra-high heat pasteurization is another type, but it uses extremely high heat for a very brief time. Finally, extended shelf-life pasteurization is a new method that can help products like milk stay fresh for many more days than conventionally treated milk.

Mastering the Subject C p.258

1 Ⓒ   2 Ⓒ   3 Ⓓ   4 **3**   5 Jovian Planet:
2, **5**, **7** Terrestrial Planet: **1**, **4**

1 [Rhetorical Purpose Question]

The author states that Eris is a dwarf planet in order to mention another one besides Pluto.

2 [Reference Question]

The "them" upon which carbon-based life forms cannot exist are gas giants.

3 [Negative Factual Question]

Venus, although it is covered by a dense cloud of gas, is still a rocky planet.

4 [Insert Text Question]

The sentence before the third square notes the characteristics of some of the gas giants' moons. The sentence to be inserted continues by mentioning two more moons that belong to gas giants.

5 [Fill in a Table Question]

According to the passage, the Jovian planets are bigger than everything in the solar system except for the sun, take at least twelve years to orbit the sun, and cannot support life because they are comprised of gas. The terrestrial planets, meanwhile, are composed of rock and have no more than two moons orbiting them.

Summarizing ▶

> The planets orbiting the sun belong to three groups: gas giants, terrestrial planets, and dwarf planets. The gas giants are Jupiter, Saturn, Uranus, and Neptune; they orbit the sun from afar. They are huge balls of gas with conditions toxic to humans. They also have rings and large numbers of satellites and take years to orbit the sun. The terrestrial planets are Mercury, Venus, Earth, and Mars. They are all rocky, have minerals, have few moons, and take a short period of time to orbit the sun. The dwarf planets are Pluto, Ceres, and three others. Most of them are very distant from the sun, so little is known about them.

Mastering the Subject D
p.261

1 (B)   2 (D)   3 (B)   4 (D)   5 [1], [3], [6]

1 [Vocabulary Question]

Research that is pioneering is original.

2 [Factual Question]

Concerning Hales, the paragraph reads, "Unlike many so-called scientists of his day, he did not rely on farfetched theories with no basis in truth."

3 [Sentence Simplification Question]

The highlighted sentence notes that pneumatic chemists both discovered and learned much about certain gases. This fact is best expressed in answer choice (B).

4 [Inference Question]

The passage reads, "However, Hales contrived a device similar to the bellows system used to operate an organ which could circulate air. When used in Savoy Prison in England, the mortality rate dropped considerably. His idea was quickly copied and used in ships, hospitals, and other places with similar results." This implies that it was his invention that was directly responsible for saving many people's lives.

5 [Prose Summary Question]

According to the passage, Hales learned about the

composition of the atmosphere by studying two separate fields, he learned a lot about plants, and he developed an air circulation machine as well.

Summarizing ▶

> Stephen Hales was a scientist who lived during the seventeenth and eighteenth centuries. He conducted work on plants and in chemistry and also was responsible for inventions in the field of medical science. Hales conducted many experiments on plants, which led him to do work in pneumatic chemistry, a branch of chemistry that no longer exists but which, during his lifetime, had many adherents and was responsible for much groundbreaking work on gases. Hales also investigated the contents of the atmosphere because of his interest in plants. Finally, he invented a circulation system for closed places that helped save many lives.

TOEFL Practice Tests A
p.264

1 (D)   2 (C)   3 (C)   4 (A)   5 (D)
6 (C)   7 (D)   8 (A)   9 **4**
10 [2], [4], [6]

1 [Vocabulary Question]

Acute danger is a very serious situation.

2 [Inference Question]

When commenting on volcanic eruptions, the author writes, "If people are living nearby, this may result in disaster," which implies that people in the vicinity can be injured.

3 [Sentence Simplification Question]

The highlighted sentence notes that volcanologists have problems because volcanoes can suddenly change their status. This is best expressed in answer choice (C).

4 [Negative Factual Question]

While dormant volcanoes may become active after centuries of dormancy, they do not erupt for centuries at a time.

5 [Factual Question]

The passage reads, "Long before most volcanoes erupt, the earth begins shaking. This is frequently the first obvious sign of growing instability. As the region becomes more unstable, the number of tremors grows while the intervals between them shorten."

6 [Rhetorical Purpose Question]

The paragraph reads, "Despite many successes in volcanic eruption prediction, it remains an imperfect science facing several major obstacles." Then, the paragraph describes some of these obstacles in detail.

7 [Vocabulary Question]

When bumper crops are produced, there are an abundant amount of crops.

8 [Rhetorical Purpose Question]

The author writes, "However, given enough warning, if the eruption is of the nonviolent type that frequently occurs in Hawaii, barriers can be built and property sometimes saved." Thus, people can be protected from volcanic eruptions.

9 [Insert Text Question]

The sentence in front of the fourth square mentions that some people refuse to evacuate an area before a volcanic eruption, and the sentence to be inserted gives one effect of what happened in the past when people did not leave and a volcano erupted.

10 [Prose Summary Question]

According to the passage, volcanoes might not erupt despite all of the signs of an eruption being present. Sometimes active volcanoes suddenly erupt without any predictions of an impending eruption having been made. And because of the damage volcanoes can cause, people have been trying to predict them for thousands of years.

TOEFL Practice Tests B
p.268

1 Ⓓ 2 Ⓑ 3 Ⓓ 4 Ⓐ 5 Ⓒ
6 Ⓑ 7 Ⓐ 8 Ⓓ 9 **2**
10 Yellow Dwarf: ①, ③, ⑥ Red Giant: ②, ⑦

1 [Rhetorical Purpose Question]

The sentence in which the Milky Way Galaxy is mentioned gives the number of stars that are estimated to be in it.

2 [Factual Question]

That author writes, "All stars form in a similar fashion, progress through specific stages, and then eventually die."

3 [Inference Question]

The passage reads, "From a small point in whatever existed prior to the presence of the universe," which implies that no one knows what existed before the big bang happened.

4 [Vocabulary Question]

When a star exhausts its hydrogen supply, it runs out of hydrogen, so it has all been expended.

5 [Factual Question]

It is written, "At some point, the helium extant in the star starts burning, so the star heats up again; however, this time, it expands tremendously, becoming what astronomers call a red giant."

6 [Negative Factual Question]

The paragraph mentions that there are sub-stages in the life of a star, but it does not name any of them or describe them.

7 [Vocabulary Question]

Something that happens paradoxically is said to occur ironically.

8 [Inference Question]

The author writes, "Some of these stars may not actually collapse but instead explode in what is called a supernova," which implies that it takes the death of a giant star for a supernova to be created.

9 [Insert Text Question]

The sentence in front of the second square describes how strong black holes are. The sentence to be inserted begins with "in fact," and it provides even more information about how powerful black holes are.

10 [Fill in a Table Question]

According to the passage, yellow dwarves shrink when they leave that stage, and they are the most common type of star in the galaxy. The sun is also a yellow dwarf. As for red giants, they do not have any hydrogen to burn, and they can increase in size to be hundreds of times bigger than they once were.

Vocabulary **Review**
p.275

1 Ⓒ 2 Ⓐ 3 Ⓐ 4 Ⓓ 5 Ⓑ
6 Ⓒ 7 Ⓓ 8 Ⓑ 9 Ⓑ 10 Ⓑ
11 Ⓓ 12 Ⓐ 13 Ⓒ 14 Ⓓ 15 Ⓐ
16 Ⓐ 17 Ⓓ 18 Ⓑ 19 Ⓐ 20 Ⓒ

Chapter **08** | Environmental Sciences

Mastering Question Types A1
p.278

1 Ⓒ 2 Ⓒ 3 Ⓐ 4 ②, ④, ⑤

1 [Vocabulary Question]

When a problem is overcome, it is defeated.

2 [Rhetorical Purpose Question]

The author writes, "Groups in Indonesia, Brazil, and the Congo, among other places, have planted millions of trees in recent years. Their efforts have led to parts of many rainforests making speedy recoveries while also maintaining the biodiversity of the forests."

3 [Sentence Simplification Question]

The highlighted sentence claims that Costa Rica is a positive example for countries and that the country has proven that rainforests can be restored quickly. This thought is best expressed in answer choice Ⓐ.

4 [Prose Summary Question]

According to the passage, governments and NGOs are fighting deforestation by passing laws and by planting trees. In addition, the Costa Rican PES program is helping the country get over its deforestation problems. Finally, endangered plants and animals are being saved in countries where rainforests have recovered.

Mastering Question Types A2   p.280

1 Ⓓ   2 Ⓑ   3 Ⓐ   4 Rain Shadow Desert:
③, ⑥, ⑦   Coastal Desert: ②, ⑤

1 [Negative Factual Question]

Desert land is said to be "uncultivable," and thus it is not fertile.

2 [Reference Question]

The "it" that transforms into a desert is the land.

3 [Inference Question]

The passage reads, "They exist right next to large bodies of water—oceans or seas—yet receive little rainfall themselves. The reason for this is currents in the ocean." This implies that the water next to the deserts is not stagnant.

4 [Fill in a Table Question]

According to the passage, rain shadow deserts are caused by the wind blowing dry air, are next to mountain ranges, and often see the land right next to them get a large amount of rain. Coastal deserts, meanwhile, are the result of currents in the water and are found in South Africa and Mexico.

Mastering Question Types B1   p.282

1 Ⓑ   2 Ⓐ   3 Ⓒ   4 ③, ④, ⑥

1 [Factual Question]

The author notes, "At certain times during the Earth's history, the planet has witnessed hot, cold, wet, and dry weather both at extreme and moderate levels. parts of the planet—no matter how far north or south they may be—have seen varying types of weather, particularly with regard to temperature. While these changes frequently affect the topology of the planet . . ."

2 [Sentence Simplification Question]

The highlighted passage states that every so often, an object from space strikes the Earth and eliminates a large amount of life on the planet. This is best expressed in answer choice Ⓐ.

3 [Rhetorical Purpose Question]

The author writes, "Some, such as Krakatoa, an Indonesian volcano that violently erupted in 1883, may cause the entire planet's weather to change."

4 [Prose Summary Question]

According to the passage, climate change may result in animals moving to warmer places. In addition, asteroid strikes and volcanic eruptions can cause serious disruption in the Earth's weather.

Mastering Question Types B2   p.284

1 Ⓒ   2 Ⓐ   3 ❹   4 Water: ④, ⑦   Gravity:
①, ⑤, ⑥

1 [Negative Factual Question]

The author writes, "Water is the most important of all the forms of erosion and is arguably the most powerful force."

2 [Inference Question]

The passage reads, "The Dust Bowl in Oklahoma, Texas, and other Western states was caused primarily by wind removing much of the fertile topsoil from the land," which implies that the fertile land there was once farmed.

3 [Insert Text Question]

The sentence before the fourth square notes that the "landscape of the Mississippi area" is constantly being changed, and the sentence to be inserted states that because of the changes, maps of the area must be updated all the time.

4 [Fill in a Table Question]

According to the passage, water erosion created the Grand Canyon and can move earth through rivers. As for gravity erosion, it can happen just as quickly as ice erosion, it involves earth moving from one altitude to a lower one, and it is exemplified by falling rocks.

Mastering the Subject A

p.286

1 D 2 B 3 C 4 **3** 5 [2], [3], [4]

1 [Factual Question]

The passage notes, "Savannas are tropical grasslands replete with various kinds of grasses, shrubs, and even a few trees and cover approximately one-fifth of the Earth's entire land surface."

2 [Rhetorical Purpose Question]

The author states that grasshoppers, among other insects, often die in savanna fires.

3 [Negative Factual Question]

The author writes, "Furthermore, other trees frequently retain certain amounts of moisture in their aboveground parts—their trunk, branches, and leaves—which provides them with some modicum of protection as well," but there is no mention of which trees do that.

4 [Insert Text Question]

When describing how savanna fires start, the sentence before the third square includes "the vast majority of them are simply acts of nature," and the sentence to be inserted then describes how lightning strikes—which are acts of nature—can cause savanna fires.

5 [Prose Summary Question]

According to the passage, plant life grows back after savanna fires because the soil has become rich in nutrients. The few animals that die in the fires serve a purpose by being eating by other animals. And the fires on savannas often occur during the dry season.

Summarizing ▶

Savannas are hot, dry areas found in many places. They endure both a rainy and a dry season. During the dry season, they experience fires, almost all of which break out naturally. These fires are actually beneficial to the savannas. First, the few animals that die are typically just insects, and their bodies serve as food for many animals. Next, the roots of grasses survive and immediately grow back once the rains return. Trees also have natural protections to help them survive the fires. And the burned vegetation helps replenish the soil, giving it more nutrients to let plants grow better and faster.

Mastering the Subject B

p.289

1 B 2 B 3 A 4 D 5 [1], [2], [5]

1 [Vocabulary Question]

When something comes into play, it is involved in a

situation.

2 [Factual Question]

It is written, "During the last great ice age about 18,000 years ago, the enormous amount of frozen water reduced sea levels everywhere by as many as 130 meters."

3 [Inference Question]

The author writes, "For example, if the entire Greenland ice shelf melted and no water returned, worldwide sea levels could rise by as much as seven meters," which implies that Greenland has enough ice on it that, if it were to melt, would affect the entire world.

4 [Reference Question]

The "it" that will perhaps not occur during the current population's lifetime is a massive rise in sea levels.

5 [Prose Summary Question]

According to the passage, ice at the polar caps and in Greenland can affect ocean levels. In addition, the levels of the oceans can be affected by rain and water evaporation. And even the movement of the continents can affect the levels of the oceans.

Summarizing ▶

The sea levels of the Earth's oceans are difficult to measure for a variety of reasons. In addition, they are constantly rising and falling depending on certain factors. In the last great ice age around 18,000 years ago, sea levels were up to 130 meters lower than they are today. Much of the Earth's water was frozen in ice, which changed the way many landmasses looked. However, today, people are concerned more about sea levels rising, not falling. Yet while the polar caps are smaller, the sea level has not risen much for reasons no one is sure about. However, the Earth is likely to experience higher sea levels sometime in the future.

Mastering the Subject C

p.292

1 C 2 D 3 D 4 **3** 5 Barrage: [1], [5]
Tidal Turbine: [2], [3], [7]

1 [Negative Factual Question]

It is written, "They are called renewable because, while producing electricity, they do not consume their energy source, unlike fossil-fuel-fired electric plants or nuclear power plants."

2 [Rhetorical Purpose Question]

The paragraph reads, "Once the tide begins receding, the sluice gates are closed, trapping the water."

3 [Reference Question]

The "they" that may kill fish if they are spinning fast enough are the turbines.

4 [Insert Text Question]

The sentence before the third square notes that there are a limited number of places where tidal power systems can be constructed, and the sentence to be inserted follows up on this theme.

5 [Fill in a Table Question]

According to the passage, barrage systems can harm sea life in the area, and one of these systems is in use at La Rance, France. As for tidal turbine systems, the part of them that creates electricity is fixed on the bottom of the water, they can be designed not to kill so many fish, and they are not overly expensive.

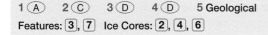

There are many forms of renewable energy, but they are not used nearly as much as fossil fuels are. One promising form of renewable energy is using wave and tidal power. Tidal power is an inexhaustible energy source that creates almost no pollution. Yet it cannot be used everywhere, and it can harm marine life. Both barrage and turbine systems are in use. Barrage systems are expensive and can only be located in a few places. Turbine systems are cheaper but can also kill many fish. There are many issues with tidal power, so it is likely not to be used very much in the future.

Mastering the Subject D

p.295

| 1 Ⓐ | 2 Ⓒ | 3 Ⓓ | 4 Ⓓ | 5 Geological |

Features: ③, ⑦ Ice Cores: ②, ④, ⑥

1 [Vocabulary Question]

Something that is postulated is theorized.

2 [Sentence Simplification Question]

The highlighted sentence notes that some places without glaciers today show evidence that they had them in the past. This notion is best expressed in answer choice Ⓒ.

3 [Inference Question]

The paragraph reads, "This most recent ice age is often called the Little Ice Age because it was not as severe as previous ones." This implies that past ice ages had varying cold temperatures.

4 [Factual Question]

The author notes, "Unfortunately, this method of determining if and when ice ages occurred depends on finding these fossils in the first place, which is not

particularly easy."

5 [Fill in a Table Question]

According to the passage, geologists study geological features in that they look for rocks in places where they should not exist, and they look for evidence of past glaciers in areas. As for ice cores, they are studied in the Arctic, they require the drilling of deep holes, and they have taught scientists very much about past ice ages.

There are no written records of the last ice age, which took place around 18,000 years ago. So scientists must examine the geological, ice core, and fossil evidence to learn about it. The geological evidence in North America and Europe comes from the changes that glaciers made as they receded toward the north. For ice core evidence, scientists examine ice from the Arctic and Greenland to examine its quality. This can tell them many things about the past. They can also examine old fossils to learn different things about the animals that once lived during the ice age.

TOEFL Practice Tests A

p.298

| 1 Ⓒ | 2 Ⓓ | 3 Ⓐ | 4 Ⓓ | 5 Ⓐ |
| 6 Ⓐ | 7 Ⓓ | 8 Ⓒ | 9 **2** | |

10 ①, ④, ⑥

1 [Negative Factual Question]

The writer mentions, "Coral is a living organism plant-like in appearance and is composed of thousands of polyps of coral grouped together."

2 [Inference Question]

It is written, "Coral reefs are in danger as pollution and other manmade problems threaten their existence," which implies that coral reefs are able to be killed by outside forces.

3 [Vocabulary Question]

Something that is secreted is emitted.

4 [Factual Question]

The writer mentions, "Sometimes these polyps detach and establish their own colonies in different areas."

5 [Sentence Simplification Question]

The highlighted sentence explains that coral reefs do not appear in places where rivers such as the Amazon release fresh water into the ocean. This is best expressed in answer choice Ⓐ.

6 [Vocabulary Question]

Something that fringes the coastline borders it.

7 [Inference Question]

When the author writes "a ship can find a passageway through them" while describing coral reefs, it is implied that there are gaps in some of them that enable ships to pass.

8 [Rhetorical Purpose Question]

About Hanauma Bay, the author states that it "witness[es] hordes of visitors each year," which emphasizes that it is popular with tourists.

9 [Insert Text Question]

The sentence before the second square mentions that algae grow in enormous quantities. The sentence to be inserted mentions that this growth causes a number of problems.

10 [Prose Summary Question]

According to the passage, coral reefs are in danger because some people take coral home with them or fish in the reefs while others dump garbage in the reefs, which kills the coral. Additionally, the reefs are unique ecosystems in that thousands of fish and animal species live in them.

TOEFL Practice Tests B
p.302

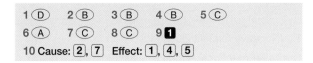

1 D   2 B   3 B   4 B   5 C
6 A   7 C   8 C   9 **1**
10 Cause: **2**, **7**   Effect: **1**, **4**, **5**

1 [Vocabulary Question]

The weathering of rock refers to its disintegrating because of erosive factors.

2 [Negative Factual Question]

The author writes, "Soil is crucial to all life on Earth because, without it, not much life could exist on land;" however, this does not include life that lives in the water or in the air.

3 [Vocabulary Question]

Soil that is rich is very productive.

4 [Rhetorical Purpose Question]

The passage claims, "Volcanoes can also produce soil, which is quite good for agriculture."

5 [Factual Question]

The author describes several factors involved in the creating of humus here: "Plant roots bind the soil together to prevent further eroding, trees prevent rain from washing it away, and bacteria and fungi

decompose the decaying matter of plants, animals, and animal feces. The final result is humus, a dark, extremely fertile soil ideal for growing crops."

6 [Vocabulary Question]

When trees and roots are anchoring soil to the ground, they are securing it so that it will not be blown or washed away.

7 [Inference Question]

The author writes, "The ecosystem of animals, fungi, and bacteria helps maintain soil's fertility and preserves it; earthworms are additionally considered essential to this." In noting that earthworms are essential and by not mentioning any other animals, the author implies that earthworms are more important to soil preservation than other animals.

8 [Factual Question]

The passage reads, "Deforestation is, essentially, the bane of soil, and when combined with water, it can have a devastating effect on the land."

9 [Insert Text Question]

The sentence located prior to the first square mentions that several civilizations throughout history declined because of deforestation. The sentence to be inserted then names the Maya as an example of a civilization to which this happened.

10 [Fill in a Table Question]

According to the passage, soil can be formed when rocks get broken down over time and when water frozen in rocks causes them to break up. The effects of soil formation are that tree roots anchor it to the soil to keep it from blowing away, humus gets created, and the land becomes fertile enough so that crops can be grown on it.

Vocabulary Review
p.309

1 D	2 A	3 A	4 A	5 B
6 C	7 A	8 D	9 B	10 C
11 C	12 B	13 C	14 C	15 D
16 A	17 A	18 C	19 A	20 D

Part C
Experiencing the TOEFL iBT Actual Tests

≡ Actual Test 01

p.312

1 B	2 D	3 B	4 C	5 D
6 A	7 B	8 C	9 **2**	

10 **2**, **4**, **6**

11 C	12 C	13 B	14 D	15 A
16 C	17 A	18 B	19 **3**	

20 **1**, **2**, **5**

21 D	22 A	23 B	24 D	25 D
26 B	27 D	28 C	29 **4**	

30 Freshwater: **3**, **6** Marine: **1**, **4**, **7**

31 B	32 B	33 C	34 C	35 D
36 B	37 C	38 C	39 **4**	

40 **2**, **3**, **5**

1 [Factual Question]

About the Ottoman Empire, the passage reads, "For centuries, the Turks had been encroaching on European lands. More than a century earlier, in 1453, they had conquered Constantinople, the capital of the Byzantine Empire, and they were making significant inroads in the Balkans in Southeastern Europe and in other areas around the Mediterranean Sea."

2 [Vocabulary Question]

When a person is agitating for something, that individual is insisting upon some kind of action being done.

3 [Inference Question]

The author notes that one of the main possessions of the Hapsburg Empire was Spain. Then, when writing about Don Juan, he is called "the Spaniard Don Juan." This implies that Don Juan had some kind of a connection with the Hapsburg Empire.

4 [Sentence Simplification Question]

The highlighted passage notes the difference between the rowers used by the Turks and the Holy League. This difference is best expressed in answer choice C.

5 [Vocabulary Question]

The climax of a battle is its apex.

6 [Rhetorical Purpose Question]

In describing their different tactics, the author contrasts the way that both sides made battle.

7 [Negative Factual Question]

Don Juan's and Ali Pasha's flagships both fought directly, and there was hand-to-hand combat, but Don Juan and Ali Pasha did not fight each other hand to hand.

8 [Factual Question]

The author writes, "With their treasury exhausted, the Venetians had no choice but to make peace with the Turks in 1574, so they formally ceded Cyprus to the Turks."

9 [Insert Text Question]

The passage before the second square describes the kind of damage that the galleasses did to the Turks' ships. The sentence to be inserted begins with "in addition," which means that it provides further information on the effects of the galleasses.

10 [Prose Summary Question]

According to the passage, at Lepanto, the Europeans were encouraged by their victory, which was the first time in years that the Ottoman Empire had been defeated. In addition, during the battle, the Holy League's galleasses annihilated the Turkish navy.

11 [Factual Question]

The passage notes that people could take black and white photographs and could also manage to take color photographs.

12 [Factual Question]

The author notes, "The only triumph required the use of a process in which the subject was photographed with three cameras, each of which had different-colored filters. The three images were then superimposed on one another to form a single color photograph. However, this process was time consuming and had severe limitations." This shows the complicated procedure involved in taking color photographs.

13 [Negative Factual Question]

Dye, not silver bromide emulsion, was mixed with the potato grains.

14 [Sentence Simplification Question]

The highlighted sentence notes that the developing of the autochrome process led to many artists quitting painting and becoming photographers. This idea is best expressed in answer choice D.

15 [Factual Question]

The author writes, "Within a few years, the autochrome process was so popular that the Lumiere's factory in Lyon had difficulty keeping up with the demand for photographic plates."

16 [Vocabulary Question]

When something is in vogue, it is fashionable.

17 [Inference Question]

It is written, "One problem with the technique was that the camera lens needed to stay open for at least one minute, requiring the subject to remain absolutely still for a perfect photograph." This is can be inferred that landscapes, in which the subjects do not move, were ideal for autochrome photography.

18 [Rhetorical Purpose Question]

The author writes, "Coupled with new photo processing methods developed by the Kodak and Agfa companies," which notes the new ways to make photographs that these companies had developed.

19 [Insert Text Question]

The sentence before the third square reads, "After he retired, the brothers took over and set off in a new direction: motion pictures." The field that the brothers believed there was more potential in was that of motion pictures, so the sentence to be inserted provides a reason why the brothers set off in a new direction.

20 [Prose Summary Question]

According to the passage, autochrome photography enabled one camera, not three, to be used to take color photographs. In addition, many people were inspired to become photographers, which showed its popularity. And it was the potato grains used that enabled color photographs to be taken.

21 [Negative Factual Question]

The author writes, "Aquaculture, otherwise referred to as fish farming, refers to the breeding, raising, and harvesting of marine life, including fish, shellfish, crustaceans, and algae, for various purposes."

22 [Inference Question]

In writing, "Since then, it was practiced at times at various places around the world until it became much more prominent during the twentieth century," the author implies that aquaculture is practiced more now than it was at any other time in the past.

23 [Factual Question]

The author writes, "Freshwater aquaculture is frequently practiced in small ponds or tanks." Then, the author adds, "There are also large fisheries that also raise great numbers of fish to sell commercially."

24 [Vocabulary Question]

When something is economically unfeasible, it is impractical for people to do.

25 [Rhetorical Purpose Question]

The passage reads, "Farmers can keep the water clean and algae-free by introducing filtration systems."

26 [Vocabulary Question]

When fish farmers must be wary of diseases, they must be cautious of them.

27 [Factual Question]

The passage reads, "As genetically modified fish are being raised by some farmers, there are worries by environmentalists that these fish will escape and then interbreed with wild fish."

28 [Rhetorical Purpose Question]

The author describes how aquaponics is done in order for people to raise fish and to grow vegetables.

29 [Insert Text Question]

The sentence to be inserted reads, "Cages for fish may be floating ones or those set up on the ocean floor." Since it, like the sentence to be inserted, mentions "cages," the two sentences go well together.

30 [Fill in a Table Question]

According to the passage, freshwater aquaculture is easy to keep track of the amount of food the fish eat and often takes place in a closed environment. As for marine aquaculture, it may require using cages floating on the water, it raises a wide variety of fish and other aquatic creatures, and it can expose fish to a variety of pollutants in the water.

31 [Vocabulary Question]

The barrenness of an area refers to its desolateness.

32 [Negative Factual Question]

The Sahel is not directly north of the Sahara Desert but is in fact directly south of it.

33 [Inference Question]

The author writes, "The north-south boundaries of the Sahel are not set in stone though; instead, they are determined by the amount of rainfall the region gets," which implies that the Sahel's borders are always changing.

34 [Factual Question]

Concerning the Sahel, the author notes, "Between 1931 and 1960, the southern boundary was about sixty miles further north than it was between 1966 and 1997. This shifting of lesser amounts of rainfall to the south is the result of rising ocean temperatures causing changes in African rainfall patterns."

35 [Vocabulary Question]

When the desert is encroaching on an area, it is

invading it.

36 [Factual Question]

The paragraph notes, "Niger is one such example: The country's northern lands are mostly desert whereas its southern part is a long, wide plain of vegetation. In addition, it has almost 20,000 square miles more land with vegetation than it did a mere two decades ago." This shows how the changes in the Sahel have benefitted Niger.

37 [Rhetorical Purpose Question]

About Darfur, it is written, "In the Darfur region of Sudan in the center of the Sahel, almost 200,000 people have perished in recent years, and more than two million have been made homeless." This sentence stresses the destructiveness of the wars there.

38 [Factual Question]

The passage notes that Timbuktu "is now a tourist destination and a civilized area in the almost featureless desert lands which surround it."

39 [Insert Text Question]

The sentence before the fourth square reads, "Another suggestion is that some regions are undergoing climate change, causing them to receive more rainfall than before." This is the "latter theory" mentioned in the sentence to be added, so the two sentences go well together.

40 [Prose Summary Question]

According to the passage, the Sahel stretches from one coast of Africa to the other. In addition, it has seen a constant state of warfare in many places, and the constant changes that it undergoes have turned millions of people there into refugees.

1 Ⓑ	2 Ⓑ	3 Ⓐ	4 Ⓓ	5 Ⓐ
6 Ⓑ	7 Ⓓ	8 Ⓑ	9 **2**	
10 ③, ④, ⑤				
11 Ⓓ	12 Ⓑ	13 Ⓑ	14 Ⓒ	15 Ⓐ
16 Ⓐ	17 Ⓓ	18 Ⓐ	19 **1**	
20 Cause: ③, ④ Effect: ①, ②, ⑦				
21 Ⓒ	22 Ⓓ	23 Ⓐ	24 Ⓑ	25 Ⓑ
26 Ⓒ	27 Ⓐ	28 Ⓐ	29 **3**	
30 ①, ②, ⑥				

1 [Vocabulary Question]

When animals show aggressive intent toward others, they are showing that they are willing to attack those animals.

2 [Negative Factual Question]

The author writes, "Instead, they rely upon various nonverbal and verbal means of communication. Not all animals use every method of communication though; what they use depend on the species."

3 [Factual Question]

The author mentions, "Birds, whose songs are imprinted at birth, may use them as part of their mating rituals."

4 [Reference Question]

The "it" that is shared with others is a food source.

5 [Inference Question]

The author writes, "Female lions can emit powerful pheromones that indicate to any male within range—which is often a great distance—that they are ready for copulation," which implies that many males may respond to her.

6 [Rhetorical Purpose Question]

The author notes that hyenas, leopards, rabbits, and members of the canine family all communicate through urination.

7 [Sentence Simplification Question]

The highlighted sentence states that bees return to their hive upon finding a food source and then do a series of movements indicating where the food source is and how much of it is available. This description is best expressed in answer choice Ⓓ.

8 [Factual Question]

The author explains, "Other animals can change the color of parts of their bodies to send messages to other members of their species."

9 [Insert Text Question]

The sentence before the second square explains why animals urinate to mark their territory, and the sentence to be inserted notes how this affects animals that are entering another's territory.

10 [Prose Summary Question]

According to the passage, animals communicate by releasing scents, they can vocalize to some extent, and they can use colors as a nonverbal means of communication.

11 [Rhetorical Purpose Question]

The author writes, "The primary threat is that of large objects striking the smaller terrestrial planets—Mercury, Venus, Earth, and Mars," so the terrestrial planets are mentioned to show how they are in danger of being struck by celestial objects.

12 [Sentence Simplification Question]

The highlighted sentence mentions that Earth has been hit by large objects in the past and states that one such impact may have killed the dinosaurs millions of years ago. This is best expressed in answer choice Ⓑ.

13 [Factual Question]

The author claims, "In recorded history, comets and large asteroids have passed close to Earth, but none has impacted the planet."

14 [Factual Question]

The paragraph includes the statement, "Additionally, visible impact craters around the planet provide evidence that much larger meteorites have struck in the past."

15 [Vocabulary Question]

Something that lingers for a long time remains in one place.

16 [Negative Factual Question]

The passage does not mention how long the massive fires on the Earth would burn for.

17 [Inference Question]

When the author claims that astronomers "had predicted the collision before it happened," it can be inferred that they knew its orbit before it crashed into Jupiter.

18 [Factual Question]

The author claims, "In fact, Jupiter has likely saved Earth—and the other terrestrial planets—from similar impacts in the past and will undoubtedly do so in the future, too."

19 [Insert Text Question]

The sentence located before the first square declares that places in the solar system other than Earth have been hit by major strikes. The sentence to be inserted then gives an example of all of the impact craters on the moon.

20 [Fill in a Table Question]

According to the passage, the gravitational pull of a large object and the intersecting orbits of celestial objects are both causes of planetary strikes. As for their effects, the strikes may alter a planet's atmosphere, they may wipe out entire species of animals, and they may create an impact crater.

21 [Factual Question]

The passage reads, "They may be caused by many factors, the most common of which are excessive rainfall, rapid snowmelt, and oceanic surges accompanying storm systems such as hurricanes, typhoons, and cyclones. In rarer situations, the collapse of a dam or the sudden blocking of a river with ice or debris from landslides can result in flooding."

22 [Vocabulary Question]

People who dread floods fear their occurrence.

23 [Factual Question]

The author writes, "Once the water level recedes, enormous amounts of silt and debris such as rocks and even garbage will remain until people remove it to make the region livable once again," but there is no mention of how long the cleanup normally takes.

24 [Rhetorical Purpose Question]

The author mentions tsunamis to compare their power with that of a storm surge.

25 [Negative Factual Question]

There is no mention in the passage of how powerful Hurricane Katrina was.

26 [Factual Question]

The author notes, "Hurricane Katrina's storm surge caused water to breach the levees of New Orleans, which caused much of the city to be flooded and resulted in more than one thousand deaths."

27 [Vocabulary Question]

The author notes, "Hurricane Katrina's storm surge caused water to breach the levees of New Orleans, which caused much of the city to be flooded and resulted in more than one thousand deaths."

28 [Inference Question]

The author mentions, "If crops are still in fields when floods strike, they may be washed away while farmland is made unsuitable for agriculture. This is especially true when oceanic storm surges bring water with a high saline content." This implies that farmland reacts poorly to salt.

29 [Insert Text Question]

The sentence located before the third square notes that farmers were able to grow surplus food. The sentence to be inserted then names an effect of that, which was that these farming communities eventually began to develop civilization.

30 [Prose Summary Question]

According to the passage, humans often live in areas that flood since they benefit from being near water. In addition, floods can happen either quickly or slowly, and each type of flood causes different amounts of damage. And even when the flooding stops, there can still be problems in their aftermaths.

MEMO

TOEFL®
MAP New TOEFL® Edition
Reading

Advanced